AF898284

Investor-State Dispute Settlement and International Investment Agreements

This book examines the international investment agreements and the dispute settlement mechanisms contained therein, which bind the Gulf Cooperation Council member States.

The Gulf Cooperation Council (GCC), comprising Bahrain, Kuwait, Oman, Qatar, Saudi Arabia, and the United Arab Emirates, is complex and unique. Recently, all member States have experienced increasing investor–state arbitration claims, while their nationals are increasingly instituting investor–state arbitrations to protect their own foreign investments. Intra-GCC disputes, though relatively rare, have also appeared, largely as a result of the recent Gulf crisis. While focussing particularly upon the investor–state dispute settlement experience of member States as respondents, the book also explores the experiences of their nationals as claimants to determine how they can approach investor– state dispute settlement in the future. The book also reflects on existing treaty-making practices, making recommendations for regional-level dispute settlement to improve upon investor–state dispute settlement outcomes.

This book provides a detailed analysis of the global investor–state dispute settlement regime and international investment agreements, and it will be of interest to students, academics, and practitioners with an interest in international investment law and arbitration.

David Price is Emeritus Professor, Public International Law and Intellectual Property Law, School of Law, Charles Darwin University, Australia. His primary research area is the intersection of public international law, international trade agreements, and intellectual property law. This work has extended to the settlement of disputes encompassing the application of investor–state dispute settlement causes and outcomes. He has published extensively in these areas, focussing upon the GCC, ASEAN, Indonesia, and Australia as exemplars. David has worked, consulted, and researched in institutions in Australia, Indonesia, the UK, Europe, and the Middle East, and held visiting professorships in Indonesia and China.

Amelia Hallam is a research associate with the School of Law, Charles Darwin University, Australia. She has been admitted as a legal practitioner in the Supreme Court of the Australian Capital Territory. In 2020 Amy completed her PhD on investor–state dispute settlement at Charles Darwin University, with Emeritus Professor David Price. Amy has an active research interest in investor–state arbitration and the Gulf, having presented at the Gulf Research Council's International Meetings in the UK, and subsequently published. Amy has also published on ISDS provisions in Gulf free trade agreements, and new knowledge societies and economic development in the GCC.

Contributing author:

Nadia Naim is an Associate Dean of International Law and Social Sciences and a Senior Lecturer in Law at Aston University. She is a qualified barrister and a fellow of the HEA. She has published many scholarly articles in the areas of international intellectual property law, intangible asset financing and development, comparative law, and international law. She has authored books in the intellectual property field and specialises in emerging areas of intellectual property development. Her most recent publication is *Islamic Legal Principles and Intellectual Property Rights in the Gulf* with Gerlach Press and her upcoming publication is with Palgrave McMillan on *Intellectual Property Law Developments*.

Routledge Research in International Economic Law

The Legality of Economic Activities in Occupied Territories
International, EU Law and Business and Human Rights Perspectives
Antoine Duval and Eva Kassoti

International Investment Protection within Europe
The EU's Assertion of Control
Julien Berger

Trade, Migration and Law
Free Movement of Persons in the South African Development Community
Victor Amadi

The Americanization of the World Trade Order
Asif H Qureshi

Reform and Regulation of Economic Institutions in Afghanistan
Haroun Rahimi

The Freest Market in the World
The Constitutional Logic of Economic Liberty in Hong Kong
Gonzalo Villalta Puig and Eric C Ip

International Trade Regulation
Evolving Dynamics and Shifting Foundations
Zhiqiong June Wang and Jianfu Chen

India and Investor-State Dispute Settlement
Affronting Sovereignty or Indicting Capriciousness?
Prabhash Ranjan

Investor-State Dispute Settlement and International Investment Agreements
The Case of the Gulf Cooperation Council Member States
David Price and Amelia Hallam

For more information about this series, please visit https://www.routledge.com/Routledge-Research-in-International-Economic-Law/book-series/INTECONLAW

Investor-State Dispute Settlement and International Investment Agreements

The Case of the Gulf Cooperation Council Member States

David Price and Amelia Hallam

Routledge
Taylor & Francis Group
LONDON AND NEW YORK

First published 2024
by Routledge
4 Park Square, Milton Park, Abingdon, Oxon OX14 4RN

and by Routledge
605 Third Avenue, New York, NY 10158

Routledge is an imprint of the Taylor & Francis Group, an informa business

© 2024 David Price and Amelia Hallam; Chapter 8, Nadia Naim

The right of David Price and Amelia Hallam to be identified as authors of this work, and of Nadia Naim as author of Chapter 8 of this work, has been asserted in accordance with sections 77 and 78 of the Copyright, Designs and Patents Act 1988.

All rights reserved. No part of this book may be reprinted or reproduced or utilised in any form or by any electronic, mechanical, or other means, now known or hereafter invented, including photocopying and recording, or in any information storage or retrieval system, without permission in writing from the publishers.

Trademark notice: Product or corporate names may be trademarks or registered trademarks, and are used only for identification and explanation without intent to infringe.

British Library Cataloguing-in-Publication Data
A catalogue record for this book is available from the British Library

Library of Congress Cataloging-in-Publication Data
Names: Price, David S. (Lawyer), author. | Hallam, Amelia, author. | Naim, Nadia, author.
Title: Investor-state dispute settlement and international investment agreements : the case of the Gulf Cooperation Council member states / David Price, Amelia Hallam, and Nadia Naim.
Description: Abingdon, Oxon [UK] ; New York, NY : Routledge, 2024. | Series: Routledge research in international economic law | Includes bibliographical references and index.
Identifiers: LCCN 2023055471 (print) | LCCN 2023055472 (ebook) | ISBN 9781032614496 (hardback) | ISBN 9781032770635 (paperback) | ISBN 9781003481072 (ebook)
Subjects: LCSH: Arbitration agreements, Commercial--Persian Gulf States. | Arbitration and award--Persian Gulf States. | International commercial arbitration--Persian Gulf States. | Investments, Foreign--Law and legislation--Persian Gulf States. | Dispute resolution (Law)--Persian Gulf States. | Investments, Foreign (International law) | Gulf Cooperation Council.
Classification: LCC KMC500 .P75 2024 (print) | LCC KMC500 (ebook) | DDC 346.536/092--dc23/eng/20231214
LC record available at https://lccn.loc.gov/2023055471
LC ebook record available at https://lccn.loc.gov/2023055472

ISBN: 978-1-032-61449-6 (hbk)
ISBN: 978-1-032-77063-5 (pbk)
ISBN: 978-1-003-48107-2 (ebk)

DOI: 10.4324/9781003481072

Typeset in Times New Roman
by Deanta Global Publishing Services, Chennai, India

Contents

List of Figures *viii*
List of Tables *ix*
Preface *x*

1 Introduction: Investor–State Dispute Settlement and the GCC Member State Experience 1

2 The GCC Member States and Their International Arbitration Frameworks 19

3 Elements and Emerging Themes in Investor–State Arbitration in the GCC Context 42

4 The GCC Member States as Respondents in ISDS Arbitrations 79

5 The GCC Member States as Home States of Claimants in ISDS Arbitrations 124

6 Intra-GCC Investor–State Arbitrations and Divergence in Approaches 166

7 Domestic Investment Protection and Promotion Legislative and Regulatory Frameworks in the GCC 192

8 ISDS, Islamic Law-Based Investment Agreements and Islamic Finance Principles 228

9 Reflections and Recommendations 252

Index *271*

Figures

2.1 GCC member State BIT agreements 21
4.1 Investor–state dispute settlement and the GCC member State experience 117
5.1 GCC member States as home state of claimants 160
9.1 GCC member States as respondents and claimant home states 263

Tables

3.1 Definition of "Investor" and Nationality Requirements 54
3.2 Definition of "Investment" 55
3.3 Fair and Equitable Treatment 60
3.4 Non-Expropriation Provisions 64
3.5 Anti-Discrimination: The National Treatment Provisions 68
3.6 Anti-Discrimination: Most-Favoured-Nation Treatment Provisions 70
3.7 Dispute Resolution by Arbitration Provisions 72
4.1 Bahrain as Respondent 84
4.2 Kuwait as Respondent 90
4.3 Oman as Respondent 99
4.4 Qatar as Respondent 102
4.5 Saudi Arabia as Respondent 103
4.6 UAE as Respondent 111
5.1 Bahrain as Home State of Investor 126
5.2 Kuwait as Home State of Investor 128
5.3 Oman as Home State of Investor 136
5.4 Qatar as Home State of Investor 139
5.5 Saudi Arabia as Home State of Investor 143
5.6 UAE as Home State of Investor 146
6.1 Intra-GCC ISDS Cases 168
7.1 GCC Economies: FDI Inflows and Outflows 2021 and 2022 222

Preface

This study examines the status and application of the global investor–state dispute settlement (ISDS) regime within the Gulf Cooperation Council (GCC), and the experiences of its member States, namely Bahrain, Kuwait, Oman, Qatar, Saudi Arabia, and the United Arab Emirates, as participants in that regime. It provides a general background in respect of the accession of the States to international investment and regional agreements (IIAs) and notably bilateral trade agreements (BITs) with ISDS provisions.

The study also provides a brief account of the rather recent history of the emergence of ISDS-based disputations involving the GCC member States as both respondents to arbitration claims and as the respective home states of investor/claimants. In so doing, it draws attention to the significant difference that exists between the number of intra-GCC disputations and those involving parties from outside the GCC. It also introduces the question as to whether the nature of ISDS-based arbitration disputes involving the States reveals a particular region-specific character.

The GCC and its member States have had relatively little exposure to investor–state arbitration, such exposure being a fairly recent occurrence of less than two decades. However, this is changing. The States are becoming increasingly subject to investor–state arbitration claims. Nationals from the States are increasingly instituting investor–state arbitration, and intra-GCC disputes, though relatively rare, are growing, largely as a result of the recent Gulf diplomatic crisis.

The GCC is a complex, unique, and at times fractious union. The GCC is also at a critical point in its development, with its States diversifying away from oil and implementing policy measures designed to open their economies to foreign direct investment. This study examines the international investment agreements which bind the States and the dispute settlement bodies which arbitrate on matters of dispute brought before them. It focusses particularly on the ISDS experience of the States as respondents and that of their nationals, in the capacity as claimants, to determine how they can approach ISDS into the future. It offers suggestions in relation to treaty-making practices and regional-level dispute settlement, hopefully making a worthy contribution to the present active debate on the current international investment arbitration regime and the current calls for change.

The impetus for this study arose from earlier research by Professor David Price and Dr Amelia Hallam of Charles Darwin University into international investment agreements, and bilateral investment treaties in particular, and the outcome of ISDS provisions enshrined in those agreements when disputation requiring arbitration arose. A simple question as to the general situation within the Gulf and in respect of the Gulf States was denied even a reasonably comprehensive and current answer. This study now endeavours to answer, at least in part, that simple question but with a rather complex answer.

Chapters 1 to 7 and 9 are jointly authored by Professor David Price and Dr Amelia Hallam. Chapter 8 is contributed by colleague Dr Nadia Naim of Aston University, who offers insight into the question of whether ISDS should be, or can become, Shariah compliant – particularly in view of the status of the Shariah across the MENA region and beyond, and the extensive and growing acceptance of Islamic finance and banking principles within both the Islamic and Western economies and investment regimes.

1 Introduction

Investor–State Dispute Settlement and the GCC Member State Experience

1.1 Introduction

This study examines the nature and application of the Investor–State Dispute Settlement (ISDS) regime within the international investment agreements (IIAs) and free trade agreements (FTAs) to which the member States of the Gulf Cooperation Council (GCC), namely Bahrain, Kuwait, Oman, Qatar, Saudi Arabia, and the United Arab Emirates (UAE), are parties, both severally and separately. It considers the experiences and performances of each State both as respondents to claims brought by foreign investors as nationals of those countries with whom the States have entered into agreements, and as the home states of investor claimants seeking redress from other parties for alleged violation of the terms of those agreements. In so doing, it reflects upon the scope of contemporary global ISDS standards, as well as Arab-based regional standards and practices, and discusses distinctions between the two regimes both in terms of their structure and their operation. It contemplates the impact of the States' exposure to investor–state arbitration upon their apparent inclination to agree to the inclusion of ISDS in future trade and investment treaties as well as the design of future investment protection provisions and dispute settlement mechanisms.

The study also questions the efficacy and fitness for purpose of the ISDS regime in its contemporary form in the GCC context in both protecting and promoting foreign investment. It notes shifting attitudes and approaches to the inclusion of certain investment provisions within IIAs, specifically bilateral investment treaties (BITs), and other broader international and regional agreements such as FTAs, and other treaties containing investment provisions. It also notes relatively recent changes in the domestic legislative and regulatory regimes concerned with foreign direct investment, reflecting the respective implementation of policies designed to attract foreign direct investment and transition towards knowledge-based economies. The efficacy of the ISDS regime is examined in the context of its ability to promote and protect foreign investment, and its fitness for purpose is analysed by questioning whether the current regime strikes an appropriate balance between sovereignty, particularly the right to regulate in the public interest, and ISDS regime autonomy.

DOI: 10.4324/9781003481072-1

1.2 Background and Context: The ISDS Context

ISDS provisions are essentially a group of provisions in a trade or investment agreement that serve as an instrument for investors to address foreign investment risk at a macro-level. They are complex and risky instruments that are broadly scoped. ISDS provisions potentially allow for acts of a state, including decisions made by the executive, judiciary, and legislature, at a national or sub-national level that foreign investors consider to be arbitrary, discriminatory, or unjust to be challenged before an international arbitral tribunal. Hence, they can be both far-reaching and controversial. ISDS provisions have been proffered as a way forward for countries to protect local investors investing in foreign states by providing a centralised process for resolving investment disputes, outside of or in addition to domestic dispute settlement options and state-to-state dispute settlement or diplomatic protection. While these are just some of the benefits of ISDS provisions, there are significant limitations to the mechanism that may have far-reaching implications for both parties to such a dispute and beyond.

As a complex and supranational dispute settlement system, ISDS requires four key elements, namely:

- treaties containing ISDS provisions, namely IIAs;
- independent institutions that facilitate the settling and developing of rules to govern investor–state disputes and promote consensus in treaty design and harmonising rules and sustainable development;
- rules regarding the conduct of investor–state disputes; and
- arbitral tribunals that adjudicate investor–state disputes on an administered or ad hoc basis by interpreting and applying IIAs.

Investment treaties are the most important element of the ISDS regime. They form the legal basis of the investor–state arbitration and are agreements between pairs or groups of countries "that have the protection of foreign investment as the primary, or only, subject matter".[1] They are international legal instruments signed by consent and executed through ratification. While these agreements are most commonly bilateral, they can also be multilateral, such as the United States–Mexico–Canada Agreement (USMCA) and the Regional Comprehensive Economic Partnership Agreement (RCEP).[2]

The treaties or IIAs are also public international law instruments that govern the relationship between states and foreign investors, with respect to their investment interests.[3] This is an important feature, as IIAs operate to protect and promote the

1 Jonathon Bonnitcha, Lauge Skovgaard Poulsen and Michael Waibel, *The Political Economy of the Investment Treaty Regime* (Oxford University Press, 2017) 2–3.

2 The RCEP entered into force on 1 January 2022 for ten of the original parties: Australia, Brunei Darussalam, Cambodia, China, Japan, Laos, New Zealand, Singapore, Thailand, and Vietnam. South Korea, Malaysia, Indonesia, and the Philippines have since also joined.

3 Jeswald W Salacuse, 'BIT by BIT: The Growth of Bilateral Investment Treaties and Their Impact on Foreign Investment in Developing Countries' (1990) 24(3) *International Lawyer* 655.

investment interests of a special class of third-party private beneficiaries, namely foreign investors. IIAs typically enable foreign investors to submit international investment disputes to binding private arbitration for alleged breaches of the substantive investment protections outside or in addition to conventional domestic remedies. The outcome of domestic judicial proceedings, if sought, is irrelevant to investor–state arbitration. Integration with domestic juridical procedures is limited, and there is typically no requirement to resolve related litigation in municipal channels as a precondition to advancing international arbitration. This is significant because the requirement to exhaust domestic remedies before seeking relief in international action is a well-established principle of international law known as the local remedies rule.[4] Further, this feature of IIAs is problematic because it potentially either allows concurrent litigation in multiple dispute resolution fora or enables foreign investors to bypass conventional domestic remedies, thereby undermining their legitimacy.

ISDS is also a complex and evolving mechanism for dispute settlement contained within the investment chapters of IIAs. It confers a right upon foreign investors to submit claims to binding international arbitration (the procedural mechanism) for alleged breaches of a group of broadly scoped investment protections also contained within the investment chapter of an IIA (the substantive investment protections). Historically, these substantive investment protections have been broadly drafted, opening the door to potential arbitral review of legitimate regulatory decisions or legal judgments, as well as inviting at times inconsistency in interpretation and application by arbitral tribunals. In fact, arbitral tribunals hearing investor–state disputes are not bound by conventional standards; in *Itisaluna v Iraq*,[5] for example, the majority of the tribunal declined to follow an earlier decision made by another arbitral tribunal on a relevant issue, which the dissenting arbitrator also noted in their judgment:

> just as the majority of the Tribunal here considers that they are not bound by the *Al-Warraq* award, the arbitral tribunals in subsequent cases that will deal with a similar issue will not be bound by this award, because this award does not set a precedent for similar situations.[6]

The procedural mechanism enables claimant investors to submit claims to arbitration for alleged breaches of one or more investment protections without necessarily having to first initiate or exhaust local remedies or rely on traditional state-to-state dispute settlement mechanisms, namely diplomatic protection. Under the state-to-state dispute settlement mechanisms, claimant investors would first have to petition their home sovereign or government to intervene on their behalf in respect of

4 *Interhandel (Switzerland v United States of America)* [1959] ICJ Rep 46.
5 *Itisaluna Iraq LLC and Others v Republic of Iraq*, ICSID Case No. ARB/17/10 (Award, 3 April 2020) at [229](*'Itisaluna v Iraq')*.
6 Ibid (Award, 3 April 2020), [229].

investment disputes. The claimant's home sovereign or government might then exercise its absolute discretion as to whether to intervene and, if so, to what degree. State-to-state dispute resolution carries a risk that disputes will potentially be politicised or escalate into militarised conflict. Avoiding this potential pitfall is touted as a perceived benefit of access to investor–state arbitration.

ISDS, however, enables claimant investors to challenge their host state directly. In enabling claimant investors to directly challenge their host state, ISDS is intended to facilitate neutral dispute settlement. The procedural mechanism contained within the investment chapter of IIAs is particularly controversial because it enables a non-sovereign entity to challenge the acts of sovereign states in private international arbitration, with limited review or appellate mechanisms. According to Gus Van Harten, ISDS, namely arbitration, "is an exceptional form of adjudication" which is "unique in its use of a for-profit asymmetrical model of adjudication to resolve finally questions about sovereign authority and public compensation for private actors … It is asymmetrical because only one class of claimants brings claims against the other".[7]

ISDS provisions have a dual purpose. Firstly, they constitute operative provisions which typically include non-discrimination and non-expropriation protections afforded by the signatory host state for foreign investors. Secondly, the host state creates a right for foreign investors to bring about an arbitration for alleged infringements of the operative provisions. To some degree, the provisions may be viewed as a form of political and/or judicial risk insurance held by host states on behalf of foreign investors. ISDS provisions are broad in construction and operation and are a cause for concern upon reflection, particularly in circumstances where there are questions about the procedural and substantive nature of arbitral tribunals constituted to hear such matters.

ISDS provisions typically create a positive obligation upon host states to ensure that the investments of investors or nationals of the subscribing jurisdiction under a BIT or a FTA are treated in accordance with the BIT, which usually requires treatment that is just and fair and protection against expropriation and, of course, provides a mechanism for the resolution of investment disputes through the creation of a right for foreign investors to seek redress from an international tribunal.[8] Under most international investment agreements today, investors are also protected against "indirect" expropriation, which can be interpreted to mean regulations and other government actions that reduce the value of a foreign investment.[9] Thus, expropriation of a foreign investor's property rights can be direct or indirect and

7 Gus Van Harten, 'Arbitrator Behaviour in Asymmetrical Adjudication (Part Two): An Examination of Hypotheses of Bias in Investment Treaty Arbitration' (Research Paper No. 31) (2016) 12(7) *Osgoode Hall Law School.*

8 Department of Foreign Affairs and Trade, Commonwealth of Australia, *ISDS*, at <http://www.dfat.gov.au/trade/topics/Pages/isds.aspx>.

9 J. Kelsey and L. Wallach, 'Investor-State Disputes in Trade Pacts Threaten Fundamental Principles of National Judicial Systems,' *Public Citizen* (April 2012), at <http://www.citizen.org/documents/isds-domestic-legal-process-background-brief.pdf>.

need not be an actual acquisition. Indeed, in the case of intangible property, it is more likely than not that the form of the "offensive" acquisition would occur through the prohibition or revocation of an existing right or group of rights held by the foreign investor. The scope of these provisions is broad in nature, and the formulation and technical construction of expropriation provisions, in particular, will require special consideration by negotiating parties to a prospective agreement. Allegations of expropriation are a significant element of investor–state arbitration impacting upon the GCC.

The GCC member States have a unique geographical, socio-legal, and economic composition, including a rich and sophisticated blend of religious tradition, Shariah law, tribal hierarchy, and customs. The States have a broader treaty relationship with Islamic partners and are undertaking ambitious economic and social reform plans as they diversify and emerge as new knowledge societies. Arbitration as a form of dispute settlement is perhaps not unfamiliar. Mary Ayad argues that

> [i]t is helpful to remember that arbitration grew from the region as an indigenous and legitimate form of dispute resolution, beginning with the early arbitrations of the Prophet Mohammed at Banu Qurazyah and in the Quranic Verses dealing with the arbitration of marriage disputes.[10]

However, in the context of the unique melting pot of features influencing the States and, critically, as a non-Western supranational union, the GCC faces sui generis challenges in the context of the broader international investment treaty and arbitration environment, which has at least historically been a Western-centric and secular framework developed by and promoting the interests of developed economies. In some respects, this is still the case.

What might be of some concern to developing countries is that, according to UNCTAD, the large majority of ISDS claims in 2022 were instituted by Western investors, predominantly hailing from the United States, Western Europe, and Canada. For developing economies, this type of risk can be classified as non-systemic risk because it is not risk assumed by contracting States as intrinsic to the nature of ISDS provisions and their operation. This increases the risk of including ISDS provisions in Gulf trade agreements beyond the level of systematic risk and is a risk that may not necessarily be diversified. In these circumstances, the States may consider the inclusion of ISDS provisions in future regional and bilateral trade agreements as undesirable. Certainly, the track record of successful claims by investor claimants from the GCC member states would warrant questioning the current merit of the ISDS regime and thus be a catalyst for at least a review of their prevailing approach to the incorporation of ISDS provisions in their current form

10 Mary Ayad, 'Legal Matters Impacting the Oil and Gas Industry in the Gulf Cooperation Council (GCC) Countries: Keeping Legal Reform and Regulatory Frameworks Current in a Changing Energy Landscape' in Gawdat Bahgat (ed.) *The Changing Energy Landscape in the Gulf* (Gerlach Press, 2015) 124, 135, citing the Quran, Surah an-Nisa, verse 34.

or negotiating a more favourable approach when negotiating future agreements. Such a response may not be achievable in the short term but may be in the fullness of time in respect of bilateral agreements and would not be inconsistent with the approaches of other developing countries or even highly developed countries. But it is hardly practicable in respect of regional agreements.

In recent years, a number of developing and developed economies "have become critical of the ISDS regime and rejected the process", as well as the tribunals that deliver it, in favour of alternative dispute resolution models.[11] Both Indonesia and South Africa have demonstrated an intention to withdraw from the international investment agreement framework. Indonesia cancelled its BIT with the Netherlands in March 2014, as the first symbolic step in cancelling all its BITs, allegedly in part as a reaction to the unfavourable decision in an ICSID tribunal in the action brought by foreign mining companies. Ecuador, Venezuela and Nicaragua have opted to terminate BITs with ISDS provisions, Romania attempted to withdraw from its BIT with Sweden, and the Philippines have excluded ISDS provisions in the Japan–Philippines Economic Partnership Agreement.[12] Australia has had a skittish approach to investment and trade agreements, including an ISDS provision, adopting a sceptical and conservative non-adoption approach under a former Labour government, returning to a supportive position under a following conservative government, and currently adopting a case-by-case approach to the inclusion of ISDS provisions.

The ISDS regime continues to evolve internally in terms of IIA complexity, as well as the definitions of its key terms and conditions arising from tribunal history. It is also evolving externally insofar as the recalibration of older IIAs concluded in trade or geopolitical power imbalances and a growing trend for some developing economies to seriously consider and withdraw from IIAs reflect that the original power imbalance is no longer fit-for-purpose.

1.3 Background and Context: International Investment Agreements and the GCC Member States

The GCC member States have individually entered into a significant number of investment and trade treaties with foreign countries, while Bahrain and Oman (and neighbouring Jordan) have also entered into comprehensive FTAs with foreign investment protection and dispute settlement provisions with the United States. Many of the agreements are with developed Western economies which generally adhere to conventional ISDS rules, conventions, and organisations, notably those of the United Nations Commission on International Trade Law (UNCITRAL) or the World Bank's International Centre for Settlement of Investment Disputes (ICSID) Rules and Regulations, as the default agreement provisions for settling a

11 Leon Trakman and Kunal Sharma, 'Locating Australia on the Pacific Rim: Trade, Investment and the Asian Century' (2015) 12(1) *Transnational Dispute Management (TDM)*.

12 Ibid.

foreign investment dispute.[13] In many instances, the economy displays a willingness to invoke ISDS provisions both to settle grievances and to also use them as a strategic tool in its international trade and geopolitical arsenal.

But they have also entered into a range of BITs with fellow Arab states and states across the Middle East-North Africa (MENA) region. The very first BIT agreement by a GCC member State, for example, is recorded as the *Iraq–Kuwait BIT* of 25 October 1964, which has since been replaced by a subsequent agreement. Since then, the States have entered into a wide range and varying number of IIAs, primarily BITs, although quite a few of those have never entered into force or lapsed and were not replaced.

There are also multilateral agreements in an Islamic context with membership drawn from right across the MENA region which are relied upon as the foundations for ISDS-based arbitration claims. Two regional agreements in particular are the *Organisation of Islamic Cooperation Agreement on Promotion, Protection and Guarantee of Investments among Member States of the Organisation of the Islamic Conference* (hereinafter the "*OIC Agreement*")[14] and the *Unified Agreement for the Investment of Arab Capital in the Arab States* (hereinafter the "*Arab Investment Agreement*").[15] All GCC member States are signatories to these two agreements. The investor–state dispute settlement component of these two agreements is particularly significant in the context of intra-GCC disputes where the parties have ignored applicable BITs or there is no other applicable BIT available. However, these two agreements also have their shortcomings and inadequacies. The *OIC Agreement*, which is also the agreement most commonly applied in these situations, has attracted particular criticism; the majority of the tribunal in the leading case of *Itisaluna v Iraq*, for example, opining that:

> The Agreement is not a model of clarity in all its terms, leaving some uncertainty about elements of its interpretation and application. There is particular debate about the operation of the dispute settlement provisions of the Agreement, in respect of which there has so far, such that the Tribunal is aware, been no attempt at clarification by the OIC General Secretariat, Secretary General, Member States or OIC Agreement Contracting Parties.[16]

13 See UNCITRAL, 'Arbitration Rules', *United Nations Commission on International Trade Law*, at <https://uncitral.un.org/en/texts/arbitration/contractualtexts/arbitration>; see also ICSID, 'Rules and Regulations' *International Centre for Settlement of Investment Disputes,* at <https://icsid.worldbank.org/rules-regulations>.

14 *Organisation of Islamic Cooperation Agreement on Promotion, Protection and Guarantee of Investments among Member States of the Islamic Conference*, signed 5 June 1981 (entered into force February 1988) ('*OIC Agreement').*

15 *Unified Agreement for the Investment of Arab Capital in the Arab States* signed 26 November 1980 (entered into force 7 September 1981); amendment protocol signed 22 January 2013 ('*Arab Investment Agreement').*

16 *Itisaluna v Iraq*, (n 5) [214].

The GCC as a union has had even less, in fact very little, experience with respect to entering into IIAs, BITs, FTAs, or other treaties with investment provisions. It has concluded FTAs with Syria, with Singapore, and with the European Free Trade Association (EFTA), all of which contain limited to very limited investment encouragement provisions and dispute settlement provisions. For example, the agreement with the EFTA membership comprising Iceland, Liechtenstein, Norway, and Switzerland largely mirrors the WTO's rules and procedures for dispute settlement,[17] with participation limited to the EFTA parties (rather than investors), emphasis on good offices to informally resolve disputes or facilitate procedures, consultation and mediation as settlement strategies, and the removal or cessation of non-conforming measures or regulations.

The GCC has also commenced or re-activated long-standing negotiations for trade and investment agreements with China, New Zealand, and Australia – all of which may also incorporate investment protection provisions and dispute settlement mechanisms in various forms.

1.4 Background and Context: The GCC Member States' Introduction to ISDS

ISDS cases involving the GCC and its member States, either as a respondent state or as an investor claimant home state, are still not at all common in terms of the total number of cases registered globally annually, although there is evidence of an emerging trend for increasing frequency in recent years. This presents somewhat of a challenge for the States, in terms of reviewing their exposure to investor–state arbitration and, potentially, regulatory chill and striking an appropriate balance between investment protection and state sovereignty.

There appears to be a lack of consensus on which arbitration might represent the first ISDS arbitration arising among the GCC member States and relying upon a BIT or other IIA as a basis for a claim – whether initiated by a citizen of a State as claimant or against a State as respondent. This goes to the multifaceted and complex nature of investor–state disputes, which often involve contracts, licences, or permits and thus can potentially be litigated in domestic courts or potentially submitted as investor–state dispute settlement claims and/or as state-to-state disputes. For example, Ghaith Pharaon, a Saudi investor and controversial international business figure, initiated an ISDS arbitration against Tunisia under ICSID Rules in 1986.[18] However, the claim relied on breach of contract law and Tunisia domestic law. The first ISDS case in which a State was the respondent was arguably *Impregilo v UAE*,[19] in which Italian claimants brought a claim related to a

17 As stipulated in Annex 2 'Understanding on Rules and Procedures Governing the Settlement of Disputes' to the *Marrakesh Agreement Establishing the World Trade Organisation*.

18 *Ghaith R Pharaon v Republic of Tunisia* (ICSID Case no. ARB 86/1) ('*Pharaon v Tunisia*').

19 *Impregilo, S.p.A and Rizzani De Eccher S.p.A v United Arab Emirates* (ICSID Case No. ARB/01/1), ('*Impregilo v UAE*'). *Agreement between the Government of the United Arab Emirates and the Gov-*

mosque construction project in 2001, relying on the *UAE–Italy BIT (1995)* and seeking to apply ICSID rules.

The first case under the *Arab Investment Agreement* is recorded as *Tanmiah v Tunisia*,[20] initiated on 13 January 2003 by a Saudi company, Tanmiah for Consultancy Management & Marketing, over claimed sponsorship contract violations in respect of the Mediterranean Games held in Tunisia in September 2001.[21]

In any case, without placing undue emphasis on the occasional early case as a trend-setter or exemplar, what becomes strikingly clear, as demonstrated in the tables that follow in chapters 4 to 6, is that the application of ISDS as a dispute settlement regime is a fairly recent phenomenon, really only appearing in the last two decades and gaining momentum in just the last decade. This is despite the fact that each of the GCC member States has entered into significant numbers of IIFs, BITs, and other related agreements since the 1960s. Should this positive trend continue, the GCC member states will need to recalibrate their attitudes and approaches to the inclusion of ISDS provisions within investment treaties over the short to medium term.

1.5 The Current Debate on Investment Arbitration in the Gulf Region

The nature of the ISDS regime, its legal constructs, objectives, and purposes, and the long reach of its application and outcomes have long been subject to critical and at times intense and savage examination, prompting calls from numerous quarters for review and potential overhaul. José Alvarez summarises the approaches of critics of ISDS as follows:

> The international investment regime has been under the shadow of two hydra-headed monsters for some time. To critics in the Global South, such as Professor M Sornarajah, international investment agreements (IIAs) are an abomination bearing the visage of rapacious greed. They are exemplars of global capitalism run amuck: "neoliberal" tools that violate sovereign equality to grease an empire of capital. To critics in the North, like US Senator Elizabeth Warren, IIAs are top-down undemocratic constraints on

ernment of the Italian Republic for the Promotion and Protection of Investments, signed 22 January 1995 (entered into force 29 April 1997).

20 *Tanmiah for Consultancy Management & Marketing v. Republic of Tunisia and the Organising Committee for the Mediterranean Games 2001 in Tunis,* Arab Investment Court Case No. 1/1.

21 See Walid Ben Hamida, 'The First Arab Investment Court Decision' (2006) 7(5) *Journal of World Investment and Trade* 699–721; see also Gordon Blanke, 'Investment Arbitration in the Middle East: Basic Trends and Developments (Part 2)', *Thomson Reuters Practical Law Arbitration Blog* (17 September 2018) at <http://arbitrationblog.practicallaw.com/investment-arbitration-in-the-middle-east-basic-trends-and-developments-part-2 />.

governments' ability to channel market capitalism to protect labor rights, the environment and income equality.[22]

More generally, the operations and international arbitrations and dispute settlement strategies and campaigns of major international corporations in mining and energy-resource fields, often against least-developed and developing economies, receive particular and ongoing attention.

The nature and operation of the ISDS regime have been exhaustively examined from almost every perspective in regional groupings of nation states with complex overarching governmental and legal frameworks, such as the European Union, and between neighbouring nations with complex free trade agreements such as the United States–Mexico–Canada (free trade) Agreement. ISDS in groupings of nations with greater individual flexibility and less rigidity, such as ASEAN, have also received critical attention.

There is also a significant body of research and writing on aspects of the nature and operation of ISDS in the Gulf region. For example, Charles Brower and Jeremy Sharpe have examined the evolution of international arbitration in a broader context, namely across Islamic countries.[23] Caline Mouawad and Lillian Khoury examined investment arbitration in Arab states, with a focus on the settlement of intra-Arab disputes under the *OIC Agreement* and the *Arab Investment Agreement*.[24] Wolfgang Alschner, Dimitry Skougarevskiy and Mengyi Wang examined the BIT practices of GCC member States in 2016, identifying two trends, namely that they "are global champions of investment protection" and they "have yet to cultivate a uniform practice when it comes to investment treaty-making to speak with one voice in future negotiations with the European Union or the United States".[25] Nadia Naim has examined current international dispute settlement mechanisms in the Shariah context and the impact on the GCC,[26] while Pei Xiao has analysed the Arab Investment Court and its role as a dispute settlement forum.[27] Mohamed Abdel Wahab and Kabir Duggal have investigated the OIC Agreement and the

22 José Alvarez, 'ISDS Reform: The Long View' (2021) 36(2) ICSID Review – *Foreign Investment Law Journal* 253.

23 Charles Brower and Jeremy Sharpe, 'International Arbitration and the Islamic World: The Third Phase' (2003) 97(3) *The American Journal of International Law* 643.

24 Caline Mouawad and Lillian Khoury, 'Investment Arbitration under Multilateral Treaties in the Middle East' (2016) 2(3) *Bahrain Chamber for Dispute Resolution International Arbitration Review* 243–265.

25 Wolfgang Alschner, Dimitry Skougarevskiy and Mengyi Wang, 'Champions of Protection? A Text-as-Data Analysis of the Bilateral Investment Treaties of GCC Countries' (2016) 5(3) *International Review of Law* 1–19.

26 Nadia Naim, 'The International Trojan Horse – Investor to State Dispute Settlements and the Spillover Effects for the Gulf Co-Operation Council' (2017) 31(1) *International Review of Law, Computers and Technology* 131–148.

27 Pei Xiao, 'The Arab Investment Court: Is There Potential for the Innovation of ISDS Mechanism?' (Conference Paper, 5th International Conference on Economics, Management Engineering and Education Technology, 4–6 June 2021).

Unified Agreement for the Investment of Arab Capital in the Arab States.[28] Ahmed Almutawa and AFM Maniruzzaman have conducted a survey of issues associated with the enforcement of arbitral awards in the GCC, for the purpose of identifying how practitioners perceive arbitration, as well as the enforcement of awards, in the GCC.[29] Almutawa and Maniruzzaman also examined "the recent legislative and institutional developments and international arbitral practice in the UAE" as well as assessing "Dubai's prospect to be a Middle East business hub".[30] Nassib Ziadé has published on the topic of arbitration applying Middle East and North Africa IIAs, addressing the treaty-making practices of GCC member States.[31] Gonzallo Villalta Puig and Alice Tung Ho Yee have investigated the anticipated China–GCC FTA.[32] There are many other contributors not mentioned specifically here who have contributed to the current debate on aspects of investment arbitration between countries in the MENA region and beyond.

However, there appears to be relatively little contemporary research into the broader ISDS outcomes with respect to the approach of the GCC member States and the GCC itself as a union to the inclusion or otherwise and design of investment protection and dispute settlement within emerging treaties, particularly in the context of the recent Gulf crisis that severely negatively impacted upon intra-GCC relations and harmonies. To the best of the authors' knowledge at the time of writing, there is yet to be a global study of the experiences of the States with respect to investor–state arbitration. This book therefore endeavours to contribute to academic debate on this topic and the broader topic of Arab states participation in international arbitration, with the hope that it may serve as a useful reference for regulators, practitioners, and investors alike.

Various aspects of leading and precedent-setting ISDS cases, such as *Al-Warraq v Indonesia* and *Itisaluna v Iraq*, have received close scrutiny. But the international context in which the parties to such leading cases exist does not always receive a similar level of attention that they otherwise warrant. Nor is there consolidated attention and analysis of the GCC member State as a respondent or as the home state of claimants, both of which can reveal interesting and valid perspectives in respect of that State's attitudes to attracting incoming foreign investment or

28 Mohamed S Abdel Wahab and Kabir Duggal, *The Resurgence of the Unified Arab Investment Agreement and the Organisation for Islamic Cooperation Investment Agreement: A Dawn of a New Chapter on Investment Protection?* (BRILL, 2022).

29 Ahmed Almutawa and A F M Maniruzzaman, 'Problems of Enforcement of Foreign Arbitral Awards in the Gulf Cooperation Council States and the Prospect of a Uniform GCC Arbitration Law: An Empirical Study' (2014) *University of Portsmouth* <Microsoft Word - AHMED ALMUTAWA_EMPIRICAL STUDY_OCTOBER_2014.doc (port.ac.uk)>.

30 Ahmed Almutawa and A F M Maniruzzaman, 'The UAE's Pilgrimage to International Arbitration Stardom' (2014) 15(1–2) *The Journal of World Investment & Trade* 193, 194.

31 Nassib Ziadé, 'Arbitration under MENA Regional Investment Treaties' (2017) 83(1) *International Journal of Arbitration, Mediation and Dispute Management* 48.

32 Gonzalo Villata Puig and Alice Tung Ho Yee, 'Challenges and Opportunities of the China-Gulf Cooperation Council Free Trade Agreement' (2017) 40(1) *Hastings International and Comparative Law Review* 123.

encouraging and protecting outgoing investment. Critically, while *Al-Warraq v Indonesia* and *Itisaluna v Iraq* involve parties from the States, the interpretation and application of the *OIC Agreement* have broader implications for all OIC treaty partners and investor-claimants seeking to rely on it in the future, particularly with respect to ICSID-administered cases.

However, arising from the authors' own recent experiences in endeavouring to gain a qualitative and quantitative in-depth appreciation of the performance of the GCC and of its member States, both individually and collectively, in international arbitration and dispute settlement, it is suggested that there are some shortcomings in this area of academic research that warrant addressing. This study endeavours to initiate and contribute to addressing at least a few of those shortcomings.

The study draws from and adds to analysis relating to the ISDS experience of the GCC member States and their approach, if any, to reform.[33] It builds upon earlier examinations of the quantitative analysis of the treaty-making practices of the GCC and the States[34] and qualitative research into whether ISDS provisions belong in a Gulf free trade or investment agreement.[35] There is a growing body of research on the emerging trend of some countries publicly proposing to withdraw from their IIAs (such as Indonesia) or reduce their number (such as South Africa) or deal with them on the merits on a case-by-case basis depending on the political party in government (such as Australia). It is suggested that, considering the States' individual and collective long-standing history on entering into IIAs, BITs, and FTAs, and their emerging experiences with ISDS cases, there would be merit in their undertaking policy reviews of a similar nature.

Hence, the study also explores the network of IIAs, BITs, and other treaties containing investment provisions to which the GCC and its member states are a party and examines trends in their treaty-making practices by analysing institutions which facilitate investor–state disputes within the GCC. It does so by examining reported arbitrations involving the GCC member states as either the respondent state or the home state of a claimant investor, and consequently the extent to which ISDS disputes are intra-GCC in the context of the GCC's unique socio-legal construct. The study concludes by exploring possible positions within the GCC with respect to forging new agreements containing investment protection.

1.6 Study Parameters and Methodology

Generally, the information gathered, examined, and eventually tabulated in this study is primarily, but by no means entirely, derived from the UNCTAD Investment

33 Farouk El-Hosseny and Ruba Ghandour,Investor-State-Dispute-Settlement in the Arab world: Is there a clear path? (2018) 10(2) *International Journal of Arab Arbitration* 7–29.

34 Alschner, Skougarevskiy and Wang (n 25).

35 Amelia Hallam and David Price, 'Do Investor-State Dispute Settlement (ISDS) Provisions Belong in a Gulf Trade or Investment Agreement?' in David Price and Alhanoof Al Debasi (eds) *Intellectual Property Rights: Development and Enforcement in the Arab States of the Gulf* (Gerlach Press, 2017).

Dispute Settlement Navigator[36] in respect of cases and, to a lesser extent, its corresponding International Investment Agreements Navigator databases in respect of agreements.[37] UNCTAD describes its Dispute Settlement Navigator as containing information about known international arbitration cases initiated by investors against states pursuant to IIAs.[38]

It should be noted, however, that UNCTAD advises that its data is collected from publicly available sources, with primary sources such as official documents relating to the case and information provided by the administering institutions the main and preferred source of information. It utilises secondary sources, such as specialised reporting services and other sources deemed reliable, to supplement primary sources and/or obtain case information otherwise unavailable. Accordingly, UNCTAD formally acknowledges that the Dispute Settlement Navigator is not necessarily complete; it generally does not include non-reported arbitrations that may have been conducted through private, generally confidential, or restricted-access tribunals, such as the Permanent Court of Arbitration (PCA), the International Chamber of Commerce (ICC), or the London Court of International Arbitration (LCIA) (which have all been used for GCC arbitrations). This is particularly the case in respect of arbitrations conducted through the Arab treaty-based tribunals and the ad hoc tribunals, which are not included or cross-referenced in UNCTAD. The Navigator carries the disclaimer that the site is limited to publicly known IIA-based international investor–state arbitration proceedings, and that "as some proceedings (or certain aspects of proceedings) as well as outcomes and damages awarded can remain confidential, the information contained in the Navigator cannot be deemed exhaustive".[39]

Accordingly, this study errs on the side of inclusion in the interests of gaining as comprehensive a picture as practicable of international arbitration involving the GCC member States in either role. A case that is not referenced in UNCTAD but emerges from the restricted-access commercial arbitration institutions or is referenced in the arbitration reporting services or established media and still appears to have a foreign investor–state fundamental character will usually be included in the following chapter tables. Where there is still doubt as to whether available limited information about a case sufficiently justifies its tabular inclusion, or where preliminary information about a possible emerging case comes to attention, a brief mention will be included in the introductory text to the appropriate table. The aforementioned *Pharaon v Tunisia* is a case in point. The case involved a foreign claimant and State as parties, proceeded under ICSID rules, but relied on contract law and Tunisia's investment law rather than an IIA and appears in ICSID. Had the

36 UNCTAD, Investment Dispute Settlement Navigator, at <https://investmentpolicy.unctad.org/investment-dispute-settlement>.

37 UNCTAD, Investment Agreement Navigator, at <https://investmentpolicy.unctad.org/international-investment-agreements>.

38 UNCTAD (n 36).

39 Ibid, Methodology.

circumstances surrounding the respective parties been somewhat different, it may well have proceeded under an IIA or other international agreement.

Hence, the chapter tables herein, although compiled primarily from UNCTAD's Dispute Settlement Navigator database, adopt a more flexible approach, and ensuing discussions include arbitration reporting services, particularly by the *Investment Arbitration Reporter* subscription service[40] as well as the informed academic discourse on relevant ISDS cases, and occasional other third-party sources such as local media reports and materials from legal professional sources. It is acknowledged that these third-party sources may not be as authoritative as UNCTAD secondary sources, but they often throw some light on basic case facts and ISDS parties' strategies behind a particular claim and/or response and outcomes.

The study's tables include columns for the year of initiation of the claim, a short case name with number, a summary of the case investment and basis of the claim, the outcome of the original proceedings, and, in respect of the GCC member States as respondents (Chapter 4), the home state of the investor claimant. The year of initiation refers to the year that the claim was registered with the arbitrating body, and not the year that the actual arbitration commenced (which may be some years later). The short case name column is taken directly from the UNCTAD or other administering body records. However, where desirable and to avoid confusion, the full case name is also footnoted where considered desirable. The column also includes the administering body case number. The summary of case investment/basis of claim and outcome of original proceedings generally follow the UNCTAD or administering body, but with further clarification where available (for example in cases that are deemed settled or rejected by a tribunal on jurisdiction grounds). The column also includes the IIA on which the claimant is relying.

The information in the outcome of original proceedings column generally is based on the UNCTAD database parameters and information and follows their six options of decided in favour of State, decided in favour of neither party (liability found but no damages awarded), settled, discontinued, pending, and data not available – albeit with slight departures where appropriate (for example where more recent and reliable information is available).

Where a final award has been rendered but the case is subject to follow-on (post-award) proceedings, such as further submissions to the tribunal, annulment proceedings before an ad hoc body, or domestic judicial review, the award is retained in the outcome column (contrary to UNCTAD practice), but the post-award proceedings, to the extent reliably known, will be the subject of a brief case note following the relevant State's table.

The brief case notes also often include further information that the authors consider worthy of note, such as substantial or token damages awarded in relation to the nature of the complaint, moral damages, or undue distribution of costs. Whenever possible, information about amounts claimed and awarded is obtained from primary sources such as the arbitration documents. Otherwise, it is derived

40 *Investment Arbitration Reporter,* at <htpps://iareporter.com/about-us>.

from other publicly available sources that are deemed reliable. In some cases, the approximate amount may be recorded to give a broad indication of the dispute's magnitude.

1.7 Chapter Structure of the Study

This chapter introduces the purpose and objectives of this study. It provides a brief explanation of the system of the global ISDS regime and the experiences of Bahrain, Kuwait, Oman, Qatar, Saudi Arabia, and the United Arab Emirates as GCC member States, as participants in that regime. It also provides a brief introduction in respect of the member states' accession to IIAs generally and BITs particularly.

The chapter also introduces the rather recent history of the emergence of ISDS-based disputations involving the GCC member states as both respondents to claims and as the respective home states of investor claimants. In so doing, it draws attention to the significant difference that exists between the number of intra-GCC disputations and those involving parties from outside the GCC. Both of these aspects continue to be explored in subsequent chapters.

Chapter 2 examines in greater detail the international arbitration framework to the extent that certain elements directly impact or involve the GCC members States. It also conducts a similar exercise in respect of the two major Islamic-based investment agreements with dispute settlement provisions and which regularly appear in the record of disputes involving the GCC member states, namely the *OIC Agreement* and the *Arab Investment Agreement*. Through these analyses, it lays the foundations to explore changes in the treaty-making practices of the States over time.

Chapter 3 details some elements which underpin the ISDS system generally, but which seem to also emerge in the GCC context, namely developments with respect to key definitions and substantive investment protections, and giving particular attention to the definitions of "investor", "investment" and nationality requirements, the fair and equitable treatment standard (FET), the non-expropriation requirement, anti-discrimination, and dispute resolution provisions in respect of both claimants and respondents. These issues are also examined in further detail in later chapters in the context of specific cases.

Chapter 4 examines in some detail the experiences of each State in ISDS-based disputes, as respondents in claims initiated by foreign investors. It includes tables for each member state across this category, noting procedural rules and case number, a summary of investment and basis of the claim, the most recent known status of each case, and the opposing claimant or state.

Generally for each respondent state, the chapter offers commentary in respect of selected cases which have been concluded for one reason or another (for example, by tribunal determination or by mutual consent or by certain action or non-action by either party), focussing primarily on those issues discussed in Chapter 2 or because of particular circumstances of the case which had a bearing on its outcome. Particular attention is given to cases that may reveal or explain some of the issues and questions raised in the earlier chapters concerning the nature of the member states' performance (or, on occasion, non-performance) on the conduct of ISDS arbitrations.

Chapter 5 examines in detail the experiences of each State in ISDS-based disputes as home states of investors initiating arbitration claims. It includes tables for each member state across this category, noting procedural rules and case number, a summary of investment and basis of the claim, the most recent known status of each case, and the opposing claimant or state.

The chapter also offers commentary in respect of certain cases which for one reason or another (for example, because of tribunal determination or certain action or non-action by either party), focus primarily on issues discussed in the earlier chapters or because of particular circumstances of the case which had bearing on its outcome.

Chapter 6 discusses the particular nature of the few intra-GCC cases, in which both parties, claimant and respondent, are from the GCC member States. While few in number, they largely share origins and circumstances which, it could be argued, are not quite within conventional ISDS parameters. Particular attention is given to cases that may reveal or explain some of the issues and questions raised in the earlier chapters concerning the nature of the member states' performance (or, on occasion, non-performance) on the conduct of ISDS arbitrations.

Chapter 7 provides some additional context and perspective on the three ISDS dispute environments examined in the previous chapters. It commences with a brief commentary on the nature of the recent flow of foreign direct investment (FDI) funds into, from, and between the GCC member States. It then considers the nature and status of the domestic foreign investment and arbitration legislative regimes of the various GCC member States to explore the extent to which they relate to or may have a bearing – in support or in hindrance – upon a state's IIA and BIT agreements and international investment arbitration practices.

Chapter 8, authored by Dr Nadia Naim, considers the ISDS regime and its application and dispute outcomes, which may be particularly relevant to the GCC region and other Islamic countries. It explores the question of whether ISDS can be Shariah compliant – particularly in respect of intra-GCC disputes or disputes reliant on the two major Islamic-based agreements discussed in Chapter 2.

The chapter discusses Islamic finance principles incorporated by tribunals into the application of ISDS arbitration initially with the two leading Islamic-based international arbitration agreements, notably the Arab Investment Agreement and the OIC Agreement. It canvasses, for example, the appropriateness or otherwise of the possible reliance on or incorporation of speculative and thus hypothetical perceived and self-calculated potential long-term profits in an ISDS award, which would appear to be contrary to the principles of Islamic finance and investment. It considers whether these agreements might be appropriate vehicles for the application of these Islamic principles of finance and investment.

Chapter 9 endeavours to draw together the various key research outcomes as reported in the preceding chapters. It also reflects on possible changes in the regional ISDS regime that might emerge in the short- to medium-term future. In this regard, it draws in part on commentary and specific suggestions from the various GCC member states in the context of UNCITRAL's Working Group III ongoing campaign for review and reform of the ISDS regime.

1.8 Concluding Remarks

Internationally recognised public international law authority and investment dispute resolution arbitrator Charles Brower, writing in his recent memoir in respect of his time on the Iran–United States Claims Tribunal, has described international arbitration as an "international puzzle box". His description is particularly apt in respect of the application of ISDS rules and procedures in the Gulf region and the wider MENA context.[41] Hopefully this study will untangle or cast some light at least on those pieces of puzzles in the puzzle box.

Bibliography

Agreement between the Government of the United Arab Emirates and the Government of the Italian Republic for the Promotion and Protection of Investments, signed 22 January 1995 (entered into force 29 April 1997).

Almutawa, Ahmed and A. F. M. Maniruzzaman, 'Problems Of Enforcement of Foreign Arbitral Awards in the Gulf Cooperation Council States and the Prospect of a Uniform GCC Arbitration Law: An Empirical Study' (2014) *University of Portsmouth* at <Microsoft Word - AHMED ALMUTAWA_EMPIRICAL STUDY_OCTOBER_2014 .doc (port.ac.uk)>.

Almutawa, Ahmed and A. F. M. Maniruzzaman, 'The UAE's Pilgrimage to International Arbitration Stardom' (2014) 15(1–2) *The Journal of World Investment & Trade*, 193–245.

Alschner, Wolfgang, Dimitry Skougarevskiy and Mengyi Wang, 'Champions of Protection? A Text-as-Data Analysis of the Bilateral Investment Treaties of GCC Countries' (2016) 5(3) *International Review of Law*, 1–19.

Alvarez, Jose, 'ISDS Reform: The Long View' (2021) 36(2) *ICSID Review – Foreign Investment Law Journal*, 253–277.

Ayad, Mary, 'Legal Matters Impacting the Oil and Gas Industry in the Gulf Cooperation Council (GCC) Countries: Keeping Legal Reform and Regulatory Frameworks Current in a Changing Energy Landscape', in Gawdat Bahgat. *The Changing Energy Landscape in the Gulf* (Gerlach Press, 2015).

Blanke, Gordon, 'Investment Arbitration in the Middle East: Basic Trends and Developments (Part 2)', *Thomson Reuters Practical Law Arbitration* blog (17 September 2018) at <http://arbitrationblog.practicallaw.com/investment-arbitration-in-the-middle-east -basic-trends-and-developments-part-2>.

Bonnitcha, Jonathon, Lauge Skovgaard Poulsen and Michael Waibel, *The Political Economy of the Investment Treaty Regime* (Oxford University Press, 2017).

Brower, Charles and Jeremy Sharpe, 'International Arbitration and the Islamic World: The Third Phase' (2003) 97(3) *The American Journal of International Law*, 643–656.

Department of Foreign Affairs and Trade, Commonwealth of Australia, 'ISDS' at <http:// www.dfat.gov.au/trade/topics/Pages/isds.aspx>.

El-Hosseny, Farouk and Ruba Ghandour, 'Investor-State-Dispute in the Arab world: Is there a clear path?' (2018) 10(2) *International Journal of Arab Arbitration*, 1–14.

41 As described in the *Global Arbitration Reporter*, '"Judging Iran": Brower's Memoir and Defence of International Arbitration' as reported in the *Global Arbitration Reporter,* 25 April 2023.

Ghaith R Pharaon v Republic of Tunisia (ICSID Case no. ARB 86/1) (*'Pharaon v Tunisia'*).
Global Arbitration Reporter, '"Judging Iran": Brower's Memoir and Defence of International Arbitration', *Global Arbitration Reporter* (25 April 2023).
Hamida, Walid Ben, 'The First Arab Investment Court Decision' (2006) 7(5) *Journal of World Investment and Trade*, 699–721.
Hallam, Amelia and David Price, 'Do Investor-State Dispute Settlement (ISDS) Provisions Belong in a Gulf Trade or Investment Agreement?' in David Price and Alhanoof Al Debasi (eds) *Intellectual Property Rights: Development and Enforcement in the Arab States of the Gulf* (Gerlach Press, 2017).
Impregilo, S.p.A and Rizzani De Eccher S.p.A v United Arab Emirates (ICSID Case No. ARB/01/1), (*'Impregilo v UAE'*).
ICSID, 'Rules and Regulations' at <https://icsid.worldbank.org/rules-regulations>.
Interhandel (Switzerland v United States) of America [1959] ICJ Rep 46.
Itisaluna Iraq LLC and Others v Republic of Iraq, ICSID Case No. ARB/17/10 (Award, 3 April 2020) (*'Itisaluna v Iraq'*).
Kelsey, J. and L. Wallach, '"Investor-State' Disputes in Trade Pacts Threaten Fundamental Principles of National Judicial Systems', *Public Citizen* (April 2012) at <http://www.citizen.org/documents/isds-domestic-legal-process-background-brief.pdf>.
Mouawad, Caline and Lillian Khoury, 'Investment Arbitration under Multilateral Treaties in the Middle East' (2016) 2(3) *Bahrain Chamber for Dispute Resolution International Arbitration Review*, 243–266.
Naim, Nadia, 'The International Trojan Horse – Investor to State Dispute Settlements and the Spillover Effects for the Gulf Co-operation Council' (2017) 31(1) *International Review of Law, Computers and Technology*, 131–148.
Organisation of Islamic Cooperation Agreement on Promotion, Protection and Guarantee of Investments among member States of the Islamic Conference, signed 5 June 1981 (entered into force February 1988) (*'OIC Agreement'*).
Puig, Gonzalo Villata and Alice Tung Ho Yee, 'Challenges and Opportunities of the China-Gulf Cooperation Council Free Trade Agreement' (2017) 40(1) *Hastings International and Comparative Law Review*.
Salacuse, Jeswald W., 'BIT by BIT: The Growth of Bilateral Investment Treaties and Their Impact on Foreign Investment in Developing Countries' (1990) 24(3) *International Lawyer*, 123–158.
Trakman, Leon and Kunal Sharma, 'Locating Australia on the Pacific Rim: Trade, Investment and the Asian Century' (2015) 12(1) *Transnational Dispute Management, (TDM)*, 1–20.
UNCITRAL, 'Arbitration Rules' at <https://uncitral.un.org/en/texts/arbitration/contractualtexts/arbitration>.
UNCTAD, 'Investment Agreement Navigator' at <https://investmentpolicy.unctad.org/country-navigator>.
UNCTAD, 'Investment Dispute Settlement Navigator' at <https://investmentpolicy.unctad.org/investment-dispute-settlement>.
Unified Agreement for the Investment of Arab Capital in the Arab States, signed 26 November 1980 (entered into force 7 September 1981); amendment protocol signed 22 January 2013 (*'Arab Investment Agreement'*).
Van Harten, Gus, 'Arbitrator Behaviour in Asymmetrical Adjudication (Part Two): An Examination of Hypotheses of Bias in Investment Treaty Arbitration' Research Paper No. 31 (2016) 12(7) *Osgoode Hall Law School*, 1–63.
Wahab, Mohamed S. Abdel, and Kabir Duggal, *The Resurgence of the Unified Arab Investment Agreement and the Organisation for Islamic Cooperation Investment Agreement: A Dawn of a New Chapter on Investment Protection?* (BRILL, 2022).
Xiao, Pei, 'The Arab Investment Court: Is There Potential for the Innovation of ISDS Mechanism?' (Conference Paper, 5th International Conference on Economics, Management Engineering and Education Technology, 4–6 June 2021).
Ziadé, Nassib, 'Arbitration under MENA Regional Investment Treaties' (2017) 83(1) *International Journal of Arbitration, Mediation and Dispute Management*, 48–51.

2 The GCC Member States and Their International Arbitration Frameworks

2.1 Introduction

This chapter introduces the international arbitration framework to the extent of the participation of the GCC member States in that framework, focussing on certain elements that directly impact or involve the States. It briefly considers the history of the States on entering into international arbitration agreements (IIAs), primarily bilateral investment treaties (BITs), and analyses the progress of the States towards their current status in respect of such agreements. It comments on what appears to be an emerging trend, at least by most of the States, to adopt a more conservative approach to entertaining BIT memberships.

The chapter introduces in a similar manner the two major Islamic-based investment agreements with dispute settlement provisions and which regularly appear in the record of arbitration disputes involving the GCC member States, namely, the *Organisation of Islamic Cooperation Agreement on Promotion, Protection and Guarantee of Investments among Member States of the Organisation of the Islamic Conference* ('*OIC Agreement*')[1] and the *Unified Agreement for the Investment of Arab Capital in the Arab States* ('*Arab Investment Agreement*').[2]

2.2 The GCC Member States and Their Bilateral Investment Treaty Frameworks

According to the United Nations Conference on Trade and Development (UNCTAD) database, the GCC member States have entered into a significant number of BITs and other treaties containing investment provisions with foreign countries. In respect of BITs alone, the following constitutes a summary of the UNCTAD database information on the respective States' performance.[3] However,

1 *Organisation of Islamic Cooperation Agreement on Promotion, Protection and Guarantee of Investments among Member States of the Organisation of the Islamic Conference* (*'OIC Agreement')*.

2 *Unified Agreement for the Investment of Arab Capital in the Arab States* (the *'Arab Investment Agreement'). United Nations Conference on Trade and Development.* This Agreement is frequently also referred to in the literature as the "Unified Agreement".

3 United Nations Conference on Trade and Development (UNCTAD), International Investment Agreement Navigator, at <http://investmentpolicyhub.unctad.org/IIA/IiasByCountry#iiaInnerMenu>.

DOI: 10.4324/9781003481072-2

it should be noted that the figures represent the number of BITs as reported to UNCTAD and may not necessarily be a true reflection of the actual number:

- Bahrain – 38 agreements (32 in force, 4 signed but not in force, and 2 terminated/replaced). Bahrain's first BIT was with the United Kingdom, signed in October 1991, and its most recent with Japan in June 2022 (not in force);
- Kuwait – 93 (76 in force, 10 signed but not in force, and 7 terminated/replaced). Kuwait's first BIT was with Iraq, signed in October 1964, but since replaced, and its most recent was with Bangladesh in May 2016 (not in force);
- Oman – 39 (28 in force, 7 signed but not in force, and 4 terminated). Oman's first BIT was with West Germany, signed in June 1979, but since replaced, and its most recent was with Hungary in February 2022 (in force);
- Qatar – 67 (31 in force, 36 signed but not in force, and 1 terminated). Qatar's first BIT was with Tunisia, signed in May 1996, and its most recent with Kazakhstan in October 2022 (not in force);
- Saudi Arabia – 26 (21 in force, 4 signed but not in force, and 1 terminated). Saudi Arabia's first BIT was with the Philippines, signed in October 1994, and its most recent was with Iraq in April 2019 (not in force);
- UAE – 111 (73 in force, 38 signed but not in force, and 2 replaced). UAE's first BIT was with Kuwait, signed in February 1966, but is listed as not yet in force, while its most recent was with the Philippines in June 2022 (not in force).

The above figures reveal a significant variation in the willingness of the various GCC member States to enter into BITs, and thus arguably their objectives or strategies in doing so. The UAE has been the most active with 111 such agreements having been signed, and Saudi Arabia the most conservative with just 26 agreements. However, a third of the UAE's agreements have yet to come into force, including its first, with Kuwait, from 1966. Saudi Arabia, on the other hand, has not only been a more recent BIT participant, with its first agreement signed in 1996, but it has also brought a significant majority of its agreements into force. On the one hand, this active–conservative dichotomy might be viewed as illustrating the very different attitudes between the two countries in respect of attracting and willingness to open up their economies to foreign investment and the accompanying required liberalisation of investment rules to accord more closely with conventional international standards. However, on the other hand, it could also be interpreted as an inclination by resource- and national wealth-rich Saudi Arabia to follow a different strategy in undertaking international business by creating and managing an environment that enables it to largely set its own agenda and does not bind it to conditions espoused in formalised agreements of long standing with terms largely created by other parties that are not necessarily in its own interests.

Figure 2.1 demonstrates the historical aspect of the States' entry into BITs with other countries on a global basis. Apart from a post-independence surge by the UAE in the 1970s, much of the BIT acquisition by all the States has occurred in the 1990s and continued into the early part of the 2000s before significantly declining to the extent of very little in the way of acquisitions in recent years. There are many factors contributing to these performance figures, some political, economic, and trade in character, others international, regional, and domestic. For example, the global economic

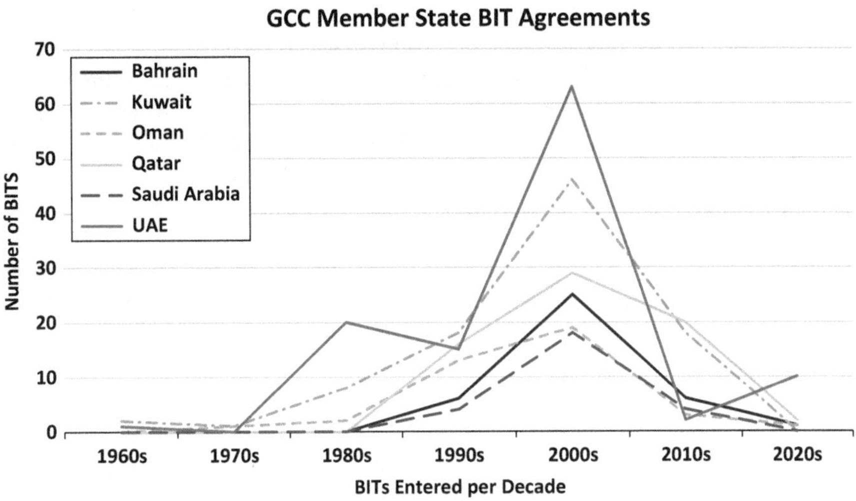

Figure 2.1 GCC member State BIT agreements.

Source: Compiled by the authors as derived from UNCTAD data.

growth along with the establishment of the World Trade Organization (WTO) in 1995 and its drive for trade liberalisation were no doubt positive influences. Bahrain, Kuwait, Qatar, and the UAE became foundation members during 1995/6, Oman was admitted in 2000, and Saudi Arabia was eventually admitted in 2005. However, factors influencing the steady decline over the following decades might well include the global and regional impact of the Iraq War, the global financial crises of 2008–9, and the social and political unrest of the Arab Spring movements. A factor behind Kuwait's acquisition against the trend during the 2000s may well have been in part attributable due to economic and trade reconstruction following the first Iraq war and its brief occupation. The 2019 global pandemic and its impact on global economies and trade must also be a significant factor in the current inactivity trend.

With the exception of the notional *UAE–Kuwait BIT (1966)* which didn't enter into force, none of the States have previously entered into, or are currently signatories to, a BIT with another GCC member State, instead seemingly relying on the GCC umbrella agreements and the two major Arab-based investment agreements (both discussed further later) in respect of intra-GCC arbitration and dispute settlement needs.[4] Between the years 1979 and 2011, all States eventually adopted both the *ICSID Convention (1965)*[5] and the *New York Convention (1958)*.[6]

4 See Chapter 6 for a detailed examination of the intra-GCC ISDS disputes.

5 *Convention on the Settlement of Investment Disputes between States and Nationals of Other States,* adopted 18 March 1965 (entered into force 14 October 1966) ('*ICSID Convention*'): Bahrain (1996), Kuwait (1979), Oman (1995), Qatar (2011), Saudi Arabia (1980), and the UAE (1982).

6 *Convention on the Recognition and Enforcement of Foreign Arbitral Awards,* adopted 10 June 1958 (entered into force 7 June 1959) ('*New York Convention*'): adopted by Bahrain (1988), Kuwait (1978), Oman (1999), Qatar (2002), Saudi Arabia (1994), and the UAE (2006).

Bahrain and Oman (as well as Jordan) have also concluded FTAs with the United States, with almost identical provisions *generally* and specifically in respect of their investment and dispute settlement provisions. Article 10.15 of the Oman–US FTA contains a specific investor–state arbitration mechanism which allows for the submission of a claim to arbitration which is considered by a disputing party not able to be settled by consultation and negotiation. While the Bahrain–US FTA contains some investment protection (e.g. national treatment and non-discrimination), it does not contain a specific mechanism for dispute settlement.[7] Bahrain and Oman's respective FTAs with the United States were the subject of contention and strong objection within the GCC, and with Saudi Arabia in particular. Anja Zorob argued in 2013 that these Agreements potentially "violated the rules of the GCC customs union, as the bilateral FTAs 'break' the common external tariff (CET) agreed on with the other with international GCC members" and further, at worst, may "undermine the credibility of the GCC as a whole".[8] The issue at the heart of the controversy was reportedly the "potential trade deflection", specifically "that the Saudi market could be flooded with highly competitive US products imported duty free via Bahrain".[9] While membership in the GCC has never precluded the individual States from entering into trade and investment treaties containing ISDS on a bilateral basis, it is suggested that the displeasure that existed at the time was not just trade-focussed but a much broader response to the then-United States administration's prevailing broader Middle East policy.

In fact, what appears to be emerging among the States is a tendency to move away from BIT-style specific arbitration agreements. Over the last five years (since 2018) and excluding the UAE, only five BITs have been entered into by the States, and only one is recorded as being in force. Over the same period, the UAE has entered into 32 BITs, only 11 of which are recorded as being in force. It has also entered into five broader-based comprehensive economic partnership agreements (CEPAs).[10] Similar to other CEPAs, these agreements generally follow the style of the established comprehensive agreements with WTO-style chapters. While investment matters and dispute settlement are briefly included, they are Party–Party based, and ISDS is not included.

In respect of the GCC, in its capacity as a regional "unifying" union of member States, it has both enacted internal statutes and entered into a limited number of agreements with external parties, which have an impact on investment and arbitration to some degree and all of which bind its members as a condition of membership. Internally, the major internal statute following on from the GCC Charter is

7 Wolfgang Alschner, Dimitry Skougarevskiy and Mengyi Wang, 'Champions of Protection? A Text-as-Data Analysis of the Bilateral Investment Treaties of GCC Countries' (2016) 5(3) *International Review of Law* 8.

8 Anja Zorob, 'Oman Caught between the GCC Customs Union and Bilateral Free Trade with the US: Is It Worth Breaking the Rules' in Steffen Wippel (ed) (2013) (6) *Regionalizing Oman* (United Nations University Series on Regionalism) (Springer, 2013) 185.

9 Ibid, 189.

10 UNCTAD, International Investment Agreement Navigator (n 3).

the *GCC Economic Agreement* of 2001;[11] externally, the GCC has entered into only seven trade and cooperation agreements, which UNCTAD classifies as IIAs, with third parties since its establishment, the first in 1988 and the most recent in 2012. Only three of the seven have entered into force.[12]

The GCC has been portrayed by its advocates as the means for the fulfilment of the aspirations of the citizens of the Gulf states for some form of Arab regional unity. Accordingly, they exhort that the decision to create the GCC was not a product of the moment but an institutional embodiment of an historical, social, and cultural reality reflecting the deep religious and cultural ties that link the six member States and the strong kin relations that prevail among their citizens.[13] From a more pragmatic perspective, arguably it was also a response to a perceived threat from an Islamic fundamentalist Iran, a Ba'athist Iraq, the state of civil war in Yemen, and the 1979 Soviet intervention in Afghanistan – all of which threatened to destabilise the ruling dynasties in the Arabian Peninsula and to involve their states in wider conflicts. The GCC's advocates further argue that the GCC establishes a cooperative framework for mutual coordination and integration in many fields in order to achieve a strong degree of regional unity.[14] According to the GCC Charter, the underpinnings for this framework are the special relations, common qualities, and similar systems founded on the creed of Islam, faith in a common destiny, and the sharing of one goal.[15]

The current *GCC Economic Agreement*, which supersedes the original Agreement of 1981 enacted on the establishment of the GCC, unifies investment-related legislation and regulations and affords GCC citizens (natural and legal persons) national treatment with respect to their investments.[16] Article 27 of the Agreement contains a mechanism for the settlement of disputes. In the first instance, disputes are heard and settled by the Secretariat General. If the Secretariat General fails to settle a dispute amicably, unresolved claims can be referred to the GCC Commercial Arbitration Centre, the headquarters of which are in Bahrain, by consent. There is scope for matters that fall outside of the competence of the

11 *Economic Agreement between the Gulf Cooperation Council States*, signed 31 December 2001 (entered into force 31 December 2001) (*'GCC Economic Agreement'*) and superseding the *Unified Economic Agreement between the Countries of the Gulf Cooperation Council*, signed 11 November 1981 (entered into force 1 December 1981) 9 (*'GCC Economic Agreement 1981'*) at <https://edit.wti.org/app.php/document/show/d444ad42-56fc-4a5f-b886-34023158dad1>.

12 See UNCTAD, International Investment Agreement Navigator, IIAs by Country Grouping, at https://investmentpolicy.unctad.org/international-investment-agreements/groupings/37/gcc-gulf-cooperation-council->. The Agreements in force are those with the European Union (1988), Singapore (2008), and the European Free Trade Association (EFTA). Those not in force are the Agreements with India (2004), Lebanon (2004), the United States (2012), and Peru (2012).

13 GCC Charter, 'The Concept and Foundations', at <http://gcc-sg.org/en-us/AboutGCC/Pages/StartingPointsAndGoals.aspx>.

14 GCC Charter, Preamble, at <http://gcc-sg.org/en-us/AboutGCC/Pages/Primarylaw.aspx>.

15 Ibid.

16 *GCC Economic Agreement* (n 11), Article 5(1) and (2).

Arbitration Centre, as well as those disputes that cannot be resolved by arbitration and the Secretariat General, to be referred to a specialised judicial commission that will be formed when considered "necessary to adjudicate disputes arising from the implementation of [the] Agreement or resolutions for its implementation".[17] It could be argued that the tenor of disagreement among members that confronted the GCC during the time of the Bahrain and Oman FTAs would have merited the establishment of such a commission, and more so the more recent diplomatic crisis between Saudi Arabia, the UAE, and Bahrain on one side and Qatar on the other side which threatened the very foundations of the GCC. Since this latest suite of disputations and ISDS claims arising therefrom have yet to be resolved (even though some degree of stability has returned to the GCC), it may be timely for that dispute settlement commission to be constituted. However, it is difficult to envisage how such an internally constituted body would effectively operate and resolve the disputes in view of the demarcation of the GCC into three distinct camps, namely the two sparring parties and the determinedly non-involved pair of Kuwait and Oman.

The GCC Financial and Economic Committee is responsible for proposing a charter for the judicial commission. Article 27(4) of the Agreement provides that until the charter of the specialised judicial commission comes into force, all disputes in which the parties do not agree to settle through arbitration and which are not "amicably settled by the Secretariat General, shall be referred to the competent GCC committees for settlement". It is not clear from the language of the Agreement specifically what these competent committees are, and how and when they were constituted. The Introduction to the Agreement refers to competent committees but does not particularise them, save for a Committee of the GCC Deputy Ministers of Finance and the Financial and Economic Committee. It then continues and refers to "other committees" and to "GCC working committees". Article 26 of the Agreement refers to unspecified committees "working under the framework of the GCC",[18] while Article 33 authorises the Financial and Economic Committee to interpret the Agreement.[19]

The GCC Commercial Arbitration Centre was established in 1995. Based in Bahrain, it is a regional-level arbitration institution, independent of the GCC member States, but its charter does not encompass ISDS cases. Its jurisdiction is limited to adjudicating "trade and business disputes between GCC nationals or between them and other nationals".[20]

As mentioned above, of the seven trade and cooperation agreements into which the GCC has entered with third parties and which UNCTAD classifies as IIAs, only three are in force. However, none of the agreements include specific reference to ISDS dispute settlement. Mention of investment and/or investment protection is

17 Ibid, Article 27.
18 Ibid, Article 26.
19 Ibid, Article 33.
20 'About the Centre' (undated), *GCC Commercial Arbitration Centre* <https://gccac.org/en/about-centre>.

only in passing or in general groupings of areas of interest within the scope of an agreement. The dispute settlement provision is limited to disputes between the parties in respect of specific terms of an agreement and generally mirrors or refers to WTO processes. For example, the *EC–GCC Cooperation Agreement*, which is in force, limits specific reference to investment in the following general terms:

> In the field of investments, the Contracting Parties shall strive to take steps for the mutual promotion and protection of investments, in particular through the extension by the Member States of the Community and the GCC countries of investment promotion and protection agreements with a view to improving reciprocal investment conditions.[21]

2.3 The GCC Member States and the Islamic-Based Investment Treaties

The GCC member States are all signatories to two key multilateral treaties containing investment provisions, namely the *OIC Agreement* (excepting Bahrain, which has not ratified the Agreement) and the *Arab Investment Agreement*. They are also signatories to an earlier brief and aspirational agreement on the promotion of investment sponsored by the Council of Arab Economic Unity within the League of Arab States, namely, the *Agreement on Investment and Free Movement of Arab Capital among Arab Countries* (*Arab League Investment Agreement*).[22] The primary purpose of that agreement was to strengthen economic ties promoting "free movement of persons and capital, freedom of residence and employment and pursuance of economic activity".[23] However it contained only the briefest passing mention of investment and its protection.

The *OIC Agreement* objective is the facilitation and promotion of an Islamic investment, economic integration, and development climate. For example, one of the objects of the *OIC Agreement* is to:

> provide and develop a favourable climate for investments, in which the economic resources of the Islamic countries could circulate between them so that optimum utilization could be made of these resources in a way that will serve their development and raise the standard of living of their peoples.[24]

The *Arab Investment Agreement,* on the other hand, promotes a much narrower vision of a pan-Arab investment climate to stimulate Arab economic resources in

21 *Cooperation Agreement between the European Economic Community, of the One Part, and the Countries Parties to the Charter of the Cooperation Council for the Arab States of the Gulf, of the Other Part*, signed 15 June 1988 (entered into force 1 January 1990), Article 7.

22 *Agreement on Investment and Free Movement of Arab Capital among Arab Countries*, signed 29 August 1970 (entered into force 29 August 1970) ('*Arab League Investment Agreement*').

23 Ibid, Preamble.

24 *OIC Agreement* (n 1), Preamble.

the field of joint Arab investment with a well-established, coherent, and integrated legal system:

> more conducive to a form of Arab economic citizenship sharing common features whereby the Arab investor, irrespective of nationality, may operate according to provisions identical to those applied by any State to its citizens, together with provision for freedom to transfer Arab capital within the Arab States and protect it by means of guarantees against non-commercial risks and a special judicial system, in addition to privileges and facilities which the investor may be granted by the host State within the context of its national sovereignty,[25]

Both Agreements also include several investment protection provisions such as the prohibition of unlawful direct and indirect expropriation, protection and security, and most favoured nation (MFN) treatment. However, contrary to many investment treaties, they do not contain provisions on fair and equitable treatment or national treatment provisions. They contain ISDS provisions which, until relatively recently, have not been used.

2.3.1 The OIC Agreement

The Organisation of Islamic Cooperation members approved and opened for signature the *OIC Agreement* at its Twelfth Islamic Conference of Foreign Ministers held in Baghdad, Iraq, on 1–5 June 1981. However, it was another seven years before the Agreement came into force in February 1988, by which date it reportedly had been ratified by 29 out of the then 36 member states. Of the GCC member States, only Kuwait and Saudi Arabia had ratified; Bahrain has still yet to sign or ratify.[26]

Although coming into force in 1988, the *OIC Investment Agreement* had "languished in obscurity"[27] until utilised by Saudi investor Hesham Al-Warraq in his ISDS claim against Indonesia in August 2011.[28] Since *Al-Warraq v Indonesia*, there have been another 21 reported disputes which have relied, or are relying, on the Agreement. Seventeen of those cases have been brought by claimants from the

25 *Arab Investment Agreement* (n 2), Preamble.

26 Report of the OIC Secretary General, 38th Session of the Follow-up Committee of the Standing Committee for Economic and Commercial Cooperation of the OIC, Ankara, Turkey, 24–5 May 2022, Appendix 1.

27 Craig Gaver and Yusuf Kumtepe, 'Checking in on the OIC Investment Agreement: New Arbitrations, but Slow Progress on Creating a Permanent Dispute Settlement Mechanism' *Kluwer Arbitration Blog* (17 March 2023), at <https://arbitrationblog.kluwerarbitration.com/2023/03/17/checking-in-on-the-oic-investment-agreement-new-arbitrations-but-slow-progress-on-creating-a-permanent-dispute-settlement-mechanism/>.

28 *Hesham Talaat M. Al-Warraq v Republic of Indonesia (Final Award)* (UNCITRAL, 15 December 2014) ('*Al-Warraq v Indonesia*'); Lexology, 'The Organisation of Islamic Cooperation Agreement on Promotion, Protection and Guarantee of Investments among Member States' (web page, 7 May 2018) <https://www.lexology.com/library/detail.aspx?g=87aca22f-7c97-4fda-bad2-6f4cdefb066>.

GCC member States, and six of those are intra-GCC disputes.[29] It has been suggested elsewhere that the value of the Agreement is that it provides protection to foreign investments between OIC members where no BIT exists.[30] This is certainly the situation with the intra-GCC cases since there are no BITs in force between the States. But it is worth noting that there are instances of BITs being in place alongside the Agreement in some cases (including *Al-Warraq v Indonesia*) initiated by the States and involving parties to the OIC. It would appear that the States would prefer to rely on the Agreement where given the choice, notwithstanding the existence of practical difficulties on occasion with arbitration administration for example, disputation over jurisdiction, or appointment of arbitrators.

Acknowledging its very broad membership base, the *OIC Agreement* defines an investor as "the Government of any contracting party or natural corporate person, who is a national of a contracting party and who owns the capital and invests it in the territory of another contracting party".[31] Nationality is determined, in the case, as any individual enjoying the nationality of a contracting party according to the provisions of the nationality law in force therein. Legal personality, on the other hand, is determined as "Any entity established in accordance with the laws in force in any contracting party and recognized by the law under which its legal personality is established", which closely parallels the equivalent definition in the first-generation BITs and the associated issues that have arisen with shell companies.

However, claimants applying the *OIC Agreement* have demonstrated an unwillingness to always comply with procedural requirements and a willingness to raise jurisdictional and interpretative objections in arbitrations, perhaps because the Agreement's language is somewhat ambiguous and anachronistic, and it contemplated a bespoke permanent judicial body to both determine and apply any interpretative uncertainties and requirements, and perhaps because respondents perceived these shortcomings to be opportunities to frustrate the process or defeat claims before they were able to proceed to the merits phase. For example, parties have failed to appoint an arbitrator, objected to the jurisdiction of a tribunal on the grounds that the Agreement does not contain an investor–state mechanism or first requires consent to arbitration or additional consent, or contested the interpretation of the most-favoured-nation provisions to import or exclude MFN conditions from other treaties.

The *Al-Warraq* case has been analysed and dissected frequently and at some length since its conclusion and has proven to be an interesting test as to how the *OIC Agreement* would be interpreted and applied. Articles 8 and 9 address MFN and national treatment provisions respectively. The MFN provisions have been utilised by claimants on more than one occasion to import into a dispute in support of their claim investor rights and privileges more favourable to their cause than those

29 Case Profiles, *Investment Arbitration Reporter* (undated), at <https://www.iareporter.com/arbitration-cases/?fwp_treaty=oic-investment-agreement&fwp_arbitration_cases_sort=year_desc&fwp_per_page=100>.

30 Gaver and Kumtepe, *Kluwer Arbitration Blog* (n 27).

31 *OIC Agreement* (n 1), Article 1(6).

within the Agreement. In *Al-Warraq v Indonesia*, the tribunal found that Article 8 (the MFN clause) "applies to import other clauses as long as the *ejusdem generis* rule applies", finding that "the subject matter of the OIC Agreement relied upon by the Claimant to import fair and equitable treatment, is the same, which is the protection of the foreign investment".[32] The tribunal also found that that "reference to "same economic activity" did not impose "a limitation on the scope of application of the MFN clause relevant".[33] The tribunal was thus prepared to take a rather liberal view of the operation of Article 8 of the Agreement.[34] However, the tribunal in *Itisaluna v Iraq* took a more conservative view of the claimant's endeavours to import arbitration consent provisions from the *Iraq–Japan BIT* into the Agreement, finding that "Article 8(1) of the OIC Agreement is subject to exception and limitation, both express and by necessary implication, that exclude its application to incorporate an ICSID consent to arbitration clause from another treaty".

Andrew Newcombe and Jean-Michel Marcoux argue that the most thought-provoking aspect of the *Al-Warraq v Indonesia* case is the "treatment of foreign investor obligations under Article 9 of the Agreement", specifically the tribunal's confirmation of "the applicability of IIA provisions imposing international obligations on foreign investors in investor-State dispute settlement".[35] Article 9 stipulates that:

> The investor shall be bound by the laws and regulations in force in the host state and shall refrain from all acts that may disturb public order or morals or that may be prejudicial to the public interest. He is also to refrain from exercising restrictive practices and from trying to achieve gains through unlawful means.

In *Al-Warraq v Indonesia*, the tribunal ultimately found that the respondent had failed to afford the claimant fair and equitable treatment in contravention of Article 9 of the Agreement. However, the tribunal held that the claimant had breached Indonesian laws and acted in a manner "prejudicial to the public interest", finding that the claimant's actions ultimately fell "within the scope of the application of the 'clean hands' doctrine" and thus could not "benefit from the protection afforded by the OIC Agreement".[36] Newcombe and Marcoux argue that "this is where the future development of the investment treaty regime lies – a symmetrical regime in which foreign investors have international rights as well as obligations".[37]

32 *Al-Warraq v Indonesia* (n 28), (Final Award, UNCITRAL, 15 December 2016) [551].

33 Ibid [552].

34 Gordon Blanke, 'The OIC Agreement and Its MFN Clause: A Question of Scope', *Thomson Reuters* (24 July 2020) at <The OIC Agreement and its MFN clause: a question of scope | Arbitration Blog (practicallaw.com)>.

35 Andrew Newcombe and Jean-Michel Marcoux, 'Hesham Talaat M. Al-Warraq v Republic of Indonesia: Imposing International Obligations on Foreign Investors' (2015) 30(3) *ICSID Review* 525, 531–2.

36 *Al-Warraq v Indonesia* (n 28), [647].

37 Newcombe and Marcoux (n 35), 532.

Article 16 of the *OIC Agreement* provides that host states (of an investment) will undertake to afford claimant-investors the right to institute proceedings through domestic institutions. However, it continues to effectively preclude investors from duplicating proceedings and seeking relief through domestic courts and in arbitration, thus requiring the claimant to make a choice.[38] Under the Agreement, decisions by the arbitral tribunal are binding and enforceable, with the force of judicial decisions by the contracting parties in their respective territories, whether or not they are a party to the relevant dispute and regardless "of whether the investor against whom the decision was passed is one of its nationals or residents or not, as if it were a final and enforceable decision of its national courts".[39] However, this has not prevented either a losing party or a disappointed party from seeking judicial redress over a perceived wrong or from exploiting a strategic opportunity in another jurisdiction.

In respect of the establishment of the arbitration procedure itself, the *OIC Agreement* stipulates straightforward and conventional steps, namely, the claimant lodges a request for arbitration with details and advises the respondent of their appointment as arbitrator. The respondent in turn advises of their arbitrator appointment, and then both parties collaborate on the appointment of an arbitration panel chair. If the second party does not appoint an arbitrator, or if the two arbitrators do not agree on the appointment of a chair within the prescribed time, either party may request the Secretary-General of the Organisation of the Islamic Conference to complete the composition of the Arbitration Tribunal. Simple. However, the refusal of a party to appoint an arbitrator, followed by the Secretary-General declining to so act pursuant to the Agreement and thus frustrate the creation of the tribunal and the arbitration, has plagued cases brought under the Agreement. In some instances, this was because of appointment time limitations and "political pressure" from some OIC members relating to an objection to consent to arbitrate, prompting the Permanent Court of Arbitration (PCA) to intervene and designate an appointing authority upon request by frustrated claimants.[40]

The PCA has certainly demonstrated a willingness to intervene in both intra-GCC and extra-GCC cases to facilitate the constitution of tribunals when respondent states and the OIC Secretary-General have failed to act. In *Bin Sulaiman v Oman*,[41] the claimant apparently requested assistance from the PCA with respect to

38 *OIC Agreement* (n 1), Article 16.

39 Ibid, Article 17(2)(d).

40 Yusuf Kumtepe and Riccardo Loschi, 'Investment Dispute Settlement Body of the Organisation of Islamic Cooperation: A Dead End for Claims under the OIC Investment Agreement?' (29 December 2019) *Kluwer Arbitration Blog* at <Kluwer Arbitration Blog>; referring to Jarrod Hepburn and Luke Eric Peterson, 'Investigation: As New Cases Emerge under Islamic Investment Treaty, Initial Viability of Claims Seems to Hinge on Willingness of Respondents to Appoint Arbitrators', *Investment Arbitration Reporter* (2 March 2017).

41 Luke Eric Peterson, 'OIC Round up: An Update on Pending Arbitration Cases Lodged under the OIC Investment Agreement', *Investment Arbitration Reporter* (11 August 2020) at <OIC round up: An update on pending arbitration cases lodged under the OIC Investment Agreement | Investment Arbitration Reporter (openathens.net)>.

constituting a tribunal (London being the seat of arbitration).[42] The PCA designated an appointing authority to make an appointment.[43] Similar instances of arbitrator non-appointment by the OIC Secretary-General and consequent PCA intervention occurred with respect to the *beIN v Saudi Arabia* case and the *Al-Medhar v Egypt* case.[44] However, in the case of *D.S. Constructions v Libya*, the PCA determined it had competence to intervene and appointed an arbitrator after the respondent and the Secretary-General failed to do so. On appeal by Libya to the Paris Court of Appeal (Paris being the seat of arbitration), the Court annulled the preliminary award, relevantly finding that the *OIC Agreement* did not allow for the PCA Secretary-General to intervene if the OIC Secretary-General didn't make an appointment.

The most recent series of arbitrations involving GCC member States in which the *OIC Agreement* is applicable relates to disputes over Qatar Airways Group's right to operate in Bahrain, Saudi Arabia, and the UAE and the revocation of Qatar Airways' licences by these States. The *Arab Investment Agreement* is also being applied with respect to these three disputes.[45] In a related action, Qatar Airways has also brought a claim against a non-GCC country, namely Egypt, with the *OIC Agreement* and the *Arab Investment Agreement* again being applied in addition to the *Egypt–Qatar BIT (1999)*.[46] The disputes appear to be ongoing notwithstanding the January 2021 GCC Summit during which Saudi Arabia, the UAE, and Bahrain "agreed to lift their blockade of Qatar in the interest of moving past the 2017–2021 Gulf crisis".[47] The outcome of the arbitrations initiated against Bahrain, Saudi Arabia, and the UAE by Qatar Airways will be an exemplar of the settlement of intra-GCC investor–state disputes under regional agreements in the absence of an applicable BIT.

The *OIC Agreement* has been the subject of frequent analysis and recent review. Joel Dahlquist and Luke Eric Peterson reported in 2019 that states party to the Agreement were working towards replacing the dispute settlement mechanism with a permanent mechanism and revising the substantive investment protections, arguing that concern about exposure to investor–state claims has contributed to reform endeavours.[48] In particular, the reforms are intended to address concerns

42 Damien Charlotin, 'Breaking: Paris Court Finds That PCA Secretary General Lacked Power to Step into Libya Arbitration When OIC Secretary General Failed to Appoint Arbitrator', *Investment Arbitration Reporter* (26 March 2021) at <Breaking: Paris Court finds that PCA Secretary General lacked power to step into Libya arbitration when OIC Secretary General failed to appoint arbitrator | Investment Arbitration Reporter (openathens.net)>.

43 Luke Eric Peterson (n 41).

44 Ibid.

45 UNCTAD (n 3).

46 Ibid at <Qatar Airways v. Egypt | Investment Dispute Settlement Navigator | UNCTAD Investment Policy Hub>.

47 Giorgio Cafiero, '42nd GCC Summit: An Opportunity for Reconciliation', *Gulf International Forum* (10 December 2021) at <42nd GCC Summit: An Opportunity for Reconciliation - Gulf International Forum (gulfif.org)>.

48 Joel Dahlquist and Luke Eric Peterson, 'Governments Working to Rein in Use of OIC Investment Treaty's Investor-State Arbitration Offer', *Investment Arbitration Reporter* (3 April 2019) at <Gov-

relating to the impact of ISDS in terms of "sovereignty, legitimacy and capacity".[49] The creation of a permanent dispute settlement body with an appellate mechanism and an effective review process, together with procedural rules and appointment mechanisms that promote the rule of law, such as an independent panel of tribunal members with security of tenure, would make a substantive contribution to addressing those concerns. However, arguably, more needs to be done to modernise and improve the substantive protections.

2.3.2 The Arab Investment Agreement

In 1980, the members of the League of Arab States (LAS) adopted and opened for signature the *Arab Investment Agreement* on 26 November 1980 during the Eleventh Arab Summit Conference in Amman, Jordan. The Agreement entered into force on 7 September 1981, by when all but 2 of their 22 members had ratified it. It was amended in 2012, with the Amendment adopted in January 2013 at the Riyadh Economic Summit, and entered into force on 24 April 2016. However, the broad authority across the membership of the LAS of the Amendment seems unclear. Article 44 of the original Agreement stipulates that amendments shall enter into force for the ratifying States three months after the lodgement of their instruments of ratification, while Article 30 of the Amendment document affirms that the amendments shall apply to those Arab States which have ratified or acceded to the Amendment document by submission of their instruments of ratification or accession. And the number of Amendment ratifications seems equally unclear. This raises an interesting conjecture on the validity of certain of its elements in a dispute. For example, the Agreement generally parallels the *OIC Agreement* in respect of national treatment and MFN provisions.[50] However, notwithstanding its earlier MFN provision, the Agreement in its original form also provides for discretionary preferential treatment atop minimum standards applications: Article 16 provides that:

> The State Party may establish additional privileges for the Arab investor in excess of the minimum stipulated within this Agreement. In the according of preferential privileges, regard shall be had, in particular, for the following considerations:

- The importance of the project with regard to the future development of the national economy;
- Joint Arab projects;
- The size of Arab participation in administration of the project;
- The extent of Arab possession of the technology employed;

ernments working to rein in use of OIC investment treaty's investor-state arbitration offer | Investment Arbitration Reporter (openathens.net)>.

49 Yusuf Kumptepe and Riccardo Loschi (n 40).

50 See *OIC Agreement* (n 1), Article 14 and *Arab Investment Agreement* (n 2), Article 5.

- The achievement of greater Arab control over the administration and the technology employed;
- The creation of employment opportunities for nationals of the host State and Arabs and the capital contribution to the State in which the investment is made;
- The sector in which the investment is made.

The State Party in which the investment is made may similarly establish preferential treatment according to the foregoing considerations for Arab investment projects which are essentially owned by Arab nationals.

A more cautious preferential treatment provision still appears in a more general form in the Amendments as Article 16, although the specific detail has been deleted:

1. the Council may, at the request of any State Party, agree to suspend enforcement in that State of any of the provisions of the Agreement and may impose limits of time, place, or subject-matter accordingly. The competent authorities within the State must be guided by the observations and recommendations of the Council in order to ensure a return to compliance with the Agreement;
2. the provision of Paragraph (1) of this Article shall not include privileges and guarantees previously accorded to any Arab investor in the scope of this Agreement.

Amr Hassan suggests that Arab investors tended not to refer their inter-Arab disputes to ISDS under the Agreement primarily because it was ostensibly anonymous to Arab investors.[51] Even in 2019, "Arab investors are more enthusiastic in referring disputes to other forums, such as the Permanent Court of Arbitration (PCA), Organisation of Islamic Cooperation (OIC) Investment Treaty, and especially ICSID".[52]

However, the major critical difference between these two Islamic-based agreements is that the *Arab Investment Agreement* is the first investment agreement to establish a permanent forum for the settlement of investor–state disputes with its Arab Investment Court. As Michael Farchakh states, "critics of Investor-State Arbitration who have called for the creation of a permanent investment court have often neglected the fact that such a jurisdiction has existed for quite some time".[53]

Not unlike the *OIC Agreement*, the *Arab Investment Agreement* also includes a fork-in-the-road provision, which requires complainants to make an election about relief. However, it is somewhat different in that it is a choice between domestic

51 Amr Arafa Hassan, 'The 2013 Amendments to the Arab Investment Agreement' (2019) 34(1) *ICSID Review* 107–35.

52 Ibid.

53 Michael Farchakh, 'The Arab Investment Court and Intra-Arab BITs: A Potential New Frontier?', *Kluwer Arbitration Blog* (29 December 2020) at <The Arab Investment Court and Intra-Arab BITs: a Potential New Frontier? - Kluwer Arbitration Blog>.

litigation or the Arab Investment Court, as opposed to arbitration more generally. Article 25 of the original version of the Agreement states that "Disputes arising from the application of this Agreement shall be settled by way of conciliation or arbitration or by recourse to the Arab Investment Court". The Agreement also contains a "fork-in-the-road provision", whereby Article 31 states that "where the Arab investor brings an action before one authority, he must refrain from so doing before the other".[54] Similarly, Article 21 (of the amended 2013 version) states that "whether the Arab investor initiates legal action before one authority, said investor may not initiate legal action before the other".

The Agreement includes an Annex which deals with conciliation and arbitration. Article 2(1) of the Annex states that where the parties fail to agree to engage in conciliation or where the conciliator is not able to hand down a decision within the time limit or the parties do not agree to accept the proposed solutions, the parties may resort to arbitration by agreement. Article 2(9) imposes a strict time limit, requiring the relevant arbitral tribunal to hand down a decision within six months of the tribunal first convening, although the LAS Secretary-General may extend the period once for no more than six months if deemed necessary and upon the substantiated request of the tribunal.

Article 27 deals with access to legal action and does not require "a prior specific consent", but rather creates a "compulsory", yet "subsidiary" jurisdiction of the Arab Investment Court, providing that each party may seek recourse to legal action in order to settle a dispute in the following instances of failure:

- of the two parties to agree to the expedient of conciliation;
- of the conciliator to award his decision within the period specified;
- of the two parties to agree on accepting the solutions proposed in the decision of the conciliator;
- of the two parties to resort to arbitration;
- of the arbitral panel to award a decision within the prescribed period for whatever reason.

While the *OIC Agreement* merely contemplates the establishment of an organ for the settlement of investment disputes, the *Arab Investment Agreement* expressly addresses the creation and workings of an Arab Investment Court, in anticipation of the future establishment of the Arab Court of Justice. Article 28 states that the Court will be composed of at least five judges plus several reserve judges, each of whom shall have a different Arab nationality and shall have the necessary academic and moral qualifications to assume high-ranking legal positions nominated by each State party. The Council shall appoint the Chairman of the Court from among the Court. Appointment shall be on a full-time basis for a period of three years with provision for renewal.

54 Ahmed Kotb, 'Egypt: The Arab Investment Court' (2016) *International Financial Law Review* at <Egypt: The Arab Investment Court | International Financial Law Review (iflr.com)>.

Article 29 provides that the Court shall have jurisdiction to settle disputes brought before it by either party to an investment that relate to or arise from application of the provisions of the Agreement. The disputes must have occurred between:

(a) any State Party and another State Party or between a State Party and the public institutions and organisations of the other parties or between the public institutions and organisations of more than one State Party;
(b) the persons referred to in paragraph 1 and Arab investors;
(c) the persons referred to in paragraphs 1 and 2 and the authorities providing investment guarantees in accordance with this Agreement.

Article 30 allows for the referral of disputes capable of being settled by international arbitration to the Arab Investment Court, by agreement. It provides that where an international Arab agreement setting up an Arab investment or any agreement related to investment within the scope of the LAS stipulates that a matter of dispute should be referred to international arbitration or to an international court, the parties involved may agree to regard it as being within the jurisdiction of the Court.

Some BITs concluded between GCC member States and other Arab states incorporate access to the Arab Investment Court, for example the *Bahrain–Jordan BIT*, which states in Article 7(B):

> All disputes related to investments between any of the two contracting parties and an investor from the other contracting party concerning his investment, if the dispute cannot be settled friendly within six months of the dispute notification date by either party it may submitted by the investor request either to:
>
> …
>
> Or according to the provisions of the chapter related to disputes settlement of the consolidated agreement for Arab capital investment in the Arab country for 1986.

Consent to submit disputes to the Arab Investment Court, whether in the form of express prior consent or otherwise in BITs, may encourage claimants to forgo access to relief under the *Arab Investment Agreement* and apply instead more favourable investment protections or broadly scoped definitions in BITs. Certainly, the cases mentioned below applying the *Arab Investment Agreement* seem to reflect the fact that generally, claimants are less inclined to apply the treaty if an alternative is available.

The Court, based in Cairo, was established in 1983. Its Statute came into force on 2 February 1985, and its internal rules were adopted by the General Assembly of the Court during its first session between 25 February and 3 March 1986. Although operational in principle from 1986, it did not consider its first case until 2003, when a Saudi company, Tanmiah for Consultancy Management & Marketing (Tanmiah), brought an action before the Court for alleged violation of the terms of the contract which it had concluded in 1999 with the Organising Committee for the Mediterranean Games for the exclusive marketing of the Games. Tanmiah sought damages of USD68 million, including moral damages. The Court rendered its decision on 12 October 2004.[55] The Court rejected the claims on both jurisdictional grounds and on the merits, in the latter matter holding in part that Tanmiah's failure to meet his obligations under the contract nullified his claim.[56] Since then, the Court has reportedly rendered 20 judgments by the end of 2020,[57] with further matters presumably pending.

There have been very few investor–state arbitrations submitted by claimants from GCC home states or against GCC host states which seek to apply the Agreement. However, there appears to be a trend emerging where claimants seek to apply the *OIC Investment Agreement* in the absence of a more favourable applicable BIT or incorporate (mostly unsuccessfully) the more favourable provisions of a BIT through the MFN clause in the *OIC Agreement*, as opposed to the *Arab Investment Agreement.* One notable exception to this trend is the suite of Qatar Airways claims, suggesting that claimants from GCC-home states are more comfortable applying the *Arab Investment Agreement*, compared with claimants external to the GCC.

Michael Farchakh speculates that there are three key reasons for the neglect and underutilisation of the *Arab Investment Agreement*, namely that proceedings in the Arab Investment Court are conducted in Arabic; that claimants and their legal representatives may prefer to submit claims to arbitration in which they can appoint arbitrators, and, being the most paramount consideration, the narrow scope of the definition of investors.[58] Farchakh argues that although the definition of "investor" was relaxed somewhat in the Amendment Protocol, the original language applies if the respondent or home state of the claimant hasn't ratified the revision; and notwithstanding which definition applies, this "presents a clear hurdle" for multinational companies operating through entities incorporated in the region. Certainly, the distribution and nationality of claimants in cases arbitrated on an intra-GCC or extra-GCC basis support this argument.[59] Given that a key element of the planned diversification of GCC economies is to encourage or require foreign investors to establish a local presence, it is likely the application of investor–state disputes and recourse to the Arab Investment Court by extension will continue to be underutilised until the language of the treaty is further modernised and perhaps broadened so that investors are not applying more favourable BITs, the appointment of arbitrators is more party-directed, and the proceedings of the Arab Investment Court are conducted on a more inclusive basis and are more international in flavour.

55 See Walid Ben Hamida, 'The First Arab Investment Court Decision' (2006) 7(5) *Journal of World Investment and Trade* for an extensive analysis of the Tanmiah case; see also Gordon Blanke (n 35).
56 Hamida (n 55), 20–1.
57 Michael Farchakh (n 53).
58 Ibid.
59 Ibid.

2.4 Concluding Remarks: A Region-Specific Character

The GCC or any of its member States does not have model agreements, and there appears little inclination to proceed down that path. The States may benefit from developing a model treaty, which may go some way towards improving consistency in the drafting of future trade and investment treaties containing investment protections and treaty-making practices of the States. However, this may be difficult to achieve in practice because of the complex and tenuous relationships between them.

These potential agreements are significant because, for example, China, New Zealand, and Australia each has different investment relationships with the GCC, and all have been in extended and at times suspended negotiations over proposed FTAs. They have also adopted different positions in relation to ISDS and ISDS reform. Therefore, the design of investment protection provisions and dispute settlement mechanisms within these instruments is likely to differ and expose the GCC member States to different levels of adverse arbitral awards and non-arbitrated outcomes, for example, regulatory chill.

There are a number of examples discussed above where GCC member States named as respondents have tried to undermine or frustrate the dispute settlement process by, for example, not complying by failing to appoint an arbitrator or objecting to jurisdiction (as occurred in *Al-Medhar v Egypt*, for example*)*. Perhaps unsurprisingly, there is evidence of an unwillingness of the Secretary-General to step in and appoint arbitrators in circumstances where the respondent state has failed or declined to do so. However, the PCA has demonstrated a willingness to facilitate the constitution of tribunals by acting as an appointing authority. There are also examples of claimants attempting to apply the MFN provision in a multilateral investment agreement in order to obtain access to a more favourable BIT (as in *Alyafei v. Jordan (1)*). In some instances, claimants have experienced difficulty enforcing awards, despite making seemingly *bona fide* attempts to settle prior to arbitration (*Al-Kharafi v. Libya and others*). Together these actions demonstrate a consensus that both the substantive investment protections, the dispute settlement protections, and the broader IIA network need careful review and updating. More generally, there is a lack of transparency in the progress of claims submitted to arbitration, indicating a degree of disinclination in publicising disputes, which are not conducted or reported in as public a manner as in other treaty partnerships.

In addition, there is a fundamental disjunct between the number of claims submitted to arbitration on an extra-GCC basis and a marked reluctance to submit disputes to arbitration on an intra-GCC basis, outside of extenuating circumstances. These factors suggest a region-specific culture that is characterised by a somewhat dichotomous attitude towards investor–state arbitration; a general wariness of the deficiencies of investment protection standards and the dispute settlement mechanism contained in the *OIC Agreement* and the *Arab Investment Agreement*; a reluctance to publicise disputes; and, from a foreign policy perspective, a certain complacency with antiquated agreements that arguably are not fit for purpose.

The GCC is also a complex and arguably unique union, with respect to its composition and the dynamic and at times fractious relationships between its members, as well as the legal systems contained within, and its religious practices and social constructs. The attitudes and approaches adopted by GCC member States reflect this complexity. Mutasim Ahmad Alqudah argues that the States "have been slow in accepting modern arbitration practices" and further that some members "have only started to modernize their arbitration laws to bring them in line with these modern practices".[60] Alqudah also notes that Shariah, a "primary source of law in the GCC" is perceived "by many western scholars and lawyers as being responsible for the incompleteness of some of these countries' arbitration systems".[61] He suggests that this perception is worth challenging because there is an argument to be made that Shariah and arbitration, including ISDS, are not necessarily incompatible.[62] The GCC needs to restore confidence in the ability of claimants, particularly those from Western home states, to pursue investor–state claims within the GCC.

It is suggested that, following the lessons of *Al-Warraq v Indonesia* and other leading cases, it would be prudent for GCC member States to contemplate what standards, both domestic and international, can be imposed to regulate the conduct of foreign investors operating in the Gulf. Potentially, this action could preclude aggrieved investors from accessing remedies for established breaches of an IIA's substantive investment protections if those investors as claimants have breached their obligations under the applicable IIA.

The GCC member States are in the midst of a transformational period, undertaking programmes of economic diversification, together with investment in human capital and technology as they shift towards a digital economy. Part of this process involves investment in industry. CEO of the Qatar Development Bank, Abdulaziz Al-Khalifa, argues that industrial SMEs need access to money, training, and markets if the GCC is to leave its "single resource identity" behind.[63] The dispute settlement framework needs to be radically overhauled to meet possible increased demand in a manner that strikes a better balance between reflecting the unique socio-legal and economic objectives of the States with enhancing investor confidence in the region. It is likely that a union-specific IIA might better serve the purposes of both GCC host states and claimants therein. Given the comparatively low rate of intra-GCC disputes, it is probably not necessary to have an intra-GCC investment treaty, although it may be of use in resolving disputes if there was, for example, another Gulf crisis in the future. Certainly, there is an argument to be

60 Mutashim Ahmad Alqudah, 'The Impact of Sharia on the Acceptance of International Commercial Arbitration in the Countries of the Gulf Cooperation Council' (2017) 20(1) *Journal of Legal, Ethical and Regulatory Issues* 1–2.

61 Ibid.

62 Amel Abdallah, 'Islamic Sharia and Arbitration in GCC States: The Way ahead' (2020) 9(2) *International Review of Law* 316.

63 Alexandre Raffoul and Fatima Al Zahra Hewaidi, 'How Industrialisation Could Future-Proof MENA's Gulf Economies', *World Economic Forum* (28 June 2021) at <Industrialisation is key to GCC economic diversification | World Economic Forum (weforum.org)>.

made for the States to develop a model investment treaty and promote initiatives to update both the *OIC Agreement* and the *Arab Investment Agreement* in a significant way – although this is no doubt easier said than done given the dynamic nature of regional, MENA, and broader geopolitics, as well as the multilateral nature of these agreements. There is a need for more precise language, particularly around consent to arbitrate, the appointment of arbitrators, and enforcement. In addition, the States would likely benefit from working further towards the establishment of an organ for the settlement of disputes under the *OIC Agreement* and consolidating and promoting the procedures of the Arab Investment Court. A review and consolidation of the other GCC investor–state dispute settlement adjudicatory centres would also be of benefit. It is suggested that a regional review and overhaul of the existing GCC-related BIT network would be beneficial so that duplication can be avoided and gaps can be addressed to avoid the application of treaties of last resort.

The application of the *OIC Agreement* and the *Arab Investment Agreement* in the Qatar Airways disputes is an example of renewed interest in applying the two treaties as part of a broader trend in the settlement of intra-Arab disputes. Mouawad and Khoury contend that the two Agreements were dormant for decades until there was a surge in arbitrations following the Arab Spring. Arab investor-claimants began to view the two Agreements as an alternative to remedies available under conventional BITs or as a "stop-gap" measure where there was no applicable BIT.[64]

However, despite the surge in intra-Arab arbitrations, both Agreements continue to be underutilised by claimants because of their imprecisions – specifically "textual ambiguity" and "procedural unpredictability".[65] The GCC member States may benefit from reviewing the investment protections and dispute settlement mechanisms contained within existing regional agreements such as these two Agreements, to incorporate greater precision about the scope of the investment protections afforded and the dispute settlement mechanism, particularly the requirement to exhaust local remedies as a precondition to access arbitration. For example, the uncertainty of "fork-in-the-road" clauses, allowing claimant investors to choose "to resort to domestic remedies", and thereby foreclosing "the option of resorting to international arbitration",[66] warrants or rather requires clarity. There is uncertainty as to whether a claim has to be exhausted in one forum to lose the right of recourse to the other. The States could improve the uncertainty of the article by requiring claimant investors to first exhaust domestic remedies and obtain a final decision from a local superior court before initiating arbitral proceedings. This would bring the Agreements into line with the exhaustion of local remedies rule and give the member States the ability to appeal within domestic institutions before

64 Caline Mouawad and Lillian Khoury, 'Investment Arbitration under Multilateral Treaties in the Middle East' (2016) 2(3) *Bahrain Chamber for Dispute Resolution International Arbitration Review* 243–4.

65 Ibid, 264–5.

66 Martin Dietrich Brauch, 'Exhaustion of Local Remedies in International Investment' (2017) *IISD.org* (IISD Best Practice Series, 2 January) at <Exhaustion of Local Remedies in International Investment Law (iisd.org)>.

being exposed to costly and potentially risky investor–state arbitration. The member States could mitigate against this kind of mischief by including a requirement to exhaust local remedies in future international investment treaties.

Bibliography

Abdallah, Amel, 'Islamic Sharia and Arbitration in GCC States: The Way Ahead' (2020) 9(2) *International Review of Law*, 316–334.

Agreement on Investment and Free Movement of Arab Capital among Arab Countries, signed 29 August 1970 (entered into force 29 August 1970) (*'Arab League Investment Agreement'*).

Alqudah, Mutashim Ahmad, 'The Impact of Sharia on the Acceptance of International Commercial Arbitration in the Countries of the Gulf Cooperation Council' (2017) 20(1) *Journal of Legal, Ethical and Regulatory Issues*, 1–17.

Alschner, Wolfgang, Dimitry Skougarevskiy and Mengyi Wang, 'Champions of Protection? A Text-as-Data Analysis of the Bilateral Investment Treaties of GCC Countries' (2016) 5(3) *International Review of Law*, 1–19.

Blanke, Gordon, 'The OIC Agreement and its MFN Clause: A Question of Scope', *Thomson Reuters* (24 July 2020) at <The OIC Agreement and its MFN clause: a question of scope | Arbitration Blog (practicallaw.com)>.

Brauch, Martin Dietrich, 'Exhaustion of Local Remedies in International Investment', *IISD.org*, IISD Best Practice Series (2 January 2017) at <Exhaustion of Local Remedies in International Investment Law (iisd.org)>.

Cafiero, 'Giorgio, 42nd GCC Summit: An Opportunity to Reconciliation', *Gulf International Forum* (10 December 2021) at <42nd GCC Summit: An Opportunity for Reconciliation - Gulf International Forum (gulfif.org)>.

Case Profiles, 'Investment Arbitration Reporter' (undated) at <https://www.iareporter.com/arbitration-cases/?fwp_treaty=oic-investment-agreement&fwp_arbitration_cases_sort=year_desc&fwp_per_page=100>.

Charlotin, Damien, ' Breaking: Paris Court Finds That PCA Secretary General Lacked Power to Sep Into Libya Arbitration When OIC Secretary General Failed to Appoint Arbitrator', *Investment Arbitration Reporter* (26 March 2021) at <Breaking: Paris Court finds that PCA Secretary General lacked power to step into Libya arbitration when OIC Secretary General failed to appoint arbitrator | Investment Arbitration Reporter (openathens.net)>.

Convention on the Recognition and Enforcement of Foreign Arbitral Awards, adopted 10 June 1958 (entered into force 7 June 1959) (*'New York Convention'*).

Convention on the Settlement of Investment Disputes between States and Nationals of Other States, adopted 18 March 1965 (entered into force 14 October 1966) (*'ICSID Convention'*).

Cooperation Agreement between the European Economic Community, of the One Part, and the Countries Parties to the Charter of the Cooperation Council for the Arab States of the Gulf, of the Other Part, signed 15 June 1988 (entered into force 1 January 1990).

Dahlquist, Joel and Luke Eric Peterson, 'Governments Working To Rein In Use Of OIC Investment Treaty's Investor-State Arbitration Offer', *Investment Arbitration Reporter* (3 April 2019) at <Governments working to rein in use of OIC investment treaty's investor-state arbitration offer | Investment Arbitration Reporter (openathens.net)>.

Farchakh, Michael, 'The Arab Investment Court and Intra-Arab BITs: A Potential New Frontier?', *Kluwer Arbitration Blog* (29 December 2020) at <The Arab Investment Court and Intra-Arab BITs: a Potential New Frontier? - Kluwer Arbitration Blog>.

Gaver, Craig and Yusuf Kumtepe, 'Checking in on the OIC Investment Agreement: New Arbitrations, But Slow Progress on Creating A Permanent Dispute Settlement

Mechanism', *Kluwer Arbitration Blog* (17 March 2023) at <https://arbitrationblog.kluwerarbitration.com/2023/03/17/checking-in-on-the-oic-investment-agreement-new-arbitrations-but-slow-progress-on-creating-a-permanent-dispute-settlement-mechanism/>.

Gulf Cooperation Council, *Economic Agreement Between the Gulf Cooperation Council States*, signed 31 December 2001 (entered into force 31 December 2001) (*'GCC Economic Agreement'*).

Gulf Cooperation Council, GCC Charter, 'The Concept and Foundations' at <http://gcc-sg.org/en-us/AboutGCC/Pages/StartingPointsAndGoals.aspx>.

Gulf Cooperation Council, GCC Charter, 'Preamble' at <http://gcc-sg.org/en-us/AboutGCC/Pages/Primarylaw.aspx>.

Gulf Cooperation Council, 'About the Centre', *G.C.C Commercial Arbitration Centre* (undated) at <G.C.C Commercial Arbitration Centre - About-centre (gcccac.org)>.

Gulf Cooperation Council, *Unified Economic Agreement between the Countries of the Gulf Cooperation Council*, signed 11 November 1981 (entered into force 1 December 1981) 9 (*'GCC Economic Agreement 1981'*) at <https://edit.wti.org/app.php/document/show/d444ad42-56fc-4a5f-b886-34023158dad1>.

Hamida, Walid Ben, 'The First Arab Investment Court Decision' (2006) 7(5) *Journal of World Investment and Trade*, 699–721.

Hassan, Amra Arafa, 'The 2013 Amendments to the Arab Investment Agreement' (2019) 43(1) *ICSID Review*, 107–135.

Hesham Talaat, M., *Al-Warraq v Republic of Indonesia (Final Award)* (UNCITRAL, 15 December 2014) (*'Al-Warraq v Indonesia'*).

Kotb, Ahmed, 'Egypt: The Arab Investment Court' (2016) *International Financial Law Review* at <Egypt: The Arab Investment Court | International Financial Law Review (iflr.com)>.

Kumtepe, Yusuf and Riccardo Loschi, 'Investment Dispute Settlement Body of the Organisation of Islamic Cooperation: A Dead End for Claims under the OIC Investment Agreement?', *Kluwer Arbitration Blog* (29 December 2019) at <Kluwer Arbitration Blog>.

Lexology, 'The Organisation of Islamic Cooperation Agreement on Promotion, Protection and Guarantee of Investments among Member States', *bilaterals.org* (web page, 7 May 2018) at <The Organisation of Islamic Cooperation Agreement on Promotion, Protection and Guarantee of Investments among Member States | bilaterals.org>.

Mouawad, Caline and Lillian Khoury, 'Investment Arbitration under Multilateral Treaties in the Middle East' (2016) 2(3) *Bahrain Chamber for Dispute Resolution International Arbitration Review*, 243–266.

Newcombe, Andrew and Jean-Michel Marcoux, 'Hesham Talaat M. Al-Warraq v Republic of Indonesia: Imposing International Obligations on Foreign Investors' (2015) 30(3) *ICSID Review*, 525–532.

Organisation of Islamic Cooperation Agreement on Promotion, Protection and Guarantee of Investments among Member States of the Organisation of the Islamic Conference (*'OIC Agreement'*)

Peterson, Luke Eric 'OIC Round UP: An Update On Pending Arbitration Cases Lodged Under The OIC Investment Agreement', *Investment Arbitration Reporter* (11 August 2020) at <OIC round up: An update on pending arbitration cases lodged under the OIC Investment Agreement | Investment Arbitration Reporter (openathens.net)>.

Raffoul, Alexandre and Fatima Al Zahra Hewaidi, 'How Industrialisation Could Future-Proof MENA's Gulf Economies', *World Economic Forum* (28 June 2021) at <Industrialisation is key to GCC economic diversification | World Economic Forum (weforum.org)>.

Report of the OIC Secretary General, 38th Session of the Follow-up Committee of the Standing Committee for Economic and Commercial Cooperation of the OIC, Ankara, Turkey, 24–25 May 2022, Appendix 1.

UNCTAD, 'Investment Policy Hub, International Investment Agreement Navigator', *IIAs by Country Grouping* at <https://investmentpolicy.unctad.org/international-investment-agreements/groupings/37/gcc-gulf-cooperation-council->.

Unified Agreement for the Investment of Arab Capital in the Arab State, signed 26 November 1980 (entered into force 7 September 1981) (*'Arab Investment Agreement'*).

Zorob, 'Anja, Oman Caught Between the GCC Customs Union and Bilateral Free Trade with the US: Is It Worth Breaking the Rules', in Steffen Wippel (ed) *Regionalizing Oman*, United Nations University Series on Regionalism, vol. 6 (Springer, 2013).

3 Elements and Emerging Themes in Investor–State Arbitration in the GCC Context

3.1 Introduction

This chapter outlines some elements which underpin the ISDS system generally, but which seem to also emerge in the GCC context, namely developments with respect to key definitions and substantive investment protections, and giving particular attention to the definitions of "investor", "investment" and nationality requirements, the fair and equitable treatment (FET) standard, the non-expropriation requirement, and dispute settlement provisions. Investor–state dispute arbitrations applying these elements demonstrate these issues arising in GCC-related cases, including nationality and the scope of the "investor" and "investment" requirements (often challenged as objections to jurisdiction *ratione personae* and *ratione materiae*, although also integral to the merits) and "clean hands" issues in respect of both claimants and respondents, which will be examined in further detail in later chapters in the context of specific cases.

The chapter considers the scope of these definitions and protections in the *Arab Investment Agreement* (1980)[1] and the *OIC Agreement* (1981),[2] both of which are examples of contemporaneous Islamic-based historical and multilateral agreements, the *France–Kuwait BIT* (1989),[3] the *France–Saudi Arabia BIT* (2002),[4] and the *United States–Oman* FTA (2006).[5] These bilateral investment treaties (BITs) and international investment agreements (IIAs) are relevant because

1 *Unified Agreement for the Investment of Arab Capital in the Arab States* signed 26 November 1980 (entered into force 7 September 1981) ('*Arab Investment Agreement'*); Amendment protocol signed 22 January 2013.

2 *Organisation of Islamic Cooperation Agreement on Promotion, Protection and Guarantee of Investments among Member States of the Islamic Conference*, signed 5 June 1981 (entered into force February 1988) ('*OIC Agreement*').

3 *Agreement between the Government of the French Republic and the State of Kuwait on the Encouragement and Reciprocal Protection of Investments*, signed 27 September 1989 (entered into force 16 May 1991) ('*France–Kuwait BIT*').

4 *Agreement between the Government of the French Republic and the Government of the Kingdom of Saudi Arabia on the Reciprocal Encouragement and Protection of Investments*, signed 26 June 2002 (entered into force 18 March 2004) ('*France–Saudi Arabia BIT*').

5 *Agreement between the Government of the United States of America and the Government of the Sultanate of Oman on the Establishment of a Free Trade Area*, signed 19 January 2006 (entered into force 1 January 2009) ('*United States–Oman FTA*').

DOI: 10.4324/9781003481072-3

of their application in arbitrations involving the GCC member States and because they usefully demonstrate changes in the treaty-making practices of the States over time. The *Arab Investment Agreement* and the *OIC Agreement* are contemporaneous and pre-date the experience of the States in the ISDS environment. However, the *Arab Investment Agreement* underwent significant updating in early 2013, with its improvements including enhancing standards of protection for investments and investors, and introducing the FET principle, as well as formally acknowledging the UNCITRAL arbitration rules.[6] Where there has been a specific change of note on a key issue examined, the following tables include specific reference to both the 1981 and post-2013 forms of that Agreement. The two French-related BITs encompass the early period of that developing experience. The provisions of the French BITs have been translated into English from the original versions for the convenience of readers. The *United States–Oman FTA* is included in this analysis since it represents a divergence from the prominence of BITs as grounds for regional ISDS-based arbitrations. While the selected agreements display commonalities, they also reveal variations and, in some instances, shortcomings, in respect of the key definitions selected for examination.

Historically, the GCC member States have had rather limited exposure to ISDS, although this has been changing over the last decade or so. In some cases, claimant investors are pursuing a cause of action in multiple fora, for example, utilising both Islamic-based and more generic international agreements. The recent Gulf diplomatic crisis between Qatar and Saudi Arabia, the United Arab Emirates (UAE), and Bahrain (including Egypt) has highlighted the fault lines underpinning the GCC union. These factors have arguably created a need for the States to evaluate their exposure to ISDS and recalibrate their attitudes and approaches to this risk, taking into account the need to potentially manage and facilitate greater levels of intra-GCC investor–state disputes into the future.

3.2 The GCC Member States, IIAs, and Definitional Frameworks

The GCC faces challenges due to the complexity of the vast network of IIAs binding both its individual member States and itself as a union. According to the United Nations Conference on Trade and Development (UNCTAD), the IIAs currently in force create a network of more than 4,400 bilateral IIA relationships between pairs of economies, with variation not only in form but also, to a much greater degree, in content.[7] Almost a third of them overlap with at least one other IIA between the same economies. Over 88% of IIA relationships are based on IIAs signed before

6 See Amr Arafa Hasaan, 'The 2013 Amendments to the Arab Investment Agreement' (2019) 34(1) *ICSID Review* 107–35, doi:10.1093/icsidreview/siz003, for an extensive review of the 2013 amendments to the *Arab Investment Agreement*.

7 United Nations Conference on Trade and Development (UNCTAD), 'Trends in the Investment Treaty Regime and a Reform Toolbox for the Energy Transition' (IIA Issues Note, Issue. 2, August 2023, p. 2) at <https://investmentpolicy.unctad.org/publications/1285/trends-in-the-investment-treaty-regime-and-a-reform-toolbox-for-the-energy-transition>.

2012, and the IIA networks of almost all economies contain such first-generation IIAs. In addition, at least 40% of the relationships created by new-generation IIAs coexist with an earlier one between the same economies.[8] However, for the third year in a row, the number of terminations in 2022 exceeded the number of newly concluded IIAs, broadly demonstrating reservations about the scope and operation of investment protections and access to dispute settlement mechanisms and inviting a review of future treaty-based obligations. The UNCTAD database records that GCC member States have entered into 429 IIAs, of which 375 are BITs, the first being the *Kuwait–Iraq BIT* (1964)[9] and the most recent being the *Cambodia–UAE CEPA* (2023).[10]

Diversity across the network of IIAs has generated contention in the literature regarding whether conceiving a regime or system of ISDS is even possible. Stephen Krasner defined a regime as the "sets of principles, norms, rules and decision-making procedures around which actors' expectations converge in a given area of international relations".[11] Bonnitcha, Poulsen, and Waibel asserted that there is an ISDS regime based on the regularities across thousands of treaties and hundreds of arbitrations.[12] This view has institution-level support. For example, UNCITRAL has argued that investment treaties follow a similar structure and contain numerous core principles, thereby making it possible to conceive a "regime" of international investment protection.[13] Conversely, considering the number of treaties in operation, the decentralisation of arbitral tribunals, the lack of appellate capacity, and the preclusion of domestic investors from the system, Rachel Wellhausen argued that there is a "*de facto*" ISDS regime.[14] Alternatively, instead of there being no system that can be reformed, there is a "fragmented collection of bilateral and regional treaties negotiated based on individualized circumstances over the span of several decades".[15] Additionally, IIAs are highly atomised because they contain differing

8 Ibid, 1.

9 *Protocol between the Governments of the State of Kuwait and the Republic of Iraq on the Promotion of the Movement of Capital and Investments between the Two Countries*, signed 25 October 1964 (entered into force 7 June 1966) ('*Kuwait–Iraq BIT*').

10 *Comprehensive Economic Partnership Agreement (CEPA) between the Kingdom of Cambodia and the Government of the United Arab Emirates (UAE)* (2022), signed 8 June 2023 ('*Cambodia–UAE BIT*').

11 Stephen Krasner, 'Structural Causes and Regime Consequences: Regimes as Intervening Variables', in Beth Simmons and Richard Steinberg (eds) *International Law and International Relations* (Cambridge University Press, 2006) 3.

12 Bonnitcha, Jonathon, Lauge Skovgaard Poulsen, and Michael Waibel, *The Political Economy of the Investment Treaty Regime* (Oxford University Press, 2017) 3.

13 UNCITRAL Secretariat, *Possible Reform of Investor-State Dispute Settlement (ISDS),* UN GAOR, 34th sess, UN Doc A/CN.9/WG.III/WP.142 <http://www.uncitral.org/pdf/english/workinggroups/wg_3/142-e.pdf>, citing David Gaukrodger and Kathryn Gordon, 'Investor-State Dispute Settlement: A Scoping Paper for the Investment Policy Community' (2012) *OECD,* Working Paper No. 3, 64.

14 Rachel Wellhausen, 'Recent Trends in Investor-State Dispute Settlement' (2016) 7(1) *Journal of International Dispute Settlement* 117.

15 James Saulino and Josh Kallmer, 'The Emperor Has No Clothes: A Critique of the Debate over Reform of the ISDS System' in Jean Kalicki and Anna Joubin-Bret (eds) *Reshaping the Investor-State Dispute Settlement System: Journeys for the 21st Century* (Brill, 2015) 560.

formulations of ISDS and investors' substantive rights.[16] Although some decentralisation and variability exist across IIAs, discerning key institutions and broad commonalities in ISDS design through analysing treaty content and legal principles through their application by arbitral tribunals is possible. While the regime lacks the procedural fairness, certainty, and consistency that typify traditional domestic legal regimes, IIAs establish a system of ISDS within the ordinary meaning of the term "regime".

IIAs are currently the subject of profound review and there is immense pressure for reform because of deeply held concerns regarding their design, implementation, and scope of operation. Many real and perceived sources of discontent exist with IIAs. These issues are wide-ranging and include asymmetry of both a substantive and procedural nature and the elevation of the rights of foreign investors above those of sovereign states. Factors contributing to this asymmetry are the breadth, imprecise construction, and variability across the substantive protections for foreign investors. IIA design flaws have enabled the institution of vexatious or frivolous claims, and the limited procedural equality within IIAs as well as the absence of an effective appellate mechanism arguably exacerbate this issue. The high cost of instituting and, most concerningly, defending ISDS claims creates doubt about equality of access to cost-effective and fair dispute settlement proceedings. For example, a study by Matthew Hodgson and Alastair Campbell across a pool of 324 cases outlined the average costs for each party, including the claimant party (USD6,019,000), the respondent party (USD4,855,000), the tribunal (USD333,000), the ICSID (USD920,000), and the UNCITRAL (USD1,089,000).[17] The large size of arbitral awards and difficulties in enforcing awards made under IIAs also underscore access and fairness issues.

The constitution, diversity, and method of appointment of arbitral tribunals are also an issue. Arbitral tribunals are drawn from a narrow pool of technical experts, often lawyers who may have previously acted for claimants, thereby posing a risk of a conflict of issue. Arbitrators are typically male and come from North American or European backgrounds. This presents a particular obstacle for the GCC and its member States, which may have to contend with Western bias and language differences in the interpretation and application of IIAs, often concluded by country pairs in a MENA context or otherwise between the States and Western states. The broad scope of arbitral discretion is also of concern. For example, alleged breaches often involve consideration of or decisions regarding legislative or executive acts which are a legitimate function of sovereign states. Arbitral review of the subject matter of claims has promoted concern regarding the appropriate degree to which arbitral review can and should occur. The discussion and case outlined below highlight the approaches to interpretation and application of IIAs taken by tribunals in arbitrations involving the States and nationals thereof.

16 Arseni Matveev, 'Investor-State Dispute Settlement: The Evolving Balance between Investor Protection and State Sovereignty' (2015) 40(1) *University of Western Australia Law Review* 348, 357.

17 Matthew Hodgson and Alastair Campbell, 'Investment Treaty Arbitration: Cost, Duration and Size of Claims All Show Steady Increase', *ISDS Platform* (14 December 2017) at <https://isds.bilaterals.org/?investment-treaty-arbitration-cost>.

3.3 Defining "Investor" and "Investment"

The definitions of "investor" and "investment" within IIAs are critical and not only create a class of potential claimants but also define the protected bundle of investors' investment interests. The definitions are closely related because claimants need to establish first that they are investors and second that they had or would have made an investment worthy of protection under the relevant agreement.[18] Additionally, the nationality of claimant investors is also important with respect to determining whether a claimant is eligible to benefit from the IIA upon which they are seeking to apply.

The breadth of these definitions is arguably an issue that GCC member States need to address in IIAs to which they are a party, as the cases below demonstrate. Dual or multiple nationality is a potential issue that the States may need to address at both the natural person and legal person levels, in order to avoid the potential for claimants to institute multiple proceedings arising out of the one cause of action and to "treaty-shop" to obtain the best perceived benefit when determining which IIA to apply in the circumstances where multiple potentially apply.

The case of *Al-Warraq v Indonesia*[19] involved "claims arising out of the Government's bailout of a bank in which the claimant had allegedly invested, followed by criminal investigations and the subsequent prosecution of Al-Warraq for fraudulent activities in the Indonesian financial sector".[20] The respondent submitted preliminary objections to the jurisdiction and admissibility of the claims. The tribunal considered the definition of "investor" and the nationality requirements as set out in Article 1 of the *OIC Agreement*. The respondent questioned "whether the Claimant personally held shares in Bank Century at the time it was placed in administration", with the tribunal requiring "further evidence and submissions on the Claimant's condition as an 'investor' for the purposes of the *OIC Agreement*" and reserved the question for the merits phase.[21] The tribunal dismissed the claimant's allegation that its investment was made in part by the claimant and in part through First Gulf Asia Holdings Ltd, finding that the company was registered in the Bahamas, that the Bahamas were not a Contracting Party, and that First Gulf therefore could not be an "investor" within the meaning of the term as contained in the *OIC Agreement*.[22]

In its final award, dated 15 December 2014, the tribunal addressed the issue of the definition of "investor" within the *OIC Agreement*. The tribunal referred

18 Sergio Puig and Meg Kinnear, 'NAFTA Chapter Eleven at Fifteen: Contributions to a Systemic Approach in Investment Arbitration', citing *S D Myers Inc v Government of Canada (Partial Award),* (2010) 25(2) *ICSID Review – Foreign Investment Law Journal* 229.

19 *Hesham Talaat M. Al-Warraq v The Republic of Indonesia, Award on Respondent's Preliminary Objections to Jurisdiction and Admissibility of the Claims* (UNCITRAL, 21 June 2012) [90] *('Al-Warraq v Indonesia')*.

20 UNCTAD, 'Al Warraq v. Indonesia' (undated) *UNCTAD* <Al Warraq v. Indonesia | Investment Dispute Settlement Navigator | UNCTAD Investment Policy Hub>.

21 *Al-Warraq v Indonesia* (n 19), [91].

22 Ibid.

to Article 31 of the Vienna Convention (1969)[23] for interpretive purposes, before examining the definitions of "capital" and "investment" contained within Articles 1(4) and 1(5) of the Agreement, and before turning to the definition of "investor" as set out in Article 6(1) of the Agreement.[24] The tribunal noted "that there is no explicit reference to direct or indirect investments in the Agreement, and in particular in Article 1(4) and 1(5)".[25] The tribunal considered whether the claimant held a direct investment in Bank Century, finding that it did not because it did not own "a single share" in Bank Century at the date of the bailout, according to the Financial Services Authority which administers the Indonesian Stock Exchange; and contrary to the claimant's submissions, there was no evidence that his shares were held by ABN Amro Private Banking or Clearstream, a Luxembourg company. Furthermore, even if his shares were held by Clearstream on his behalf, such an arrangement would not be recognised under Indonesia's Law No. 40 of 2007 the Company Law, specifically Article 48.[26]

The tribunal then considered indirect ownership, ultimately finding that the claimant qualified as an "investor" within the meaning of the *OIC Agreement* by virtue of his ownership of shares in Bank Century through First Gulf Asia Holdings Ltd.[27] In responding to the respondent's submission that the IIAs must expressly allow for indirect investments, otherwise the protection afforded to investments is limited to direct investments only, the tribunal noted that "contemporary arbitral jurisprudence adopts a broader definition of 'investment'".[28] The tribunal also noted that "several contemporary commentators have confirmed that the definitions given to 'capital' and 'investment' in modern international investment treaties refer broadly – as is the case with Article 1 of the Agreement – to 'all assets'".[29]

In *Soufraki v United Arab Emirates*,[30] the tribunal considered the nationality of a natural person claimant who identified as an Italian national, seeking to apply the *United Arab Emirates–Italy BIT*[31] after the respondent raised an objection to jurisdiction, challenging the claimant's Italian nationality. In its Award, the tribunal assessed[32] whether the claimant had established his Italian nationality to the satisfaction of Article 25(2)(a) of the *Convention on the Settlement of Investment*

23 *Vienna Convention on the Law of Treaties,* signed 23 May 1969 (entered into force 27 January 1980) 1155 UNTS 331 ('*Vienna Convention 1969*').

24 *Al-Warraq v Indonesia (Final Award)* (UNCITRAL, 15 December 2014) [498]–[501].

25 Ibid [498]–[503].

26 Ibid [505]–[510].

27 Ibid [511].

28 Ibid [541], citing *Fedax N.V. v Republic of Venezuela* (ICSID Case No. ARB/96/3).

29 Ibid [516].

30 *Hussein Nauman Soufraki v United Arab Emirates* (ICSID Case No. ARB/02/7, 18 June 2002) ('*Soufraki v United Arab Emirates*').

31 *Agreement between the Government of the United Arab Emirates and the Government of the Italian Republic for the Promotion and Protection of Investments,* signed 22 January 1995 (entered into force 29 April 1997) ('*UAE–Italy BIT*').

32 *Soufraki v United Arab Emirates (Award),* (ICSID Case No. ARB/02/7, 7 July 2004).

Disputes between States and Nationals of Other States.[33] Although the tribunal relevantly stated that nationality was within the domestic jurisdiction of the State, it also found that:

> when, in international arbitral or judicial proceedings, the nationality of a person is challenged, the international tribunal is competent to pass upon that challenge, it will accord great weight to the nationality law of the State in question and to the interpretation and application of that law by its authorities. But it will decide for itself whether, on the facts and law before it, the person whose nationality is at issue was or was not a national of the State in question and when, and what follows from that finding. Where, as in the instant case, the jurisdiction of an international tribunal turns on an issue of nationality, the international tribunal is empowered, indeed bound, to decide that issue.[34]

The tribunal ultimately declined jurisdiction on the basis that the claimant was not an Italian national, having failed to demonstrate that he had both established and maintained a residence in Italy during the relevant period. Consequently, the claimant did not belong "to the class of investors in respect of whom the Respondent has consented to ICSID jurisdiction".[35]

An example of a natural person investor-claimant arguing multiple citizenships occurred in the case of *Bachar Kiwan v Kuwait*.[36] Bachar Kiwan, a natural person holding Syrian and French citizenship,[37] and a former adviser and business associate of the Kuwaiti Al-Sabah Royal Family, brought a claim against Kuwait under the ICSID Convention Arbitration Rules and applying the *France–Kuwait BIT* (1989).[38] Kiwan likely instituted proceedings under the *France–Kuwait BIT* rather than the *Syria–Kuwait BIT* (2001)[39] because the investment protections under the former were perceived as more favourable and his prospects for success were deemed greater, and/or it was considered politically expedient to do so given his former role.

In addition to the breadth of the definition of "investor", the nationality requirements, and the construction of "investment", the GCC has entered into

33 *Convention on the Settlement of Investment Disputes between States and Nationals of Other States*, signed 18 March 1965 (entered into force 14 October 1966) 575 UNTS 159.

34 *Soufraki v United Arab Emirates* (n 32), [55].

35 Ibid [58], [81], and [84].

36 *Bachar Kiwan v The State of Kuwait* (ICSID Case No. ARB/20/53) ('*Kiwan v Kuwait*').

37 Sarawak Report, 'How a Kuwaiti Royal Sheikh Jailed a 1MDB Whistleblower Whilst Laundering China Kickbacks for Najib' *Sarawakreport* (29 May 2020) <How A Kuwaiti Royal Sheikh Jailed A 1MDB Whistleblower Whilst Laundering China Kickbacks For Najib - EXCLUSIVE | Sarawak Report>.

38 *Agreement between the Government of the French Republic and the State of Kuwait on the Encouragement and Reciprocal Protection of Investments*, signed 27 September 1989 (entered into force 16 May 1991) ('*France–Kuwait BIT*').

39 *Agreement between the Government of the Syrian Arab Republic and the State of Kuwait for the Mutual Promotion and Protection of Investments*), signed 16 August 2001 (entered into force 23 March 2004) (*Syria–Kuwait BIT*).

agreements containing ISDS provisions and investment chapters in its capacity as a regional union. Individual GCC member States have also entered into agreements at the state-to-state level, thereby creating the potential for overlap, resulting in multiple actions arising out of one set of facts. An example of this overlapping issue is the *OIC Agreement*, which coexists with multiple IIAs, notably including the *Arab Investment Agreement* between the League of Arab States.[40] It is suggested that States would benefit from reviewing their treaty stock to assess the scope of this risk and take care when entering into new treaties to mitigate against adverse exposure by limiting the scope of the definitions.

GCC member States could also benefit from developing a model construction of the terms for "investor", the related nationality requirements, and "investment", and improving the precision with respect to claimant eligibility to bring claims. Narrowing the scope of these definitions would go some way to limiting the class of potential claimants and avoiding the adoption of a wide range of interpretations by arbitral tribunals. According to UNCTAD, none of the six States have an individual model BIT recorded.[41] There is also no record of a model GCC BIT at the regional level.[42] The lack of a model BIT is a significant policy gap that warrants addressing by the States and which could go some way to improving clarity and consistency in the negotiation of investment protection provisions, treaty form, interpretation, and application by arbitral tribunals.

For example, in *MAKAE v Saudi Arabia*, the claimant, a French company, initiated arbitration proceedings against Saudi Arabia for measures allegedly amounting to the "effective destruction and indirect expropriation of its" investment, namely "various retail and restaurant businesses",[43] in contravention of its obligations pursuant to the *Saudi Arabia–France BIT* (2002).[44] The Respondent raised preliminary objections to jurisdiction *ratione personae*, *ratione materiae*, and *ratione temporis*,[45] arguing *inter alia* that the claimant did not constitute an investor for the purposes of the BIT because it was not constituted in accordance with French law, nor did it have its *siège social* in France.[46] The Respondent also argued that the interests of the claimant did not amount to a covered investment within the meaning of the Agreement because the claimant neither owned nor controlled an

40 See UNCTAD, 'Agreement on Promotion, Protection and Guarantee of Investments amongst the Member States of the Organization of the Islamic Conference' (OIC Agreement) (undated) *UNCTAD* <OIC Investment Agreement (1981) | International Investment Agreements Navigator | UNCTAD Investment Policy Hub>, for a list of the *OIC Agreement's* relationships with other agreements.

41 UNCTAD, 'International Investment Agreements Navigator: Model Agreements' (undated) <International Investment Agreements Navigator | UNCTAD Investment Policy Hub>.

42 Ibid.

43 *MAKAE Europe SARL v Kingdom of Saudi Arabia (Award)* (ICSID Case No. ARB/17/42, 30 August 2021) [1]–[5] ('*MAKAE v Saudi Arabia*').

44 *Agreement between the Government of the Kingdom of Saudi Arabia and the Government of the French Republic Concerning the Encouragement and Reciprocal Protection of Investments*, signed 26 June 2002 (entered into force 18 March 2004) ('*Saudi Arabia–France BIT*').

45 *MAKAE v Saudi Arabia* (n 43), [52].

46 Ibid [54].

investment in Saudi Arabia, and that if the claimant did, he would be in contravention of Saudi law.[47]

In its award, the tribunal considered whether or not it had jurisdiction to proceed to the merits, assessing whether or not there was a "qualifying investor", "covered investment", "owned or controlled by the investor" and in accordance with domestic law in the Kingdom.[48] The relevant part of Article 1(1) of the BIT, which sets out the definition of "investment", states that investment means "all assets of any kind, such as property, rights and income, owned or controlled by an investor of one of the Contracting Parties in the territory of the other Contracting Party".

In addressing the claim and the Respondent's objection to the award, the tribunal focussed particularly on the element of control. It noted that the tribunal in *Perenco Ecuador Ltd v Republic of Ecuador*[49] observed that "an absence of detailed general or conventional rules of international law governing the organisation, operation, management and control of an enterprise" exists and that the parties had agreed that the meaning of control needed to be determined pursuant to the customary international law rules of treaty interpretation, as reflected in Article 21 of the Vienna Convention.[50]

A significant issue related to the inclusion of the term "control". The parties agreed that de facto control would meet the standard contained in the BIT and further that it was appropriate to determine whether the element of control was satisfied on the facts. However they disagreed as to (a) the character or weight of the evidence required to prove *de facto* control, and (b) whether a claimant must demonstrate that it has decision-making authority over the allegedly controlled investment, combined with some form of ownership or other economic interest involving an expectation of financial return.[51] The tribunal observed that the normal standard was the balance of probabilities and that nothing in the Agreement warranted deviating from this standard, referring to the tribunal's comments in *Pezold and others v Republic of Zimbabwe*,[52] but noted that, as Rule 34 of the ICSID Arbitration Rules applied, the tribunal "is the judge of the probative value of any evidence adduced".[53] The tribunal found that the BIT "clearly establishes ownership or control as alternative bases of jurisdiction"[54] and went on to accept the claimant's submission that "[t]here can be *de facto* control where the evidence establishes that a small and specialized component of a corporate family performs a role or roles that determine the overall character and direction of an enterprise".[55]

47 Ibid [65].
48 Ibid [109].
49 *Perenco Ecuador Ltd v Republic of Ecuador, Decision on Remaining Issues of Jurisdiction and on Liability* (ICSID Case No ARB/08/6, 12 September 2014) [522].
50 *MAKAE v Saudi Arabia* (n 43), [115].
51 Ibid [118].
52 *Bernard Friedrich Arnd Rüdiger von Pezold et. al. v Republic of Zimbabwe (Award)* (ICSID Case No. ARB/10/15, 28 July 2015) [177]–[178].
53 *MAKAE v Saudi Arabia* (n 43), [122]–[123].
54 Ibid [132].
55 Ibid [135].

The tribunal relevantly determined that while *de facto* control can be sufficient to satisfy the definition of "investment" contained in Article 1(1) of the BIT,[56] ultimately in this particular case, the claimant did not exercise *de facto* control in respect of the investment "at any relevant time" and thus, the tribunal lacked the requisite jurisdiction.[57] The tribunal stated that the evidence:

> indicates that for roughly two-and-a-half years the Claimant had a physical presence in France, its activities were modest and limited in scope and that it did not take over Mr Alenezi's [the founder, general manager and authorized representative of MAKAE Europe] significant role in developing and managing relationships with premium brands or in determining brands and products for sale.[58]

In *Al Tamimi v Oman*,[59] the tribunal considered the definitions of "investor of a Party" as defined in Article 10.7 of the *United States–Oman FTA*, the meaning of "national" as defined in Article 1.2 of the FTA, and the meaning of "national of another Contracting State" as defined by Article 25(2) of the ICSID Convention. The tribunal relevantly determined that it would have jurisdiction *ratione personae* in respect of the claimant if it was established that "(a) he is a national of the United States, as defined in Title III of the Immigration and Nationality Act; and (b) he has made, or has attempted to make, an investment in the territory of Oman".[60] The tribunal considered the Respondent's submission that the claimant's "dominant and effective" nationality as contained within the definition of Article 10.7 was Emirati, finding that there was insufficient evidence to find that he was a dual national.[61] Relevantly, the tribunal did not consider that:

> the language of "dominant and effective nationality" is intended to prevent dual citizens of both the United States and a third-party State, such as the UAE, from invoking the US-Oman BIT – even where the nationality of the third-party State is predominant. Rather, the Tribunal considers that the provision is aimed at preventing claims by dual nationals of both State parties (i.e. the United States and Oman) from seeking to use the FTA to claim against their own State of dominant and effective nationality – thereby defeating the purpose of the FTA to apply investment protection only to "investors of the other Party".[62]

56 Ibid [118].
57 Ibid [171]–[172].
58 Ibid [170].
59 *Adel A Hamadi Al Tamimi v Sultanate of Oman (Award)* (ICSID Case No. ARB/11/33, 3 November 2015) ('*Al Tamimi v Oman*').
60 Ibid [269].
61 Ibid [271].
62 Ibid [274].

The tribunal went on to state that it was unnecessary "to definitively determine this interpretive point because the evidence does not disclose that Mr Al Tamimi is a national of any country other than the United States".[63] As such, GCC member States may benefit from including a dominant and effective nationality requirement to avoid any risks with respect to the multiplicity of proceedings in the case of natural person claimants.

There is also arguably a strong case for GCC member States to review and improve upon the definition of legal person to require those entities, particularly companies, to directly invest in the local economy in their host state. Such a measure may go some way towards preventing potential claimants from incorporating and registering companies in a particular jurisdiction for the purpose of obtaining favourable investment protections and arbitral relief without necessarily having a legitimate cause for complaint. Nationality-related issues in investor–state disputes involving the States or claimants from those states may become more prolific as the States endeavour to shift away from hydrocarbon-based economies towards knowledge-based economies. Incorporating, for example, a requirement that legal person investors have "substantial business" activities in IIAs, as has been done in Article 1 of the 2019 Dutch Model BIT, may be beneficial. Kabbir Duggal and Laurens van de Ven argue that the new "substantial business requirement rule will likely exclude purely mailbox companies",[64] which has historically been problematic because Dutch BITs have often been used by mailbox companies. Until the 2019 Dutch Model BIT was published, "only the Netherlands-Chile BIT contain[ed] an express substantial business requirement 'the term "nationals" shall comprise … legal persons … having real economies activities, in the territory of that same Contracting Party'".[65] Moreover, none of the States have entered into a BIT with the Netherlands invoking the 2019 Dutch Model BIT incorporating the substantial activities test.[66] Relevantly, Article 1(b) and (c) of the Model BIT states that:

(a) "investor" means with regard to either Contracting Party:
    (i) any natural person having the nationality of that Contracting Party under its applicable law;
    (ii) any legal person constituted under the law of that Contracting Party and having substantial business activities in the territory of that Contracting Party; or

63 Ibid.

64 Kabir Duggal and Laurens van de Ven, 'The 2019 Netherlands Model BIT: Riding the New Investment Treaty Waves' (2019) 35(3) *Arbitration International* 359.

65 Ibid, citing Article 1(b) of the *Agreement on Encouragement and Reciprocal Protection of Investments between the Kingdom of the Netherlands and the Republic of Chile*, signed 30 November 1998 (not yet entered into force).

66 The *Netherlands–UAE BIT* was signed on 26 November 2013, but it has not entered into force; the original *Netherlands–Oman BIT* was signed 19 September 1987 and entered into force 1 February 1989, while a subsequent BIT signed on 17 January 2009 has not entered into force; the *Bahrain–Netherlands BIT* was signed on 5 February 2007 and entered into force 1 December 2009; the *Kuwait–Netherlands BIT* was signed 29 May 2001 and entered into force 31 May 2002.

(iii) any legal person that is constituted under the law of that Contracting Party and is directly or indirectly owned or controlled by a natural person as defined in (i) or by a legal person as defined in (ii). A natural person who has the nationality of the Kingdom of the Netherlands and the other Contracting Party is deemed to be exclusively a natural person of the Contracting Party of his or her dominant and effective nationality.

(b) Indications of having 'substantive business activities' in a Contracting Party may include:
- (i) the undertaking's registered office and/or administration is established in that Contracting Party;
- (ii) the undertaking's headquarters and/or management is established in that Contracting Party;
- (iii) the number of employees and their qualifications based in that Contracting Party;
- (iv) the turnover generated in that Contracting Party; and
- (v) an office, production facility and/or research laboratory is established in that Contracting Party;

These indications should be assessed in each specific case, taking into account the total number of employees and turnover of the undertaking concerned, and taking account of the nature and maturity of the activities carried out by the undertaking in the Contracting Party in which it is established.

According to Duggal and van de Ven, "[s]ubstantial business requirement rules are common among recent other BITs, and multilateral investment treaties".[67] While the GCC member States would benefit from the inclusion of a substantive business activities requirement, it would need to be more carefully construed to prevent arbitral tribunals from adopting subjective and inconsistent approaches to the application of the requirement. There is a risk that the inclusion of a non-exhaustive list of indicia for "substantive business activities" does not go far enough in terms of protecting the States from exposure to claims being raised by shell companies. This may be addressed by requiring claimants to prove a direct nexus between legitimate expenditure (whether capital or otherwise) in the relevant host state and the alleged injury to the investment, the subject of the claim. Claimants should also be positively required to establish that they had made the relevant investment before the cause of action arose as a precondition to accessing relief, making consideration of *ratione temporis* necessary at the time of instituting proceedings, not in the objections or jurisdictional phases. This measure should be made together with a requirement that the operation of the substantive investment protections is temporally limited to investments covered by the relevant IIA.[68]

67 Kabir Duggal and Laurens van de Ven (n 64), 74.

68 *Philip Morris v Australia (Award on Jurisdiction and Admissibility)* (PCA Case No. 2012-12, 17 December 2015) [528].

Table 3.1 demonstrates the evolving construction of the definition of "investor" across the *Arab Investment Agreement*, the *OIC Agreement*, the *Saudi Arabia–France BIT*, the *France–Kuwait BIT*, and the *United States–Oman FTA*.

Table 3.1 Definition of "Investor" and Nationality Requirements

IIA	*Definition of "Investor"*
Arab Investment Agreement 2013 Amendment Protocol Art 1.8	Arab investor: The natural or juridical person who/which owns Arab capital which it invests in the territory of a State Party of which it is not a national, provided that the Arab investor holds directly at least (51%) of the share capital of the relevant juridical person.
OIC Agreement Art. 1.6	The Government of any contracting party or natural corporate person, who is a national of a contracting party and who owns the capital and invests it in the territory of another contracting party. Nationality shall be determined as follows: (a) Natural Person: Any individual enjoying the nationality of a contracting party according to the provisions of the nationality law in force therein. (b) Legal Personality: Any entity established in accordance with the laws in force in any contracting party and recognized by the law under which its legal personality is established.
France–Kuwait BIT Art. 1(2)	The term "investor" shall designate any national of one of the Contracting States or any legal person, including the Government of a Contracting State, which invests in the territory of the other Contracting State.
Saudi Arabia–France BIT Art. 1(2)	The term "investor" means: - any natural person possessing the nationality of one of the Contracting Parties, in accordance with the legislation of that Contracting Party; - any legal person constituted in the territory of one of the Contracting Parties, in accordance with the legislation of that Contracting Party, having its registered office there, or controlled directly or indirectly by nationals of one of the Contracting Parties, or by legal persons having their head office in the territory of one of the Contracting Parties and constituted in accordance with the legislation of that Contracting Party, such as joint-stock companies, enterprises, cooperatives, limited liability companies, partnerships, offices, institutions, funds, organizations, trade associations and other similar entities, whether limited liability or not; - either Contracting Party and its financial institutions and authorities, public funds and other similar governmental institutions.
US–Oman FTA Art. 10.27	Investor of a Party means a Party or state enterprise thereof, or a national or an enterprise of a Party, that attempts to make, is making, or has made an investment in the territory of the other Party; provided, however, that a natural person who is a dual national shall be deemed to be exclusively a national of the State of his or her dominant and effective nationality.

Table 3.2 illustrates the approaches to defining "investment" over the same agreements.

Table 3.2 Definition of "Investment"

IIA	*Definition of "Investment"*
Arab Investment Agreement 2013 Amendment Protocol Art. 1.6–7	6. Arab capital: Funds owned by an Arab investor comprising any material and immaterial rights which have a monetary value; 7. Investment of Arab capital: The use of Arab capital in an economic or social field in the territory of a State Party other than the State of which the Arab investor is a national, or its transfer to said State with a view to obtaining a return in accordance with the provisions of this Agreement;
OIC Agreement Art. 1.5	The employment of capital in one of the permissible fields in the territories of a contracting party with a view to achieving a profitable return, or the transfer of capital to a contracting party for the same purpose, in accordance with this Agreement.
France–Kuwait BIT Art. 1(1)	The term "investment" refers to assets such as property, rights and interests of all kinds, directly or indirectly under the control of a natural or legal person, including the Government of a Contracting State, and invested in the territory and maritime areas of the other Contracting State, in accordance with the laws and regulations of that State. Without limiting the general scope of the foregoing, the term ((investment) includes: (a) Movable and immovable property, as well as any other rights in rem such as mortgages, liens, usufructs, bonds, and similar rights; (b) Shares, issue premiums and other forms of participation, whether minority or indirect, in companies constituted in the territory of one of the Contracting States; c) Obligations, creances and rights to all benefits having economic value; d) Copyright, intellectual and industrial property rights (such as patents, licenses, trademarks, trade secrets, models and industrial models), technical processes, names filed and customers; (e) Privileges granted by law or by virtue of a contract, including privileges relating to the prospection, cultivation, extraction or exploitation of natural resources, including those situated in adjacent maritime areas over which the Contracting States exercise sovereign rights; (f) Income not invested.

(*Continued*)

Table 3.2 (Continued)

IIA	*Definition of "Investment"*
Saudi Arabia–France BIT Art. 1(1)	The term "investment" means all assets of any kind, such as property, rights and income, held or controlled by an investor of one of the Contracting Parties in the territory of the other Contracting Party in accordance with the law of that Contracting Party and, more particularly but not exclusively: a) movable and immovable property, as well as all other rights in rem such as mortgages, liens, usufructs, guarantees and all similar rights; b) interests, shares and obligations of companies incorporated in the territory of one of the Contracting Parties and other forms of rights or participation in such companies, whether or not minority or indirect, as well as securities issued by one of the Contracting Parties or any of its investors; c) claims or obligations, or rights to any benefits having economic value; d) intellectual, commercial and industrial property rights including, but not limited to, copyrights and related rights, patents, licenses, industrial designs, technical processes, know-how, trademarks, trade secrets and trade secrets, registered names and customers; e) rights conferred by law or under a public or private contract or any license, authorization or concession granted by legal means. No change in the form of investment of assets shall affect their classification as investment, provided that such modification is not contrary to the law of the Contracting Party in the territory or maritime area of which the investment is made.
US–Oman FTA Art. 10.27	Investment means every asset that an investor owns or controls, directly or indirectly, that has the characteristics of an investment, including such characteristics as the commitment of capital or other resources, the expectation of gain or profit, or the assumption of risk. Forms that an investment may take include: (a) an enterprise; (b) shares, stock, and other forms of equity participation in an enterprise; (c) bonds, debentures, other debt instruments, and loans; (d) futures, options, and other derivatives; (e) turnkey, construction, management, production, concession, revenue-sharing, and other similar contracts; (f) intellectual property rights; (g) licenses, authorizations, permits, and similar rights conferred pursuant to domestic law; and (h) other tangible or intangible, movable or immovable property, and related property rights, such as leases, mortgages, liens, and pledges.

3.4. Fair and Equitable Treatment Standard and Doctrine of Legitimate Expectations

The fair and equitable treatment (FET) standard is a frequently cited protection that is included in the majority of trade agreements and is pleaded in most claims.[69] Its purpose is to protect foreign investors against unfair and unreasonable conduct by a host state. State measures that may constitute a breach of the FET standard are measures that negatively affect covered investments and may involve legislative measures or the revocation of a licence, for example. The FET standard has been used to ensure attentiveness and protection, due process, protection from arbitrariness and discrimination, transparency, and constancy.[70] Jacob Stone has argued that, in addition to these obligations, the FET standard has been found to incorporate the requirement of good faith, provision of justice, and freedom from coercion and harassment.[71] Stone has argued that, even though "these obligations have been identified by various tribunals, there is no consensus among academics (and states in particular) as to their scope and content, much less their existence".[72] It is therefore critical for GCC member States to carefully consider the scope of FET standards contained within existing treaties and in negotiations for future treaties to mitigate against inconsistent and arbitrary interpretation and application of this protection.

The doctrine of legitimate expectations is an element of the FET standard that operates to protect investors' expectations regarding their investments. However, this standard is subject to much controversy because of its broad scope and variability in its application. The doctrine is a legal doctrine derived from domestic administrative law; however, there is no classical definition of this doctrine, inviting variability in applying arbitral discretion and conjecture.[73] The question as to whether the States have an obligation to respect and protect the legitimate expectations held by foreign investors has been particularly controversial.

Neither the *Arab Investment Agreement* in its original form nor the *OIC Agreement* included any FET provisions, although the former rectified this omission in its 2013 Amendment Protocol. A specific FET reference in Article 2 replaced the original vague and inadequate "protect[ing] the investor, safeguard his investment and its related revenues and rights and, to the extent possible, ensuring the stability

69 James Billingsley, 'Eli Lilly and Company v The Government of Canada and the Perils of Investor-State Arbitration' (2015) 20 *Appeal: Review of the Current Law and Law Reform* 27, 32.

70 Ibid.

71 Jacob Stone, 'Arbitrariness, the Fair and Equitable Treatment Standard, and the International Law of Investment' (2012) 25 *Leiden Journal of International Law* 77, 83–4.

72 Ibid, 84.

73 Laura Zielinksi, '"Legitimate Expectations" in the Vattenfall Case: At the Heart of the Debate over ISDS' on *Kluwer Arbitration Blog* (10 January 2017) <http://arbitrationblog.kluwerarbitration.com/2017/01/10/legitimate-expectations-in-the-vattenfall-case-at-the-heart-of-the-debate-over-isds/>.

of the pertinent legal provisions". In the absence of specific FET provisions, the *OIC Agreement*'s closest provision to some form of FET protection arguably was, and remains, the potential availability of importing such a protection from another IIA by virtue of an MFN clause. For example, in *Al-Warraq v Indonesia*, the claimant alleged that Indonesia was "subject to a fair and equitable treatment obligation by virtue of the most-favoured-nation clause in Article 8 of the OIC Agreement".[74] Relevantly, the arbitral tribunal noted that:

> the most-favoured-nation clause has been applied to matters of dispute-settlement as well as substantive treaty guarantees. This issue has been dealt with by a number of contemporary arbitral decisions, which also recognized the application of most-favoured-nation clauses to import fair and equitable treatment.[75]

The tribunal ultimately found that the MFN clause can operate to import clauses from other IIAs on the condition that the "the *ejusdem generis* rule applies".[76] The respondent submitted that Article 8 of the *OIC Agreement* has a limitation, and that the MFN treatment only applies within the context of the same economic activity, and that in this respect Article 8 is different from a typical MFN clause found in BITs that do not contain such a limitation.[77] The tribunal found that the term "same economic activity" did not impose a limitation on the scope of operation of the MFN clause in *Al-Warraq v Indonesia*.[78]

In *Desert Line v Yemen*,[79] the claimant (an Omani construction company) brought a claim against Yemen after conflict arose over a contractual relationship between the claimant and respondent in respect of road construction projects. Specifically, the claims arose out of disputes relating to amounts owed for work already completed, leading to the suspension of further work, arbitration in the Yemeni Commercial Court, company personnel being arrested, and the signature of a settlement arrangement allegedly made under duress.[80] The claimant initiated

74 *Hesham Talaat M. Al-Warraq v The Republic of Indonesia, Final Award* (UNCITRAL, 15 December 2014 [540]).

75 *Hesham Talaat M. Al-Warraq v The Republic of Indonesia, Final Award* (UNCITRAL, 15 December 2014 [541]); Patrick Dumberry, 'The Importation of the FET Standard through MFN Clauses: An Empirical Study of BITs (2017) *ICSID Review* 32(1) 126.

76 *Al-Warraq v Indonesia* (n 75), [551]; Patrick Dumberry (n 75), 126–7.

77 *Al-Warraq v Indonesia (*n 75), [552].

78 Ibid.

79 *Desert Line Projects LLC v The Republic of Yemen* (ICSID Case No. ARB/05/17, 30 September 2005) ('*Desert Line v Yemen*').

80 UNCTAD, 'Investment Dispute Settlement Navigator' <Desert Line v. Yemen | Investment Dispute Settlement Navigator | UNCTAD Investment Policy Hub>.

arbitration proceedings, applying the *Oman–Yemen BIT* (1998),[81] seeking relief for alleged breaches of the FET protection in respect of its investment, specifically in relation to the respondent's conduct in respect of the settlement agreement. Article 3 of the BIT provides:

> The two Contracting Parties undertake to ensure fair and equitable treatment to the investments of investors of the other Contracting Party. They also undertake not to subject in any way to discriminatory or legally unjustified measures the management, maintenance, use, transfer, enjoyment, assignment of an investment mad by the investors of one of the two Contracting Parties in the territory of the other Contracting Party, as well as companies and projects in which such investments have been made.

In relation to the requirement for contracting parties to provide fair and equitable treatment and to ensure measures are legally justified, the tribunal found that "[t]he application of these norms is dictated by the specific circumstances of the case".[82] The tribunal found that the respondent contravened Article 3 of the BIT "by inadmissibly pressuring the Claimant to accept and execute the Settlement Agreement instead of the final and binding Yemeni Arbitral Award".[83] In addition, the tribunal concluded that the claimant had entered into the disputed settlement agreement under "financial and physical duress" and, critically, that its conclusion was in breach of Article 3 and therefore "not entitled to international effect".[84] The tribunal further determined that in consequence, the Yemeni Arbitral Award was to be reinstated for the purpose of determining Yemen's liability in respect of the BIT.[85] GCC member States should therefore carefully consider the scope of the FET standard when negotiating IIAs, noting that tribunals will consider each set of facts on a case-by-case basis. Moreover, failure to discharge equitable considerations such as the doctrine of "clean hands" with respect to the conduct of the respondent may be sufficient (in this case, the duress to conclude the settlement agreement), in the eyes of an arbitral tribunal, to constitute a breach of a substantive investment protection contained within an IIA.

Table 3.3 demonstrates the construction of the FET standard across the *Arab Investment Agreement*, the *OIC Agreement*, the *Saudi Arabia–France BIT*, the *France–Kuwait BIT*, and the *United States–Oman FTA*.

81 *Agreement for the Reciprocal Promotion and Protection of Investments between the Government of the Sultanate of Oman and the Government of the Republic of Yemen*, signed 20 September 1998 (entered into force 1 April 2000).

82 *Desert Line v Yemen (Award)* (6 February 2008) [192].

83 Ibid [193].

84 Ibid [194].

85 Ibid [195].

Table 3.3 Fair and Equitable Treatment

IIA	*Fair and Equitable Treatment Standard*
Arab Investment Agreement 2013 Amendment Protocol Arts (2) and (4)	2. The States Parties to this Agreement shall … undertake to protect investors, investments and their revenues. Arab capital in the State Party shall benefit from fair and equitable treatment at all times and shall not impose any Performance requirements or barriers to entry which could be harmful to investment or have a negative impact on it or its ownership. 4. Conclusions and interpretations derived from the provisions of this Agreement shall be guided by the principles on which it is based and the aims which inspired it, followed by the rules and principles common to the respective legislation of the States members of the League of Arab States and, then, the principles of international trade.
OIC Agreement	Nil specific reference
France–Kuwait BIT Art. 4	Each of the Contracting States undertakes to ensure, in accordance with the principles of international law, fair and equitable treatment of investments and offences by investors of the other Contracting State in its territory and in its maritime areas and to ensure that the exercise of the right thus recognized is not impeded either in law or in fact.
Saudi Arabia–France BIT Art. 2(1)	Each Contracting Party shall make every effort to encourage investments in its territory and maritime area by investors of the other Party and shall admit them within the framework of its legislation. It grants these investments, in all circumstances, fair and equitable treatment.
US–Oman FTA Art. 10.5(1)	1. Each Party shall accord to covered investments treatment in accordance with customary international law, including fair and equitable treatment and full protection and security. 2. For greater certainty, paragraph 1 prescribes the customary international law minimum standard of treatment of aliens as the minimum standard of treatment to be afforded to covered investments. The concepts of "fair and equitable treatment" and "full protection and security" do not require treatment in addition to or beyond that which is required by that standard, and do not create additional substantive rights. The obligation in paragraph 1 to provide: (a) "fair and equitable treatment" includes the obligation not to deny justice in criminal, civil, or administrative adjudicatory proceedings in accordance with the principle of due process embodied in the principal legal systems of the world; and (b) "full protection and security" requires each Party to provide the level of police protection required under customary international law.

3.5 Expropriation

Expropriation occurs when a state takes or otherwise deprives a foreign investor of its investment or an element thereof, on unjust terms or otherwise, without making compensation. There are two types of expropriation – direct (host state acquisition of asset) and indirect (deprivation of investment) – that may attract treaty protection.[86] International arbitrators determine:

> the threshold between a government act that simply amounts to a diminution of value and does not constitute expropriation, on one hand, and a measure that constitutes a property rights violation and does give rise to expropriation, on the other.[87]

Shawn Nichols has argued that arbitral tribunals "generally apply one of two juridical litmus tests, or some combination of the two, to determine if a state must compensate investors for the costs associated with a given regulatory measure".[88] The first test (the public interest test) involves determining the objective of a government measure. This reflects the state's right to regulate in the public interest without needing to pay compensation provided the measure or series of measures is not discriminatory or protectionist. The second, and narrower, test is the pecuniary injury test. In the following case, the definition of 'investment' and the operation of the anti-expropriation protection were closely linked considerations.

The case of *Navodaya v Gabon*[89] involved claims arising out of Gabon's alleged expropriation of a mining concession in respect of a manganese deposit in Okondja, eastern Gabon, applying the *OIC Agreement*.[90] The home state of the claimant was the UAE, although the claimant was "backed and managed by Indian investors".[91] The claimant alleged several breaches, arguing that the acts of terminating, failing to review, and designating to a third party the relevant licence constituted an indirect expropriation in contravention of Article 10 of the Agreement.[92] The respondent submitted a counter-argument that the claimant did not have an investment capable of being expropriated, despite the claimant arguing that the respondent's submission was jurisdictional and inadmissible. The tribunal reportedly found "the existence of an investment pertains as much to jurisdiction as to the merits, since

86 Julien Chaisse and Christian Bellak, 'Navigating the Expanding Universe of International Treaties on Foreign Investment' (2015) 18(1) *Journal of International Economic Law* 79, 94.

87 Shawn Nichols, Expanding Property Rights under Investor-State Dispute Settlement (ISDS): Class Struggle in the Era of Transnational Capital (2018) 25(2) *Review of International Political Economy* 243, 245.

88 Ibid.

89 *Navodaya Trading DMCC v The Gabonese Republic* (2018) UNCTAD, *'Investment Dispute Settlement Navigator'* <Navodaya v Gabon | United Arab Emirates | Investment Dispute Settlement Navigator | UNCTAD Investment Policy Hub> ('*Navodaya v Gabon*').

90 Ibid.

91 Damien Charlotin, 'Uncovered: Kaufmann-Kohler Chaired Tribunal Confirms That OIC Agreement Contains Consent to Arbitration, but Ultimately Dismisses Mining Claims on the Merits', *Investment Arbitration Reporter* (17 February 2021) <Uncovered: Kaufmann-Kohler chaired tribunal confirms that OIC Agreement contains consent to arbitration, but ultimately dismisses mining claims on the merits | Investment Arbitration Reporter (openathens.net)>.

92 Ibid.

there could not be an expropriation or other breach of the investor's rights absent an investment".[93] The tribunal ultimately found the claimant had made an investment through its participation in a joint venture with the respondent and rejected the respondent's argument that the licence did not amount to an investment and was expropriable on the basis that "the licence was a manifestation of Navodaya's investment".[94] The tribunal adopted a rather broad view of the construction of the term "investment", rejecting the respondent's argument that the claimant had not generated revenue and finding instead that "the definition merely indicated that revenue generation was the purpose of the investment, and there was no doubt that Navodaya had invested in view of earning a return".[95] With respect to the acts alleged to amount to an expropriation, the tribunal found that the respondent had not in fact terminated the relevant licence but rather had merely threatened to do so; and that the respondent was justified in refusing to renew the licence because of the claimant's non-compliance with the licence and local laws and obligations. Consequently, the respondent's grant of the licence to a third party could not constitute an expropriation.[96]

In *Almasryia v Kuwait*,[97] the tribunal considered the legal merit of the claimant's (an Egyptian company) expropriation claim made under Article 7 of the *Egypt–Kuwait BIT* (2001).[98] The dispute arose out of a joint venture agreement between the claimant and Faisal Bandar Al-Otaibi and Bin Samar Contracting for the purpose of developing and constructing hotels for tourists, real estate, and other projects. Subsequently, Mr Al-Otaibi attempted to obtain a deed of ownership in respect of land in Wafra, Kuwait, but failed. The claimant argued that the failure of Kuwait to grant a deed injured its joint venture investment in contravention of the *Egypt–Kuwait BIT*, specifically Articles 6 and 7.[99] The respondent sought dismissal of the claims on the basis that they were manifestly without legal merit.[100] Article 7 of the BIT states:

> 1 – (a) Investments made by investors belonging to either of the two Contracting States in the territory of the other Contracting State shall not be subject to nationalisation, expropriation, or confiscation, nor shall they be subject, directly or indirectly, to measures whose effect is equivalent to nationalisation, expropriation, or confiscation (referred to collectively hereinafter as "expropriation") by the other Contracting State, except for a public

93 Ibid.
94 Ibid.
95 Ibid.
96 Ibid.
97 *Almasryia for Operating & Maintaining Touristic Construction Co. L.L.C. v State of Kuwait, (Award on the Respondent's Application under Rule 41(5) of the ICSID Arbitration Rules)* (ICSID Case No. ARB/18/2, 1 November 2019) ('*Almasryia v Kuwait*').
98 *Agreement between the Government of the Arab Republic of Egypt and the Government of the State of Kuwait for the Promotion and Reciprocal of Investments*, signed 17 April 2001 (entered into force 26 April 2002).
99 *Almasryia v Kuwait* (n 97), [4].
100 Ibid [5].

> purpose relating to a national interest of that Contracting State, and then in return for compensation that is immediate, sufficient and effective, and on the condition that those measures are taken on a non-discriminatory basis, and in accordance with legal procedures in general usage.
>
> . . .
>
> 3 – "Expropriation" also includes cases when a Contracting State expropriates the assets of a company or enterprise which was set up or founded in accordance with the laws in force in its territory, in which an investor belonging to the other Contracting State has a majority or important share, through owning stocks, shares, bonds, rights, or other interests.
>
> 4 – The term "expropriation" also includes any interference or regulatory procedures carried out by a Contracting State such as incorporating or restricting the investment, or the forced sale of all or part of the investment, or any other similar procedures having the same effect of seizing the property or expropriating it, and arising from which procedures, the investor is in actuality dispossessed of his property, or his majority or substantial interest in his investment, or suffers loss or damage to the economic value of the investment.

In relation to the expropriation claim, the tribunal considered as a starting point that "investment tribunals have recognized the existence of rights under the relevant domestic law within the context of expropriation claims".[101] The tribunal relevantly found that the private joint venture agreement was "a promise between two private parties contained in a private instrument, which has not been sanctioned or recognized by the host state, cannot be the basis of a property title".[102] The tribunal went on to conclude that "an essential element for the Claimant's expropriation claim is missing, namely, the existence of property rights in accordance with the laws of Kuwait", ultimately finding that the expropriation claim manifestly lacked legal merit.[103] GCC member States need to carefully manage the domestic laws creating covered investments to limit exposure to potential arbitration. The creation of domestic registers of foreign-owned property, for example, may go some way to identifying and managing exposure to risk.

Tribunals have also been prepared to decline jurisdiction in relation to claims including breaches of expropriation provisions. In *Khadamat v Saudi Arabia*,[104] the tribunal reportedly found that it did not have temporal jurisdiction because the alleged expropriation of the relevant investment (land) held by a Saudi company indirectly owned by the Indian company and again by a Kuwait company had occurred before the claimant bought rights in the Saudi company.[105] GCC member

101 Ibid [53].

102 Ibid [56].

103 Ibid [58].

104 *Khadamat Integrated Solutions Private Limited (India) v The Kingdom of Saudi Arabia* (PCA Case No. 2019–24), ('*Khadamat v Saudi Arabia*').

105 'Saudi Arabia Defeats Indian Investor's BIT Arbitration Claim', *Investment Arbitration Reporter* (28 February 2020) at <Saudi Arabia defeats Indian investor's BIT arbitration claim | Investment Arbitration Reporter (openathens.net)>.

States could improve upon the certainty of investment provisions contained within IIAs by expressly incorporating a provision addressing this issue, for example, a provision that expressly limits access to relief in investor–state arbitration to covered investments already owned by foreign claimant-investors at the time of the alleged expropriation.

Table 3.4 demonstrates the construction of the non-expropriation provisions across the *Arab Investment Agreement*, the *OIC Agreement*, the *France–Saudi Arabia BIT*, the *France–Kuwait BIT*, and the *United States–Oman FTA*.

Table 3.4 Non-Expropriation Provisions

IIA	*The Non-Expropriation Standard*
Arab Investment Agreement 2013 Amendment Protocol Art. 8(1) and (2)	1. In accordance with the provisions of this Agreement, Invested Arab capital shall not be subject to any special or general measures, whether permanent or temporary, irrespective of their legal form, which wholly or partially affect any of the assets, reserves or revenues of the investor and which lead to … expropriation … or any other action which infringes the right of ownership itself or prejudices the intrinsic authority of the owner in terms of his control and possession of the investment, his right to administer it, his acquisition of the revenues therefrom or the fulfilment of his rights and the discharge of his obligations. 2. It shall, however, be permissible to: (a) Expropriate for public benefit in accordance with the authority vested in the State or its institutions to perform their functions in carrying out public projects, provided that this is done on a non-discriminatory basis, in accordance with general legal provisions governing expropriation and in return for fair compensation equal to the market value of the investment.
OIC Agreement Art. 10(1) and (2)	1. The host state shall undertake not to adopt or permit the adoption of any measure – itself or through one of its organs, institutions or local authorities – if such a measure may directly or indirectly affect the ownership of the investor's capital or investment by depriving him totally or partially of his ownership or of all or part of his basic rights or the exercise of his authority on the ownership, possession or utilization of his capital, or of his actual control over the investment, its management, making use out of it, enjoying its utilities, the realization of its benefits or guaranteeing its development and growth. 2. It will, however, be permissible to: (a) Expropriate the investment in the public interest in accordance with the law, without discrimination and on prompt payment of adequate and effective compensation to the investor in accordance with the laws of the host state regulating such compensation, provided that the investor shall have the right to contest the measure of expropriation in the competent court of the host state. (b) Adopt preventive measures issued in accordance with an order from a competent legal authority and the execution measures of the decision given by competent judicial authority.

(*Continued*)

Table 3.4 (Continued)

IIA	*The Non-Expropriation Standard*
France–Kuwait BIT Art. 7(2)	Contracting States shall not take, in their territory and in their maritime zones, measures of expropriation or nationalisation or any other measure the purpose of which is to impose, directly or indirectly, investors in the other State investments belonging to them, except on grounds of public utility and provided that such measures are not discriminatory, nor contrary to a particular commitment.
Saudi Arabia–France BIT Art. 4(2)	The Contracting Parties shall not take measures of expropriation, nationalization or freezing of assets, or any other measure the effect of which is to dispossess, directly or indirectly, investors of the other Party of investments made in its territory and in its maritime zone, except for reasons of public utility and provided that such measures are not discriminatory, or contrary to a particular commitment. Any measures of dispossession which may be taken must give rise to the payment of prompt, adequate and effective compensation, the amount of which, equal to the value of the investments concerned, must be assessed in relation to the normal economic situation prevailing before any threat of dispossession. This indemnity, its amount and its terms of payment shall be fixed at the latest on the date of dispossession. This compensation is indeed achievable, paid without delay and freely transferable. It shall, until the date of its payment, earn interest calculated at the appropriate market interest rate.
US–Oman FTA Art. 10.6(1); Annex 10-B	Neither Party may expropriate or nationalize a covered investment either directly or indirectly through measures equivalent to expropriation or nationalization ("expropriation"), except: (a) for a public purpose; (b) in a non-discriminatory manner; (c) on payment of prompt, adequate, and effective compensation; and (d) in accordance with due process of law and Article 10.5.1 through 10.5.3.

3.6. Anti-Discrimination

Anti-discrimination provisions comprise two standards – the national treatment and the most-favoured-nation (MFN) provisions. In some instances, IIAs contain guidance stipulating which standard should be applied. Broadly, the national treatment standard protects foreign investors against host state treatment that treats foreign investors less favourably than domestic investors. The MFN standard protects foreign investors against being treated less favourably than investors from a third country. Both provisions are relative standards that require analysing a party's treatment of foreign investors and their investments in the context of the treatment of domestic or other foreign investors in like circumstances.[106]

One of the key issues addressed by the tribunal in its award in the case of *Itisaluna v Iraq* was whether the claimants were "able to incorporate into the OIC Agreement, by operation of its MFN clause, the ICSID arbitration clause in the *Iraq–Japan BIT*".[107] The case related to an agreement between Munir Sukhitan Investment (a Jordanian incorporated company) and the National Communications and Media Commission in Iraq in respect of a licence to provide telecommunication services within Iraq.[108] The claimants, Itisaluna Iraq LLC (also a Jordanian incorporated company), Munir Sukihitan Investment, VTEL Holdings, and VTEL Middle East and Africa (both incorporated in Dubai), initiated arbitration in March 2017 claiming that their right to operate "their own international gateways" pursuant to the licencing arrangement was injured in 2008 when the General Secretariat of the Iraqi Council of Ministers banned the operation of their gateways. The claimants further argued that the respondent did not allow them to lay optical fibre cables, and that the Iraq Communications and Media Commission raised fees, failed in its duties as a regulator, and did not undertake good faith negotiations in respect of the renewal of the licence at the heart of the dispute.[109] The tribunal relevantly determined that:

> The operation of the MFN clause to incorporate into the OIC Agreement from another treaty "consent in writing to submit [the dispute in question] to the Centre", as required by Article 25(1) of the ICSID Convention, is the essential bridge that the Claimants must cross if they are to succeed.[110]

The tribunal ultimately concluded that the claimants could not rely on Article 8 of the *OIC Agreement* to incorporate into it "the consent in writing to submit the present dispute to ICSID arbitration derived from the Iraq–Japan BIT", specifically Article 17(4)(a); thereby upholding the respondent's *ratione voluntatis* jurisdictional objection.[111] In drawing this conclusion, the tribunal recognised the "multilateral character" of the BIT,[112] the relationship between Articles 16 (right of complaint in the host state's domestic judicial system) and 17 (conciliation

106 Harm Schepel, 'Investment Protection, ISDS, and EU Law' (speech delivered at the Investor-State Dispute Settlement in EU law and International Law Public Conference, European Parliament, 2 March 2015).

107 *Itisaluna Iraq LLC and others v Republic of Iraq (*AWARD*)* (ICSID Case No. ARB/17/10, 3 April 2020) [80] and [146] (*'Itisaluna v Iraq')*.

108 Lisa Bohmer, 'Breaking: Majority in Itisaluna v Iraq Declines Jurisdiction over OIC Claims; Dissenter Would Have Granted Access to ICSID Arbitration through MFN Clause', *Investment Arbitration Reporter* (5 April 2020) at <Breaking: Majority in Itisaluna v. Iraq declines jurisdiction over OIC claims; dissenter would have granted access to ICSID arbitration through MFN clause | Investment Arbitration Reporter (openathens.net)>.

109 Ibid.

110 *Itisaluna v Iraq* (n 107), [146].

111 Ibid [148].

112 Ibid [152].

and arbitration), as well as the interpretation of Article 17 and interpretation and application of Article 8.[113] With respect to the multilateral character of the *OIC Agreement*, the tribunal resolved to "exercise considerable caution" in formulating an interpretation of the Agreement based not on its terms or the practices of all contracting parties but "rather on the contested practice of one of its Contracting Parties alone".[114] The tribunal went on to find that:

> An MFN clause in a multilateral treaty cannot be used as a foundation on which to construct (even if only potentially) a variable framework of application in respect of its individual Contracting Parties by reference to their distinct and unrelated bilateral treaty practice. That would be the very antithesis of the principle underlying the MFN clause.[115]

However, the tribunal did emphasise "that its conclusion on recourse to ICSID arbitration under the framework of the OIC Agreement is without prejudice to the availability and sustainability of any other point", potentially leaving the door open to re-litigation of the dispute in another forum.[116]

With respect to the relationship between Articles 16 and 17 of the *OIC Agreement*, the tribunal found that "a treaty must be interpreted holistically" and as such the two provisions "cannot be detached" and "read in isolation".[117] The tribunal also found that the terms of Article 16 contemplate ISDS, not just from the words contained within the provision but from the broader agreement.[118] The tribunal adopted the view that Article 16 should be interpreted as containing a "fork-in-the-road provision" and the inclusion of a "reference to an arbitral tribunal" supported "the contention that the Agreement has in contemplation the possibility of internationalised investor-State arbitration".[119]

The tribunal further found that Article 17 both "contemplates and addresses investor-State disputes" and further that "it is incontrovertible that no OIC Agreement dispute settlement Organ is presently operational and available to address investor-State claims", meaning that the rules and procedures contained in Article 17 were applicable.[120] The tribunal also found "that resort to arbitration is conditional on the prior resort to conciliation"[121] and also that consent to arbitration was afforded by Article 17(2) following the institution and exhaustion of conciliation.[122] Conversely, the tribunal in *Navodaya v Gabon* found that recourse to and exhaustion of conciliation was not mandatory under Article 17 of the Agreement before a claimant could access arbitration.

113 Ibid [156].
114 Ibid [153]
115 Ibid [153].
116 Ibid [149]. See also Lisa Bohmer (n 108).
117 *Itisaluna v Iraq* (n 107), [160].
118 Ibid [161].
119 Ibid [164]–[165].
120 Ibid [169]–[171].
121 Ibid [183].
122 Ibid [80] and [190].

In regard to the application of Article 8 of the *OIC Agreement*, the tribunal in *Itisaluna v Iraq* found that the most-favoured-nation principle is:

> a principle of treaty law that must be expressly stated and is amenable to limitation, whether expressly or implicitly, having regard to the terms in which the principle is expressed and its purpose in the context of the instrument in which it is found …
>
> Article 8(1) of the OIC Agreement is subject to exception and limitation, both express and by necessary implication, that exclude its application to incorporate an ICSID consent to arbitration clause from another treaty …
>
> [T]he Tribunal does not consider that the MFN principle can properly be used to derive from another treaty consent to ICSID arbitration that is not only absent from the principal treaty but evidently intentionally so, given the bespoke nature of the dispute settlement arrangements in the principle treaty.[123]

Table 3.5 sets out the content of the national treatment provisions across the *Arab Investment Agreement*, the *OIC Agreement*, the *Saudi Arabia–France BIT*, the *France–Kuwait BIT*, and the *United States–Oman FTA*.

Table 3.5 Anti-Discrimination: The National Treatment Provisions

IIA	*National Treatment*
Arab Investment Agreement 2013 Amendment Protocol Art. 5	2. In the host State, invested Arab capital shall be treated in a manner not less favourable than the capital owned by the citizens of said State or a third State, whichever is more favourable and without discrimination. 4. The provisions of this Article shall not apply to the following: (a) The privileges granted by any contract party to the investors of a third state pursuant to its membership of a free trade area, customs union or common market. (b) Tax or *zakat* treatment. (c) Ownership of land and real estate.
OIC Agreement Art. 14	The investor shall be accorded a treatment not less than that accorded by the host state to its national investors or others regarding the compensation of damage that may befall the physical assets of investment due to hostilities of international nature committed by any international body or due to civil disturbances or violent acts of general nature.

(*Continued*)

123 Ibid [196]–[197], [221].

Table 3.5 (Continued)

France–Kuwait BIT Art. 5	1. Each Contracting State shall apply, in its territory and in its maritime areas, to investors of the other State, in respect of their investments and associated activities, the treatment accorded to its investors, or the treatment accorded to investors of the most favoured nation, if the latter is more advantageous … 2. Subject to the provisions of Article II, each Contracting State shall grant investors from other contracting States, under such terms and conditions as favourable as it may, in similar situations, to its own investors to investors of a third State, in particular, the right of access to its courts, administrative jurisdictions and administrations, as well as to any other institution exercising an authority of jurisdiction and, on the other hand, the right to employ persons of their choice, empowered, under the applicable laws and internal regulations, to assert and exercise the rights relating to their investments.
Saudi Arabia–France BIT Art. 3(2)	In accordance with its laws and regulations, each Contracting Party shall accord to the investments it has admitted and to the investment income of investors of the other Contracting Party treatment no less favourable than that accorded to the investments and investment income of its own investors.
US–Oman FTA Art. 10.3	1. Each Party shall accord to investors of the other Party treatment no less favourable than that it accords, in like circumstances, to its own investors with respect to the establishment, acquisition, expansion, management, conduct, operation, and sale or other disposition of investments in its territory. 2. Each Party shall accord to covered investments treatment no less favourable than that it accords, in like circumstances, to investments in its territory of its own investors with respect to the establishment, acquisition, expansion, management, conduct, operation, and sale or other disposition of investments. 3. The treatment to be accorded by a Party under paragraphs 1 and 2 means, with respect to a regional level of government, treatment no less favourable than the treatment accorded, in like circumstances, by that regional level of government to natural persons resident in and enterprises constituted under the laws of other regional levels of government of the Party of which it forms a part, and to their respective investments.

Table 3.6 sets out the changes to the MFN provisions across the same agreements.

Table 3.6 Anti-Discrimination: Most-Favoured-Nation Treatment Provisions

IIA	*Most-Favoured-Nation Treatment*
Arab Investment Agreement	(See Article 5 as detailed in Table 3.5 Anti-Discrimination: The National Treatment Provisions, above)
OIC Agreement Art. 8	1. The investors of any contracting party shall enjoy, within the context of economic activity in which they have employed their investments in the territories of another contracting party, a treatment not less favourable than the treatment accorded to investors belonging to another State not party to this Agreement, in the context of that activity and in respect of rights and privileges accorded to those investors. 2. Provisions of paragraph 1 above shall not be applied to any better treatment given by a contracting party in the following cases: a) Rights and privileges given to investors of one contracting party by another contracting party in accordance with an international agreement, law or special preferential arrangement. b) Rights and privileges arising from an international agreement currently in force or to be concluded in the future and to which any contracting party may become a member and under which an economic union, customs union or mutual tax exemption arrangement is set up. c) Rights and privileges given by a contracting party for a specific project due to its special importance to that state.
France–Kuwait BIT	(See Article 5 as detailed in Table 3.5 Anti-Discrimination: The National Treatment Provisions above.)
Saudi Arabia–France BIT Art. 3(1)	Each Contracting Party shall accord to the investments which it has admitted and to the investment income of investors of the other Contracting Party treatment no less favourable than that accorded to investments and investment income of investors of a third State.
US–Oman FTA Art. 10.4	1. Each Party shall accord to investors of the other Party treatment no less favourable than that it accords, in like circumstances, to investors of any non-Party with respect to the establishment, acquisition, expansion, management, conduct, operation, and sale or other disposition of investments in its territory. 2. Each Party shall accord to covered investments treatment no less favourable than that it accords, in like circumstances, to investments in its territory of investors of any non-Party with respect to the establishment, acquisition, expansion, management, conduct, operation, and sale or other disposition of investments.

3.7 Dispute Resolution

The purpose of including dispute resolution provisions within IIAs is to enable claimants to submit disputes to a neutral, third-party, and (supposedly) independent body of arbitrators outside of or potentially in addition to domestic legal institutions. In doing so, they are perceived to mitigate against the risk of politicisation of disputes and enhance the timeliness and cost-effectiveness of dispute settlement proceedings. However, access to international investment arbitration is not always contained within IIAs and even when it is, there are varying degrees to which the provisions guarantee such access, the notion and requirement of consent to submit to arbitration being one of the key issues relating to the dispute settlement mechanisms. The dispute settlement mechanisms are a central, and at times, contentious part of dispute settlement involving GCC member States or investor-claimants hailing from the States.

In *Al-Warraq v Indonesia*,[124] for example, the claimant relied upon Article 17 of the *OIC Agreement* in order to bring about the arbitration, arguing that in ratifying the Agreement, the respondent had "made an offer to arbitrate to investors which the Claimant can accept and thereby establish a valid arbitration agreement without any additional consent on the part of the State". The Respondent argued that Article 17 "does not contain any offer to arbitrate or consent to arbitrate on the part of the State".[125] The tribunal found that Article 17 does constitute an investor–state arbitration clause, taking into account the treaty's "object and purpose", Article 16 being a fork-in-the-road clause, and the language used in Articles 16 and 17.[126]

In *Ali Alyafei v Jordan* (I)[127] the claimant reportedly sought to rely upon the MFN clause (Article 6(2)) in the *Arab Investment Agreement* in order "to import the dispute resolution clause of the Italy–Jordan BIT, which allows for ICSID arbitration" because the Agreement "does not expressly provide for ICSID arbitration" and moreover, there is doubt as to "whether this treaty even offers the advance consent of states to arbitration". A tribunal was appointed to hear the matter, but the case was reportedly discontinued in mid-2016 "for non-payment of advances". The claimant sought relief in a fresh arbitration applying the *OIC Agreement*; however this case was dismissed.[128]

124 *Hesham Talaat M. Al-Warraq v The Republic of Indonesia, Award on Respondent's Preliminary Objections to Jurisdiction and Admissibility of the Claims* (UNCITRAL, 21 June 2012) [67].

125 Ibid [68].

126 *Al-Warraq v Indonesia, Award on Respondent's Preliminary Objections to Jurisdiction and Admissibility of the Claims* (UNCITRAL, 21 June 2012) [73]–[76].

127 *Ali Alyafei v Hashemite Kingdom of Jordan (1)* (ICSID Case No. ARB/15/24); Joel Dahlquist, 'Qatari Businessman Contends That MFN Clause in Regional Treaty Can Provide Foothold for an ICSID Claim against Jordan', *Investment Arbitration Reporter* (15 June 2015), at <Qatari businessman contends that MFN clause in regional treaty can provide foothold for an ICSID claim against Jordan | Investment Arbitration Reporter (openathens.net)>.

128 Luke Eric Peterson, 'Panels Finalized for Three ICSID Treaty-Based Arbitrations: ALPIQ v. Romania, PT Ventures v. Cabo Verde and Ali Alyafei v Jordan', *Investment Arbitration Reporter* (16 September 2015) at <Panels finalized for three ICSID treaty-based arbitrations: Alpiq v. Romania, PT Ventures v. Cabo Verde and Ali Alyafei v. Jordan | Investment Arbitration Reporter (openathens.net)>; Jarrod Hepburn and Luke Eric Peterson, 'Investigation: As New Cases Emerge under Islamic Investment Treaty, Initial Viability of Claims Seems to Hinge on Willingness of Respondents to Appoint Arbitrators', *Investment Arbitration Reporter* (2 March 2017) at <Investigation: As new cases emerge under Islamic investment treaty, initial viability of claims seems to hinge on willingness of respondents to appoint arbitrators | Investment Arbitration Reporter (openathens.net)>.

Table 3.7 Dispute Resolution by Arbitration Provisions

IIA	*Dispute Resolution Treatment*
Arab Investment Agreement 2013 Amendment Protocol Arts 23–25	23. The Arab investor may resort to courts in the host State in accordance to the rules of jurisdiction within such State in the case of matters which fall within the jurisdiction of the Arab Investment Court. However, where the Arab investor initiates legal action before one authority, said investor may not initiate legal action before the other. 24. If it is not possible to settle the dispute through the means agreed upon by the parties to the investment, the matter shall be referred to the Arab Investment Court. 25. If it is stated in an Arab-international agreement establishing an Arab investment or in any agreement regarding investment within the scope of the Arab League or between its members that an issue or a dispute shall be referred to international arbitration or to international courts, the parties involved may agree to deem said issue or dispute falling within jurisdiction of the Court.
OIC Agreement Arts 16 and 17	16. The host state undertakes to allow the investor the right to resort to its national judicial system to complain against a measure adopted by its authorities against him, or to contest the extent of its conformity with the provisions of the regulations and laws in force in its territory, or to complain against the non-adoption by the host state of a certain measure which is in the interest of the investor, and which the state should have adopted, irrespective of whether the complaint is related, or otherwise, to the implementation of the provisions of the Agreement to the relationship between the investor and the host state. Provided that if the investor chooses to raise the complaint before the national courts or before an arbitral tribunal then having done so before one of the two quarters he loses the right of recourse to the other. 17. Until an Organ for the settlement of disputes arising under the Agreement is established, disputes that may arise shall be entitled through conciliation or arbitration.
France–Kuwait BIT Art. 11	1. Any investment dispute between one of the Contracting States and an investor of the other Contracting State shall be settled amicably between the two parties concerned. If such a dispute has not been settled within six months from the time it was raised by either party to the dispute, it shall, at the request of either party, be submitted to arbitration by the International Centre for Settlement of Investment Disputes (ICSID) … 2. Each of the Contracting States hereby agrees to submit to the Centre any investment dispute for settlement by conciliation or binding arbitration. 3. The Contracting States shall not deal with a case submitted to arbitration through diplomatic channels or contacts until the proceedings have been completed and one of the contracting States has not complied with or implemented the decision rendered by the ICSID, except to the extent that diplomatic contacts will facilitate the settlement of the dispute in respect of the case concerned. 4. In the event that the Agreement is not applicable, the dispute shall be settled by ad hoc arbitration.

(*Continued*)

Table 3.7 (Continued)

IIA	*Dispute Resolution Treatment*
Saudi Arabia–France BIT Art. 6	1. Any investment dispute between one of the Contracting Parties and an investor of the other Contracting Party shall be settled amicably to the extent possible. 2. If the dispute has not been settled in accordance with the procedure described in paragraph 1 of this Article within six months from the date on which the request for settlement was filed, it shall, at the request of the investor, be submitted to the competent court of the Contracting Party in whose territory the investment was made, or be submitted to arbitration in accordance with … [ICSID] … If the investor opts for arbitration, the Contracting Party undertakes not to require that all local recourse procedures have been exhausted. 3. (a) If the dispute is submitted to the Contracting Party's competent court, as permitted by paragraph 2, the investor shall refrain from concurrently resorting to international arbitration and the court's award shall be binding and not subject to appeal or recourse other than as provided by the Contracting Party's law. 3. b) If the dispute is submitted to arbitration in accordance with the provisions of paragraph 2, the award shall be enforceable and not subject to appeal or recourse other than as provided for in the above-mentioned Agreement. The enforcement of the award shall be governed by the laws relating to the enforcement of judgments in force in the State in whose territories the award is enforceable.
US–Oman FTA Art. 10.14 & 10.15(1)	10.14. In the event of an investment dispute, the claimant and the respondent should initially seek to resolve the dispute through consultation and negotiation, which may include the use of non-binding, third-party procedures. 10.15(1). In the event that a disputing party considers that an investment dispute cannot be settled by consultation and negotiation: (a) the claimant, on its own behalf, may submit to arbitration under this Section a claim (i) that the respondent has breached an obligation under Section A, an investment authorization, or an investment agreement; and (ii) that the claimant has incurred loss or damage by reason of, or arising out of, that breach; and (b) the claimant, on behalf of an enterprise of the respondent that is a juridical person that the claimant owns or controls directly or indirectly, may submit to arbitration under this Section a claim (i) that the respondent has breached an obligation under … Section A, … an investment authorization, or … an investment agreement; and (ii) that the enterprise has incurred loss or damage by reason of, or arising out of, that breach, provided that a claimant may submit pursuant to … a claim for breach of an investment agreement only if the subject matter of the claim and the claimed damages directly relate to the covered investment that was established or acquired, or sought to be established or acquired, in reliance on the relevant investment agreement.

3.8 Concluding Remarks

The GCC and its member States participate in an increasingly complex and dynamic system of investor–state dispute settlement. Both are contracting parties in a number of multilateral and bilateral IIAs which in some cases overlap, creating a risk of multiplicity of dispute settlements arising out of one set of facts and/or treaty-shopping. These IIAs contain both substantive investment protections and access to investor–state arbitration, outside of domestic judicial institutions and in some instances without necessarily having had to have first commenced and/or exhausted local remedies. The content of the investment protections contained within these IIAs is rather broad and inexact and has consequently been interpreted and applied by tribunals in different ways. The lack of transparency regarding the occurrence and effect of adverse arbitrations against states, as well as regulatory chill, arguably contribute to the risk that ISDS may erode sovereign power, particularly the right to regulate in the public interest. The operation of survival or sunset clauses that continue to operate and expose governments to liability under ISDS despite termination of the relevant IIA and the possibility that arbitrations may be administered or conducted on an ad hoc basis create a risk of incoherence, inconsistency, and incorrectness of arbitral decisions.

Perhaps key among the definitions, in the GCC context, are those relating to investors and the nationality requirements. Both the substantive investment protections and dispute settlement mechanisms have been the subject of much debate and arbitral review.

It is suggested that GCC member States would benefit from a careful review of the scope of substantive investment protections, particularly expropriation, the FET standard/minimum standard of treatment, and arbitrary, unreasonable, and/or discriminatory measures contained within existing treaties and most especially within the *OIC Agreement*. For example, Article 10 of the Agreement states:

> 1. The host state shall undertake not to adopt or permit the adoption of any measure – itself or through one of its organs, institutions or local authorities – if such a measure may directly indirectly affect the ownership of the investor's capital or investment by depriving him totally or partially of his ownership or of all or part of his basic rights or the exercise of his authority on the ownership, possession or utilization of his capital, or of his actual control over the investment, its management, making use out of it, enjoying its utilities, the realization of its benefits or guaranteeing its development and growth.
> 2. It will, however, be permissible to:
>   (a) Expropriate the investment in the public interest in accordance with the law, without discrimination and on prompt payment of adequate and effective compensation to the investor in accordance with the laws of the host state regulating such compensation, provided that the investor shall have the right to contest the measure of expropriation in the competent court of the host state.

(b) Adopt preventive measures issued in accordance with an order from a competent legal authority and the execution measures of the decision given by a competent judicial authority.

The language used in the provision is inclusive and imprecise, making the scope of the protection unduly broad, and arguably needs to be redrafted in order to limit the scope for investor claimants to initiate costly arbitration for alleged harm to their investments. There would be merit in reducing the availability of relief to claimants for such a broad group of investment-related rights and properly exclude expropriation conducted for legitimate purposes, and requiring claimant investors to first exhaust local remedies before pursuing a claim for expropriation in investor–state arbitration, for example. In practice, however, revision of the *OIC Agreement* may be a controversial and lengthy process due to the number of countries which are parties to the agreement. GCC member States would also likely benefit from the creation of a model agreement which limits the scope of operation of substantive investment provisions.

It is suggested that the GCC and its member States would also benefit from a review of existing agreements and should seek to improve upon the drafting of investment provisions in order to enhance foreign investor confidence and limit the scope of inconsistency in arbitral awards. Both stand to benefit from the conclusion of IIAs containing more narrow substantive investment protections and stronger limitations on access to arbitral relief. States would also arguably benefit from a careful review of the complex relationship between domestic regulation and investor–state arbitration, including, for example, the creation of registers of foreign-owned assets (including nationality attribution) and the introduction of stricter requirements about the required nexus between foreign investment in local jurisdictions and access to ISDS, set out temporal limitations.

A key issue in contention in respect of the dispute settlement mechanism is the availability of reliance on MFN clauses by investor claimants in order to import more favourable provisions from other treaties, most especially the dispute settlement provisions. This issue and the divergent approaches adopted by various tribunals, together with another significant issue in terms of the application of the *OIC Agreement*, namely the appointment of arbitrators, are considered further in the chapters addressing the contexts of arbitrations in detail, namely Chapter 4 on the States as respondents, Chapter 5 on the States as investors claimants, and Chapter 6 specifically on the intra-GCC disputes.

Bibliography

Adel A Hamadi Al Tamimi v Sultanate of Oman (Award) (ICSID Case No. ARB/11/33, 3 November 2015) (*'Al Tamimi v Oman'*).

Agreement between the Government of the Arab Republic of Egypt and the Government of the State of Kuwait for the Promotion and Reciprocal of Investments, signed 17 April 2001 (entered into force 26 April 2002).

Agreement between the Government of the French Republic and the Government of the Kingdom of Saudi Arabia on the Reciprocal Encouragement and Protection of Investments, signed 26 June 2002 (entered into force 18 March 2004) (*'France – Saudi Arabia BIT'*).

Agreement between the Government of the French Republic and the State of Kuwait on the Encouragement and Reciprocal Protection of Investments, signed 27 September 1989 (entered into force 16 May 1991) (*'France – Kuwait BIT'*).

Agreement between the Government of the Kingdom of Saudi Arabia and the Government of the French Republic Concerning the Encouragement and Reciprocal Protection of Investments, signed 26 June 2002 (entered into force 18 March 2004) (*'Saudi Arabia - France BIT'*).

Agreement between the Government of the Syrian Arab Republic and the State of Kuwait for the Mutual Promotion and Protection of Investments) (*'Syria – Kuwait BIT'*), signed 16 August 2001 (entered into force 23 March 2004).

Agreement between the Government of the United Arab Emirates and the Government of the Italian Republic for the Promotion and Protection of Investments, signed 22 January 1995 (entered into force 29 April 1997) (*'UAE – Italy BIT'*).

Agreement between the Government of the United States of America and the Government of the Sultanate of Oman on the Establishment of a Free Trade Area, signed 19 January 2006 (entered into force 1 January 2009) (*'United States – Oman FTA'*).

Agreement for the Reciprocal Promotion and Protection of Investments between the Government of the Sultanate of Oman and the Government of the Republic of Yemen, signed 20 September 1998 (entered into force 1 April 2000).

Agreement on Encouragement and Reciprocal Protection of Investments between the Kingdom of the Netherlands and the Republic of Chile, signed 30 November 1998 (yet to enter into force).

Ali Alyafei v Hashemite Kingdom of Jordan (1) (ICSID Case No. ARB/15/24).

Almasryia for Operating & Maintaining Touristic Construction Co. L.L.C. v State of Kuwait, (Award on the Respondent's Application under Rule 41(5) of the ICSID Arbitration Rules) (ICSID Case No. ARB/18/2, 1 November 2019) (*'Almasryia v Kuwait'*).

Bachar Kiwan v The State of Kuwait (ICSID Case No. ARB/20/53) (*'Kiwan v Kuwait'*).

Bernard Friedrich Arnd Rüdiger von Pezold et. al. v Republic of Zimbabwe (Award) (ICSID Case No. ARB/10/15, 28 July 2015).

Billingsley, James, 'Eli Lilly and Company v The Government of Canada and the Perils of Investor-State Arbitration' (2015) 20 *Appeal: Review of the Current Law and Law Reform*, 27–32.

Chaisse, Julien and Christian Bellak, 'Navigating the Expanding Universe of International Treaties on Foreign Investment' (2015) 18(1) *Journal of International Economic Law*, 79–94.

Charlotin, Damian, 'Uncovered: Kaufmann-Kohler Chaired Tribunal Confirms That OIC Agreement Contains Consent To Arbitration, But Ultimately Dismisses Mining Claims On The Merits', *Investment Arbitration Reporter* (17 February 2021) <Uncovered: Kaufmann-Kohler chaired tribunal confirms that OIC Agreement contains consent to arbitration, but ultimately dismisses mining claims on the merits | Investment Arbitration Reporter (openathens.net)>.

Comprehensive Economic Partnership Agreement (CEPA) between the Kingdom of Cambodia and the Government of the United Arab Emirates (UAE) (2022), signed 8 June 2023, (*'Cambodia – UAE BIT'*).

Convention on the Settlement of Investment Disputes between States and Nationals of Other States, signed 18 March 1965 (entered into force 14 October 1966).

Dahlquist, Joel, 'Qatari Businessman Contends That MFN Clause In Regional Treaty Can Provide Foothold For An ICSID Claim Against Jordan', *Investment Arbitration Reporter*

(15 June 2015) at <Qatari businessman contends that MFN clause in regional treaty can provide foothold for an ICSID claim against Jordan | Investment Arbitration Reporter (openathens.net)>.

Desert Line Projects LLC v The Republic of Yemen (ICSID Case No. ARB/05/17, 30 September 2005) (*'Desert Line v Yemen'*).

'Dissenter Would Have Granted Access To ICSID Arbitration Through MFN Clause', *Investment Arbitration Reporter* (5 April 2020) at <Breaking: Majority in Itisaluna v. Iraq declines jurisdiction over OIC claims; dissenter would have granted access to ICSID arbitration through MFN clause | Investment Arbitration Reporter (openathens.net)>.

Duggal, Kabir and Laurens van de Ven, 'The 2019 Netherlands Model BIT: Riding the New Investment Treaty Waves' (2019) 35(3) *Arbitration International*, 359–374.

Dumberry, Patrick, 'The Importation of the FET Standard through MFN Clauses: An Empirical Study of BITs' (2017) 32(1) *ICSID Review*, 126–127.

Hasaan, Amr Arafa, 'The 2013 Amendments to the Arab Investment Agreement' (2019) 34(1) *ICSID Review*, doi:10.1093/icsidreview/siz003.

Hepburn, Jarrod and Luke Eric Peterson, 'Investigation: As New Cases Emerge Under Islamic Investment Treaty, Initial Viability of Claims Seems to Hinge On Willingness Of Respondents To Appoint Arbitrators', *Investment Arbitration Reporter* (2 March 2017) at<Investigation: As new cases emerge under Islamic investment treaty, initial viability of claims seems to hinge on willingness of respondents to appoint arbitrators | Investment Arbitration Reporter (openathens.net)>.

Hesham Talaat M. Al-Warraq v The Republic of Indonesia, Award on Respondent's Preliminary Objections to Jurisdiction and Admissibility of the Claims (UNCITRAL, 21 June 2012), (*'Al-Warraq v Indonesia'*).

Hodgson, Matthew and Alastair Campbell, 'Investment Treaty Arbitration: Cost, Duration and Size of Claims All Show Steady Increase', *ISDS Platform* (14 December 2017) at <https://isds.bilaterals.org/?investment-treaty-arbitration-cost>.

Hussein Nauman Soufraki v United Arab Emirates (ICSID Case No. ARB/02/7, 18 June 2002) (*'Soufraki v United Arab Emirates'*).

Itisaluna Iraq LLC and others v Republic of Iraq (Award) (ICSID Case No. ARB/17/10, 3 April 2020) (*'Itisaluna v Iraq'*).

Khadamat Integrated Solutions Private Limited (India) v The Kingdom of Saudi Arabia PCA Case No. 2019-24 (*'Khadamat v Saudi Arabia'*).

Krasner, Stephen, 'Structural Causes and Regime Consequences: Regimes as Intervening Variables', in Beth Simmons and Richard Steinberg (eds) *International Law and International Relations* (Cambridge University Press, 2006).

MAKAE Europe SARL v Kingdom of Saudi Arabia (Award) (ICSID Case No. ARB/17/42, 30 August 2021) (*'MAKAE v Saudi Arabia'*).

Matveev, Arseni, 'Investor-State Dispute Settlement: The Evolving Balance Between Investor Protection And State Sovereignty' (2015) 40(1) *University of Western Australia Law Review*, 348–386.

Navodaya Trading DMCC v The Gabonese Republic (2018) UNCTAD, 'Investment Dispute Settlement Navigator' <United Arab Emirates | Investment Dispute Settlement Navigator | UNCTAD Investment Policy Hub> (*'Navodaya v Gabon'*).

Nichols, Shawn, 'Expanding Property Rights under Investor-State Dispute Settlement (ISDS): Class Struggle in the Era of Transnational Capital' (2018) 25(2) *Review of International Political Economy*, 243–269.

Organisation of Islamic Cooperation Agreement on Promotion, Protection and Guarantee of Investments among member States of the Islamic Conference, signed 5 June 1981 (entered into force February 1988) (*'OIC Agreement'*).

Perenco Ecuador Ltd v Republic of Ecuador, Decision on Remaining Issues of Jurisdiction and on Liability (ICSID Case No ARB/08/6), 12 September 2014).

Peterson, Luke Eric, 'Panels Finalized For Three ICSID Treaty-Based Arbitrations: ALPIQ v. Romania, PT Ventures v. Cabo Verde And Ali Alyafei v Jordan', *Investment Arbitration Reporter* (16 September 2015) at <Panels finalized for three ICSID treaty-based arbitrations: Alpiq v. Romania, PT Ventures v. Cabo Verde and Ali Alyafei v. Jordan | Investment Arbitration Reporter (openathens.net)>.

Philip Morris v Australia (Award on Jurisdiction and Admissibility) (PCA Case No.2012-12, 17 December 2015).

Protocol between the Governments of the State of Kuwait and the Republic of Iraq on the Promotion of the Movement of Capital and Investments between the Two Countries), signed 25 October 1964 (entered into force 7 June 1966) (*'Kuwait – Iraq BIT'*).

Puig, Sergio and Meg Kinnear, 'NAFTA Chapter Eleven at Fifteen: Contributions to a Systemic Approach in Investment Arbitration, Citing S D Myers Inc v Government of Canada Partial Award' (2010) 25(2) *ICSID Review – Foreign Investment Law Journal*, 225–267.

Sarawak Report, 'How a Kuwaiti Royal Sheikh Jailed A 1MDB Whistleblower Whilst Laundering China Kickbacks For Najib' *Sarawakreport* (29 May 2020) at <How A Kuwaiti Royal Sheikh Jailed A 1MDB Whistleblower Whilst Laundering China Kickbacks For Najib - EXCLUSIVE | Sarawak Report>.

'Saudi Arabia Defeats Indian Investor's BIT Arbitration Claim', *Investment Arbitration Reporter* (28 February 2020) at <Saudi Arabia defeats Indian investor's BIT arbitration claim | Investment Arbitration Reporter (openathens.net)>.

Saulino, James and Josh Kallmer, 'The Emperor Has No Clothes: A Critique of the Debate Over Reform of the ISDS System', in Jean Kalicki and Anna Joubin-Bret (eds) *Reshaping the Investor-State Dispute Settlement System: Journeys for the 21st Century* (Brill, 2015).

Schepel, Harm, 'Investment Protection, ISDS, and EU Law' (Speech delivered at theInvestor-State Dispute Settlement in EU law and International Law Public Conference, European Parliament, 2 March 2015).

Stone, Jacob, 'Arbitrariness, the Fair and Equitable Treatment Standard, and the International Law of Investment' (2012) 25 *Leiden Journal of International Law*, 77–107.

UNCITRAL Secretariat, 'Possible Reform of Investor-State Dispute Settlement (ISDS)', UN GAOR, 34th sess, UN Doc A/CN.9/WG.III/WP.142 at<http://www.uncitral.org/pdf/english/workinggroups/wg_3/142-e.pdf>.

UNCTAD, 'International Investment Agreements Navigator: Model Agreements' (undated) at <International Investment Agreements Navigator | UNCTAD Investment Policy Hub>.

UNCTAD, 'Trends In The Investment Treaty Regime And A Reform Toolbox For The Energy Transition' (IIA Issues Note, Issue 2, August 2023) at <https://investmentpolicy.unctad.org/publications/1285/trends-in-the-investment-treaty-regime-and-a-reform-toolbox-for-the-energy-transition>.

Vienna Convention on the Law of Treaties, signed 23 May 1969 (entered into force 27 January 1980) 1155 UNTS 331 (*'Vienna Convention 1969'*).

Wellhausen, Rachel, 'Recent Trends in Investor-State Dispute Settlement' (2016) 7(1) *Journal of International Dispute Settlement*, 117–135.

Zielinksi, Laura, 'Legitimate Expectations" in the Vattenfall Case: At the Heart of the Debate over ISDS', *Kluwer Arbitration Blog* (10 January 2017) at <http://arbitrationblog.kluwerarbitration.com/2017/01/10/legitimate-expectations-in-the-vattenfall-case-at-the-heart-of-the-debate-over-isds/>.

4 The GCC Member States as Respondents in ISDS Arbitrations

4.1 Introduction

This chapter examines in detail the experiences of each GCC member State in ISDS-based disputes, as respondents in claims initiated by foreign investors. It includes tables for each member State across this category, noting procedural rules and case number, a summary of the investment and basis of claim, the most recent known status of each case, and the opposing claimant or state. Generally, the information gathered in each table is primarily derived from the United Nations Conference on Trade and Development (UNCTAD) Investment Dispute Settlement Navigator and, to a lesser extent, its corresponding International Investment Agreements Navigator databases. UNCTAD describes the Dispute Settlement Navigator – or ISDS Navigator – as containing information about known international arbitration cases initiated by investors against States pursuant to international investment agreements (IIAs), which it also refers to as treaty-based investor–state dispute settlement (ISDS) cases.[1] Although contract-based or domestic legislation-based claims thus may not be included in the tables, reference is still made to some from time to time as appropriate.

However, it should be noted that UNCTAD data is collected from publicly available sources, with primary sources such as official documents relating to the case and information provided by the administering institutions being the main and preferred source of information. Secondary sources, such as specialised reporting services and other sources deemed reliable, are used to supplement the primary sources and/or obtain indications of emerging arbitrations or case information that is otherwise unavailable. This is particularly so in instances where arbitrations are conducted on the basis of either the two Islamic-based agreements or under ad hoc arbitration rules, since these cases generally do not appear in the UNCTAD database. UNCTAD formally notes that the ISDS Navigator does not always include non-reported arbitrations that may have been conducted through private, generally confidential, or restricted-access tribunals, such as the Permanent Court of

1 UNCTAD, Investment Policy Hub, Investment Dispute Settlement Navigator, at <https://investmentpolicy.unctad.org/investment-dispute-settlement>.

DOI: 10.4324/9781003481072-4

Arbitration (PCA), the International Chamber of Commerce (ICC), or the London Court of International Arbitration (LCIA).

Tables 4.1, 4.2, 4.3, 4.4, 4.5, and 4.6 set out the details of known arbitrations initiated against each GCC member State and reliant upon BITs and other IIAs. Accordingly, they do not include international arbitration cases which have been based on contract laws and/or private or domestic-based commercial agreements. The tables, compiled primarily from UNCTAD's ISDS Navigator database and ensuing discussions have been supplemented by the *Investment Arbitration Reporter* subscription service and occasional other third-party sources such as local media reports and materials from legal professional sources. It is readily acknowledged that these third-party sources may not be as reliable as UNCTAD secondary sources, but on regular occasion they do throw some light on ISDS parties' strategies behind a particular claim and/or response. The table columns also generally adhere to the UNCTAD parameters, although information is added from other sources in respect of the case summaries where there is no UNCTAD information available.

In respect of the possible outcomes of a case, UNCTAD uses the following terminologies:

- *pending*: any of the following elements remains to be decided: jurisdiction, liability (merits), compensation. Or, for instance, a State is found to have breached one or more IIA obligations (liability) but no award or damages has been issued yet;
- *decided in favour of state*: tribunal dismisses the case for lack of jurisdiction or because respondent State has not committed any breach of the applicable IIA;
- *decided in favour of investor*: tribunal finds the respondent State committed one or more breaches of the applicable IIA and awards monetary compensation or non-pecuniary relief to the claimant;
- *decided in favour of neither party* (liability found but no damages awarded): respondent State committed one or more breaches of applicable IIA but does not award monetary compensation or non-pecuniary relief to the claimant investor;
- *settled*: disputing parties settle the case and arbitral proceedings are discontinued accordingly;
- *discontinued*: for any reason other than due to a (known) settlement, including non-payment of arbitration fees, to pursue litigation in another forum, or for any other reason (including unknown reasons);
- *no details available*: UNCTAD does not provide advice on its use of this descriptor, but it appears to be used when an original arbitration decision may be subject to further review and leading to possible change, for example, when undergoing annulment proceedings, or even when final details of a case are simply not available and pending is no longer the most appropriate descriptor.

The ICSID Rules in force in respect of the mutually agreed or non-contested cessation of a case and thus covering the "settled" and "discontinued" tribunal determinations as stated in the following tables, namely the 2006 Arbitration Rules,[2] state as follows:

> Rule 43 Settlement and Discontinuance
>
> (1) If, before the award is rendered, the parties agree on a settlement of the dispute or otherwise to discontinue the proceeding, the Tribunal, or the Secretary-General if the Tribunal has not yet been constituted, shall, at their written request, in an order take note of the discontinuance of the proceeding.
> (2) If the parties file with the Secretary-General the full and signed text of their settlement and in writing request the Tribunal to embody such settlement in an award, the Tribunal may record the settlement in the form of its award.
>
> Rule 44 Discontinuance at Request of a Party
>
> If a party requests the discontinuance of the proceeding, the Tribunal, or the Secretary-General if the Tribunal has not yet been constituted, shall in an order fix a time limit within which the other party may state whether it opposes the discontinuance. If no objection is made in writing within the time limit, the other party shall be deemed to have acquiesced in the discontinuance and the Tribunal, or if appropriate the Secretary-General, shall in an order take note of the discontinuance of the proceeding. If objection is made, the proceeding shall continue.

Rule 45, which provides for Discontinuance for Failure of Parties to Act, does not appear to have been cited in any of the following listed cases.

Generally for each GCC member State as a respondent State, this chapter also offers commentary in respect of selected cases which have been concluded for one reason or another (for example, by tribunal determination or by mutual consent or by certain action or non-action by either party), focussing primarily on those issues discussed in Chapter 3 or because of particular circumstances of the case which had bearing on its outcome.

Particular attention is given to cases that may reveal or explain some of the issues and questions raised in the earlier chapters concerning the nature of the member States' performance (or, on occasion, non-performance) on the conduct of ISDS arbitrations.

2 ICSID have introduced a new set of arbitration rules in 2022, which include changed numbering of clauses among other amendments.

The outcomes recorded in Tables 4.1 to 4.6 generally accord with the UNCTAD formula. However, where a different outcome is available from a deemed reliable source, including media sources, which provides greater detail or is subsequent to the UNCTAD information, particularly as it changes UNCTAD's application of the terms "Pending" or "Data not Available", then that detailed or subsequent information is utilised in the tables. This can occur when the outcome of the initial arbitration has become subject to further proceedings, such as an annulment application or judicial review.

4.2 ISDS in the Gulf: GCC Member States as Respondents

The GCC member States have had relatively little exposure as respondent states in investor–state arbitrations, when compared to countries with the highest number of ISDS arbitrations initiated against them, namely Argentina (62 arbitrations), Venezuela (62 arbitrations), and Spain (56 arbitrations).[3] However, there has been an increasing trend in arbitrations initiated against the GCC member States, particularly in recent years.

As at the time of this writing, UNCTAD data shows a total of 1,303 known treaty-based ISDS cases, 924 of which have been concluded, 357 still pending, and 22 with status unknown. It reports a total of 33 reported arbitrations initiated against the GCC member States, some of which have been concluded and others still pending. The majority of these arbitrations have occurred over the last 5 years, with 19 initiated since early 2018.

The first ISDS arbitration initiated against a GCC member State and relying upon a BIT or other IIA, namely *Impregilo v UAE*, was brought in 2001, applying the *UAE–Italy BIT*.[4] The claim, brought by Italian claimants, related to a mosque construction project in the UAE, is believed to "have been settled on confidential terms",[5] having been discontinued pursuant to Rule 44 of the ICSID Arbitration Rules. Rule 44 provides in part that

> If a party requests the discontinuance of the proceeding … the other party may state whether it opposes the discontinuance. If no objection is made in writing within the time limit, the other party shall be deemed to have acquiesced … If objection is made, the proceeding shall continue.

3 As of 31 December 2022, according to the UNCTAD (n 1), at <https://investmentpolicy.unctad.org/investment-dispute-settlement?status=100>.>.

4 *Impregilo, S.p.A and Rizzani De Eccher S.p.A v United Arab Emirates* (ICSID Case No. ARB/01/1) ('*Impregilo v UAE*'); *Agreement between the Government of the United Arab Emirates and the Government of the Italian Republic for the Promotion and Protection of Investments*, signed 22 January 1995 (entered into force 29 April 1997).

5 Janine Maillis and Craig Shepard, 'Investment Treaty Arbitration in United Arab Emirates' *Lexology.com* (16 November 2018) <Investment Treaty Arbitration in United Arab Emirates - Lexology>.

The most recent series of arbitrations initiated against GCC member States since 2022 includes the claims against Bahrain and Qatar (one each) and Saudi Arabia (two). Saudi Arabia was the only State to be subject to an arbitration claim in 2023. However, a claim against Qatar that does not appear in UNCTAD, namely, Keppel Seghers Engineering of Singapore, reportedly commenced arbitration proceedings against Qatar's Public Works authority with the ICC in Paris, in May 2022, according to the Singapore press.[6] However, according to *Jus Mundi,* this may be a commercial case rather than an ISDS case.[7]

Since *Impregilo v UAE* in 2001, Saudi Arabia has been the most frequently named respondent, appearing in ten cases, followed by Kuwait and the UAE which have been named as respondents in seven and six cases respectively. Bahrain and Oman have been evenly named as respondents in four cases each, while Qatar has been the least frequently named respondent, appearing in just two cases.

4.3 The Kingdom of Bahrain

Bahrain has had a very limited exposure as a respondent within the ISDS environment, both in terms of the number of arbitrations and the time frame in which these cases have occurred, with only four cases being listed in UNCTAD with Bahrain as respondent, and the first case not occurring until 2017. That first case was *Bank Melli Iran and Bank Saderat Iran v Bahrain,* in the PCA on 18 February 2017 under the terms of the *Bahrain–Iran BIT* of 2002. Although the claim was lodged in February 2017, the tribunal did not hand down its ruling until 19 November 2021. The case warrants closer analysis since it is the only case to date among the GCC member States as respondents where a tribunal has found in favour of the claimant/s. The three other cases to date involving Bahrain are all listed by UNCTAD as still pending.

6 Jude Chan, 'Keppel Unit Begins Arbitration Proceedings to Claim S$173 Million in Qatar Project Spat', *Business Times* (Singapore) (31 May 2022) at <https://www.businesstimes.com.sg/companies-markets/keppel-unit-begins-arbitration-proceedings-to-claim-s173-million-in-qatar-project>.

7 *Keppel Seghers v. Qatar Public Works Authority,* Jus Mundi, at <https://jusmundi.com/en/document/decision/en-keppel-seghers-engineering-singapore-pte-ltd-v-qatar-public-works-authority-party-representatives>.

Table 4.1 Bahrain as Respondent

No.	*Year Initiated*	*Short Name Case*	*Summary*	*Outcome of Original Proceedings*	*Home State of Investor*
1	2022	Naftiran Intertrade v Bahrain ICSID case no. ARB/22/34	Investment: banking and financial services Details of claim not listed Proceeding under *Bahrain–Malaysia BIT* (1999)	Pending	Malaysia
2	2021	Central Bank of Iran v Bahrain	Investment: financial and banking activities but further details not listed Claim details not listed but reportedly USD7 billion in respect of Bahrain's participation in the 2015 international Joint Comprehensive Action Plan ("Iran Nuclear deal") and freeze on Iranian investments in Bahrain. Proceeding under *Bahrain–Iran BIT* (2002)	Pending	Iran
3	2020	Qatar Airways v Bahrain	Investment: licences and permits to conduct air transport activities Claims arising out of the Government's alleged actions to block Qatar Airways operations in Bahrain, including the closure of airspace to the claimant and revocation of licences to operate. Proceeding under *OIC Agreement* (1981) and *Arab Investment Agreement* (1980)[a]	Pending	Qatar
4	2017	Bank Melli v Bahrain PCA case no. 2017-25	Investment: investments in Future Bank, a local commercial bank Claims arising from Bahrain's central bank decision to close Future Bank in 2016, after placing it under forced administration in 2015. Proceeded under *Bahrain–Iran BIT* (2002)	Decided in favour of the claimants	Iran

Source: compiled by the authors primarily from UNCTAD, Investment Policy Hub, Investment Dispute Settlement Navigator, at <https://investmentpolicy.unctad.org/investment-dispute-settlement/country/15/bahrain> and *Investment Arbitration Reporter*, at <https://www-iareporter-com.eu1.proxy.openathens.net/>.

[a]See further discussion on this and other cases brought by Qatar collectively against Bahrain, Saudi Arabia, and the UAE in Chapter 6.

The *Central Bank of Iran v Bahrain* case is part of an ongoing saga involving both countries and their respective entities and is some respects a direct sequel to *Bank Melli*. The claim reportedly seeks investment reimbursements and the return of foreign exchange reserves allegedly not handed over by Bahrain following the *Bank Melli* saga. The saga also involves criminal cases recently concluded against Iran's Central Bank and its senior officials. In a judgment handed down in August 2021 by the Bahrain High Criminal Court, the Bank and six of its senior officials were found guilty of money laundering on a significant scale and imposed fines of 1 million Bahraini dinars on each defendant and ordered the confiscation of the alleged laundered funds. Bahrain's public prosecutor and state-owned news service claimed that the prosecution was "the largest money laundering case in the history of the defendant kingdom".[8] On 3 October of the same year, the Bahrain High Court of Appeal confirmed the judgment and reportedly increased the severity of the penalties at the request of the Bahrain Public Prosecutor.[9] The Public Prosecution had argued that its investigations revealed a huge scheme to launder billions of dollars through the Iranian Future Bank, established in Bahrain and controlled by the National Iranian Bank, Bank Melli Iran, and Bank Saderat Iran.[10] Criminal investigations are reportedly continuing by Bahrain authorities.

4.4 Case Study: *Bank Melli Iran and Bank Saderat Iran v Bahrain*

In *Bank Melli and Bank Saderat Iran v Bahrain*,[11] the Iranian claimants initiated an arbitration against Bahrain, administered by the PCA, applying the *Bahrain–Iran BIT* (2002)[12] under the UNCITRAL Arbitration Rules 1976. The claim arose as a result of the Central Bank of Bahrain's decision to shut down Future Bank, following a period during which Future Bank was under administration.[13]

Future Bank was a joint venture between Ahli United Bank (Bahraini), Bank Melli (Iranian), and Bank Saderat (Iranian) which was set up in 2004 as Bahrain attempted to improve its relationship with Iran.[14] Future Bank was designated by

8 As reported in the *Tehran Times*, 'CBI and the other Iranian banks were handed fines of 1 million Bahraini dinars each, and that confiscation was ordered of laundered funds', *Tehran Times* (8 August 2021) at <https://www.tehrantimes.com/news/463688/Iran-s-central-bank-takes-legal-action-against-Bahrain>.

9 As reported via the *Bahrain News Agency*, 'High Court of Appeal Upholds Ruling against Future Bank and Officials, Central Bank of Iran and Other Iranian Banks', *Bahrain News Agency* (31 October 2021) at <https://www.bna.bh/en/news?cms=q8FmFJgiscL2fwIzON1%2BDj3D0Kqbr8W5hjB5G6BIOmQ%3D>.

10 Ibid.

11 *Bank Melli and Bank Saderat v Bahrain (Statement of Claim) (PCA Case No 2017-25, 16 October 2017) ('Bank Melli').*

12 *Agreement on Reciprocal Promotion and Protection of Investments between the Government of Islamic Republic of Iran and the Government of the Kingdom of Bahrain*, signed 19 October 2002 (entered into force 12 October 2004) ('*Bahrain–Iran BIT*').

13 UNCTAD (n 1), at <https://investmentpolicy.unctad.org/investment-dispute-settlement/cases/817/bank-melli-and-bank-saderat-v-bahrain>.

14 'Court Orders Bahrain to Pay Damages to Iran for "Political Expropriation"', *Press TV* (24 November 2021) at <Court orders Bahrain to pay damages to Iran for 'political expropriation' (presstv.ir)>.

the United States Department of the Treasury on 12 March 2008 as an "entity of proliferation concern" because it was controlled by Bank Melli, which had been designated by Treasury on 25 October 2007 as a "Weapons of Mass Destruction (WMD)" supporter pursuant to Executive Order 13382.[15] Bank Saderat was designated by Treasury for financing terrorism, pursuant to Executive Order 13224[16] and had been refused access to finance in the United States on 8 September 2006 in an attempt to mitigate against Iranian "support for terrorism", through transfers "to Hizballah and other terrorist organizations".[17] Future Bank was designated under the same Executive Order, with the objective of "freezing the assets of proliferators of weapons of mass destruction (WMD) and their supporters".[18] The United Nations Security Council also issued resolutions with respect to the proliferation of weapons of mass destruction, particularly concerning nuclear activity in Iran, namely Resolution 1969 and Resolution 1737.[19]

The Central Bank of Bahrain took steps to close Future Bank in January 2016 when the Bahrain–Iran relationship soured following rising tension between Saudi Arabia and Iran.[20] The claimants argued that, in forcing the closure of Future Bank, Bahrain had expropriated their investments without compensation, in contravention of the *Bahrain–Iran BIT*.[21] Article 6(1) of the BIT states:[22]

> Investments of investors of either Contracting Party shall not be nationalized, confiscated, expropriated or subjected, to similar measures by the other Contracting Party except such measures are taken for public purposes, in accordance with due process of law, in a non-discriminatory manner and effective and appropriate compensation is envisaged. The amount of compensation shall be paid without delay.

Proportionality was a significant issue in the case. The claimants argued that the expropriation was disproportionate in the context of allegations that Future Bank had contravened sanctions and that it was open to the Central Bank of Bahrain to use other "more moderate regulatory tools".[23]

15 United States Department of the Treasury, 'Treasury Designates Iran-Controlled Bank for Proliferation Future Bank Controlled by Iran's Bank Melli', *U.S. Department of the Treasury* (12 March 2008) at <Treasury Designates Iran-Controlled Bank for Proliferation Future Bank Controlled by Iran's Bank Melli>.

16 United States Department of the Treasury, 'Fact Sheet: Designation of Iranian Entities and Individuals for Proliferation Activities and Support for Terrorism', *U.S. Department of the Treasury* (25 October 2007) at <Fact Sheet: Designation of Iranian Entities and Individuals for Proliferation Activities and Support for Terrorism (treasury.gov)>.

17 United States Department of the Treasury, 'Treasury Cuts Iran's Bank Saderat off from U.S. Financial System', *U.S. Department of the Treasury* (8 September 2006) at <Treasury Cuts Iran's Bank Saderat Off From U.S. Financial System>.

18 Ibid.

19 See *Bank Melli v Bahrain* (n 11), [189–96] for an overview of sanctions applied.

20 Ibid. See also *Press TV* (n 14).

21 *Bank Melli v Bahrain* (n 11), [5].

22 *Bahrain–Iran BIT (2002)*, Article 6(1).

23 *Bank Melli v Bahrain* (n 11), [581–3].

Bahrain denied the claims and argued that they were inadmissible by reason of the claimants' illegal operations.[24] Bahrain argued that the "Claimants' violations of Bahraini law and international sanctions against Iran result in the lack of jurisdiction of the Tribunal and/or render the claims inadmissible on grounds of the clean hands doctrine and of international public policy".[25]

Bahrain submitted that the closure of Future Bank was required in order to shield investors from "alleged corruption and sanctions violations by Future Bank's senior management", some of which were later convicted of criminal financial activities in domestic proceedings in Bahrain.[26] It also claimed that Future Bank conducted its activities in contravention of local laws, specifically "record-keeping, monitoring and reporting of suspicious transactions", making it difficult to ascertain the extent of Iran's alleged circumvention of sanctions relating to nuclear-related activity.[27] Article 1 of the BIT contains a requirement that an investment be made in accordance with local laws, relevantly stating:[28]

> The term "investment refers to every kind of asset, invested by the investors of one Contracting Party in the territory of the other Contracting Party in accordance with the laws and regulations of the other Contracting Party."

The PCA tribunal considered its jurisdiction and the admissibility of the claim in the context of Future Bank's wrongdoings, noting that Article 1 of the BIT is silent as to the consequences of illegality in which the investor may participate following the relevant investment.[29] With respect to its competence to hear the matter, the tribunal held that a BIT is not "an insurance policy for an investor who engages in unlawful activities", but if an investment is made legally and other jurisdictional obligations have been satisfied, the "Contracting States have consented to give the treaty tribunal the competence to adjudicate the disputes arising out of such investment, including disputes about alleged subsequent illegal activities and their consequences".[30] The requirement for compliance with domestic laws and regulations in Article 1 was "temporally limited" to the time that the investment was made, and that this interpretation was consistently applied by arbitral tribunals with respect to similar requirements.[31] In regards to the impact of the illegal actions of Future Bank upon the admissibility of the claim, the tribunal stated that it was possible for illegal activities to effectively:

24 Ibid [594].
25 Ibid [351].
26 Joby Warrick and Souad Mehennet, 'Iranian Banks Notch Win in Dispute over Sanctions Enforcement', *Washington Post* (26 November 2021) at <Iranian banks notch win in dispute over sanctions enforcement - The Washington Post>.
27 Ibid.
28 *Bahrain–Iran BIT (2002)*, Article 1.
29 *Bank Melli v Bahrain* (n 11), [355].
30 Ibid [356].
31 Ibid [357].

> "bar the admissibility of claims" because "international adjudicatory bodies have a duty not to entertain claims tainted by violations of certain universally accepted norms pursuant to general principles of good faith and *nemo auditor propiam turpitudinem allegans*".[32]

The tribunal also stated that, with respect to admissibility, the relevant consideration is "whether the unlawful conduct taints the claims".[33] It declared that illegality sufficient to attract a bar to admissibility must be "(i) serious and widespread and (ii) bear a close relationship to the claims".[34]

The tribunal determined that the sanction violations in this case, while relevant to assessment of the case on the merits and with respect to quantum, were insufficiently severe and/or systematic to render the claims inadmissible.[35] The tribunal also considered whether Future Bank's illegality tainted the claim, distinguishing the claim, which arose out of regulatory measures made by Bahraini authorities, from "a transaction tainted by Future Bank's unlawful conduct".[36] The tribunal ultimately determined that the unlawful activities did not attract a bar to jurisdiction or admissibility. It reasoned that an assessment of the outcome of the illegalities was a merits issue and that it was necessary to focus particularly on whether the regulatory activity was "a bona fide and proportionate response" and/or whether the illegalities would impact compensation.[37]

The tribunal accepted the Bahraini claim that Future Bank had not complied with its local laws and regulations, concluding that Bahrain's treatment of Future Bank did not amount to "genuine regulatory measures aimed at addressing Future Bank's illegal conduct" but, rather, that its closure constituted an expropriation without properly considering alternative measures.[38] The tribunal made this determination having found that there was no trace of a contemporaneous examination of reasons for the regulatory activities, that there was evidence the regulatory measures taken against Future Bank were politically motivated, that there was limited evidence of warnings about the alleged breaches of regulations with Future Bank or within the regulatory authority leading up to the regulatory measures, and that there was no indication that alternative measures less harmful than administration and ultimately liquidation, namely the suspension of its licence, had been considered.[39] The tribunal found that the regulatory measures taken against Future Bank amounted to an indirect expropriation of the interests held by the claimants in the Bank.[40]

32 Ibid [365].
33 Ibid [370].
34 Ibid [376].
35 Ibid [503].
36 Ibid [505].
37 Ibid [506–7].
38 Warrick and Mekhennet (n 26).
39 *Bank Melli v Bahrain* (n 11), [652–90].
40 Ibid [690].

The tribunal handed down an award in favour of the claimants on 19 November 2021. It determined that Bahrain contravened Article 6 of the *Bahrain–Iran BIT* and ordered Bahrain to pay the claimants EUR243 million in damages plus costs and simple interest. However, the tribunal dismissed their claim for additional moral and/or reputational damages.[41]

Bahrain reportedly plans to appeal the PCA decision[42] and has also submitted further proceedings with respect to an alleged currency error relating to damages.[43]

As reported above, while the arbitration was still in progress, the Bahraini High Court of Appeal upheld convictions against Future Bank, the Central Bank of Iran, and other Iranian Banks by the First Instance Court, sentencing six of its senior officials to terms of imprisonment, imposing fines on both the individuals and the banks, and confiscating Future Bank's assets.[44] Twelve months later, in October 2022, the High Court accepted an appeal by the Public Prosecution "demanding the punishments be toughened up in accordance with the requirements of the law".[45]

Another claim has been brought in December 2021 by the Central Bank of Iran against Bahrain under the *Bahrain–Iran BIT*, seeking some USD7 billion in damages (*Central Bank of Iran v. Bahrain*).[46] Details of the basis of the claim and the administering institution are not yet available.

4.5 The State of Kuwait

Kuwait has also had a fairly short and recent exposure to the ISDS regime as a respondent with its first case not occurring until 2017. It has since attracted a further six cases, the most recent known being lodged in 2020 and is continuing. The most recent information on this case from ICSID is that the tribunal held a hearing on jurisdiction and the merits in Paris in late July 2023.[47] At this stage, Kuwait has had positive outcomes in the cases it has faced with those concluded either being withdrawn or discontinued on jurisdictional grounds.

41 Ibid [836].

42 Warrick and Mekhennet (n 26).

43 Lisa Bohmer, 'Revealed: A Comprehensive Account of the Heretofore Unpublished Bank Melli v. Bahrain Award; Some Details Have Leaked, but Review of Award Gives Full Picture of Tribunal's Findings on Iranian Sanctions Questions, Political Expropriation, and Potential Set-Offs', *International Arbitration Reporter* (14 December 2021) at <Revealed: A comprehensive account of the heretofore unpublished Bank Melli v. Bahrain award; some details have leaked, but review of award gives full picture of tribunal's findings on Iranian sanctions questions, political expropriation, and potential set-offs | Investment Arbitration Reporter (openathens.net)>.

44 'High Court of Appeal Upholds Ruling against Future Bank Officials, Central Bank of Iran and Other Iranian Banks', *Bahrain News Agency* (31 October 2021) at <https://www.bna.bh/en/news?cms=q8FmFJgiscL2fwIzON1%2BDj3D0Kqbr8W5hjB5G6BIOmQ%3D>.

45 'Higher Court of Appeal Toughens up Sentences in One of Biggest Money Laundering Cases in Bahrain's History', *Bahrain News Agency* (3 October 2022) at <https://www.bna.bh/en/news?cms=q8FmFJgiscL2fwIzON1%2BDhtdM0rFmdnRT2P1YS86rVk%3D>.

46 See UNCTAD (n 1), at < Central Bank of Iran v. Kingdom of Bahrain | Investment Dispute Settlement Navigator | UNCTAD Investment Policy Hub>. See also Bohmer (n 43).

47 ICSID at <https://icsid.worldbank.org/cases/case-database/case-detail?CaseNo=ARB/20/53>.

Table 4.2 Kuwait as Respondent

No.	*Year Initiated*	*Short Case Name*	*Summary*	*Outcome of Original Proceedings*	*Home State of Investor*
1	2020	Kiwan v Kuwait ICSID case no. ARB/20/53	Investment: indirect 45% shareholding in Al Waseet Int'l, a group of companies in the media and publishing sector, via a holding company. Claims arising from Government's alleged seizure of claimant's investments following criminal investigations on fraud charges and claimant's imprisonment. Proceeding under *France–Kuwait BIT* (1989).	Pending	France
2	2019	Alcoser and Lucidos de Yeso v Kuwait PCA case	Investment: health screening services for immigrant workers through local entity Public Services Company (PSC). Claims arising from Government's termination of certain health services contracts between Ministry of Health and PSC. Initiated under *Kuwait–Spain BIT* (2005).	Discontinued – withdrawn by claimants before tribunal appointed	Spain
3	2019	Sumrain v Kuwait[a] ICSID case no. ARB/19/20	Investment: real estate build-operate-transfer joint venture and building restoration in the Sharq heritage village complex in Kuwait City. Claims arising from financial penalties imposed and cancellation and transfer of contract. Proceeded under *Egypt–Kuwait BIT* (2001).	Settled pursuant to ICSID Rule 43(1)	Egypt

(*Continued*)

Table 4.2 (Continued)

No.	*Year Initiated*	*Short Case Name*	*Summary*	*Outcome of Original Proceedings*	*Home State of Investor*
4	2018	Almasryia v Kuwait ICSID case no. ARB/18/2	Investment: joint venture with a Kuwaiti national to develop and construct tourist hotels near Al-Khafji city in Wafra region. Claims arising from alleged Government conduct preventing claimant from taking ownership of land for a real estate development project. Proceeded under *Egypt–Kuwait BIT* 2001.	Initially decided in favour of the State (jurisdiction declined), but subsequently annulled	Egypt
5	2018	Conseil Economique v Kuwait PCA case no. 2018-35	Investment: health screening services for immigrant workers. Claims arising from Kuwait's Ministry of Health termination of a contract for foreign worker medical examinations. Proceeded under *Switzerland–Kuwait BIT.*	Discontinued	Switzerland
6	2018	Lazareva v Kuwait ICSID case no. UNCT/19/1	Investment: shareholding in KGL Investment Kuwaiti investment company, and private equity company operating in Kuwait. Claims arising from a series of measures by Kuwait, including unsubstantiated charges against the claimant, including embezzlement, wrongful imprisonment, and general harassment. Proceeded under *Kuwait–Russian Federation BIT* (1994).	Decided in favour of the State (jurisdiction declined)	Russian Federation

(*Continued*)

Table 4.2 (Continued)

No.	*Year Initiated*	*Short Case Name*	*Summary*	*Outcome of Original Proceedings*	*Home State of Investor*
7	2017	OHL and others v Kuwait[a] ICSID case no. ARB/17/8	Investment: highway construction project. Claims arising from Kuwait's actions to delay and disrupt project's regular progress and continual harassment and threats against claimant staff. Proceeded under *Kuwait–Spain BIT* and *Italy–Kuwait BIT.*	Decided in favour of the State	Spain and Italy

Source: compiled by the authors primarily from UNCTAD, Investment Policy Hub, Investment Dispute Settlement Navigator, at https://investmentpolicy.unctad.org/investment-dispute-settlement/country/112/kuwait and *Investment Arbitration Reporter*, <https://www-iareporter-com.eu1.proxy.openathens.net/>.

[a]*Alaa Nizar Raja Sumrain, Ayat Nizar Raja Sumrain, Eshraka Nizar Raja Sumrain and Mohamed Nizar Raja Sumrain v. State of Kuwait* (ICSID Case No. ARB/19/20) (*'Sumrain v Kuwait').*

[b]*Obrascón Huarte Lain S.A., Rizzani de Eccher S.p.A. and Trevi S.p.A. v. State of Kuwait* (ICSID Case No. ARB/17/8) ('*OHL and others v Kuwait*').

The tribunal in *OHL and others v Kuwait* rendered its award in December 2022, finding in favour of the respondent. ICSID reports that an application for partial annulment of the award by the claimants was registered on 23 March 2023, with an ad hoc committee appointed on 7 June 2023.[48]

The tribunal in *Sumrain v Kuwait* issued an order on 11 February 2022, taking note of the discontinuance of the proceeding pursuant to ICSID Arbitration Rule 43(1). Rule 43(1) provides that

> If, before the award is rendered, the parties agree on a settlement of the dispute or otherwise to discontinue the proceeding, the Tribunal, or the Secretary-General if the Tribunal has not yet been constituted, shall, at their written request, in an order take note of the discontinuance of the proceeding.

The Rule does not require parties to also detail the terms or conditions of any such settlement.

In *Almasryia v Kuwait*, the tribunal accepted the respondent's preliminary objection that the claimant's claims manifestly lacked legal merit due to the claimant's non-compliance with Article 10(2) of the BIT, which required attempted amicable settlement of a dispute during a specified timeframe prior to lodgement

48 Ibid, Procedural Details.

of an arbitration claim, as well as the lack of evidential substantiation of title in respect of the claim of expropriation of the disputed land for the development.[49] The tribunal ordered the claimant to bear full costs of the proceedings. Almasryia lodged an application with ICSID for annulment of the award on 12 March 2023. According to a statement posted by Almasryia's legal representative on the firm's website, the ICSID adhoc committee issued a full annulment on 28 December 2023.[50]

On 9 June 2020, the tribunal in the *Conseil Economique v Kuwait*[51] arbitration dismissed the claimant's case with prejudice, reportedly based on substantiated allegations by Kuwait that the basis for the claim was fraudulent, and on the previous withdrawal of claims.[52] The claimant sought to withdraw its claim and proposed a discounted costs settlement, which Kuwait rejected, and Kuwait requested the tribunal to issue an award and the dismissal of the claim with prejudice. The tribunal ordered the claimant to bear 50% of the arbitration costs, as well as 100% of Kuwait's legal fees and expenses.[53] *Counseil Economique* also withdrew another case based on similar claims in respect of health services for immigrant workers, prior to a tribunal being appointed.[54]

In *Maria Lazareva v The State of Kuwait*, the claimant (also known as Marsha) instituted arbitral proceedings against Kuwait, seeking USD100 million for damage to her shareholding in a Kuwait-based investment company for actions taken by Kuwaiti authorities including "the allegedly unsubstantiated charges against the claimant, her harassment, improper detention and the allegedly wrongful 10-year imprisonment, causing injury to the investment".[55]

49 *Almasryia for Operating & Maintaining Touristic Construction Co. L.L.C. v. State of Kuwait*, Final Award [67]–[69] (ICSID Case No. ARB/18/2) (*'Almasryia v Kuwait'*).

50 Lisa Bohmer, 'Egyptian investor claims success in bid for annulment of Rule 41(5) award that favored Kuwait' (4 January 2024) at <https://www-iareporter-com.eu1.proxy.openathens.net/articles/egyptian-investor-claims-success-in-bid-for-annulment-of-rule-415-award-that-favored-kuwait/>.

51 *Conseil Economique des Pays Musulmans v. The State of Kuwait* ('PCA Case No. 2018-35) (*'Conseil Economique v Kuwait'*); relying on the *Agreement between the Swiss Confederation and the State of Kuwait for the Encouragement and Reciprocal Protection of Investments*, signed on 31 October 1998 (entered into force 17 December 2000).

52 Paolo Bossi, 'Conseil Economique des Pays Musulmans v. The State of Kuwait', *Global Legal Chronicle* (undated) at <https://globallegalchronicle.com/conseil-economique-des-pays-musulmans-v-the-state-of-kuwait/>.

53 Ibid.

54 Lisa Bohmer, 'Second Group of Investors in Health Screening Services Withdraws Its Arbitration Claims against Kuwait', *Investment Arbitration Reporter* (17 June 2020) at <https://www-iareporter-com.eu1.proxy.openathens.net/articles/a-second-group-of-investors-in-health-screening-services-withdraws-its-arbitration-claims-against-kuwait/>.

55 UNCTAD (n 1), 'Maria Lazareva v. The State of Kuwait' (last updated 31 December 2021) <Lazareva v. Kuwait | Investment Dispute Settlement Navigator | UNCTAD Investment Policy Hub>; *Kuwait–Russian Federation BIT* (1994), signed 21 November 1994 (entered into force 30 May 1996).

The claimant was vice chairperson and managing director of the Kuwaiti private equity fund KGL Investment, which managed the Kuwait's Port Fund in which both the Kuwait Ports Authority and other government authorities held interest. Kuwaiti authorities reportedly accused the claimant of "intelligence gathering for a foreign power, and subsequently of embezzling funds from the Kuwait Ports Authority".[56] The claimant was arrested and imprisoned.

Two of the three tribunal members declined jurisdiction on the basis that the claimant's investment was not protected under the *Kuwait–Russian Federation BIT*, concluding that she did not exercise sufficient control over KGL Investment to qualify as an investor under the BIT. The tribunal awarded Kuwait around USD3.8 million in legal costs.

On 14 November 2022, Marsha Lazareva lodged an appeal at the Paris Court of Appeal to set aside the arbitration award in the dispute against Kuwait.[57]

4.6 Case Study: *Bachar Kiwan v State of Kuwait*

Bachar Kiwan, who holds joint Syrian and French citizenship, has lodged an arbitration with ICSID and is applying the ICSID Rules.[58] Kiwan was an adviser and business associate to the Kuwaiti Al-Sabah Royal Family, including Prime Minister Sheikh Jaber Al-Mubarak Al-Hamad Al-Sabah and his eldest son Sheikh Sabah Jaber Al-Mubarak Al-Hamad Al-Sabah. According to the media and political blog *Sarawak Report*, the eldest son fell from grace with Malaysian national Jho Low over the Al-Sabah relationship and the family's alleged agreement "to launder billions of dollars in kickbacks provided by the Chinese state company CCCC as 'commission' to Malaysia's then prime minister Najib Razak".[59]

Jho Low ultimately determined to divert the alleged kickbacks through the Al-Waseet Group, which was owned by Kiwan and Sheikh Sabah Jaber, in order to avoid potential scrutiny by authorities for money laundering, rather than the Kuwaiti company Komoros Gulf General Trading & Contracting, also owned by Kiwan and Sheikh Sabah Jaber and which was set up for the purpose of receiving

56 'Russian Managing Director of Private Equity Fund Commences BIT Arbitration against State of Kuwait', *Investment Arbitration Reporter* (17 July 2018) at <https://www-iareporter-com.eu1.proxy.openathens.net/articles/russian-managing-director-of-private-equity-fund-commences-bit-arbitration-against-state-of-kuwait/>.

57 'Marsha Lazareva Appeals to the Paris Court of Appeal against the State of Kuwait', *Omnia Strategy LLP* (16 November 2020) at <https://www.google.com/search?client=firefox-b-e&q=Marsha+Lazareva>.

58 UNCTAD (n 1), at <Kiwan v. Kuwait | Investment Dispute Settlement Navigator | UNCTAD Investment Policy Hub>; *France–Kuwait BIT*, signed 27 September 1989 (entered into force 16 May 1991).

59 Sarawak Report, 'How a Kuwaiti Royal Sheikh Jailed a 1MDB Whistleblower whilst Laundering China Kickbacks for Najib' *Sarawakreport* (29 May 2020) at <How A Kuwaiti Royal Sheikh Jailed A 1MDB Whistleblower Whilst Laundering China Kickbacks For Najib - EXCLUSIVE | Sarawak Report>.

the payments.[60] Kiwan reportedly deemed the diversion too risky when he was alerted to Jho Low's actions with respect to the developing 1 Malaysia Development Berhad (1MDB) scandal, causing a deep rift with both Jho Low and the Al-Sabah family. The rift resulted in Kiwan's imprisonment and subsequent departure from Kuwait via Spain (where at one point he avoided extradition back to Kuwait) to reside in Paris. The extradition request by Kuwait was denied by Spain on the basis of a perceived risk to Kiwan of both "torture and persecution".[61] ICSID reportedly rejected Kiwan's request for provisional measures, possibly prompted by the extradition attempts, on the basis that they were unnecessary.[62] This could be construed as an early indication that the claimant may face difficulties in successfully making out his claims.

There is little authoritative information available about the investor–state dispute itself. However, according to UNCTAD, Kiwan's claims arise out of the Kuwaiti "Government's alleged seizure of the claimant's investments following criminal investigations on fraud charges and the claimant's imprisonment".[63] Specifically, Kiwan claimed that the seizures amount to a breach of the fair and equitable treatment (FET) protection, the full protection and security, and the effective means protection, as well as claiming that the respondent contravened "his rights against arbitrary imprisonment and to an impartial judicial system, as protected by the International Covenant for Civil and Political Rights".[64] Kiwan has claimed USD439 million, arguing that Kuwait was in violation of the *France–Kuwait BIT*, breaching the FET minimum standard of treatment, full protection and security, and indirect expropriation protections.[65]

Kiwan's claim is the first reported arbitration initiated which seeks to apply the *France–Kuwait BIT* and, as such, will be a test case as to how the FET, minimum standard of treatment, full protection and security, and indirect expropriation provisions will be interpreted and applied.[66] It is unclear as to why the claim was not initiated applying the *Kuwait–Syria BIT*,[67] the *OIC Agreement*, the *Arab*

60 Ibid.

61 Damian Charlotin, 'ICSID Tribunal Rejects Request for Provisional Measures Triggered by Kuwait's Efforts to Extradite Investor', *Investment Arbitration Reporter* (4 January 2022) at <ICSID tribunal rejects request for provisional measures triggered by Kuwait's efforts to extradite investor | Investment Arbitration Reporter (iareporter.com)>.

62 Ibid.

63 UNCTAD (n 1), at <Kiwan v. Kuwait | Investment Dispute Settlement Navigator | UNCTAD Investment Policy Hub>.

64 Damien Charlotin, 'French Businessman Involved in 1MDB Scandal Lodges ICSID Claim against Kuwait', *Investment Arbitration Reporter* (18 December 2020) at <French businessman involved in 1MDB scandal lodges ICSID claim against Kuwait | Investment Arbitration Reporter (openathens.net)>.

65 UNCTAD (n 1), at <https://investmentpolicy.unctad.org/investment-dispute-settlement/cases/1073/kiwan-v-kuwait>.

66 Ibid.

67 *Kuwait–Syrian Arab Republic BIT*, signed 16 August 2001 (entered into force 23 March 2004).

Investment Agreement, and/or the *Arab League Investment Agreement*. As an example of forum-shopping, perhaps it was considered that the broad construction of investment protections and clearer construction of key terms and defined provisions contained within the *France–Kuwait BIT* would be more favourable, while the issue of alleged unclean hands would be a more difficult obstacle to overcome or cause additional issues if alternative IIAs were applied.

As a claimant, Kiwan has some significant obstacles to overcome in order to make a successful claim. The ICSID tribunal might be inclined to dismiss the case on a jurisdiction or an admissibility basis. Alternatively, it may determine that the claim fails on the merits or reduce compensation,[68] given that the business relationship from which the dispute arose was allegedly tainted by illegality or had an illegal purpose, specifically money laundering. Further, Kiwan has arguably not initiated the arbitration with "clean hands" having allegedly been involved in the money laundering plan from the outset via his interest in Komoros Gulf General Trading & Contracting. What also remains to be seen is the degree to which Sheikh Sabah Jaber's role in the alleged illegality impacts upon the tribunal's deliberations in this regard, or the extent (if any) to which Kuwait may ignore an unfavourable outcome, which appears to be occurring in the Swifthold Foundation case (see entry under Qatar).

While the *France–Kuwait BIT* contains a requirement that an investment must be made "in accordance with state laws",[69] the alleged plan to launder money may not necessarily be fatal to Kiwan's claim. Martin Jarrett, Sergio Puig, and Steven Ratner argue that, although the majority of IIAs contain a qualification in terms of protected investments required to be compliant with domestic laws, "tribunals have overall been unreceptive to claims that illegal investor conduct deprives them of jurisdiction, though tribunals have considered allegations of bribery".[70] Agata Zwolankiewicz, on the other hand, argues that "there is a prevailing view that the illegality of the investment would deprive the investor of a treaty protection to a certain extent", although there is some contention about whether or not illegality and the doctrine of clean hands are separate or linked considerations.[71] In any event, and in the view of the authors, the ICSID tribunal may well take an

68 Agata Zwolankiewicz, 'The Principle of Clean Hands in International Investment Arbitration: What Is the Extent of Investment Protection in Investor-State Disputes? (2021) 3(1) *Institute for Transnational Arbitration* 4, citing Marcin Kaldunski, 'Principle of Clean Hands and Protection of Human Rights in International Investment Arbitration' (2015) 4 *Polish Review of International and European Law* 69.

69 UNCTAD (n 1), at <France - Kuwait BIT (1989) | International Investment Agreements Navigator | UNCTAD Investment Policy Hub>.

70 Martin Jarrett, Sergio Puig and Steven Ratner, 'New Options for Investor Accountability in ISDS', *JIL:Talk!* (22 December 2022) at <New Options for Investor Accountability in ISDS – EJIL: Talk! (ejiltalk.org)>.

71 Agata Zwolankiewicz (n 68).

unfavourable view of the claimant's actions in light of the alleged mutual illegal money laundering purpose.

The case of *Al-Warraq v Indonesia*, to which the *OIC Agreement* applied, provides some guidance. In *Al-Warraq*, the tribunal considered the requirement that an investment be made in compliance with local laws and the common law doctrine of "clean hands". Relevantly, Article 9 of the Agreement states:

> The investor shall be bound by the laws and regulations in force in the host state and shall refrain from all acts that may disturb public order or morals or that may be prejudicial to the public interest. He is also to refrain from exercising restrictive practices and from trying to achieve gains through unlawful means.

The tribunal found that the claimant's conduct in undertaking "duties on the Board of Commissioners in a major bank without understanding their significance is clearly prejudicial to the public interest prohibited by Article 9" which refers to the investor's being "bound by the laws and regulations in force in the host state".[72] The tribunal went on to find that, by breaching the domestic laws and acting in a manner which risked the public interest, the claimant had "deprived himself of the protection afforded by the OIC Agreement" and further, that the doctrine of "*clean hands*" rendered the claim inadmissible."[73] The tribunal specifically referred to "the decision of Lord Mansfield in *Holman v Johnson* (1775)" which stated:[74]

> No court will lend its aid to a man who founds his cause of action upon an immoral or illegal act. If, from the plaintiff's own stating or otherwise, the cause of action appears to arise *ex turpi causa*, or the transgression of a positive law of this country, there the court says he has no right to be assisted.

Kiwan's alleged involvement in the money laundering is thus likely to be considered to have occurred in contravention of Kuwaiti laws and to fall within the scope of the doctrine of clean hands, effectively precluding admissibility of the claim and protection under the *France–Kuwait BIT*.

One of the law firms representing the claimant in *Kiwan v Kuwait*, Aceris Law, argues that arbitration in Kuwait is a work in progress and "in need of

72 *Hesham Talaat M. Al-Warraq v The Republic of Indonesia, ('Al-Warraq v Indonesia') Award* [644] at <https://jusmundi.com/fr/document/decision/en-hesham-talaat-m-al-warraq-v-the-republic-of-indonesia-final-award-monday-15th-december-2014#decision>.

73 Ibid [645]–[646].

74 Ibid [646].

reform", lacking "a standalone comprehensive procedural arbitration law based on the UNCITRAL Model Law [and] adequate English-friendly arbitration facilities".[75] Instead, dispute settlement provisions are to be found in "Islamic law, international law and institutional regulations".[76] Aceris Law suggests that this dispute may prompt Kuwait to review its arbitration laws and the adequacy of its dispute settlement mechanisms, including the need to "make a clear distinction between international and domestic arbitration" in the key laws that govern arbitration in Kuwait, specifically the *Code of Civil and Commercial Procedure (1980)* and the *Judicial Arbitration in Civil and Commercial Matter Law (1995)*.[77] However, such a review may only go ahead if the dispute proceeds and a significant award is handed down against Kuwait in favour of Kiwan, particularly if the tribunal finds that Kuwait also had unclean hands and potentially was involved in an illegal undertaking.

4.7 The Sultanate of Oman

Oman has faced just four ISDS cases as a respondent, with the first, *Al-Tamimi v Oman*, being an early BIT case in the GCC and which was found in Oman's favour. Anecdotal information indicates that none of the cases have involved significant financial claims as seen in some of the other GCC member State cases. The latest case, *Bin Sulaiman v Oman*, proceeding through the PCA, London, under UNCITRAL Rules, is in the arbitration phase according to ICSID, but has been apparently decided in favour of the State. Being intra-GCC, this case is discussed in further detail in Chapter 6.

Table 4.3 Oman as Respondent

No.	*Year Initiated*	*Short Case Name*	*Summary*	*Outcome of Original Proceedings*	*Home State of Investor*
1	2017	Bin Sulaiman v Oman[a] PCA case no. 2017-32	Investment: in Oman construction sector. Details of claim not available. Proceeding under *OIC Agreement* (1981).	Decided in favour of the State	Saudi Arabia

(*Continued*)

75 Aceris Law LLC, 'International Arbitration in Kuwait', *Aceris Law* (14 March 2021) at <International Arbitration in Kuwait • Aceris Law LLC>.

76 Ibid.

77 Ibid.

Table 4.3 (Continued)

No.	*Year Initiated*	*Short Case Name*	*Summary*	*Outcome of Original Proceedings*	*Home State of Investor*
2	2016	Attila Doğan v Oman ICSID case no. ARB/16/7	Investment: engineering and construction concession contract for oil and gas project with State-owned Petroleum Development of Oman. Claims arising from Government's frustration of claimant's engineering and construction contract. Including delaying or preventing entry of qualified foreign personnel and requiring hiring extra local labour from local construction company. PDO directed contract work to prior local contract-holder and eventually terminated contract in favour of local contractors. Proceeded under *Oman–Turkey BIT* (2007).	Data not available	Turkiye
3	2015	Samsung v Oman ICSID case no. ARB/15/30	Investment: contract bid bond for a refinery improvement project. Claims arising out of State discriminatory treatment towards claimant in connection with bidding process for Sohar refinery improvements run by state-owned Oman Refineries and Petroleum Industries Company (ORPIC) in 2013. Proceeded under *South Korea–Oman BIT* (2003).	Settled	South Korea
4	2011	Al Tamimi v Oman ICSID case no. ARB/11/33	Investment: controlling shareholding in two investment vehicle companies with 25-year lease agreements with State-owned mining company OMCO to quarry limestone in Buraimi region. Claims arising from Government's alleged harassment and interference in claimant's mining company operations in Oman, leading to termination of lease agreements and confiscation of mining facilities by Oman Police. Proceeded under *US–Oman FTA* 2006.	Decided in favour of the State	United States

Source: compiled by the authors primarily from UNCTAD, Investment Policy Hub, Investment Dispute Settlement Navigator, at https://investmentpolicy.unctad.org/investment-dispute-settlement/country/159/oman and *Investment Arbitration Reporter*, <https://www-iareporter-com.eu1.proxy.openathens.net/>.
[a]*Omar Bin Sulaiman Abdul Aziz Al Rajhi v. Oman* (PCA Case No. 2017-32) ('*Bin Sulaiman v Oman*'). This case, being an intra-GCC arbitration, is discussed in Chapter 6.

The tribunal in *Attila Doğan v Oman* rendered its award in a majority decision on 1 February 2021, although UNCTAD records the current status as "data not available". However, it has been reported that the claimant filed an application for annulment of the award on 9 June 2021, indicating that the award would have been in Oman's favour to a lesser or greater extent.[78] The ad hoc committee was constituted in July 2021. Reportedly, there have been disputations involving a number of requests relating to "security for costs and the termination of the proceedings",[79] primarily by Oman. On 27 September 2023, the claimant reportedly registered a submission proposing the disqualification of all members of the ad hoc annulment committee, and it remains unclear whether or not this proposal is related to prior rulings with respect to "security for costs and the termination of the proceedings".[80] According to ICSID, on 12 October 2023, Oman in response has filed "observations on the proposal for disqualification".[81]

The *Samsung v Oman*[82] arbitration is recorded as having been "Settled". Although no guidance is provided as to what "settled" in this particular case may constitute, it would appear not to be a discontinuation under ICSID Rule 43(1) or Rule 44.

Samsung Engineering filed its arbitration claim with ICSID concerning a refinery improvement project in Sohar in the north of the Sultanate. Samsung alleged discriminatory treatment in 2013 in respect of the bidding process for a USD1 billion project for improvements to the refinery run by the state-owned Oman Refineries and Petroleum Industries Company (ORPIC).[83] Samsung alleged that it had been selected as the preferred bidder by ORPIC for the project. Despite advanced negotiations, the two sides were unable to finalise a contract for the project because of disagreement on the project's construction timeline. During the protracted tender negotiations, ORPIC issued a "bond call" on Samsung's tender guarantee, which precipitated the ICSID claim lodgement. Samsung sought compensation for its tender guarantee plus reimbursement for its project planning and bidding expenses.

ICSID records that on 17 January 2018, the tribunal rendered its award in respect of the case, although media reported the outcome as proceedings declared closed

78 *Attila Doğan Construction & Installation Co. Inc. v. Sultanate of Oman* (ICSID Case No. ARB/16/7) ('*Attila Dogan v Oman*').

79 Lisa Bohmer, 'Turkish Construction Firm Challenges All Three Ad Hoc Committee Members in Opaque ICSID Case against Oman', *Investment Arbitration Reporter* (5 October 2023) at <Turkish construction firm challenges all three ad hoc committee members in opaque ICSID case against Oman | Investment Arbitration Reporter (openathens.net)>.

80 Ibid.

81 ICSID, 'Attila Dŏgan Construction & Installation Co. Inc. v. Sultanate of Oman (ICSID Case No. ARB/16/7)' (October 2023) at <Case Details | ICSID (worldbank.org)>.

82 *Samsung Engineering Co., Ltd. v. Sultanate of Oman* (ICSID Case No. ARB/15/30) ('*Samsung v Oman*').

83 See Kim Jae-won, 'Samsung Engineering Files for Arbitration with Oman', *Korea Times* (24 July 2015) at <http://isds.bilaterals.org/?samsung-engineering-files-for-arbitration-with-Oman>.

after the parties came to an agreement without an intervention from the tribunal.[84] It appears that the agreement between the parties was reached before the claim was considered on its merits. In late January 2018, media reported that the dispute had been resolved, with industry insiders expecting the resolution to lead to increased business activity between the two "down the road".[85] Details of the settlement have not been made public. Media also quoted a so-called industry insider as stating that "following the conclusion of the Omani government and Samsung Engineering's dissension, it can be expected that the latter will find success with future Oman bids going forward".[86]

4.8 The State of Qatar

Qatar has the leanest record of ISDS casework as a respondent with just two cases listed, the earliest not occurring until 2018 and subsequently discontinued/settled at an early stage, and the remaining case still continuing and recorded as pending. In respect of this latter case, namely *Benabderrahmane v. Qatar*, a tribunal was constituted in January 2023; in May 2023, the tribunal determined as a procedural order that the ICSID Arbitration Rules applicable to the case were the 2022 rules rather than the 2006 rules.[87]

84 Ibid.

85 See 'Samsung Engineering Settles Dispute with Oman, ISDS Withdrawn', *Korea Bizwire* (29 January 2018) at <http://koreabizwire.com/samsung-engineering-settles-dispute-with-oman-isds-withdrawn/109298>.

86 Ibid.

87 Damien Charlotin, 'ICSID Tribunal Decides that 2022 Arbitration Rules Are Applicable in Case Where Notice of Dispute Was Filed before July 2022, but Request for Arbitration Was Lodged after the New Rules' Entry into Force', *Investment Arbitration Reporter* (15 March 2023) at <https://www-iareporter-com.eu1.proxy.openathens.net/articles/icsid-tribunal-decides-that-2022-arbitration-rules-are-applicable-to-treaty-dispute-that-was-notified-before-july-2022-but-lodged-after-the-new-rules-were-adopted/>.

Table 4.4 Qatar as Respondent

No.	*Year Initiated*	*Short Case Name*	*Summary*	*Outcome of Original Proceedings*	*Home State of Investor*
1	2022	Benabderrahmane v Qatar ICSID case no. ARB/22/23	Investment: details not listed but appears to be related to "consulting service specialized in public relations and international affairs".[a] Proceeding under *France–Qatar BIT* (1996).	Pending	Algeria/ France
2	2018	Al Awamleh and others v Qatar ICSID case no. ARB/18/38	Investment: details not available. Claims arising from Government's non-payment for claimants' services to create television shows and seizure of claimants' assets in the country. Proceeding under Jordan–Qatar BIT (2009).	Discontinued pursuant to ICSID Rule 43(1), July 2019	Jordan

Source: compiled by the authors primarily from UNCTAD, Investment Policy Hub, Investment Dispute Settlement Navigator, at https://investmentpolicy.unctad.org/investment-dispute-settlement/country/171/qatar and *Investment Arbitration Reporter*, <https://www-iareporter-com.eu1.proxy.openathens.net/>.

[a]'French-Algerian Consulting Investor Lodges ICSID Claim against Qatar', *Investment Arbitration Reporter* (15 September 2022) at <https://www-iareporter-com.eu1.proxy.openathens.net/articles/french-algerian-consulting-investor-lodges-icsid-claim-against-qatar/>.

There were a number of media reports during 2022 of an emerging dispute against Qatar, with the State being put on notice by a Swifthold Foundation applying the *Panama–Qatar BIT 2010*.[88] The claim relates to the alleged frustration of the enforcement of a USD6 billion judgment against a Qatari corporation, Fast International Trading Group, which is owned by Sheikh Fahd bin Ahmed bin Mohammed bin Al-Thani, a member of the Qatari Ruling Family.[89] While it seems

88 Girish Deepak, 'Panama-Based Foundation Puts Qatar on Notice of Dispute, Alleging That the State Obstructed Enforcement of 6 Billion USD English High Court Judgement', *Investment Arbitration Reporter* (15 February 2022) at <Panama-based foundation puts Qatar on notice of dispute, alleging that the state obstructed enforcement of 6 billion USD English High Court judgment | Investment Arbitration Reporter (openathens.net)>.

89 Ibid.

that Swifthold is at the ultimate stage of informal negotiation, lodgement of a claim may still occur following Swifthold's favourable judgment in the UK courts. This case has not been incorporated into the listing above in the absence of formal notice of such lodgement. However, it is worthy of note because of the amount at the heart of the dispute and the avoidance actions of Sheikh Fahad and his relationship within the Ruling Family. This is also an issue in another GCC arbitration, namely *Kiwan v Kuwait*, as discussed earlier. At this stage it seems that a formal claim has yet to be registered (or publicly reported to have been registered).

4.9 The Kingdom of Saudi Arabia

Saudi Arabia's track record as a respondent in ISDS claims stands in stark contrast to the majority of GGC member States, in terms of both the dimension and its history of claims. The Kingdom has experienced 11 such claims over a 20-year period, with the great majority occurring in the last 5 years or so. The earliest claim, *Ed Zublin v Saudi Arabia* in 2003, was one of the first claims in the region. However, the next case did not arise until 2017. Four of the cases are recorded as still pending, with the most recent claim reported as having been lodged as recently as August 2023.

As appears to be the most common outcome across the region, most of the claims against the Kingdom have been either settled by mutual agreement under Rule 43 or decided in favour of the State on jurisdictional grounds.

Table 4.5 Saudi Arabia as Respondent

No.	*Year Initiated*	*Short Case Name*	*Summary*	*Outcome of Original Proceedings*	*Home State of Investor*
1	2023	Mühendislik v Saudi Arabia[a] ICSID case no. ARB/23/36	Investment: participation in the Jeddah sewerage system construction system Claim: details still uncertain but investor reportedly involved in litigation in Saudi courts for over ten years. Allegations of Saudi Arabia denial of justice, in violation of the BIT.[b] Proceeding under *Turkiye–Saudi Arabia* BIT (2006).	Pending	Turkiye

(*Continued*)

Table 4.5 (Continued)

No.	*Year Initiated*	*Short Case Name*	*Summary*	*Outcome of Original Proceedings*	*Home State of Investor*
2	2022	PCCW Cascade (Middle East) v Saudi Arabia ICSID case no. ARB/22/20	Investment details unavailable, but possibly joint venture for fixed-line and broadband communications services in 2008, with a local private investment fund, Mawarid Group. Details on claims not available, but possibly relating to Saudi withdrawal of investment licence and forced winding up of the joint venture in 2011.[c] Proceeding under *China–Saudi Arabia BIT* (1996).	Pending	China
3	2020	Qatar Airways v Saudi Arabia	Investment: licences and permits to conduct air transport activities. Claims arising from Government's actions to block Qatar Airways operations in the country, including closure of airspace to claimant and revocation of claimant's operating licences. Proceeding under *OIC Agreement* (1981) and *Arab Investment Agreement* (1980).[d]	Pending	Qatar

(*Continued*)

Table 4.5 (Continued)

No.	*Year Initiated*	*Short Case Name*	*Summary*	*Outcome of Original Proceedings*	*Home State of Investor*
4	2019	DSG v Saudi Arabia ICSID case no. ARB/19/32	Investment: projects for the construction of schools in Saudi Arabia. Further details not available. Details of claims not available other than alleged violation of *Turkiye–Saudi Arabia BIT* (2006).	Discontinued pursuant to ICSID Rule 43(1)	Turkiye
5	2019	Qatar Pharma and Al Sulaiti v Saudi Arabia	Investment: investments in two locally incorporated pharmaceutical companies and three warehouses for products in Riyadh, Jeddah, and Dammam. Claims arising from repudiation of long-term sales contracts between claimants and Saudi Ministry of Health after suspension of diplomatic relations with Qatar in 2017. Ministry's measures included failure to pay for contract products supplied by claimants forcing closure of local warehouses. Proceeding under *OIC Agreement* (1981).	Pending	Qatar

(*Continued*)

Table 4.5 (Continued)

No.	*Year Initiated*	*Short Case Name*	*Summary*	*Outcome of Original Proceedings*	*Home State of Investor*
6	2018	beIN v Saudi Arabia	Investment: broadcasting licence for pay TV services in Saudi Arabia and local subsidiary ownership, Oula Al Raeda Trading Company, for retail operations. Claims arising from Government measures to stop claimant's broadcasting operations in Saudi Arabia after suspension of diplomatic relations with Qatar in 2017. Included non-renewal of claimant's broadcasting licence and denial of its subsidiary licence. Proceeding under *OIC Agreement* (1981).	Pending	Qatar
7	2018	HOCHTIEF Infrastructure v Saudi Arabia ICSID case no. ARB/18/14	Investment: 55% shareholding in joint venture for contract to redesign, upgrade, and expand terminals at King Khaled International Airport in Riyadh. Claims arising from Government cancellation of the airport project and its subsequent reassignment to a different joint venture. Proceeded under *Saudi Arabia–Germany BIT* (1996).	Settled, pursuant to ICSID Rule 43(1)	Germany

(*Continued*)

Table 4.5 (Continued)

No.	*Year Initiated*	*Short Case Name*	*Summary*	*Outcome of Original Proceedings*	*Home State of Investor*
8	2018	Khadamat v Saudi Arabia PCA case no. 2019-24	Investment: large-scale land development through a local company acquired by the claimant. Claims arising from expropriation from the local company of the land intended for development. Proceeded under *India–Saudi Arabia BIT*- (2006).	Decided in favour of the State (jurisdiction declined)	India
9	2017	MAKAE Europe v Saudi Arabia ICSID case no. ARB/17/42	Investment: investments in Saudi Arabia's fashion retail sector. Claims arising from alleged Government systematic and unwarranted harassment leading to destruction of claimant's fashion retail business in the country. Proceeded under *France–Saudi Arabia BIT* 2002.	Decided in favour of the State (jurisdiction declined)	France
10	2017	Samsung v Saudi Arabia ICSID case no. ARB/17/43	Investment: construction of the Yanbu 3 Power and Seawater Desalination Plant project on the Red Sea coast. Claims arising from alleged termination of a power plant construction contract. Proceeded under *Saudi Arabia–South Korea BIT* 2007.	Data unavailable	South Korea

(*Continued*)

Table 4.5 (Continued)

No.	*Year Initiated*	*Short Case Name*	*Summary*	*Outcome of Original Proceedings*	*Home State of Investor*
11	2003	Ed. Züblin v Saudi Arabia ICSID case no. ARB/03/01	Investment: data not available. Claims arising from investor's construction of university facilities in Saudi Arabia. Proceeded under *Saudi Arabia–Germany* BIT (1996).	Settled pursuant to ICSID Rule 44	Germany

Source: compiled by the authors primarily from UNCTAD, Investment Policy Hub, Investment Dispute Settlement Navigator, at https://investmentpolicy.unctad.org/investment-dispute-settlement/country/185/saudi-arabia and *Investment Arbitration Reporter*, <https://www-iareporter-com.eu1.proxy.openathens.net/>.

[a]Güriş İnşaat ve Mühendislik Anonim Şirketi v. Kingdom of Saudi Arabia (ICSID Case No. ARB/23/36) ('Mühendislik v Saudi Arabia').

[b]Lisa Boehmer, '[Updated] Saudi Arabia Is Facing Denial of Justice Claim at ICSID', Investment Arbitration Reporter (22 August 2023) at <https://www-iareporter-com.eu1.proxy.openathens.net/articles/construction-investor-lodges-treaty-arbitration-against-saudi-arabia/>.

[c]Damien Charlotin, 'Chinese Investor Lodges BIT Arbitration against Saudi Arabia', Investment Arbitration Reporter (27 July 2022) at <https://www-iareporter-com.eu1.proxy.openathens.net/articles/chinese-investor-lodges-bit-arbitration-against-saudi-arabia/>. See also 'Saudi Telecoms Company SITC to Be Dissolved after Losing License', Al Arabiya (7 May 2013) at <https://english.alarabiya.net/business/technology/2013/05/07/Saudi-telecoms-company-SITC-to-be-dissolved>.

[d]See further discussion on this and other cases brought by Qatar Airways, Qatar Pharma, and beIn broadcasting against Bahrain, Saudi Arabia, and the UAE in Chapter 6.

Because of their particular regional geopolitical factors involving the fracturing of diplomatic relations, the suite of cases brought jointly against Saudi Arabia, Bahrain, and the UAE (and Egypt), jointly by Qatar Airways, Qatari broadcaster beIN, and Qatar Pharma, are discussed in greater detail in Chapter 6 on intra-GCC cases.

Neither the UNCTAD nor ICSID databases provide details of the basis of claim in *DSG v Saudi Arabia.*[90] The dispute may relate to one or more of a number of construction projects in Saudi Arabia in which DSG has been, or is currently, involved, including works on water pipelines, a water supply project, a bauxite mine, a petrochemical complex, a sports stadium, and Terminal 5 at Riyadh's King Khalid International Airport. UNCTAD lists *DSG v Saudi Arabia* as simply discontinued. However, the ICSID database reports that the proceedings were suspended from November 2021, pursuant to the parties' agreement. On 15 December 2022, the

90 *DSG Yapi Sanayi Ticaret Anonim Sirketi v. Saudi Arabia* (ICSID case No. ARB/19/32) ('*DSG v Saudi Arabia*').

tribunal took note that the action was discontinued pursuant to ICSID Rule 43(1),[91] perhaps indicating that the dispute may not have been entirely project-specific but arising from issues with the client–contractor relationship.

In *Khadamat v Saudi Arabia*,[92] the claimant alleged expropriation of land earmarked for development owned by a local company. The tribunal declined jurisdiction on the grounds that the alleged expropriation of the land held by the local company (which was indirectly owned by Khadamat through a Kuwaiti company) occurred *prior* to the claimant's acquisition of ownership rights in that local company.

Jurisdiction was also declined in *MAKAE Europe v Saudi Arabia*.[93] The claimant argued that Saudi Arabia had violated the *France–Saudi Arabia BIT* (2002) by allegedly destroying its investment in the Saudi fashion retail and restaurant industries through government actions that included the imprisonment of the claimant's founder and manager. However, the tribunal considered that the claimant, as a French company, did not have direct or *de facto* control over the Saudi investment and therefore was not a qualifying investor under the BIT cited as the basis for the claim.

In the case of *Samsung v Saudi Arabia*, the tribunal rendered its award in December 2021. However, the award remains closed and UNCTAD reports that data is not available in respect of the outcome of this arbitration. However, other sources indicate that the arbitration was concluded in favour of the claimant, thus perhaps mirroring the similar case involving Oman a few years earlier.[94] And, as with the Oman situation, the parties' commercial relationship appears to be undisturbed by the arbitration, as on 1 December 2021, Samsung advised that it had been awarded a USD1.23 billion contract for the development of the first shale gas project in Saudi Arabia.[95]

4.10 The United Arab Emirates

The UAE has been presented with just six ISDS cases lodged against it as respondent, with another emerging case likely. It is worth noting that none of the cases to date have reached the stage of being determined on the merits, having generally been withdrawn by mutual consent of the parties or declined by the tribunal on

91 ICSID, Case Details, *DSG v Saudi Arabia* <https://icsid.worldbank.org/cases/case-database/case-detail?CaseNo=ARB/19/32>.

92 *Khadamat Integrated Solutions Private Limited (India) v. The Kingdom of Saudi Arabia* (PCA Case No. 2019-24) ('*Khadamat v Saudi Arabia*').

93 *MAKAE Europe SARL v. Kingdom of Saudi Arabia* (ICSID Case No. ARB/17/42) ('*MAKAE Europe v Saudi Arabia*').

94 Namely, *Samsung v Oman* (ICSID Case No. 15/30).

95 Girish Deepak, 'Power Generation Arbitration against Saudi Arabia Concludes with an Award', *Investment Arbitrator Reporter* (15 December 2021) at <https://www-iareporter-com.eu1.proxy.openathens.net/articles/power-generation-arbitration-against-saudi-arabia-concludes-with-an-award/>.

jurisdictional grounds. The very first case raised against the UAE as respondent, namely *Impregilo v United Arab Emirates* of 2001, is arguably the first ISDS arbitration brought against a GCC member State relying on violation of a BIT as a basis of claim.

Jus Mundi reports that Andrea Constantino, an Italian national, gave Notice of Intent on 1 May 2023 of a claim against the UAE, alleging wrongful imprisonment, inhumane treatment, and the seizure of assets in violation of the *Italy–UAE BIT* (1995).[96] Arrested by UAE authorities in early 2021 over the alleged illegal shipment of oil to Yemen contrary to Saudi and Emirates embargoes during the Yemen conflict, he was released after an Italian Government diplomatic intervention. Considering the nature of the circumstances surrounding his claim, including the Yemen conflict and parties involved therein and the diplomatic interventions to date, and the considerable uncertainty as to whether this matter will evolve into a "conventional" ISDS case, it is suggested that it would be somewhat premature to list it in Table 4.6.

It is quite likely that the Qatari series of cases arising out of the recent diplomatic crisis between Qatar and Saudi Arabia, the UAE, and Bahrain, including those listed in Table 4.6 against the UAE, will eventually be resolved by intense rounds of diplomatic negotiations outside the formal arbitration context, perhaps leading to the withdrawal of the above claim pursuant to ICSID Rule 43 or 44. As previously stated, these cases are discussed in greater detail in Chapter 6 on intra-GCC cases.

96 *Andrea Constantino v UAE*, Jus Mundi, at <https://jusmundi.com/en/document/other/en-andrea-costantino-v-united-arab-emirates-notice-of-dispute-monday-15th-may-2023>. See also Lisa Bohmer, 'Italian National in the Oil and Gas Business Puts the UAE on Notice of Dispute, Alleging BIT Violations through His Wrongful Imprisonment, Inhumane Treatment, and the Seizure of His Asset', *Investment Arbitration Reporter* (1 June 2023) at <https://www-iareporter-com.eu1.proxy.openathens.net/articles/italian-national-in-the-oil-and-gas-business-puts-the-uae-on-notice-of-dispute-alleging-bit-violations-through-his-wrongful-imprisonment-inhumane-treatment-and-the-seizure-of-his-assets/>

Table 4.6 UAE as Respondent

No.	*Year Initiated*	*Short Case Name*	*Summary*	*Outcome of Original Proceedings*	*Home State of Investor*
1	2021	Taheri v United Arab Emirates ICSID case no. ARB/21/19	Investment: distribution and trading enterprises, further details not available. Claims arising out of the Government's failure to renew claimant's permit to reside in the country, affecting investments in import-export activities and general commodities trading. Proceeded under *Sweden–UAE BIT*.	Settled pursuant to ICSID Rule 43(2)	Sweden
2	2020	Qatar Airways v United Arab Emirates	Investment: licences and permits to conduct air transport activities. Claims arising from Government actions to block Qatar Airways operations, including closure of airspace to claimant and revocation of claimant's operating licences. Proceeding under *OIC Agreement* (1980) and *Arab Investment Agreement* (1981).[a]	Pending	Qatar
3	2019	Dalal v United Arab Emirates ICSID case no. ARB/19/10	Investment: investment in three plots on Dubai's "The World" island developed by Nakheel PJSC and The World LLC. Claims arising from Nakheel non-development of island infrastructure to enable returns on land investment. Proceeded under *UK–UAE BIT* (1992).	Discontinued pursuant to ICSID Rule 43(1)	United Kingdom

(*Continued*)

Table 4.6 (*Continued*)

No.	*Year Initiated*	*Short Case Name*	*Summary*	*Outcome of Original Proceedings*	*Home State of Investor*
4	2017	BM Mühendislik v United Arab Emirates ICSID case no. ARB/17/20	Investment: road construction. Claimant removed from prominent road extension project as contractor and project put out for a new tender. Proceeded under *Turkey–UAE BIT* (2005).	Data not available	Turkiye
5	2002	Soufraki v UAE ICSID case no. ARB/02/7	Investment: rights under a port concession agreement. Claims arising from cancellation of concession agreement between investor and Dubai Department of Ports and Customs to develop, manage, and operation Al Hamriya Port and surrounds. Proceeded under *Italy–UAE BIT* (1995).	Decided in favour of the State (jurisdiction declined)	Italy
6	2001	Impregilo v UAE ICSID case no. ARB/01/1	Investment: data not available. Claims arising from mosque construction project in the UAE. Proceeded under *Italy–UAE BIT* (1995).	Discontinued pursuant to ICSID Rule 44	Italy

Source: compiled by the authors primarily from UNCTAD, Investment Policy Hub, Investment Dispute Settlement Navigator, at https://investmentpolicy.unctad.org/investment-dispute-settlement/country/220/united-arab-emirates and *Investment Arbitration Reporter*, <https://www-iareporter-com.eu1.proxy.openathens.net/>.

See further discussion on this and other cases brought by Qatar collectively against Bahrain, Saudi ArabiaArabia, and the UAE in Chapter 6.

The most recent of UAE's cases as respondent, namely, *Taheri v UAE*, was settled by mutual agreement of the parties pursuant to ICSID Rule 43(2) in November 2022. The claimant sought damages of USD11 million following the government's failure to renew his residence permit, thus adversely affecting his local import-export business. However, the recent public release of the tribunal's award acknowledging the settlement sheds further interesting light on the case. The award indicates that the settlement was initiated by the claimant, following certain allegations raised by the UAE regarding the authenticity of key evidence in the dispute.[97] The claimant proposed a settlement which the UAE accepted, and the parties notified the settlement to the tribunal. As a result of this settlement agreement, the claim was withdrawn with prejudice.

The award reveals that the claimant disclosed that the claim was receiving third party funding. At the UAE's request, the tribunal determined that the funder's identity needed to be disclosed to the extent required for conflict purposes and ordered the claimant to disclose whether there were any provisions for adverse costs within the funding agreement.[98] The UAE next raised objections to certain key documents provided by the claimant, which allegedly evidenced "incongruities and possible tampering or manipulation". During the ensuing forensic review of this key evidence, the parties reached an agreement to settle the dispute. Under the terms of the settlement agreement, the claimant agreed to discontinue the arbitration proceedings by withdrawing, "with prejudice", all claims in the arbitration proceedings.[99] The claimant further agreed to pay all fees and expenses of the tribunal, as well as the administrative charges and direct costs of ICSID. The parties also agreed to bear their respective legal costs in the proceedings and for the settlement award to be published.[100]

The case of *BM Mühendislik v United Arab Emirates*, which commenced in February 2017, involved a dispute over the claimant's investment in the construction of a road extension project in western Abu Dhabi (the Corniche Road). The arbitration is still proceeding, with UNCTAD using its standard annotation under the relevant circumstances that data on the original proceedings is not available. The tribunal rendered its award on 23 December 2022, with a concurring and dissenting opinion by the claimant-appointed arbitrator. On 14 February 2023, the claimant registered a request for rectification and a supplementary decision of the award filed. On 10 March, the UAE lodged observations on the claimant's request, with the claimant responding to the UAE's observations on 31 March 2023.[101]

In the *Soufraki v United Arab Emirates* case, another very early case against the UAE, the tribunal held that it lacked jurisdiction to hear the case on the grounds that the claimant, who claimed to hold both Italian and Canadian citizenship, no longer held Italian nationality, but rather Canadian nationality on the grounds of more recent residence and business-related declarations.[102] The claimant had relied on the *Italy–UAE BIT*(1995) as the basis of the claim. A subsequent application by

97 Girish Deepak, 'Settlement Award between Amir Masood Taheri and UAE Comes to Light; Claim Was Withdrawn Following Discrepancy in Evidence and Disclosure of Third-Party Funding', *Investment Arbitration Reporter* (6 December 2022) at <https://www-iareporter-com.eu1.proxy.openathens.net/articles/settlement-award-between-mr-taheri-and-uae-comes-to-light-claim-was-withdrawn-following-discrepancy-in-evidence-and-disclosure-of-third-party-funding/>.

98 Ibid.

99 Ibid.

100 Ibid.

101 *BM Mühendislik ve İnşaat A.Ş. v. United Arab Emirates* (ICSID Case No. ARB/17/20).

102 *Hussain Nuaman Soufraki v United Arab Emirates* (ICSID Case No. ARB/02/07) ('*Soufraki v United Arab Emirates*').

the claimant to an ad hoc committee for annulment of the tribunal determination seems to have been unsuccessful.

4.11 General Regional Case Commentary

Of the total arbitrations initiated against GCC member States as listed in Tables 4.1, 4.2, 4.3, 4.4, 4.5, and 4.6, 12 cases (35%) are recorded as still pending, the longest standing appearing to be *beIn v Saudi Arabia* from 2017. This number of pending cases is somewhat higher than the UNCTAD percentage (<27%), but it should be noted that the great majority of these pending cases were first registered since 2020, demonstrating the extent of the recent surge in ISDS arbitrations involving various GCC member States as respondents. Eight cases have been decided in favour of the State, with a tribunal declining jurisdiction in five of those cases. But, in stark contrast, only one case is formally recorded as having been determined in favour of the claimant (namely, Bank Melli).

A total of 11 cases together have been settled or discontinued – and at times the UNCTAD nomenclature does not distinguish in detail between the two. ICSID Rules 43(1) or (2) or Rule 44, applying to mutually agreed or non-contested discontinuations, have generally been invoked as the basis for settlement or discontinuation. Rule 45, which applies to discontinuations for the failure of a party to act, does not appear to have been invoked in an original proceedings. Data is not available on three cases.

The *Bank Melli v Bahrain* arbitration has been considered earlier as a case study because it is a highly significant dispute, being the only case brought against a GCC member State (Bahrain) in which the claimants prevailed and because of the issues that the tribunal considered in relation to the preliminary objections and the merits. Particularly pertinent in this regard are the issues of "clean hands" in relation to jurisdiction, admissibility, and the merits, which are currently being considered in other disputes involving the States (such as occurring in *Kiwan v Kuwait*). The outcome of the pending disputes will likely inform the treaty-making practices of the States into the future and may reflect the complex nature of relationships internal to the union in the case of intra-GCC disputes such as the Qatar Airways suite of disputes. They may also give greater credence to the suggested creation of a GCC-level dispute settlement body.

The data available for damages claimed in arbitrations initiated against GCC member States is rather limited. Some data on amounts is available in 12 of the disputes, which range from USD15.5 million in *Dalal v United Arab Emirates*[103] (which did not proceed to final determination) to USD1 billion in the Qatari case of *beIN v Saudi Arabia* (which is still pending) and USD7 billion in *Central Bank of Iran v Bahrain*. There is no data available at all about the amounts awarded or

103 *Shokat Mohammed Dalal v United Arab Emirates* (ICSID Case No. ARB/19/10) ('*Dalal v United Arab Emirates*').

settled, except for the case of *Bank Melli v Bahrain*,[104] in which EUR514.2 million was claimed and EUR243 million plus costs plus interest was awarded. A figure of USD7 billion in damages has been speculated for the *Central Bank of Iran v. Bahrain* claim, but this needs confirmation.

Most arbitrations, namely 18 (62%), were conducted under the ICSID Rules, with a further 7 arbitrations (24%) conducted under the UNCITRAL Rules. Again, there is no data concerning the applicable rules in respect of the remaining disputes.

There has been a relatively wide spread of applicable IIAs allegedly infringed in arbitrations initiated against GCC member States. The distribution is fairly even with the exception of disputes applying the *OIC Agreement*. That Agreement was applied in three (9%) cases, and both the Agreement and the *Arab Investment Agreement* were applied in a further three (9%) cases. The *Egypt–Kuwait BIT* (2001) was applied in two (6%) cases, as were the *Germany–Saudi Arabia BIT* (1996) and the *Italy–UAE BIT* (1995). All other disputes were brought under other BITs, with the exception of the *United States–Oman FTA*[105] which was applied in *Tamimi v Oman*.[106] Given the relatively high application rate for the *OIC Agreement*, the GCC member States would arguably benefit from a careful review of the construction of the substantive investment protections and dispute settlement mechanisms contained within each agreement.

A fairly wide distribution exists in terms of the nationality of claimants in arbitrations initiated against GCC member States. Except for *OHL and others v Kuwait*, which is a construction-related dispute involving two investors from Italy and one from Spain, all arbitrations were initiated by investors from individual home states. This exception case has been treated as its own category so as not to overstate the number of claimants. The ICSID tribunal reportedly dismissed the claimants' request for provisional measures, although the nature of the request has not been disclosed.[107]

Arbitrations initiated against GCC member States were most commonly brought against Saudi Arabia with 11 arbitrations (32%), followed by seven (20%) arbitrations initiated against Kuwait, six (18%) against the UAE, four (12%) each against Oman and Bahrain, and just two (6%) against Qatar.

The most common home state of investors in cases brought against other GCC member States was Qatar, which occurred in six (15%) cases. But this is a unique situation, reflecting the recent Gulf diplomatic crisis between the GCC member States. Next was Turkiye as the home state of the claimant, which occurred in three cases (9%). Six (21%) cases brought against member States were by investors from home states within the GCC, namely Qatar and, to a lesser extent, Saudi

104 *Bank Melli v Bahrain* (n 11).

105 *Free Trade Agreement between the United States and Oman*, signed 19 January 2006 (entered into force 1 January 2009) ('*United States–Oman FTA*').

106 *Adel A Hamadi Al Tamimi v Sultanate of Oman* (ICSID Case No. ARB/11/33) ('*Tamimi v Oman*').

107 Girish Deepak, 'Kuwait Round up: An Update on Arbitration Proceedings against the State', *Investment Arbitration Reporter* (3 December 2021) at <Kuwait Round Up: An update on arbitration proceedings against the state | Investment Arbitration Reporter (openathens.net)>.

Arabia. Other claimants came from a wide range of developed, transitioning, and developing economies, namely Algeria, China, Egypt, France, Germany, India, Iran, Italy, Jordan, Malaysia, South Korea, Russia, Spain, Sweden, Switzerland, the United Kingdom, and the United States. It is anticipated that disputes with non-GCC member States will increase with respect to the economic diversification programmes adopted by the States.

Detailed information is available on the breaches alleged in only 8 of the 34 arbitrations initiated against GCC member States, with the claimants alleging multiple breaches in 7 of the 8 cases. Commonly alleged breaches included the fair and equitable treatment/minimum standards of treatment protection, full protection and security (or other), and expropriation. In *Almasryia v Kuwait*, the claimants alleged a single breach, namely direct expropriation.[108] In *Soufraki v United Arab Emirates*, however, the breaches alleged are unclear. Data is not available from UNCTAD with respect to the remainder.

With respect to breaches found, the case was settled or discontinued before a decision on liability in eight instances, jurisdiction was declined in four instances, data is not available in two instances (although subsequent information from other sources clarifies), all claims were dismissed at the merits stage in one instance, and indirect expropriation was found in one instance. Therefore, it is rare that breaches alleged have been successfully made out in cases instituted against GCC member States, noting, however, that a significant number of all cases are yet to be finalised.

Investor–state disputes initiated against GCC member States as respondents have arisen out of a broad range of economic sectors. However, a significant proportion of disputes involved the construction sector, with 11 (38%) cases arising out of construction, three (10%) from information and communication, three (10%) from transportation and storage, two (7%) from real estate activities, two (7%) from the financial and insurance sector, two (7%) from wholesale and retail trade, vehicles, and motorcycles, one (3%) from manufacturing, and one (3%) from mining and quarrying. Data was not available in of the cases.

It is expected that disputes arising from the construction sector will continue to be a significant proportion of arbitrations initiated against the States into the future. This is likely because "construction disputes are inevitable due to activity in the construction industry and arbitration is the preferred dispute resolution mechanism for such disputes, especially for foreign parties".[109] However, the most recent arbitrations have arisen out of the information, communications, and public relations sectors, as demonstrated by the *Kiwan v Kuwait*, *Benabderrahmane v Qatar*, and *PCCW Cascade (Middle East) v Saudi Arabia* cases, and exceptionally the transportation and storage sector, in the series of arbitrations initiated by Qatar Airways against Bahrain, Saudi Arabia, and the UAE, considered above.

108 *Almasryia for Operating & Maintaining Touristic Construction Co. L.L.C. v State of Kuwait* (ICSID Case No. ARB/18/2) ('*Almasryia v Kuwait*').

109 Aceris Law LLC (n 75).

Figure 4.1 summarises the history of the GCC member States as respondents in ISDS claims. The first case arose just over 20 years ago, followed by the further occasional case in the ensuing couple of years. Then followed a period of almost complete inactivity for over a decade, until 2017 onwards when a mini-explosion of cases involving all States with multiple cases in some instances occurred. A partial explanation for this surge could be due to the Qatari suite of cases, but the trend has continued. And it is quite possible that the slight downward trend over the last year or so may be corrected upwards as cases emerge from behind the cloak of secrecy and confidentiality maintained by the majority of the leading arbitration tribunals.

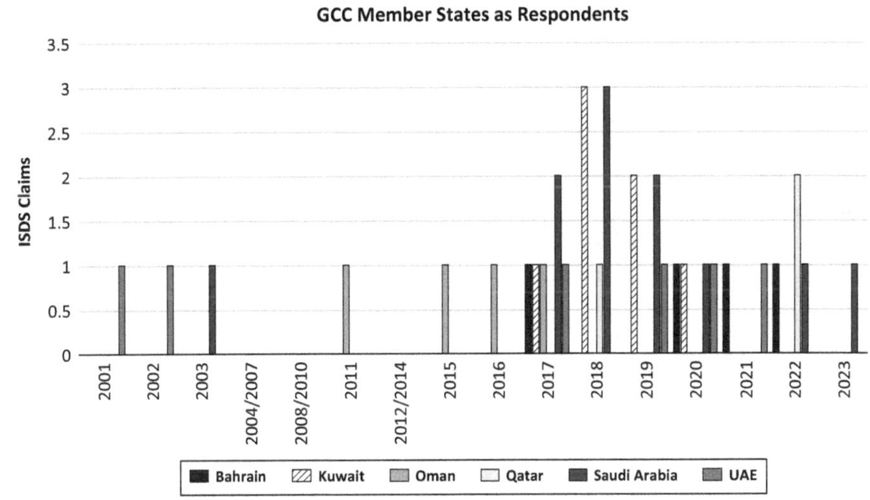

Figure 4.1 Investor–state dispute settlement and the GCC member State experience.

Source: Compiled by the authors as derived from UNCTAD data.

4.12 Concluding Remarks: Increasing Exposure to ISDS in the Future

The wealthier GCC member States are likely to have greater levels of exposure to investor–state arbitration in the future due to external environmental factors. Specifically, change may occur as a result of increased "economic competition" as a result of "high sovereign debt levels" caused by the domestic, continuing regional and international impact of the COVID-19 pandemic, regional foreign direct investment flows, and volatility in global oil markets.[110] Saudi Arabia, for example, is reportedly endeavouring to attract foreign direct investment by requiring companies to base their regional headquarters in Saudi Arabia in order to qualify for government contracts from 2024, in an effort to divert companies from basing themselves

110 Sebastian Castelier, 'GCC States Race for Foreign Investment', *AL-Monitor* (22 February 2021) <GCC states race for foreign investment - Al-Monitor: The Pulse of the Middle East>.

in the UAE, particularly Dubai.[111] Saudi Crown Prince Mohammed bin Salman has publicised an intention to "open up the kingdom and diversify its economy under a series of reforms".[112] These reforms are chiefly about diversification from oil and include Vision 2030, the National Transformation Program 2020, and a "private sector investment boost".[113] These measures, if successful, may result in an increase in adverse non-litigated ISDS investor–state disputes initiated against Saudi Arabia.

However, this is not simply a story about Saudi Arabia. In fact, all six GCC member States have demonstrated a desire to diversify their economies and emerge as new knowledge societies. One of the key features of these respective programmes is the protection and promotion of foreign direct investment. While the States are adopting different policies and endeavouring to make this transition at different rates, it is anticipated that across the board, this shift is likely to result in investor–state disputes, potentially escalating to arbitration.

Increased economic competition between the States may undermine the adoption of suitable and unified approaches to ISDS and treaty-making practices at the regional level, in addition to exposing individual member States to increased arbitration.[114] The Saudi response to foreign policy issues, particularly those arising from the disputation over relations with Iran and the consequent severance of diplomatic relations, is likely to reflect the strength of the union and the degree to which Saudi Arabia will adopt flexibility and exercise its *de facto* leadership role within the GCC with a view to neutralising perceived or potential external threats for the benefit of the union.[115]

GCC member States might mitigate against the risk of adverse arbitral liability at an individual state level despite competition and fractures within the union by reviewing their existing BITs and TIPs to narrow the scope of investment protections and limit the possibility of dispute settlement by arbitration. The States can also conclude new BITs and TIPs on this more limited basis and require claimants to first exhaust local remedies as a precondition to submitting claims to arbitration to promote domestic legal institutions and legal procedures and remove the potential for duplicity of litigation and dispute settlement "forum shopping". This is

111 Ibid; Sebastian Castelier, 'Saudi Arabia Says Foreign Companies Must Have Regional HQs in Kingdom to Access Government Contracts', *Arab News* (15 February 2021) <Saudi Arabia says foreign companies must have regional HQs in Kingdom to access government contracts (arabnews .com)>.

112 Nayera Abdallah and Alexander Cornwell, 'Saudi Arabia Won't Work with Foreign Firms without Regional HQ from 2024', *Reuters* (16 February 2021) <https://jp.reuters.com/article/saudi-company-int-idUSKBN2AF1PX/>https://www.reuters.com/article/idUSKBN2AF1PW/

113 *Mordor Intelligence*, 'Saudi Arabia Construction Market – Growth, Trends, Covid-19 Impact and Forecasts (2021–2026)', *Mordor Intelligence* (undated) <Saudi Arabia Construction Market | 2021 - 26 | Industry Share, Size, Growth - Mordor Intelligence>.

114 Giorgio Cafiero, '42nd GCC Summit: An Opportunity for Reconciliation' (10 December 2021) *Gulf International Forum* <42nd GCC Summit: An Opportunity for Reconciliation - Gulf International Forum (gulfif.org)>.

115 Ibid.

particularly important in the context of Shariah law and its influence upon the legal institutions and methods in the GCC member States, particularly Saudi Arabia.[116]

Bibliography

Abdallah, Nayera and Alexander Cornwell, 'Saudi Arabia won't work with foreign firms without regional HQ from 2024' (16 February 2021) *Reuters* at <Saudi Arabia won't work with foreign firms without regional HQ from 2024 | Reuters>.

Aceris Law LLC, 'International Arbitration in Kuwait', *Aceris Law* (14 March 2021) at <International Arbitration in Kuwait • Aceris Law LLC>.

Adel A Hamadi Al Tamimi v Sultanate of Oman (ICSID Case No. ARB/11/33) (*'Tamimi v Oman'*).

Agreement between the Government of the French Republic and the State of Kuwait on the Encouragement and Reciprocal Protection of Investments, signed 27 September 1989 (entered into force 16 May 1991) (*'France – Kuwait BIT'*).

Agreement between the Government of the United Arab Emirates and the Government of the Italian Republic for the Promotion and Protection of Investments, signed 22 January 1995 (entered into force 29 April 1997).

Agreement between the Government of the United States of America and the Government of the Sultanate of Oman on the Establishment of a Free Trade Area, (entered into force 1 January 2009).

Agreement between the Swiss Confederation and the State of Kuwait for the Encouragement and Reciprocal Protection of Investments, signed on 31st October 1998 (entered into force 17 December 2000).

Agreement on Reciprocal Promotion and Protection of Investments between the Government of Islamic Republic of Iran and the Government of the Kingdom of Bahrain, signed 19 October 2002 (entered into force 12 October 2004) (*'Bahrain – Iran BIT'*).

Alaa Nizar Raja Sumrain, Ayat Nizar Raja Sumrain, Eshraka Nizar Raja Sumrain and Mohamed Nizar Raja Sumrain v. State of Kuwait (ICSID Case No. ARB/19/20) (*'Sumrain v Kuwait'*).

Almasryia for Operating & Maintaining Touristic Construction Co. L.L.C. v. State of Kuwait, Final Award (ICSID Case No. ARB/18/2) (*'Almasryia v Kuwait'*).

Andrea Constantino v UAE, 'Jus Mundi' at <https://jusmundi.com/en/document/other/en-andrea-costantino-v-united-arab-emirates-notice-of-dispute-monday-15th-may-2023>.

Attila Doğan Construction & Installation Co. Inc. v. Sultanate of Oman (ICSID Case No. ARB/16/7) (*'Attila Dogan v Oman'*).

Bank Melli and Bank Saderat v Bahrain (Statement of Claim) (PCA Case No 2017-25, 16 October 2017) (*'Bank Melli'*).

Bohmer, Lisa, 'Italian National in the Oil and Gas Business Puts the UAE on Notice of Dispute, Alleging BIT Violations Through His Wrongful Imprisonment, Inhumane Treatment, and the Seizure of His Asset', *Investment Arbitration Reporter* (1 June 2023) at < https://www-iareporter-com.eu1.proxy.openathens.net/articles/italian-national-in-the-oil-and-gas-business-puts-the-uae-on-notice-of-dispute-alleging-bit-violations-through-his-wrongful-imprisonment-inhumane-treatment-and-the-seizure-of-his-assets/>.

Bohmer, Lisa, 'Revealed: A Comprehensive Account Of The Heretofore Unpublished Bank Melli v. Bahrain Award; Some Details Have Leaked, But Review Of Award Gives Full Picture of Tribunal's Findings on Iranian Sanctions Questions, Political Expropriation,

116 Aceris Law LLC (n 78).

And Potential Set-Offs', *International Arbitration Reporter* (14 December 2023) at <Revealed: A comprehensive account of the heretofore unpublished Bank Melli v. Bahrain award; some details have leaked, but review of award gives full picture of tribunal's findings on Iranian sanctions questions, political expropriation, and potential set-offs | Investment Arbitration Reporter (openathens.net)>.

Bohmer, Lisa, 'Second Group of Investors in Health Screening Services Withdraws its Arbitration Claims against Kuwait', *Investment Arbitration Reporter* (17 June 2020) at <https://www-iareporter-com.eu1.proxy.openathens.net/articles/a-second-group-of-investors-in-health-screening-services-withdraws-its-arbitration-claims-against-kuwait/>.

Bohmer, Lisa, 'Turkish Construction Firm Challenges All Three Ad Hoc Committee members in Opaque ICSID Case Against Oman', *Investment Arbitration Reporter* (5 October 2023) at <Turkish construction firm challenges all three ad hoc committee members in opaque ICSID case against Oman | Investment Arbitration Reporter (openathens.net) *Investment Arbitration Reporter*, 22 August 2023.

Bohmer, Lisa, '[Updated] Saudi Arabia is facing denial of justice claim at ICSID', *Investment Arbitration Reporter* (22 August 2023) at <https://www-iareporter-com.eu1.proxy.openathens.net/articles/construction-investor-lodges-treaty-arbitration-against-saudi-arabia/>.

Bossi, Paolo, 'Conseil Economique des Pays Musulmans v. The State of Kuwait', *Global Legal Chronicle* at <https://globallegalchronicle.com/conseil-economique-des-pays-musulmans-v-the-state-of-kuwait/>.

Cafiero, Giorgio, '42nd GCC Summit: An Opportunity to Reconciliation', *Gulf International Forum* (10 December 2021) at <42nd GCC Summit: An Opportunity for Reconciliation - Gulf International Forum (gulfif.org)>.

Castelier, Sedbastian, 'GCC States Race for Foreign Investment', *AL-Monitor* (22 February 2021) at <https://www.al-monitor.com/originals/2021/02/gcc-gulf-economy-rivalries-saudi-arabia-covid19-uae-riyadh.html>.

Castelier, Sebastian, 'Saudi Arabia says foreign companies must have regional HQs in Kingdom to access government contracts' *Arab News* (15 February 2021) at <Saudi Arabia says foreign companies must have regional HQs in Kingdom to access government contracts (arabnews.com)>.

Chan, Jude, 'Keppel Unit Begins Arbitration Proceedings to Claim S$173 Million in Qatar Project Spat', *Business Times* (Singapore) (31 May 2022) at <https://www.businesstimes.com.sg/companies-markets/keppel-unit-begins-arbitration-proceedings-to-claim-s173-million-in-qatar-project>.

Charlotin, Damien, 'Chinese investor lodges BIT arbitration against Saudi Arabia', *Investment Arbitration Reporter* (27 July 2022) at <https://www-iareporter-com.eu1.proxy.openathens.net/articles/chinese-investor-lodges-bit-arbitration-against-saudi-arabia/>.

Charlotin, Damien, 'French Businessman Involved in 1MDB Scandal Lodges ICSID Claim Against Kuwait', *Investment Arbitration Reporter* (18 December 2020) at <French businessman involved in 1MDB scandal lodges ICSID claim against Kuwait | Investment Arbitration Reporter (openathens.net)>.

Charlotin, Damien, 'ICSID tribunal decides that 2022 Arbitration Rules Are Applicable in Case Where Notice of Dispute Was Filed Before July 2022, but Request for Arbitration Was Lodged after the New Rules' Entry Into Force', *Investment Arbitration Reporter* (15 March 2023) at <https://www-iareporter-com.eu1.proxy.openathens.net/articles/icsid-tribunal-decides-that-2022-arbitration-rules-are-applicable-to-treaty-dispute-that-was-notified-before-july-2022-but-lodged-after-the-new-rules-were-adopted/>.

Charlotin, Damien, 'ICSID Tribunal Rejects Request for Provisional Measures Triggered by Kuwait's Efforts to Extradite Investor', *Investment Arbitration Reporter* (4 January

2022) at <ICSID tribunal rejects request for provisional measures triggered by Kuwait's efforts to extradite investor | Investment Arbitration Reporter (iareporter.com)>.

Conseil Economique des Pays Musulmans v. The State of Kuwait (PCA Case No. 2018-35) (*'Conseil Economique v Kuwait'*).

'Court Orders Bahrain to Pay Damages to Iran for Political Expropriation', *Press TV* (24 November 2021) at <Court orders Bahrain to pay damages to Iran for 'political expropriation' (presstv.ir)>.

Deepak, Girish, 'Kuwait Round Up: An Update on Arbitration Proceedings Against the State', *Investment Arbitration Reporter* (3 December 2021) at <Kuwait Round Up: An update on arbitration proceedings against the state | Investment Arbitration Reporter (openathens.net)>.

Deepak, Girish, 'Panama-Based Foundation Puts Qatar On Notice Of Dispute, Alleging That The State Obstructed Enforcement Of 6 Billion USD English High Court Judgement', *Investment Arbitration Reporter* (15 February 2022) at <Panama-based foundation puts Qatar on notice of dispute, alleging that the state obstructed enforcement of 6 billion USD English High Court judgment | Investment Arbitration Reporter (openathens.n et)>.

Deepak, Girish, 'Power Generation Arbitration Against Saudi Arabia Concludes with an Award', *Investment Arbitrator Reporter* (15 December) at <https://www-iareporter-com .eu1.proxy.openathens.net/articles/power-generation-arbitration-against-saudi-arabia -concludes-with-an-award/>.

Deepak, Girish, 'Settlement Award between Amir Masood Taheri and UAE Comes to Light; Claim Was Withdrawn Following Discrepancy in Evidence and Disclosure of Third-Party Funding', *Investment Arbitration Reporter* (6 December 2022) at <https://www -iareporter-com.eu1.proxy.openathens.net/articles/settlement-award-between-mr-taheri -and-uae-comes-to-light-claim-was-withdrawn-following-discrepancy-in-evidence-and -disclosure-of-third-party-funding>.

DSG Yapi Sanayi Ticaret Anonim Sirketi v Saudi Arabia (ICSID Case No. ARB/19/32) (*'DSG v Saudi Arabia'*).

'French-Algerian Consulting Investor Lodges ICSID Claim against Qatar', *Investment Arbitration Reporte* (15 September 2022) at <https://www-iareporter-com.eu1.proxy .openathens.net/articles/french-algerian-consulting-investor-lodges-icsid-claim-against -qatar/>.

Güriş İnşaat ve Mühendislik Anonim Şirketi v. Kingdom of Saudi Arabia (ICSID Case No. ARB/23/36) (*'Mühendislık v Saudi Arabia'*).

Hesham Talaat M. Al-Warraq v The Republic of Indonesia, ('Al-Warraq v Indonesia') Award [644] at <https://jusmundi.com/fr/document/decision/en-hesham-talaat-m-al-warraq-v -the-republic-of-indonesia-final-award-monday-15th-december-2014#decision>.

'High Court of Appeal Upholds Ruling Against Future Bank and Officials, Central Bank of Iran and Other Iranian Banks', *Bahrain News Agency* (31 October 2021) at <https://www .bna.bh/en/news?cms=q8FmFJgiscL2fwIzON1%2BDj3D0Kqbr8W5hjB5G6BIOmQ %3D>.

'Higher Court of Appeal Toughens up Sentences in one of Biggest Money Laundering Cases in Bahrain's History', *Bahrain News Agency* (3 October 2022) at <https://www.bna.bh/ en/news?cms=q8FmFJgiscL2fwIzON1%2BDj3D0Kqbr8W5hjB5G6BIOmQ%3D>.

Hussain Nuaman Soufraki v United Arab Emirates (ICSID case No. ARB/02/07) (*'Soufraki v United Arab Emirates'*).

Impregilo, S.p.A and Rizzani De Eccher S.p.A v United Arab Emirates (ICSID Case No. ARB/01/1) (*'Impregilo v UAE'*).

Jarrett, Martin, Sergio Puig and Steven Ratner, 'New Options for Investor Accountability in ISDS' *EJIL:Talk!* (22 December 2021) at <New Options for Investor Accountability in ISDS – EJIL: Talk! (ejiltalk.org)>.

Keppel Seghers v. Qatar Public Works Authority, Jus Mundi at <https://jusmundi.com/en/document/decision/en-keppel-seghers-engineering-singapore-pte-ltd-v-qatar-public-works-authority-party-representatives>.

Khadamat Integrated Solutions Private Limited (India) v. The Kingdom of Saudi Arabia (PCA Case No. 2019-24) (*'Khadamat v Saudi Arabia'*).

Kim, Jae-won, 'Samsung Engineering files for arbitration with Oman', *Korea Times* (24 July 2015) at <http://isds.bilaterals.org/?samsung-engineering-files-for-arbitration-with-Oman>.

Kuwait – Russian Federation BIT (1994), signed 21 November 1994 (entered into force 30 May 1996).

Kuwait – Syrian Arab Republic BIT, signed 16 August 2001 (entered into force 23 March 2004).

Maillis, Janine and Craig Shepard, 'Investment Treaty Arbitration in United Arab Emirates', *Lexology.com* (16 November 2018) at <Investment Treaty Arbitration in United Arab Emirates - Lexology>.

MAKAE Europe SARL v. Kingdom of Saudi Arabia (ICSID Case No. ARB/17/42) (*'MAKAE Europe v Saudi Arabia'*).

'Marsha Lazareva Appeals to the Paris Court of Appeal against the, State of Kuwait', *Omnia Strategy LLP* (16 November 2020) at <https://www.google.com/search?client=firefox-b-e&q=Marsha+Lazareva>.

Mordor Intelligence, 'Saudi Arabia Construction Market – Growth, Trends, Covid-19 Impact and Forecasts (2021–2026)', *Mordor Intelligence* (undated) at <Saudi Arabia Construction Market | 2021 - 26 | Industry Share, Size, Growth - Mordor Intelligence>.

Obrascón Huarte Lain S.A., Rizzani de Eccher S.p.A. and Trevi S.p.A. v. State of Kuwait (ICSID Case No. ARB/17/8) (*'OHL and others v Kuwait'*).

Omar Bin Sulaiman Abdul Aziz Al Rajhi v. Oman (PCA Case No. 2017-32) (*'Bin Sulaiman v Oman'*).

'Russian Managing Director of Private Equity Fund Commences BIT Arbitration against State of Kuwait', *Investment Arbitration Reporter* (17 July 2018) at <https://www-iareporter-com.eu1.proxy.openathens.net/articles/russian-managing-director-of-private-equity-fund-commences-bit-arbitration-against-state-of-kuwait/>.

Samsung Engineering Co., Ltd. v. Sultanate of Oman (ICSID Case No. ARB/15/30) (*'Samsung v Oman'*).

'Samsung Engineering Settles Dispute with Oman, ISDS Withdrawn', *Korea Bizwire* (29 January 2018) at <http://koreabizwire.com/samsung-engineering-settles-dispute-with-oman-isds-withdrawn/109298>.

Sarawak Report, 'How a Kuwaiti Royal Sheikh Jailed A 1MDB Whistleblower Whilst Laundering China Kickbacks For Najib' *Sarawakreport* (29 May 2020) at <How A Kuwaiti Royal Sheikh Jailed A 1MDB Whistleblower Whilst Laundering China Kickbacks For Najib - EXCLUSIVE | Sarawak Report>.

'Saudi Telecoms Company SITC to be Dissolved after Losing License', *Al Arabiya* (7 May 2013) at <https://english.alarabiya.net/business/technology/2013/05/07/Saudi-telecoms-company-SITC-to-be-dissolved>.

Shokat Mohammed Dalal v United Arab Emirates (ICSID Case No. ARB/19/10) (*'Dalal v United Arab Emirates'*).

Tehran Times, 'CBI and the Other Iranian Banks Were Handed Fines of 1 Million Bahraini Dinars Each, and That Confiscation Was Ordered of Laundered Funds', *Tehran Times* (8 August 2021) at <https://www.tehrantimes.com/news/463688/Iran-s-central-bank-takes-legal-action-against-Bahrain>.

UNCTAD, 'Investment Policy Hub, Investment Dispute Settlement Navigator' at <https://investmentpolicy.unctad.org/investment-dispute-settlement>.

United States Department of the Treasury, 'Fact Sheet: Designation of Iranian Entities and Individuals for Proliferation Activities and Support for Terrorism', *U.S. Department of the Treasury* (25 October 2007) at <Fact Sheet: Designation of Iranian Entities and Individuals for Proliferation Activities and Support for Terrorism (treasury.gov)>.

United States Department of the Treasury, 'Treasury Cuts Iran's Bank Saderat Off From U.S. Financial System', *U.S. Department of the Treasury* (8 September 2007) at <Treasury Cuts Iran's Bank Saderat Off From U.S. Financial System>.

United States Department of the Treasury, 'Treasury Designates Iran-Controlled Bank for Proliferation Future Bank Controlled by Iran's Bank Melli', *U.S. Department of the Treasury* (12 March 2008) at <Treasury Designates Iran-Controlled Bank for Proliferation Future Bank Controlled by Iran's Bank Melli>.

Warrick, Joby and Souad Mehennet, 'Iranian Banks Notch win in Dispute Over sanctIons Enforcement', *Washington Post* (26 November 2021) at <Iranian banks notch win in dispute over sanctions enforcement - The Washington Post>.

Zwolankiewicz, Agata, 'The Principle of Clean Hands in International Investment Arbitration: What is the Extent of Investment Protection in Investor-State Disputes? (2021) 3(1) *Institute for Transnational Arbitration*, 4–31.

5 The GCC Member States as Home States of Claimants in ISDS Arbitrations

5.1 Introduction

This chapter examines in detail the experiences of each GCC member State in ISDS-based disputes reliant on bilateral investment treaties or other international investment agreements as the basis of claim as home state of investors initiating claims. As with the previous chapter on the States as respondents in ISDS arbitrations, it includes tables for each member State across this category, noting procedural rules and case number, a summary of the investment and the basis of the claim, the most recent known status of each case, and the opposing claimant or state. Although contract-based or domestic legislation-based claims are thus not included in the tables, mention will still be made of some from time to time as appropriate.

The chapter also offers commentary in respect of selected cases which for one reason or another (for example, by tribunal determination or by mutual consent or by certain action or non-action by either party), focussing primarily on issues discussed in the earlier chapters or because of particular circumstances of the case which had a bearing on its outcome.

Attention is given to cases that may reveal or explain some of the issues and questions raised in the earlier chapters concerning the nature of the member States' performance (or on occasion, non-performance) in the conduct of ISDS arbitrations.

Again, the information gathered relies primarily, but not exclusively, on the UNCTAD Investment Dispute Settlement Navigator database, but is supplemented by secondary sources deemed reliable. The same parameters and qualifications in respect of UNCTAD terminologies and recordal methodologies as utilised for the previous chapter on the States as respondents to ISDS cases also apply to this chapter and the cases listed.

5.2 ISDS from the Gulf: GCC Member States as Home States of Claimants

As with the GCC member States as respondents, the history of ISDS claims lodged by nationals of the States is rather limited, both in terms of number and timespan. At the time of writing, nationals of the States have lodged a total of 38 ISDS claims

DOI: 10.4324/9781003481072-5

through established arbitration institutions, compared with the 34 received by the States as respondents over a fairly similar period of time. The spread of claimants across the States is very disparate but nevertheless is not unexpected and generally reflects the wealth generated by the respective economies and government policy and attitudes to outward foreign investment. The UNCTAD data shows the UAE leads the way with 13 claims upon other countries, followed by Kuwait and Qatar with nine claims each. However, Qatar's figures are a little distorted by the suite of claims brought by its investors against the other States arising out of the Gulf diplomatic crisis. UNCTAD records claims by four Saudi nationals followed by Omani (two claims) and Bahraini (one claim) nationals. However, these numbers of arbitrations pale into insignificance when compared with the home states of the most prolific group of investor claimants, notably the United States (226 claims), the Netherlands (131 claims), and the United Kingdom (104 claims).[1] The number of arbitrations has increased in the last five years or so, peaking in 2018, and then exhibiting a relative decline. These lower numbers may change in the relatively near future, however, with the diversification measures planned, particularly in Saudi Arabia, mentioned above.

The first case brought by a claimant from a GCC member State, and relying upon a bilateral investment treaty (BIT) or other international investment agreement (IIA) as the basis of the claim, was *Desert Line v Yemen*, initiated by an Omani claimant, Desert Line LLC, in 2005.[2] However, it is worthy of note that in 1986, Ghaith Rashad Pharaon, a Saudi national, brought an ISDS claim under ICSID Rules against Tunisia, but the basis of claim rested largely on contract law and host-state domestic investment law rather than a BIT or other IIA. Hence it has not been included in Table 5.5.[3]

Tables 5.1, 5.2, 5.3, 5.4, 5.5, and 5.6 detail ISDS claims submitted by investors from each GCC member State and which are reliant upon BITs and other IIAs. Accordingly, they do not include international arbitration cases which proceeded under contract laws and/or commercial agreements. The tables have been compiled primarily from UNCTAD data, supplemented by information gleaned from international arbitration centres, from the Investment Arbitration Reporter subscription service, and from occasional local media sources on individual cases.

1 Note that of these 38 cases, the original arbitration of *Ali Alyafei v Hashemite Kingdom of Jordan* (ICSID Case No. ARB/15/24) was bifurcated and counted as two arbitrations and tribunals applying two different treaties, namely the *Unified Agreement for the Investment of Arab Capital in the Arab States* signed 26 November 1980 (entered into force 7 September 1981*) ('Arab Investment Agreement')* (Alyafei Part 1) and the *Agreement on Promotion, Protection and Guarantee of Investments amongst the Member States of the Organization of the Islamic Conference*, signed 5 June 1981 (entered into force February 1988) *('OIC Agreement'*) (Alyafei Part II), both of which were later discontinued.

2 *Desert Line Projects LLC v. Republic of Yemen* (ICSID Case No. ARB/05/17 ('*Desert Line v Yemen*').

3 *Ghaith Rashad Pharaon v. Republic of Tunisia* (ICSID Case No. ARB/86/1 (*'Pharaon v Tunisia').*

5.3 The Kingdom of Bahrain

Table 5.1 Bahrain as Home State of Investor

No.	*Year Initiated*	*Short Case Name*	*Summary*	*Outcome of Original Proceedings*
1	2016	Nile Douma v Egypt PCA case no. 2107-09	Investment: licence relating to the building of a hotel and use of land in Cairo. Claims arising out of Egyptian authorities' refusal to grant the licence and register the relevant plot of land under claimant's name. Proceeded under *Bahrain–Egypt BIT* 1997.	Decided in favour of the State

Source: compiled by the authors primarily from UNCTAD, *Investment Policy Hub* <Advanced Search | Investment Dispute Settlement Navigator | UNCTAD Investment Policy Hub>, and *Investment Arbitration Reporter*, <https://www-iareporter-com.eu1.proxy.openathens.net/>.

The one identified ISDS case brought by an investor as a national of Bahrain, namely, *Nile Douma v Egypt*, was neither particularly complex nor large-scale by general ISDS standards in terms of damages sought. Nile Douma Holding, a Bahrain-registered luxury hotel developer, had acquired, with government approval, a plot of land in the Rod El Farag area of Cairo to build a new luxury hotel complex. In 2016 the company brought arbitral claims under UNCITRAL rules seeking USD29.3 million damages plus interest. The company claimed that the Egyptian government had interfered with its investment by declining to register title to the land for the project in Nile Douma's name. The tribunal handed down its award on 12 November 2021. The tribunal reportedly found in favour of the State, rejecting Nile Douma's claim.[4] The reasons for its decision remain unreported publicly.

5.4 The State of Kuwait

UNCTAD reports nine ISDS cases lodged by investors claiming Kuwait citizenship, the first being *ICRS v Jordan* as recently as 2009, and the most recent being *KGL v Egypt* in 2021. UNCTAD records that the majority of these were either found in favour of the respondent State or discontinued by mutual consent before

4 'Egypt Defeats Hotel Investor', *Garrigues Newsletter* (27 December 2021) at <https://www.garrigues.com/en_GB/new/international-arbitration-newsletter-december-2021-regional-overview-middle-east-and-africa>.

consideration of the merits, with only one case found in favour of the claimant, namely *Al-Kharafi v Libya & Or*. However, that claimant victory appears to have been short-lived, with the arbitration award subsequently overturned on judicial review (see following report). However, this figure of nine cases (even as amended) may still be out of date, as indicated by the following ISDS cases, which do not appear in UNCTAD or Table 5.2.

The *Kuwait Times* reported in June 2023 that the Kuwait Oil Company (KOC) had prevailed in an arbitration before the London Court of International Arbitration (LCIA) against one of its (unnamed) contractors under a joint venture agreement.[5] Relying on a KOC press release, the *Kuwait Times* reported that the dispute arose in the context of an undersea pipeline project, with KOC alleging that the contractor had refused to accept responsibility for delays and that amicable settlement negotiations had failed. The LCIA handed down a report in favour of KOC, awarding USD77 million, plus costs, in favour of KOC. The news item concludes with the statement that "this case is considered the second in which KOC succeeded in obtaining a ruling in its favour during the arbitration process in the London Court", although that first case is not identified.[6] Because of the absence of available information as to whether the case may have been ISDS or commercial/contract, it has not been included in the Kuwait table.

The ICSID database records an arbitration between AAN Digital Services Holding, a Kuwaiti-registered company, and the government of the Democratic Republic of the Congo (DRC) (ICSID case no. ARB/19/24) in respect of the government's conduct over the Kuwaiti company's holdings in the DRC's mobile phone network operator Sematel.[7] ICSID also records the case as having been discontinued pursuant to ICSID Arbitration Rule 45 (Discontinuance for Failure of Parties to Act). However, since the dispute in question relies on DRC investment law of 2002 and project contracts, rather than a BIT or other IIA, it has not been included in Table 5.2 and corresponding statistics.

5 See Girish Deepak, 'Kuwait Oil Company Reports Win in LCIA Arbitration against Contractor', *Investment Arbitration Reporter* (12 June 2023) at <https://www-iareporter-com.eu1.proxy.openathens.net/articles/kuwait-oil-company-reports-win-in-lcia-arbitration-against-contractor/>.

6 'KOC Wins 77 Million Dollars in Arbitration Case Filed in London Court', *Kuwait Times* (21 June 2023) at <https://timeskuwait.com/news/koc-wins-77-million-dollars-in-arbitration-case-filed-in-london-court/>.

7 *AAN Digital Services Holding Company (KSC) v. Democratic Republic of the Congo* (ICSID Case No. ARB/19/24, 11 September 2019).

Table 5.2 Kuwait as Home State of Investor

No.	*Year Initiated*	*Short Case Name*	*Summary*	*Outcome of Original Proceedings*
1	2021	KGL v Egypt ICSID case no. ARB/21/21	Investment: 2006 concession agreement for the build-transfer-operate of Egypt's Damietta Port container terminal. Claims arising from cancellation of the agreement between the Damietta Port Authority and Damietta International Ports company, in which claimant held 25% interest. Proceeded under *Egypt–Kuwait BIT* (2001).	Settled pursuant to ICSID Rule 43(1)
2	2019	Aljarallah v Turkey and TMSF PCA case no. 2020-04	Investment: minor shareholding in Aydinli Hazir Giyim Sanayi ve Ticaret, a Turkish clothing company. Claims arising from alleged non-payment of profit shares to claimant and removal from company board after company placed under trusteeship of Turkey's Savings Deposit Insurance Fund (SDIF) on suspicion of ties with alleged terrorist group accused of orchestrating the failed 2016 coup. Proceeding under *Kuwait–Turkiye BIT* (2010).	Decided in favour of the State
3	2018	International Holding Project Group and others v Egypt[a] ICSID case no. ARB/18/31	Investment: multi-billion-dollar real estate project. Further details not available. Claims by Kuwaiti corporations and nationals arising from El-Aziz Saleh Esmail Abdallah Al-Rashed from contract cancellation to build a new city in Cairo.[b] Proceeding under *Egypt–Kuwait BIT* (2002).	Pending
4	2017	Agility v Iraq ICSID case no. ARB/17/7	Investment: shareholding in Korek Telecom, an Iraqi telecommunications enterprise. Claims arising from Government regulatory agency annulment of claimant's level of shareholding in Korek Telecom and orders that excess shares be transferred back to original Iraqi shareholders. Proceeded under *Iraq–Kuwait BIT* (2013).	Decided in favour of the State (under annulment proceedings)

(*Continued*)

Table 5.2 (*Continued*)

No.	*Year Initiated*	*Short Case Name*	*Summary*	*Outcome of Original Proceedings*
5	2013	Alghanim v Jordan ICSID case no. ARB/13/38	Investment: majority shareholding (96% stake) in Umniah, a Jordanian telecommunications provider company that held a GSM operating licence. Claims arising from Government measures following Alghanim's sale of its Umniah stake to Bahraini company Batelco, including Government-levied tax assessment. Proceeded under *Kuwait–Jordan BIT* (2001).	Decided in favour of the State
6	2011	Agility v Pakistan ICSID case no. ARB/11/8	Investment: ownership of Automated Customs Clearance System software to assess import duties introduced by Pakistan Government at Karachi International Container Terminal and later extended to other ports and airports. Claims arising from Government non-payments for claimant's automated customs clearing system on imports. Proceeded under *Kuwait–Pakistan BIT* (1983).	Decided in favour of neither party (liability found but no damages awarded)
7	2011	Al-Kharafi v Libya and/or Ad hoc CRCCICA	Investment: lease agreement with Libyan Tourism Development Authority for a build-and-operate of a tourism and beachfront hotel project in Tripoli. Claims arising from the Libyan Tourism Authority's annulment of agreement with claimant for development of the tourism project. Proceeded under *Arab Investment Agreement* (1980).	Decided in favour of the claimant (annulled on judicial appeal)
8	2011	Bawabet v Egypt ICSID case no. ARB/11/6	Investment: interests in an Alexandria-based fertiliser supply company. Claims arising from Government's cancellation of the free zone status in which the claimant's fertiliser company operated, plus price increases in gas supplied under certain contract. Proceeded under *Egypt–Kuwait BIT* (2001).	Settled pursuant to ICSID Rule 43(1)

(*Continued*)

Table 5.2 (Continued)

No.	*Year Initiated*	*Short Case Name*	*Summary*	*Outcome of Original Proceedings*
9	2009	ICRS v Jordan[c] ICSID case no. ARB/09/13	Investment: rights under a light railway system agreement between Jordan and the claimant. Claims arising from Government termination of an implementation agreement between Jordan Public Transport Regulatory Commission to build, operate, and transfer a light railway system (LRS Project) connecting Amman and Zarqa. Proceeded under *Jordan–Kuwait BIT* (2001).	Discontinued pursuant to ICSID Rule 43(1)

Source: compiled by the authors primarily from UNCTAD, *Investment Policy Hub* <Advanced Search | Investment Dispute Settlement Navigator | UNCTAD Investment Policy Hub>, and *Investment Arbitration Reporter*, <https://www-iareporter-com.eu1.proxy.openathens.net/>.

[a]*Abd-El-Aziz Saleh Esmail Abdallah Al-Rashed, Awrad International Holding, International Holding Project Group and others v. Arab Republic of Egypt* (ICSID Case No. ARB/18/31) ('*International Holding Group Project v Egypt*').

[b]Kuwaitis Mount Multi-Billion Dollar Investment Arbitration against Egypt', *Investment Arbitration Reporter* (20 September 2018) at <Kuwaitis mount multi-billion dollar investment arbitration against Egypt | Investment Arbitration Reporter (openathens.net)>; Lisa Bohmer, 'Tribunal Is in Place in Egyptian Real Estate Dispute, with Pierre Tercier Tapped to Chair', *Investment Arbitration Reporter* (6 August 2019) at <Tribunal is in place in Egyptian real estate dispute, with Pierre Tercier tapped to chair | Investment Arbitration Reporter (openathens.net)>.

[c]*International Company for Railway Systems (ICRS) v. Jordan*, (ICSID Case No. ARB/09/13) ('*ICRS v Jordan*'). See also parallel case before the International Chamber of Commerce, *Government of the Hashemite Kingdom of Jordan and the Public Transport Regulatory Commission v. International Company for Railway Systems (ICRS)*, ICC Case No. 16342/EC/ND (6 February 2012) at <https://jusmundi.com/en/document/decision/en-the-government-of-the-hashemite-kingdom-of-jordan-and-the-public-transport-regulatory-commission-v-international-company-for-railway-systems-ii-award-monday-6th-february-2012>.

The case of *Waleed Aljarallah v Turkey* involved the seizure by the Turkish Government of a local textile and clothing company, in which Kuwait national Waleed Aljaralllah held a minor shareholding. Following a failed political coup in 2016, Turkish authorities seized the company and placed it under trusteeship of Turkiye's Savings Deposit Insurance Fund, on suspicions of ties with an alleged terrorist organisation accused of orchestrating the coup.

Waleed Aljarallah lodged an arbitration claim under UNCITRAL rules with the PCA in September 2020, seeking around USD38 million in damages and relying upon the *Turkey–Kuwait BIT* (2010). On 18 October 2023, the tribunal reportedly rendered its decision, dismissing all claims on the merits and awarding costs against the claimant.[8]

The two following Agility cases also raised issues of "clean hands" in both instances. In unusual circumstances, the *Agility v Pakistan* case, initiated before ICSID in 2011, was concluded on 1 August 2016, following acknowledgement by the claimant that it concurred with the argument by the respondent that the treaty upon which their claims had rested, namely the 1983 *Kuwait–Pakistan BIT*, had never entered into force.[9] However, the case also generated ongoing allegations of corruption by both parties, including supporting material proffered by the respondent late in the proceedings. Upon objection by the respondent to a requested stay in proceedings to examine the new material, and the invalidity of the BIT as a basis for claim, the claimant requested withdrawal of their claims. The tribunal awarded the respondent 90% of its legal costs against the claimant, which, it could be argued, represents a (moral?) victory for the State.

In *Agility v Iraq*, involving an Agility investment in Iraq's telecommunications sector, the claimant sought damages in excess of USD650 million plus costs.[10] Agility and the French telecoms company Orange had invested almost USD500 million in 2011 to acquire a 44% stake in Iraq's Korek Telecom following its award of a Government licence for a nationwide mobile telecommunications network. In July the Iraq Government body, Communications & Media Commission (CMC), declared the 2011 transaction to be null and void and directed that Agility's and Orange's shareholdings revert back to the original shareholders. Agility alleged that the Iraqi government had violated the *Iraq–Kuwait BIT* of 2013 when it nullified the 2011 transaction. The tribunal delivered its decision on 22 February 2021, dismissing all of Agility's claims (including the expropriation claim) and requiring the claimant meet the respondent's arbitration costs, exceeding USD5 million.

The claimant subsequently filed an application for annulment of the award. ICSID reports that the ad hoc committee held a hearing on the annulment on 15–16 November 2022.[11]

Reportedly, a subsidiary and an affiliate of Agility lodged ICC arbitration proceedings against Korek Telecom and its controlling shareholder alleging fraud and corruption orchestrated by Korek Telecom Company and its controlling

8 Lisa Bohmer, 'UNCITRAL Tribunal Dismisses under-the-Radar Treaty Claim against Turkey', *Investment Arbitration Reporter* (19 October 2023) at <https://www-iareporter-com.eu1.proxy.openathens.net/articles/turkey-is-facing-under-the-radar-uncitral-arbitration/>.

9 Luke Eric Peterson, 'After Obtaining a Jurisdictional Victory in 2013, Investor Later Concedes that Pakistani Investment Treaty Is Not in Force and Drops Its Arbitration', *Investment Arbitration Reporter* (11 August 2016) at <https://www-iareporter-com.eu1.proxy.openathens.net/articles/after-obtaining-a-jurisdictional-victory-in-2013-investor-later-concedes-that-pakistani-investment-treaty-is-not-in-force-and-drops-its-arbitration/>.

10 *Agility Public Warehousing Company K.S.C. v. Republic of Iraq* (ICSID Case No. ARB/17/7) ('*Agility v Iraq*').

11 *Agility v Iraq*, 'Proceedings', *ICSID*, at <https://icsid.worldbank.org/cases/case-database/case-detail?CaseNo=ARB/17/7>.

shareholder, with the ICC handing down an award in favour of Agility on 20 March 2023.[12] There was also reportedly a contract based on "a fraud claim between their [Agility and Orange] joint venture, Iraq Telecom, and the Intercontinental Bank of Lebanon, before the Lebanese Arbitration Centre" in which the tribunal found for Iraq Telecom in the September 2021 award.[13]

5.4.1 Case Study: **Al-Kharafi v Libya**

The case of *Al-Kharafi v Libya* is significant for a number of reasons. It represents the one Kuwaiti ISDS case to date in which the investor initially prevailed in an ISDS case, the dimension of the arbitral award including moral damages was significant among GCC member state cases, and the tribunal decision was subject to subsequent judicial intervention.[14] UNCTAD records the case as an ISDS arbitration, but it has also been suggested that it is essentially a dispute over non-compliance with contractual terms of the original build-and-operate agreement between the parties.[15]

The arbitration commenced in June 2012 and proceeded under the Cairo Regional Centre for International Commercial Arbitration ("CRCICA") rules. The claim revolved around annulment of the claimant's licence for a build-and-operate tourist development project, including a 99-year lease on land, in Tripoli, Libya. The claimant submitted that the failure of the Libyan Tourist Development Authority to transfer land that was physically and legally unencumbered to allow construction to commence, and the minister's annulment of the development licence on the grounds of the claimant's alleged inaction for four years, constituted breaches of the *Arab Investment Agreement*, as well as the Libyan Investment Law

12 Lisa Bohmer, '[Updated with a Copy of the Award] UAE Based Agility Claims Victory in Commercial Telecoms Arbitration Involving Corruption Allegations – As Related ICSID Cases Continue to Unfold', *Investment Arbitration Reporter* (21 March 2023) at <[Updated with a copy of the Award] UAE-based Agility claims victory in commercial telecoms arbitration involving corruption allegations – as related ICSID cases continue to unfold | Investment Arbitration Reporter (openathens.n et)>; ICC Arbitration No. 25194/AYZ/ELU. See also 'Agility Announces Arbitration Decision in Korek Case' *Agility Pres Release* (21 March 2023) at <Agility Announces Arbitration Decision in Korek Case | Agility>.

13 Girish Deepak, '[Updated with New Document] Iraq Round-up: Iraq Joins Mauritius Convention and New York Convention, an under-the-Radar 26 Billion USD Dispute and Updates on Other Pending Proceedings', *Investment Arbitration Reporter* (21 October 2021) at <[Updated with new document] Iraq Round-Up: Iraq joins Mauritius Convention and New York Convention, an under-the-radar 26 billion USD dispute, and updates on other pending proceedings | Investment Arbitration Reporter (openathens.net)>.

14 *Mohamed Abdulmohsen Al-Kharafi & Sons Co. v. The Republic of Libya and others (Final Award)* ('*Kharafi v Libya*').

15 Luke Eric Peterson, 'Damages Analysis: Investor Nets $900 Million Windfall for Libyan Resort That Was Never Built – And $30 Million in Moral Damages for Reputational Harm', *Investment Arbitration Reporter* (24 July 2013) at <Damages analysis: Investor nets $900 million windfall for Libyan resort that was never built - and $30 million in moral damages for reputational harm | Investment Arbitration Reporter (openathens.net)>.

and the Libyan Civil Code on contracts. The claimants sought the equivalent of USD2.056 billion in damages, account of lost profits, and costs, of which the lost profits comprised almost USD2 billion.[16]

In a majority decision rendered in March 2013, the tribunal agreed on virtually all issues of the claim and in so doing appeared rather critical of the respondent's conduct both in respect of the development issues and the arbitration. In respect of the land transfer issue the tribunal considered that

> the facts ... show a large gap between the aspirations of the Libyan State and the reality. Aspirations have been confronted by administrative corruption that perhaps was not organized or deliberate but is deemed a gross negligence and disregard of investment rules, the evidence of which is clear.[17]

In respect of the arbitration, the tribunal commented adversely on more than one occasion on aspects of the respondent's submission, counterarguments, and poor or even nil responses to expert evidence.[18] In its concluding remarks, the tribunal stated:

> The Arbitral Tribunal hopes that this arbitration will serve as an incentive to government agencies in charge of following—up governmental investment projects in the Arab countries to support the completion of investment projects successfully and without any obstacles, in the best interest of all Arabs, and to prevent "the collapse of the Arab investment for generations to come".[19]

The tribunal awarded the claimants the equivalent of USD937 million, which included components for direct damages, moral damages, lost profits over the remainder of the term of the lease, arbitration costs and expenses, plus interest from the date of the award. The moral damages and lost profits, comprising the equivalent of USD30 million and USD900 million respectively, were both significant in their quantum and very rare in GCC-related arbitration cases.

Following the arbitral award, Libya lodged an annulment action before the Egyptian courts, being the seat of the tribunal arbitration. In February 2014, the Cairo Court of Appeal rejected the appeal on the grounds that Annex Article 2(8) of the *Arab Investment Agreement* stipulated that decisions of an arbitral panel were to be final and binding and that no appeal may be made against arbitration decisions. On appeal to the Court of Cassation, the Court vacated that judgment. While acknowledging the status of the Agreement's conditions on non-appeal, it considered that Egypt's Arbitration Law No. 27 of 1994 permitted review on

16 '*Kharafi v Libya*' (n 14), *(Final Award)* [14–15].
17 Ibid [287].
18 Ibid [253–4], [357], [368–9].
19 Ibid [382].

grounds of procedural integrity, as distinct from review of facts and merits, and referred the case back to the Court of Appeal.

At its second hearing the Court of Appeal again rejected the appeal on the procedural grounds that it lacked jurisdiction over arbitration awards issued under the Agreement. On further appeal, the Court of Cassation held that the lower court had erred in declining jurisdiction and that explicit jurisdiction to hear annulment actions against international arbitration awards existed under the Egyptian Arbitration law as the umbrella over all arbitrations seated in Egypt, and directed it to decide the case on its merits.

Finally, at its third hearing in June 2020, the Court annulled the arbitration award on the basis of a serious mistake of law leading to a failure to observe the rules of public policy, the notions of equity and justice, and particularly the method of calculating the damages.[20] The Court disagreed with the tribunal's method of calculating damages, considering the USD930 million compensation awarded as being "excessively unjust" and "abusive", while noting that the claimant had invested only around USD5 million. It also rejected the tribunal's assessment that the "lost profits [were] resulting from real and certain loss opportunities".[21] The Court observed that the reports on which the calculation of damages were based lacked credibility, being based solely on data and information provided by the claimant which were not independently verified and which were based on mere "abstract assumptions" and "hypothetical speculations" that lacked factual support.[22]

The Court concluded that its ability to review an arbitral award remains very limited although it may review it when the award violates the main principles of international public policy rules such as the proportionality of damages, and when the arbitrators exceed their powers with an award that is "irrational" and is a "manifest disregard of the law".[23]

Meanwhile, and since the tribunal award, the claimant has been endeavouring to have the award recognised and executed in France. In May 2013, the Paris Tribunal de Grande Instance issued a grant of exequatur which, following Libyan appeals, was upheld by both the Paris Court of Appeal and the Cour de Cassation.[24] In a

20 'Investment Treaty Policy and Dispute Settlement', in *Middle East and North Africa Investment Policy Perspectives*, OECD Publishing, Paris, <https://doi.org/10.1787/f78a2c1b-en.>, 99.

21 Ibid. See also Fatma Salah, 'Egypt Court Annuls Award against Libya on the Substantive Ground of Fundamental Error of Law', *Kluwer Arbitration Blog (*19 July 2020) at <https://arbitrationblog.kluwerarbitration.com/2020/07/19/egypt-court-annuls-award-against-libya-on-the-substantive-ground-of-fundamental-error-of-law/>.

22 Fatma Salah, 'Egypt Court Annuls Award against Libya on the Substantive Ground of Fundamental Error of Law', *Kluwer Arbitration Blog* (9 July 2020), at <https://arbitrationblog.kluwerarbitration.com/2020/07/19/egypt-court-annuls-award-against-libya-on-the-substantive-ground-of-fundamental-error-of-law/>.

23 OECD (2021) (n 20), 99.

24 Jarrod Hepburn and Luke Eric Peterson, 'As Al Kharafi Group Try to Collect Billion Dollar Libya Award, Battles Flare in Egypt, France, and before Arab Investment Court', *Investment Arbitration Reporter* (23 November 2014) at <https://www-iareporter-com.eu1.proxy.openathens.net/articles/as-al-kharafi-group-try-to-collect-billion-dollar-libya-award-battles-flare-in-egypt-france-and-before-arab-investment-court/>.

series of claims, appeals, and counter-appeals Al-Kharafi subsequently managed to obtain attachment over funds held by the Libyan Investment Authority in the French Bank Société Générale, on the grounds that the Authority was a State entity.[25] While initially successful in the French courts in achieving the attachments, recent decisions have followed a ruling of the European Court of Justice that Libyan funds frozen under EU sanctions against the Libyan regime could not be attached without prior authorisation from the relevant domestic authorities.[26] In February 2022, the Paris Court of Appeal lifted the prior attachments which was confirmed by the Cour de Cassation in September 2022. In a judgment dated 2 February 2023, the Paris Court of Appeal has rejected the claimants' latest efforts to reinstate the attachments of the LIA's funds with Société Générale.[27]

5.5 The Sultanate of Oman

UNCTAD reports only two ISDS cases appearing from Omani investors. The first case, *Desert Line v Yemen*, brought by Desert Line LLC in 2005, was reportedly the first ISDS case brought by an investor from any GCC member State which relied upon a BIT or other IIA (as distinct from the *OIC Agreement* or the *Arab Investment Agreement*) as the basis of claim.[28] The second case, *SGRF v Bulgaria*,[29] was withdrawn by the Omani claimant before the merits stage.

25 Damien Charlotin, 'An Update on the $1 Billion Kharafi v. Libya Award', *Investment Arbitration Reporter* (4 October 2019) at <https://www-iareporter-com.eu1.proxy.openathens.net/articles/an-update-on-the-1-billion-kharafi-v-libya-award/>.

26 Damien Charlotin, 'Libya Round-Up: An Update on Arbitration Cases against the State', *Investment Arbitration Reporter* (26 April 2022) at <https://www-iareporter-com.eu1.proxy.openathens.net/articles/libya-round-up-an-update-on-arbitration-cases-against-the-state/#topic-shortcode-S22176>.

27 Damien Charlotin, 'Paris Appeal Court Confirms Lifting of Attachments against Sanctioned Libyan Entities in Battle for Enforcement of Treaty Award', *Investment Arbitration Reporter* (9 February 2023) at <https://www-iareporter-com.eu]1.proxy.openathens.net/articles/french-supreme-court-confirms-lifting-of-attachments-against-sanctioned-libyan-entities-in-battle-for-enforcement-of-treaty-award/>.

28 *Desert Line v. Yemen* (n 2).

29 *State General Reserve Fund of the Sultanate of Oman v Republic of Bulgaria* (ICSID Case No. ARB/15/43, 22 October 2015) *('SGRF v Bulgaria')*.

Table 5.3 Oman as Home State of Investor

No.	*Year Initiated*	*Short Case Name*	*Summary*	*Outcome of Original Proceedings*
1	2015	SGRF v Bulgaria ICSID case no. ARB/15/43	Investment: shareholding in Corporate Commercial Bank (Corpbank), the fourth largest bank Bulgaria. Claims arising from losses by claimant following Government revocation of Corpbank's licence and its bankruptcy. Proceeded under *Oman–Bulgaria BIT* (2007).	Decided in favour of the State
2	2005	Desert Line Projects v Yemen ICSID case no. ARB/05/17	Investment: rights under several contracts with Yemen Government for sealed road construction. Claims arising from disagreements over payments for executed works under several contracts with Yemen Government which led to the suspension of works, arbitration claims before Yemen Commercial Court, arrest of personnel, and the signing of a settlement agreement under duress. Proceeded under *Oman–Yemen BIT* (1998).	Decided in favour of the claimant

Source: compiled by the authors primarily from UNCTAD, Investment Policy Hub <Advanced Search | Investment Dispute Settlement Navigator | UNCTAD Investment Policy Hub>, and Investment Arbitration Reporter, <https://www-iareporter-com.eu1.proxy.openathens.net/>.

The *Desert Line v Yemen* dispute proceeded under ICSID Rules, relying upon on the *Oman–Yemen BIT* (1998)[30] and seeking the equivalent of approximately USD250 million in damages. Included in that sum was a claim for approximately USD100 million in moral damages. The claim involved disagreements over amounts owed for executed works under several road construction contracts concluded between the claimant, Omani construction company Desert Line, and the Government of Yemen, which led to the suspension of works, arbitration proceedings before the Yemeni Commercial Court, the arrest of personnel, and the subsequent forced signing of a settlement agreement under alleged duress.

30 *Agreement for the Reciprocal Promotion and Protection of Investments between the Government of the Sultanate of Oman and the Government of the Republic of Yemen,* signed 20 September 1998, (entered into force 1 April 2000).

The tribunal rendered its determination in just two years after the establishment of the tribunal – a rapid determination in ISDS cases – awarding Desert Line around USD19 million plus $400,000 for its legal costs against the respondent and just 30% of tribunal costs. In arriving at its determination, the tribunal noted that:

> Considering all circumstances of this case, including in particular that the Respondent breached the BIT; that it unsuccessfully challenged jurisdiction; that it insufficiently cooperated in providing documents and testimonial evidence; that not all Claimant's claims were granted; the Arbitral Tribunal deems it fair and reasonable that the cost burden be shared between the Parties as follows.[31]

In respect of the (rarely successful) claim for moral damages the tribunal's judgment is enlightening. It held that it had authority to award moral damages in "exceptional and specific circumstances". It found that the specific circumstances of this case warranted moral damages, since Yemen had acted maliciously, in particular by exerting duress upon the claimant's executives:

> the violation of the BIT by the Respondent, in particular the physical duress exerted on the executives of the Claimant, was malicious and is therefore constitutive of a fault-based liability. Therefore, the Respondent shall be liable to reparation for the injury suffered by the Claimant, whether it be bodily, moral or material in nature … Nevertheless, the amount asked by the Claimant [OMR40 million] is exaggerated and cannot be allocated in its entirety. The Arbitral Tribunal considers that, based on the information at hand and the general principles, an amount of USD 1,000,000 should be granted for moral damages, including loss of reputation. This amount is indeed more than symbolic yet modest in proportion to the vastness of the project.[32]

The case of *State General Reserve Fund (SGRF) of Oman v Bulgaria* proceeded under ICSID rules and relied on the *Oman–Bulgaria BIT* (2007).[33] In October 2015, the SGRF, Oman's largest sovereign wealth fund, lodged an arbitration claim with ICSID against Bulgaria, in respect of the collapse of Bulgaria's Corporate Commercial Bank (Corpbank). The SGRF owned a 30% stake in Corpbank, Bulgaria's fourth largest lender, before the Bulgarian National Bank (BNB) took control of Corpbank, triggering the country's worst financial crisis since the 1990s.[34]

31 *Desert Line v Yemen* (n 2), *Final Award,* 6 February 2008, [304].

32 Ibid [290]

33 *Agreement between the Government of the Sultanate of Oman and the Government of the Republic of Bulgaria on the Promotion and Reciprocal Protection of Investments*, signed 3 February 2007 (entered into force 22 October 2014).

34 See Tsvetelia Tsolova, 'Oman Fund Set to Seek Ruling against Bulgaria over Bank Collapse-Source', *Reuters* (23 July 2015) at <https://www.reuters.com/article/bulgaria-oman-banking-idusl5n1013in20150722>.

The SGRF claimed EUR80 million in compensation for an alleged violation by Bulgaria of the standards for treatment of foreign investors through the actions taken by the Bulgarian Government, the BNB, and the Bulgarian courts, whereby Corpbank was placed under administration and delicensed in 2014. The SGRF alleged that the BNB and courts had prevented it from implementing rescue measures in respect of its investment and thus breached several investment protection standards.

In December 2018, the SGRF declared that it was withdrawing its claims, the reasons for the withdrawal remaining undisclosed, before the hearing of the case on the merits. In an award issued on 13 August 2019, the Tribunal recorded the claims as "withdrawn with prejudice", dismissed the totality of SGRF's claims, and awarded Bulgaria its legal fees and costs in the arbitration.[35] The tribunal also noted that:

> in the present case the Tribunal, as was noted above, does not suppose that either Party acted in bad faith at any stage of the proceedings. The very late decision of Claimant to withdraw its claims with prejudice is certainly a salient feature of the proceedings; but the Tribunal considers that the timing of this decision is of less importance than the fact of the withdrawal of the claim.[36]

5.6 The State of Qatar

UNCTAD reports nine ISDS cases lodged by investors claiming Qatari citizenship, the first being less than a decade ago. This first case, *Alyafei v Jordan*, was bifurcated into two cases (I) and (II), with both initiated in 2015. The most recent case appears to be *Qatar National Bank v South Sudan and the South Sudan Bank*, lodged in 2020.

The remaining seven Qatari investment cases in Table 5.4 are all related to the suspension of diplomatic relations between Egypt, Bahrain, Saudi Arabia, the UAE, and Qatar (namely the four Qatar Airways, Qatar Pharma, beIN, and Al Jazeera), most of which were registered during 2020. Hence all these cases are listed as "Pending". These cases are discussed collectively at greater length as case studies in Chapter 6 as part of the separate analysis of intra-GCC cases.

The UNCTAD database does not include the case of *Qatar National Bank (QPSC) v Republic of South Sudan and Bank of South Sudan*, which appears in ICSID and is commented upon in the arbitration media.[37] Details are scant, but it appears that the dispute centres around a plan by the South Sudan Bank as the

35 *SGRF v Bulgaria* (n 29), *AWARD*, 13 August 2019 [83].

36 Ibid [73].

37 Vladislav Djanic, 'Banking Dispute Leads to South Sudan's Second Ever ICSID Arbitration', *Investment Arbitration Reporter* (9 October 2020) at <https://www-iareporter-com.eu1.proxy.openathens.net/articles/banking-dispute-leads-to-south-sudans-second-ever-icsid-arbitration/>.

country's central bank to ban the use of foreign currency nationally in a bid to curtail depreciation of the South Sudanese currency following the exhaustion of its foreign currency reserves. This determination would severely impact QPSC's business in South Sudan, having been the first foreign bank to open a branch in the country and now having an established presence. The dispute, although proceeding as an ISDS case under ICSID Arbitration Rules, is stated as being only contract-based and thus has not been included in Table 5.4.[38]

Table 5.4 Qatar as Home State of Investor

No.	*Year Initiated*	*Short Case Name*	*Summary*	*Outcome of Original Proceedings*
1	2020	Qatar Airways v Bahrain	Investment: licences and permits to conduct air transport activities. Claims arising from Government actions blocking Qatar Airways operations in the country, including closure of airspace and revocation of operating licences. Proceeding under *OIC Agreement* (1981) and *Arab Investment Agreement* (1980).	Pending
2	2020	Qatar Airways v Egypt	Investment: licences and permits to conduct air transport activities. Claims arising from Government actions blocking Qatar Airways operations in the country, including closure of airspace and revocation of operating licences. Proceeding under *OIC Agreement* (1981) and *Arab Investment Agreement* (1980).	Pending
3	2020	Qatar Airways v Saudi Arabia	Investment: licences and permits to conduct air transport activities. Claims arising from Government actions blocking Qatar Airways operations in the country, including closure of airspace and revocation of operating licences. Proceeding under *OIC Agreement* (1981) *and Arab Investment Agreement* (1980).	Pending

(*Continued*)

38 *Qatar National Bank (Q.P.S.C.) v. Republic of South Sudan and Bank of South Sudan* (ICSID Case No. ARB/20/40), Proceedings ('*Qatar National Bank v South Sudan*') at < https://icsid.worldbank.org/cases/case-database/case-detail?CaseNo=ARB/20/40>.

Table 5.4 (*Continued*)

No.	*Year Initiated*	*Short Case Name*	*Summary*	*Outcome of Original Proceedings*
4	2020	Qatar Airways v United Arab Emirates	Investment: licences and permits to conduct air transport activities. Claims arising from Government actions blocking Qatar Airways operations in the country, including closure of airspace and revocation of operating licences. Proceeding under *OIC Agreement* (1981) and *Arab Investment Agreement* (1980).	Pending
5	2019	Qatar Pharma and Al Sulaiti v Saudi Arabia	Investment: investments in two locally incorporated pharmaceutical companies and three warehouses in Riyadh, Jeddah, and Dammam. Claims arising from repudiation of long-term sales contracts with Saudi Ministry of Health after Saudi Arabia suspended diplomatic relations with Qatar in 2017. Ministry's measures included failure to pay for supplied products contracts and forced closure of warehouses. Proceeding under *OIC Agreement* (1981).	Pending
6	2018	beIN v. Saudi Arabia	Investment: broadcasting licence for pay TV in Saudi Arabia and ownership of local subsidiary, Al Oula Al Raeda Trading, for retail operations. Claims arising from Government measures to stop the claimant's broadcasting after Saudi Arabia suspended diplomatic relations with Qatar in 2017. Included non-renewal of claimant's pay TV broadcasting licence and the denial of licences required by the claimant's subsidiary. Proceeding under *OIC Agreement* (1981).	Pending

(*Continued*)

Table 5.4 (*Continued*)

No.	*Year Initiated*	*Short Case Name*	*Summary*	*Outcome of Original Proceedings*
7	2016	Al Jazeera v Egypt ICSID case no. ARB/16/1	Investment: investments in multimedia broadcasting operations. Claims arising from destruction of claimant's Egypt media business, by arrest and detention of employees, attacks on facilities, interference with transmissions and broadcasts, office closures, cancellation of broadcasting licence, and compulsory liquidation of local branch. Proceeding under *Egypt–Qatar BIT* (1999).	Pending
8	2015	Alyafei v Jordan (II)	Investment: shareholding in the Amman-based Housing Bank of Trade and Finance. Claims arising from breach of 2012 share purchase agreement with Jordan Social Security and Investment Fund for fund's shares in Housing Bank of Trade and Finance; in particular alleged non-payment of Agreement's "break-up fee". Proceeded under *Italy–Jordan BIT* (1996) and *Arab Investment Agreement* (1980).	Discontinued
9	2015	Alyafei v Jordan (I) ICSID case no. ARB/15/24	Investment: shareholding in the Amman-based Housing Bank of Trade and Finance. Claims arising from breach of 2012 share purchase agreement with Jordan Social Security and Investment Fund for fund's shares in Housing Bank of Trade and Finance; in particular alleged non-payment of Agreement's "break-up fee". Proceeded under *OIC Agreement* (1981).	Discontinued pursuant to ICSID Rule 14(3)(d)

Source: compiled by the authors primarily from UNCTAD, *Investment Policy Hub* <Advanced Search \| Investment Dispute Settlement Navigator \| UNCTAD Investment Policy Hub> and *Investment Arbitration Reporter*, <https://www-iareporter-com.eu1.proxy.openathens.net/>.

Qatari national Ali Alyafei, as the claimant in *Alyafei v. Jordan (I)*, alleges that Jordan violated the terms of a share purchase agreement by not paying a contractually agreed "break-up fee" following his failure to acquire an interest in a Jordanian bank. He initially submitted an ICSID arbitration seeking USD500 million in damages and invoking both the *Arab Investment Agreement* and the *Italy–Jordan BIT* (1996). Jordan, the respondent in the case, is a signatory to both arbitration Agreements. By initially proceeding under both treaties, the claimant reportedly was seeking to enhance the possibility of a more favourable outcome by importing into the *Arab Investment Agreement* (referred to below as the "Unified Agreement") the dispute settlement provision from the BIT by relying on the most-favoured-nation (MFN) clause in the BIT. The *Investment Arbitration Reporter* states that it has confirmed that "Mr Alyafei is relying on the most favoured nation clause in the Unified Agreement – Article 6(2) – in a bid to import the dispute resolution clause of the Italy–Jordan BIT, which allows for ICSID arbitration".[39] Both claimant and respondent appointed arbitrators, but the proceedings and thus the case were discontinued by the tribunal on 11 July 2016 "for lack of payment of the required advances, pursuant to ICSID Administrative and Financial Regulation 14(3)(d)".[40]

The claimant meanwhile initiated a new arbitration, namely, *Alyafei v. Jordan (II)* under the *OIC Agreement* and ad-hoc auspices.[41] However, the case was ultimately dismissed by the tribunal in late 2016 when the claimant failed to submit its memorial according to the timeline agreed by the tribunal.[42]

5.7 The Kingdom of Saudi Arabia

The four ISDS cases listed in Table 5.5, derived from UNCTAD, raise interest for a number of reasons. Firstly, it may appear somewhat surprising that only four cases appear in the usual databases of Saudi investors seeking redress for alleged wrongful actions of respondent states through the main international third-party ISDS avenues, particularly when one considers the status and impact of Saudi participation and investment activity in the contemporary global economy and trade arenas. It also appears surprising when compared with the number of ISDS cases listed,

39 Joel Dahlquist, 'Qatari Businessman Contends that MFN Clause in Regional Treaty Can Provide Foothold for an ICSID Claim against Jordan', *Investment Arbitration Reporter* (15 June 2015) at <https://www-iareporter-com.eu1.proxy.openathens.net/articles/qatari-businessman-contends-that-mfn-clause-in-regional-treaty-can-provide-foothold-for-an-icsid-claim-against-jordan/>.

40 *Ali Alyafei v. Hashemite Kingdom of Jordan* (ICSID case no. ARB/15/24, 11 June 2015), ('*Alyafei v. Jordan (I)*') at <https://icsid.worldbank.org/cases/case-database/case-detail?CaseNo=ARB/15/24>.

41 See Jarrod Hepburn and Luke Eric Peterson, 'Investigation: As New Cases Emerge under Islamic Investment Treaty, Initial Viability of Claims Seems to Hinge on Willingness of Respondents to Appoint Arbitrators', *Investment Arbitration Reporter* (2 March 2017) at <https://www-iareporter-com.eu1.proxy.openathens.net/articles/investigation-as-new-cases-emerge-under-islamic-investment-treaty-initial-viability-of-claims-seems-to-hinge-on-willingness-of-respondents-to-appoint-arbitrators/>.

42 Ibid.

namely ten, with the Kingdom as a respondent State, although much care needs to be taken in necessarily trying to draw a nexus between the two situations.

Putting aside for one moment the contract-based case of *Ghaith Pharaon v Tunisia* of 1986, all four cases have arisen both fairly recently and within the rather short time frame of between 2011 and 2018. All have relied on the *OIC Agreement* as the basis of the claim, with details of the administering institutions yet to be made public in two instances and the PCA listed for the remaining two cases. Three of the cases are recorded as still pending with just one, namely *Al Warraq v Indonesia*, decided in favour of neither party.

The *Ghaith Pharaon v Tunisia case* was lodged on 24 September 1986.[43] The investment concerned related to the construction of tourism and holiday resort developments, with the claim relying on violations of contract law and Tunisia's investment law of 1969. The claim was discontinued on 21 November 1988 pursuant to ICSID Arbitration Rule 43(1).

Table 5.5 Saudi Arabia as Home State of Investor

No.	*Year Initiated*	*Short Case Name*	*Summary*	*Outcome of Original Proceedings*
1	2018	Al Mehdar v Egypt (4)	Investment: Appears to be investment in Egypt's hotel and tourism sector, but further details are not available. Claims appear to relate to cancelled tourism projects, but no further details available. Proceeding under *OIC Agreement* (1981).	Pending
2	2018	Al-Tuwairqi v Pakistan[a] PCA case 2018-34	Investment: joint venture investment in steel manufacturing plant in Bin Qasim, Karachi, constructed and operated by local subsidiary, Tuwairqi Steel Mills. Proceeding under *OIC Agreement* (1981). Claims relating to pricing for gas required for the steel manufacturing process and to provide general electricity flow for the facility. Proceeding under *OIC Agreement* (1981).	Pending

(*Continued*)

43 *Pharaon v. Tunisia* (n 3).

Table 5.5 *(Continued)*

No.	*Year Initiated*	*Short Case Name*	*Summary*	*Outcome of Original Proceedings*
3	2017	Bin Sulaiman v Oman[b] PCA case 2017-32	Investment: related to Omani construction sector, but further details unknown. Basis for claims unknown. Proceeding under *OIC Agreement* (1981).	Pending
4	2011	Al Warraq v Indonesia	Investment: indirect ownership of capital in Bank Century through wholly owned company First Gulf Asia Holdings and claimant's personal shareholding via ABN Amro. Claims arising from Government bailout of a bank in which claimant had invested, followed by criminal investigations and subsequent prosecution of the claimant for fraudulent activities in the Indonesian financial sector. Proceeding under *OIC Agreement* (1981).	Decided in favour of neither party (liability found but no damages awarded)

Source: compiled by the authors primarily from UNCTAD, *Investment Policy Hub* <Advanced Search | Investment Dispute Settlement Navigator | UNCTAD Investment Policy Hub>, and *Investment Arbitration Reporter*, <https://www-iareporter-com.eu1.proxy.openathens.net/>.

[a]*Hilal Hussain Al-Tuwairqi and Al-Tuwairqi Holding v. Pakistan.*

[b]*Omar Bin Sulaiman Abdul Aziz Al Rajhi v. The Sultanate of Oman* (PCA Case No. 2017-32) *('Bin Sulaiman v Oman').*

Hashem Al Mehdar v Arab Republic of Egypt, lodged in 2018, is reportedly associated with three seemingly related claims lodged by the claimant in 2014. The claims were in relation to investments in Egypt's hotel and tourism sector. Egypt as respondent in each case reportedly refused to appoint arbitrators on the grounds that the treaty invoked by the claimants, the *OIC Agreement*, does not express the state's consent to arbitration, and the treaty-designated appointing authority (the OIC Secretary-General) was silent despite requests to make default arbitrator appointments.[44] The disputes appear to involve the cancellation of tourism pro-

44 Joel Dahlquist and Luke Eric Peterson, 'Investigation: Four Previously-Confidential Claims under the *OIC Agreement* Are Uncovered, as Controversy Continues over Treaty's Use in Arbitration', *Investment Arbitration Reporter* (16 May 2019) at <https://www-iareporter-com.eu1.proxy.openathens.net/articles/investigation-4-previously-confidential-claims-under-oic-investment-agreement-are-uncovered-as-controversy-continues-over-treatys-use-in-arbitration/>.

jects, and the earlier disputes were reportedly settled in 2017 only to the extent of enabling the claimant to restart the projects in return for abandoning the arbitrations.[45] However, according to UNCTAD, it appears that arbitrators have since been appointed for this latest arbitration.

The case of *Al Warraq v Indonesia* has been raised elsewhere on more than one occasion throughout this study, as a leading case in respect a range of issues in ISDS-based arbitrations, including non-appointment of arbitrators, "clean hands", the interpretation and application of the *OIC Agreement*, including s 17 (consent to arbitrate), and perhaps most significantly, the scope and operation of the MFN clause contained within Article 8. The decision of the arbitral tribunal in *Al-Warraq v Indonesia* is particularly significant because it was the first treaty-based dispute submitted to arbitration which applied the *OIC Agreement* and the *UNCITRAL Arbitration Rules (1976)*, and because of the relatively permissive approach adopted by the tribunal. But in another and subsequent leading arbitration, namely *Itisaluna Iraq and Others v Republic of Iraq, the tribunal* departed from *Al-Warraq v Indonesia* on some key issues and interpretations of the *OIC Agreement*.

5.8 The United Arab Emirates

As is the case with the other GCC member States (with the exception of Oman's isolated case in 2005), the experience of UAE investors in ISDS arbitration has really only developed over a period of 15 years or less, with the first claim made in 2009 against Yemen. UNCTAD records 13 ISDS cases relying on a BIT or other IIA that have been raised by UAE investors – the most by a margin of almost 50% to the next prolific GCC member States (Kuwait and Qatar with 9 claims each). The first UAE claim, *MTN v Yemen*, arose in 2009 in the telecommunications sector. Four of the claims relied on the *OIC Agreement* as the basis of the claim, but the majority of cases, including those against six other MENA countries, relied on prevailing BITs.

Only one case, namely *DP World v Belgium*, appears to have been decided in favour of the investor, DP World being a major maritime ports and container terminal operator with global reach. Both UNCTAD and ICSID record the case as still pending. However, ICSID records that the tribunal issued a decision on jurisdiction and liability in April 2021 and has since been considering the issues of *quantum* and costs,[46] indicating that at least one claim has been accepted by the tribunal.

DP World has also been engaged in a decade-long running arbitrational and legal battle with the Djibouti Government over the ownership and control of the Doraleh Container Terminal in Djibouti, reputed to be the largest in Africa. At the centre of the dispute is the Government's attempt to gain full control of the Terminal by rescinding DP World's rights in breach of the original build-operate

45 Ibid.

46 *DP World Limited v. Kingdom of Belgium (ICSID Case No. ARB/17/21) Procedural Details,* 23 June 2023 *('DP World v Belgium')* at <https://icsid.worldbank.org/cases/case-database/case-detail?CaseNo=ARB/17/21>.

Concession Agreement. As the dispute appears to be primarily over contract issues rather than IIA issues, it is not included in Table 5.6.[47]

The most common outcome for UAE investors across all the cases listed in Table 5.6 has been declining jurisdiction by a tribunal (four instances), followed by settlement under ICSID Rule 43 or Rule 44.

Table 5.6 UAE as Home State of Investor

No.	*Year Initiated*	*Short Case Name*	*Summary*	*Outcome of Original Proceedings*
1	2019	CTIP Oil & Gas v Egypt ICSID case no. ARB/19/27	Investment: rights under a gas pipeline construction and operation agreement. Claims arising from a gas pipeline construction and operation agreement. Proceeded under *Egypt–UAE BIT* (1997).	Pending
2	2019	Trasta v Libya PCA case no. 2020-09	Investment: joint venture to operate an oil refinery in Ras Lanuf, with Libya's National Oil Corporation (NOC). Claims arising from Government's failure to protect claimant's oil refinery investment during Libyan civil war from 2011, including acts and omissions by joint venture partner NOC. Oil refinery damaged due to occupation and misuse, ceasing operation in 2013. Proceeding under *OIC Agreement* (1981).	Pending
3	2018	Alcor v Czech Republic PCA case no. 2018-45	Investment: acquisition of land plots upon which City of Prague maintained public roads and utilities. Claims arising from refusal of City of Prague to conclude lease agreements for the lands on grounds that claimant no longer owned the land. Proceeded under *Czech Republic–UAE BIT* (1994).	Decided in favour of the State (jurisdiction declined)

(*Continued*)

47 Current arbitration is at the London Court of International Arbitration before a single arbitrator. *Republic of Djibouti, Port de Djibouti SA and Djibouti Ports and Free Zone Authority v. Doraleh Container Terminal (DCT), DP World Djibouti FZCO and Dubai (International) Djibouti FZE*, LCIA Case No. 142732 (*'Djibouti v DP World'*).

Table 5.6 (Continued)

No.	*Year Initiated*	*Short Case Name*	*Summary*	*Outcome of Original Proceedings*
4	2018	Borkowski and Rasia FZE v Armenia ICSID case no. ARB/18/28	Investment: concessions to construct and operate railway and highway routes in Southern Armenia. Claims arising from Government's breach of concession contracts by using other companies to implement infrastructure projects. Proceeding under *Armenia–United states BIT* (1992).	Decided in favour of the State (under annulment proceedings)
5	2018	Navodaya v Gabon PCA Case no. 2018-23	Investment: rights under manganese exploration permit as part of joint venture with state-owned Société Equatoriale des Mines mining company. Claims arising from Government's expropriation of claimant's mining concession for a manganese deposit in Okondja, eastern Gabon. Proceeded under *OIC Agreement* (1981).	Decided in favour of the State
6	2017	DP World v Belgium ICSID case no. ARB/17/21	Investment: indirect shareholding of 60% in the Antwerp Gateway container terminal at the Port of Antwerp, through a local subsidiary. Claims arising from Government reallocation of territory within subsidiary's port concession agreement, for use by another operator. Proceeded under *BLEU–UAE BIT* (2004).	Pending (seems decided in favour of the claimant)
7	2017	Itisaluna Iraq and others v Iraq ICSID case no. ARB17/10	Investment: licence for provision of telecoms services. Claims arising from Government's alleged impairment of claimants' rights under a telecommunications licence and subsequent non-renewal of the licence. Proceeded under *OIC Agreement* (1981).	Decided in favour of the State (jurisdiction declined)

(Continued)

Table 5.6 (Continued)

No.	*Year Initiated*	*Short Case Name*	*Summary*	*Outcome of Original Proceedings*
8	2017	D.S. Construction v Libya PCA case no. 2017-21	Investment: contracts for 19 construction projects in Libya. Claims arising from State's acts and omissions prior to, during, and after the Libyan revolution which allegedly caused damaged to the claimant's investment. Proceeding under *OIC Agreement* (1981).	Pending
9	2016	Ras Al Khaimah Investment Authority v India ad hoc	Investment: shareholding in ANRAK Aluminium, an Indian company, to establish and operate an alumina refinery and smelter in Andhra Pradesh in South India. Claims arising out of non-fulfillment and subsequent cancellation of 2007 MOU between Andhra Pradesh and claimant, in which State government agreed to direct a state-owned mining company to supply bauxite to ANRAK, for the operation of the refinery and smelter. Proceeded under *India–UAE BIT* (2010).	Decided in favour of the State (jurisdiction declined)
10	2016	Strategic Infrasol and Thakur Family Trust v India ad hoc	Investment: investments in two real estate projects in Mumbai. Claims arising from Government non-investigation of alleged forgery and criminal actions by claimant's Indian co-developer construction company of the Mumbai projects and forged documents to acquire control of the projects; and for Government seizure and confiscation of claimant funds pursuant to a court order against the claimants for money laundering. Proceeded under *India–UAE BIT* (2010).	Data not available

(Continued)

Table 5.6 (Continued)

No.	*Year Initiated*	*Short Case Name*	*Summary*	*Outcome of Original Proceedings*
11	2011	National Gas v Egypt ICSID case no. ARB/11/7	Investment: concession agreement between claimant and Egypt's national oil company on gas pipelines construction and operation. Claims arising from Cairo Court decision to set aside arbitration award against state-owned oil company on basis that the concession agreement arbitration clause had not been approved as required by Egyptian law. Proceeded under *Egypt–UAE BIT* (1997).	Decided in favour of the State (jurisdiction declined)
12	2011	Sajwani v. Egypt[a] ICSID case no. ARB/11/16	Investment: ownership of 30 square km of land near the Red Sea for property development project. Claims arising from Government's conviction of claimant on grounds of corruption over acquisition of land in Gamsha Bay for development of a residential complex. Proceeded under *Egypt–UAE BIT* (1997).	Settled pursuant to ICSID Rule 44
13	2009	MTN v. Yemen ICSID case no. ARB/09/07	Investment: operation of a mobile phone (GSM) network. Claims arising from Government discriminatory conduct in favour of state-controlled mobile phone operator Yemen Mobile and refusal to grant agreed exemptions on taxes and customs duties on imported equipment for the operation of the network. Proceeded under *UAE–Yemen BIT* (2001).	Settled pursuant to ICSID Rule 43(2)

Source: compiled by the authors primarily from UNCTAD, *Investment Policy Hub* <Advanced Search \| Investment Dispute Settlement Navigator \| UNCTAD Investment Policy Hub>, and *Investment Arbitration Reporter*, <https://www-iareporter-com.eu1.proxy.openathens.net/>.

[a]*Hussain Sajwani, Damac Park Avenue for Real Estate Development S.A.E., and Damac Gamsha Bay for Development S.A.E. v. Arab Republic of Egypt* (ICSID Case No. ARB/11/16) *('Sajwani v Egypt')*.

The status of *CTIP Oil & Gas v Egypt*, brought under the *Egypt–UAE BIT (*1997), is recorded by UNCTAD as pending, although as recently as June 2023 the tribunal was considering submissions from the parties on costs. CTIP's Egyptian subsidiary previously brought a claim under the Egypt–UAE BIT but reportedly failed because the claimant was unsuccessful in making out that the subsidiary was effectively under "foreign control" over the project in order to invoke the BIT, and the tribunal declined jurisdiction.[48]

In 2019 Trasta Energy Ltd (Trasta), a subsidiary of Emirati Al Ghurair group, lodged an arbitration with the PCA against Libya over the operation of the Ra's Lanuf oil refinery on the Libyan coast, relying on the *OIC Agreement.* Trasta had entered into a joint venture agreement with Libya's National Oil Corporation (NOC) to form the Libyan Emirates Oil Refining Company (LERCO) to operate the refinery.[49] The refinery had been closed for several years following various disputes between the joint venture partners, damage suffered during the Libyan civil war, and supply issues following the war and closure.[50] A tribunal was finalised for the Trasta arbitration claim in August 2020 but was reconstituted in March 2021. The arbitral phase is reportedly still pending.[51]

The ISDS arbitration claim follows a series of commercial arbitrations by Trasta and by LERCO against NOC. Trasta lodged two claims before the ICC and one before the PCA alleging breaches of its LERCO shareholder agreement with NOC.[52] LERCO also lodged claims before the ICC alleging that NOC had

48 *CTIP Oil & Gas International Limited v. Arab Republic of Egypt* (ICSID Case No. ARB/19/27) *Award,* 17 September 2019 ('*CTP Oil and Gas v Egypt*'). See also Lisa Bohmer, 'Egypt Round-up: A Bifurcation Decision, a Provisional Measures Request, and New Legislation on Arbitration Awards and Agreements', *Investment Arbitration Reporter* (25 August 2021) at <Egypt Round-Up: A bifurcation decision, a provisional measures request, and new legislation on arbitration awards and agreements | Investment Arbitration Reporter (openathens.net)>.

49 Mohamed Karbal, 'Libya: Oil and Gas Disputes: The Libyan Experience', *Mondaq* (31 March 2021) at <Oil & Gas Disputes: The Libyan Experience - Oil, Gas & Electricity - Libya (mondaq.com)>.

50 North Africa Post, 'NOC wins appeal against LERCO over Ras Lanuf Refiner dispute' (1 March 2021); and Damien Charlotin, '[Corrected] French Court Annuls Finding of Lack of Jurisdiction over Civil War Claims, but Upholds Remainder of Commercial Award in Favour of Libya's National Oil Company, Libya and NOC Are Still Facing Trio of Arbitrations Arising from Same Dispute', *Investment Arbitration Reporter* (1 March 2021) at <[CORRECTED] French court annuls finding of lack of jurisdiction over civil war claims, but upholds remainder of commercial award in favour of Libya's National Oil Company; Libya and NOC are still facing trio of arbitrations arising from same dispute | Investment Arbitration Reporter (openathens.net)>.

51 'Arbitration Cases', *Investment Arbitration Reporter* (undated) at <Arbitration Cases | Investment Arbitration Reporter (openathens.net)>.

52 Namely, *Trasta v Libya National Oil Corporation (1)* (2013) (ICC Case No. 19814/MCP), *Trasta Energy Limited (United Arab Emirates) v The State of Libya* (2018) (PCA Case No. 2020-09), and *Trasta v Libya National Oil Corporation* (2) (2019) (ICC Case No. 24722/AYZ). The two ICC cases which alleged contractual breaches and the arbitral phases have reportedly concluded. See 'Analysis: Tribunal majority in Trasta v. NOC (2) sides with the respondent, holding that Libya's National Oil Corporation could validly force its partner to sell its shares in a local refinery', *Investment Arbitration Reporter* (undated) at <https://www-iareporter-com.eu1.proxy.openathens.net/articles/88312/>.

breached its agreement on the supply of crude oil to the refinery.[53] The ICC reportedly dismissed Trasta's claim in 2017 and LERCO's claim in 2018.[54] LERCO challenged the ICC's adverse finding in Paris, and the Paris Court of Appeal declined to annul most of the award.[55]

It has been suggested that, after failing to obtain satisfaction in the ICC cases, the claimant turned to arbitration under the *OIC Agreement* in 2019.[56]

The case of *Alcor Holdings v Czech Republic*, which commenced in 2018, dealt with the investment by the claimant in a project company seeking acquisition of land in the city of Prague with the intention of entering into a long-term lease-back arrangement, contrary to the City's zoning planning regulations. Accordingly, the City declined to approve the land acquisition which caused the claimant to dispose of its investment in the project company. However, on 2 March 2022, the tribunal found that the claimant did not own an investment at the time the proceedings were instituted.[57] The tribunal determined that the claimant, having sold all its interests in the project company through which the investment was made prior to the initiation of the arbitration proceedings, did not qualify as a protected investor under the terms of the *Czech–UAE BIT* (1994) on which the claim relied. Consequently, the tribunal reportedly declined jurisdiction and dismissed the case.

The status of *D.S Construction FZCO v Libya*, which commenced under the *OIC Agreement*, appears to be one of confusion and uncertainty. On 16 October 2016, D.S Construction lodged an application for arbitration with the PCA over claims arising out of Libya's acts and omissions prior to, during, and after the Libyan revolution, which allegedly caused damages to the claimant's investment in a number of construction projects throughout the country. The claimant sought approximately USD525 in damages. Libya originally declined to appoint an arbitrator, as did the OIC Secretary-General. Consequently, the PCA Secretary-General, at the request of the claimant, arranged for the appointment of an arbitrator, enabling a tribunal to be constituted and the arbitration to commence. In March 2021, Libya lodged an appeal against the PCA appointment and thus the validity of the tribunal in the Paris Court of Appeal. The Court found the PCA appointment to be invalid and that the tribunal was improperly constituted and therefore annulled the

53 Namely, *Lerco v Libya National Oil Corporation* (1) (2013) (ICC Case No. 17958/MCP), in which the annulment/set aside has reportedly concluded, and *Lerco v Libya National Oil Corporation* (2) (2019) ICC Case No. 24408/AYZ, in which the arbitral phase is reportedly pending.

54 Mohamed Karbal (n 49).

55 Damien Charlotin (n 50).

56 Ibid.

57 *Alcor Holdings Ltd v The Czech Republic (Award, 2 March 2022)* PCA Case No. 2018-45 at [255]–[283]; Damien Charlotin, 'Uncovered: UNCITRAL Tribunal Finds That Sale of Investment Two Years Prior to Lodging the Arbitration Deprived Claimant of Investor States; Reservation of Right to Bring Treaty Claim Is Deemed to Be Irrelevant', *Investment Arbitration Reporter* (22 March 2022) at <Uncovered: UNCITRAL tribunal finds that sale of investment two years prior to lodging the arbitration deprived claimant of investor status; reservation of right to bring treaty claim is deemed to be irrelevant | Investment Arbitration Reporter (openathens.net)>.

tribunal's preliminary award.[58] D.S Construction lodged an appeal on 20 August 2021 with the Cour de Cassation, but on 21 April 2022, it was formally noted by that Court that D.S Constructions had discontinued its appeal. The reasons for the discontinuation were not provided. Hence the status of D.S Construction's claim and whether further arbitration will emerge is uncertain. What is also uncertain is the impact of the Paris Court of Appeal's judgment on other current and future PCA arbitrator appointments, and on the preference for the *OIC Agreement* as the treaty of choice for future claims by investor/claimants from states that are signatories to the Agreement.

The case of *Strategic Infrasol and Thakur Family Trust v India* appears in the UNCTAD database as an ISDS claim under UNCITRAL Rules but is a curious one. Reportedly relying on the *India–United Arab Emirates BIT* (2013), a notice of intent to submit a claim to arbitration was first lodged on 8 October 2015 and again on 20 May 2016. The claim centred around a real estate development project in Mumbai, India, with a local developer, which had commenced in 1998. Conflicts between the project partners involved claims of alleged fraud, expropriation, forged documentation, bank account seizures, wrongly assessed tax liabilities, and failure of Indian authorities to properly investigate criminal activities involved.[59] India's brief response was to assert that the matter was a private dispute not directly involving government entities, that the BIT therefore did not apply, and that the complainants were merely "forum shopping". According to media reports at the time, the proceeding was to be seated in London and administered by the LCIA under UNCITRAL rules, with the claimants seeking damages in the vicinity of USD85 billion.[60] However, apart from a few exchanges of correspondence between the claimants and the Indian government in 2016 and 2017, it appears that very little if any formal action has been undertaken, for example moves by any party to nominate tribunal members, to progress the arbitration. In 2018, it was suggested that the claimants were seeking third-party funding to pursue the arbitration.[61]

UNCTAD simply records the status as "Data not available". Nevertheless, according to the claim, the dispute would appear to encompass a whole range ISDS issues, some already discussed in Chapter 3, including investor status, jurisdiction, FET, expropriation and "clean hands", and criminal activity.

58 Damien Charlotin (n 26).

59 See Jarrod Hepburn, 'Investors Exchange Arguments with India over UNCITRAL/BIT Real Estate Dispute', *Investment Arbitration Reporter* (2 April 2017) at <https://www-iareporter-com.eu1.proxy.openathens.net/articles/investors-exchange-arguments-with-india-over-uncitralbit-real-estate-dispute/>. See also Jarrod Hepburn, 'An Update on Investment Treaty Disputes Involving the Government of India', *Investment Arbitration Reporter* (23 April 2018) at <https://www-iareporter-com.eu1.proxy.openathens.net/articles/an-update-on-investment-treaty-disputes-involving-the-government-of-india/>.

60 Lacey Yong, 'India Faces $85billion Claim from UAE Investors', *Global Arbitration Review* (11 November 2015); Nauzer Barucha, 'UAE Firms Sue India, Desi Co for Rs 5 lakh cr over Mumbai Plots', *Times of India* (5 November 2015) in *bilaterals.com*, at <https://www.bilaterals.org/?uae-firms-sue-india-desi-co-for-rs>.

61 Jarrod Hepburn (n 59) (23 April 2018).

It is debatable whether the arbitration *Borkowski and Rasia FZE v Armenia* constitutes an ISDS IIA-based case or a straightforward contract-based case. However, since both UNCTAD and ICSID include it in their respective databases and because it provides insight into IIA standing, it is also included in Table 5.6. The case is recorded as relying on both the *United States–Armenia BIT* (1992)[62] and contract terms and proceeding under ICSID Arbitration Rules. While the UAE also has a BIT with Armenia, signed on 27 July 2016, it did not come into force until 27 November 2017 and therefore could not apply to this cause of action.[63] The claimants were Joseph Borkowski, a United States national who was also chairman and CEO of Rasia FZE, and Dubai-based Rasia FZE.

In 2012, the Armenian government awarded Rasia FZE, a Dubai-based investment company, valuable long-term concession agreements in respect of the development of a high-speed rail link and road links between southern Armenia and northern Iran on a public-private partnership basis. The agreements included feasibility studies, engineering designs, project financing, and construction, with strict stage completion provisions. Disputation between the parties and lodgement of the subsequent arbitration claim arose after the Armenian government allegedly breached the concession agreement granted to the claimants by turning to other companies for the implementation of the infrastructure projects.

The tribunal rendered its award on 20 January 2023. It found that, although the Armenian government had breached certain terms by the manner in which it had awarded certain contracts to third parties, Rasia FZE claims for breach of contract were time-barred because it had presented too late for them to be actionable under the statute of limitations reflected in the Armenian Civil Code.[64] The tribunal also found that Borkowski's umbrella clause claims under the *United States–Armenia BIT* were also time-barred. Further, it held that, in any case, Borkowski had no standing to assert such claims, since Armenia's obligations were not entered into with respect to him.[65] With respect to other BIT claims asserted, the tribunal found no conduct by Armenia that violated its obligations under the BIT with respect to American investors or their investments.[66]

The claimants lodged an application for annulment of the award on 2 June 2023. The ad hoc committee has been constituted and hearings on the application have commenced.[67]

62 *Treaty between the United States of America and the Republic of Armenia Concerning the Encouragement and Reciprocal Protection of Investment,* signed 23 September 1992 (entered into force 29 March 1996).

63 *Agreement between the Government of the Republic of Armenia and the Government of the United Arab Emirates for the Promotion and Reciprocal Protection of Investments,* signed 22 July 2016 (entered into force 21 November 2017).

64 *Joseph K. Borkowski and Rasia FZE v. Republic of Armenia* (ICSID Case No. ARB/18/28/0) *('Borkowski v Armenia'), Award,* 20 January 2023, [709].

65 Ibid [710].

66 Ibid.

67 *Borkowski v Armenia*, UNCTAD Investment Dispute Settlement Navigator, at <https://investmentpolicy.unctad.org/investment-dispute-settlement/cases/934/borkowski-and-rasia-fze-v-armenia>.

5.8.1 Case Study: Itisaluna Iraq & Others v Iraq

Itisaluna Iraq & Others v Iraq (*Itisaluna v Iraq*)[68] was initiated in 2017 by claimants from Jordan and the UAE applying the *OIC Agreement* and administered by an ICSID arbitral tribunal.[69] The tribunal rendered its award on 3 April 2020. It is a landmark case, demonstrating the difficulties and divergence of opinions in relation to the interpretation and application of the Agreement. The approach adopted by the majority in *Itisaluna v Iraq* is significant in terms of its approach to the importation of dispute settlement mechanisms via the Agreement's MFN clause, and consent to ICSID arbitration, in particular.

The dispute related to investments by the claimant in a joint venture in Iraq to launch voice data and internet services.[70] The licence entitled the claimant and venture partners to install, construct, and operate a public network to provide telecommunications services and "establish, operate, or otherwise provide international gateway services to transit telecommunications traffic".[71] Iraq's General Secretariate of the Council of Ministers allegedly prohibited the investors from "operating their own international gateway under the License", without compensation, preventing them "from using and benefiting from an essential element of their investment in Iraq".[72] Attempts to renew the licence on its expiry were rejected by the Iraq national Communications and Media Commission, which instead continued "to pressure them into accepting a renewal of the expired License stripped of its key terms" causing financial injury.[73]

In its Award, the tribunal stated that the key issue was whether it had jurisdiction, given the requirement for written consent to submit the claim to ICSID pursuant to Article 25(1) of the *ICSID Convention*.[74] Article 25(1) states:

> The jurisdiction of the Centre shall extend to any legal dispute arising directly out of an investment, between a Contracting State (or any constituent subdivision or agency of a Contracting State) and a *national* of another Contracting State, which the parties to the dispute consent in writing to submit to the Centre. When the parties have given their consent, no party may withdraw its consent unilaterally.

The claimants argued that the ICSID tribunal had jurisdiction *ratione voluntatis*, submitting that Article 17 of the *OIC Agreement* amounts to Iraq's written consent

68 *Itisaluna Iraq LLC, Munir Sukhitan International Investment LLC, VTEL Holdings Ltd., VTEL Middle East and Africa Limited v. Republic of Iraq*, ICSID Case No. ARB/17/10, Award, 3 April 2020 ('*Itisaluna v Iraq*').

69 UNCTAD, 'Investment Dispute Settlement Navigator' (last updated 31 December 2022) at <Itisaluna Iraq and others v. Iraq | Investment Dispute Settlement Navigator | UNCTAD Investment Policy Hub>.

70 *Itisaluna v Iraq* (n 68), [5].

71 Ibid [26] citing Notice of Arbitration, 8 January 2017.

72 Ibid.

73 Ibid.

74 Ibid [20].

to initiate an ISDS dispute proceeding before an arbitral tribunal. Further, Article 8(1), an MFN provision, allowed for importation of Article 17(4)(1) of the *Iraq–Japan BIT* into the Agreement, thereby enabling ICSID arbitration of the dispute.[75] In contrast, the Respondent argued that the tribunal lacked jurisdiction because Article 17 did not specifically allow for ICSID administration and further, that the Agreement's MFN provision did not allow for the importation of the requisite written consent from another treaty.[76] The tribunal held that:

> *the* critical question [was] whether the Claimants are able to incorporate into the OIC Agreement, by operation of its MFN clause, the ICSID arbitration clause in the Iraq–Japan BIT.[77]

The tribunal upheld the Respondent's objection to jurisdiction (*ratione voluntatis*), finding that the Agreement's MFN clause did not operate to import consent to ICSID arbitration from another treaty and thus, the case failed.[78] The tribunal noted generally that claimants must be capable of satisfying the *ratione personae* and *ratione materiae* conditions of the treaty which they seek to apply and cannot import from another treaty by operation of an MFN provision in that other treaty.[79]

In reaching its decision, the tribunal first considered the "multilateral character" of the *OIC Agreement*, adopting a cautious approach, finding that "bilateral practice that is unrelated to the multilateral agreement, cannot be safely relied upon as a yardstick for the interpretation and application of that multilateral agreement".[80] Accordingly, it would not be sound to rely upon an MFN clause "to construct (even if only potentially) a variable framework of application in respect of its individual Contracting Parties by reference to their distinct and unrelated bilateral treaty practice"; to do so "would be the very antithesis of the principle underlying the MFN clause".[81] The tribunal distinguished the *Itisaluna v Iraq* case from cases relied upon by the Claimants, notably *RosInvest v Russia*,[82] and *Le Chèque Déjeuner v Hungary*,[83] since those cases involved the importation of consent to submit to arbitration via MFN clauses, based on the bilateral treaty practices of the respondent. Specifically, the tribunal stated:

> There is a self-evident difference between relying on the practice of a respondent, in one or more of its bilateral treaties, to derive or enlarge its consent to

75 Ibid [21]; *Agreement between the Republic of Iraq and Japan for the Promotion and Protection of Investment*, signed 7 June 2012 (entered into force 25 February 2014).

76 Ibid [20].

77 Ibid [80].

78 Ibid [148].

79 Ibid [150].

80 Ibid [152]–[153].

81 Ibid [153].

82 *RosInvest v Russia*, SCC Case No. V079/2005, Award on Jurisdiction, 1 October 2007.

83 *Le Chèque Déjeuner and C.D. Holding Internationale v. Hungary*, ICSID Case No. ARB/13/35, Decision on Preliminary Issues of Jurisdiction, 3 March 2016.

> arbitration in another of its bilateral treaties by operation of an MFN provision, and the situation in the present case, in which the Respondent's bilateral treaty practice is invoked to derive consent to arbitration in a multilateral treaty.[84]

The tribunal also considered the relationship between Articles 16 and 17 of the *OIC Agreement.* Relevantly, Article 16 second sentence states that "if the investor chooses to raise the complaint before the national courts or before an arbitral tribunal than having done so before one of the two quarters he loses the right of recourse to the other". The tribunal found that the sentence "is a fork-in-the-road provision that differentiates between domestic proceedings, via national courts or arbitral tribunals, and available international arbitral proceedings".[85] The inclusion of the phrase "an arbitral tribunal" supported "the contention that the OIC Agreement has in contemplation the possibility of internationalised investor-state arbitration".[86]

The tribunal went on to find that Article 17 of the *OIC Agreement* "contemplates and addresses investor-State disputes",[87] noting that although the Article, particularly the phrase "disputes arising under the Agreement", was "broad enough to encompass both investor-State and Contracting Party disputes", "when coupled with the phrase 'parties to the dispute' elsewhere in Article 17, it contemplates investment disputes arising under specific substantive provisions of the Agreement".[88] The tribunal also considered whether conciliation was a precondition to arbitration, finding "that the intended gateway to arbitration under this provision is prior resort to conciliation and, thereafter, the failure of the conciliation process".[89] The tribunal noted that such a requirement had not been fulfilled and thus found that even if no such requirement existed, or the Claimants had satisfied it, "Article 17(2)(1) of the Agreement establishes a 'right' to resort to arbitration".[90] Critically, it found that

> [I]t follows from the terms of Article 17(2) of the OIC Agreement, in all of its parts, that it constitutes consent to arbitration in general terms, subject (on the Tribunal's analysis) on the fulfilment of the condition precedent of prior resort to, and exhaustion of, the conciliation process.[91]

However, the tribunal emphasised that consent to submit to arbitration, derived from Article 17(2), is limited in operation and does not amount to consent to submit to ICSID arbitration, as required by Article 25(1) of the ICSID Convention.[92] The

84 *Itisaluna v Iraq* (n 68), [155].
85 Ibid [164].
86 Ibid [165].
87 Ibid [169].
88 Ibid [168].
89 Ibid [183].
90 Ibid [185]–[187].
91 Ibid [190].
92 Ibid [191].

tribunal then considered whether the requisite consent for ICSID arbitration could be imported via the MFN clause contained in Article 8(1) of the Agreement, finding that "there is a sufficiently settled body of consistent investment treaty law in favour of the proposition that MFN clauses are capable of applying, as a matter of principle, to dispute settlement provisions".[93]

The tribunal found that the MFN is

> a principle of treaty law that must be expressly stated and is amendable to limitation, whether expressly or implicitly, having regard to the terms in which the principle is expressed and its purpose in the context of the instrument in which it is found.[94]

On that basis, the tribunal considered that Article 8(2) supported the view that Article 8(1) could not be relied upon to import consent to ICSID arbitration from an external instrument.[95]

The tribunal was somewhat scathing of the claimants' submission with respect to the contention that it could import consent to ICSID arbitration by virtue of the MFN provision, stating "it is difficult to escape the whiff of overreach that casts a pall over the Claimants' case".[96] The tribunal ultimately found that the Claimants could not rely upon the MFN clause to incorporate the requisite consent to ICSID arbitration, upholding the Respondent's objection to jurisdiction *ratione voluntatis*, and the case thus failed.[97]

Craig Gaver argues that the *Itisaluna v Iraq* award "seemingly forecloses future access to ICSID under the *OIC Agreement*"; but this may be avoided if "the parties specifically consent to it" and further, that it "will have important ramifications for other arbitrations arising under the treaty".[98] However, it is unlikely that a respondent state would provide the required consent to ICSID arbitration when defending an investor–state claim applying the Agreement.

Following *Itisaluna v Iraq*, claimants may be dissuaded from seeking to import consent to ICSID arbitration into the *OIC Agreement* from another BIT, but this is not likely to impact a large number of claims. Ioannis Konstantinidis argues that the vast majority of the ongoing arbitrations under the Agreement do not operate under the ICSID Rules; indeed in some instances, "claimants use the MFN clause of the Agreement to access UNCITRAL arbitration, which does not have any such double-consent requirement and is similar in nature to the form of ad hoc arbitration provided under the OIC Investment Agreement" which may create circumstances

93 Ibid [195], citing Dissenting and Concurring Opinion, *Impregilo S.p.A v Argentine Republic*, ICSID Case No. ARB/07/17, 21 June 2011 at [14].

94 Ibid [196].

95 Ibid [197]–[199].

96 Ibid [208].

97 Ibid [223]–[225].

98 Craig Gaver, '"To the Centre": Itisaluna v. Iraq and ICSID's Entry into the OIC Debate', *Kluwer Arbitration Blog* (8 June 2020) at <"To the Centre": Itisaluna v. Iraq and ICSID's Entry into the OIC Debate - Kluwer Arbitration Blog>.

which can be distinguishable from the Itisaluna decision.[99] Mohamed Wahab argues that the tension between policy considerations and pragmatic approaches to ensuring the effectiveness of the Agreement remains unresolved.[100]

In the authors' view, it is unlikely that *Itisaluna v Iraq* will finally settle contention regarding the interpretation and application of the dispute settlement provisions contained in the Agreement. However, there may be options to improve precision in the Agreement in the future. For example, Wahab argues that the Agreement's effectiveness could be improved in circumstances where

> *(i)* The OIC Contracting parties executed an amendment or released a proper explanatory and implementation protocol *(ii)* the OIC General Secretariat under the OIC Agreement issues proper and detailed guidelines, in line with international best practices and the provisions of the Agreement, on the necessary practices for the implementation of the dispute settlement mechanisms envisaged under the Agreement; or *(iii)* a wealth of consistent decisions rendered by international tribunals regarding the dispute settlement mechanisms under the OIC Agreement.[101]

There are some practical difficulties however, in achieving these measures given the multilateral nature of the Agreement. Given the imprecision and lapse of time since the treaty was drafted, perhaps the GCC should advocate for a more radical overhaul of the *OIC Agreement*, which is arguably an anachronism and no longer fit for purpose.

5.9 General Case Commentary

Of the total 38 arbitrations initiated by claimants from GCC member States, as listed, 13 (34%) are still pending, although almost half of those are cases lodged by Qatari investors arising from the Gulf diplomatic crisis. Two of the pending cases have been under way since 2016 (notably *Al Jazeera v Saudi Arabia* and the intriguing case of *Strategic Infrasol and Thakur Family Trust v India*). Thirteen (34%) cases have been decided in favour of the State, including four that were declined on jurisdictional grounds. Six (16%) were discontinued or settled under ICSID Rule 43 or Rule 44, and two (5%) have been decided in favour of neither party (liability found but no damages awarded), indicating issues of "clean hands" impacted the judgment. Only two (8%) cases have been found in favour of the claimant, and one of those was effectively annulled on judicial appeal (*Al-Kharafi v Libya*), although *DP World v Belgium* may be a third.

99 Ioannis Konstantinidis, 'Deciphering the OIC Investment Agreement in Light of the Itisaluna v Republic of Iraq Award' (2022) 11(1) *International Review of Law*, 251, 265.

100 Mohamed Abdel Wahab, 'Itisaluna and Others v Iraq: The OIC Agreement Conundrum: Consent to ICSID Arbitration and the MFN Clauses Saga' (2021) 36(1) *ICS ID Review*, 1, 13.

101 Ibid.

Claimants from GCC member States have initiated proceedings against a range of respondent states, but a significant majority have been from the MENA states and/or signatory states to the *OIC Agreement.* Egypt has been named as the respondent state in ten (26%) arbitrations, Jordan in four (10%), Saudi Arabia and Libya in three (8%) each, and India, Iraq, Pakistan, and Yemen in two (5%) each. The remaining respondents with a single claim in each case included a range of European and Asian countries.

Nearly half of the cases, namely 18 (47%) cases, were brought under the ICSID Rules, 12 (32%) cases were brought under the UNCITRAL Rules, one (3%) case was ad hoc, and data about which rules were to be applied was not available in seven (18%) cases (primarily being the Qatari suite of cases). Almost the majority of cases were also administered by ICSID, seven (18%) cases were administered by the PCA, three (8%) had no report of the administering institution, and one case (3%) was administered by the Cairo Regional Centre For International Commercial Arbitration. Data was not available about the administering institution in 9 (24%) of the cases.

A number of different IIAs were applicable in claims brought forward by investors from GCC member States. Three of the cases applied more than one IIA, specifically the recent Qatar Airways suite of arbitrations. In the case of the Qatar Airways' dispute with Egypt, the claimant sought to rely on the *Egypt–Qatar BIT* (1999), in addition to the *Arab Investment Agreement* and the *OIC Agreement.* The other arbitrations initiated by investors from member States applied individual IIAs. The *OIC Agreement* was the most commonly applied IIA, with 15 (39%) cases either solely or in tandem with other BITs or with the *Arab Investment Agreement.* All Saudi claims proceeded under the *OIC Agreement.*

Where data is available, the amounts claimed by claimants from GCC member States ranged from USD19.6 million to USD15 billion (or equivalents). There is very limited data available about the amounts awarded or settled, with details available in only four cases. The amounts awarded in these four cases were USD18.8 million in *Desert Line Projects v Yemen* and USD935 million in *Al-Kharafi v Libya and others* (which was annulled on appeal). In the other two cases for which data is available on amounts awarded or settled, namely, *Al-Warraq v Indonesia* and *Agility v Pakistan*, the respective tribunals decided in favour of neither party (liability was found but damages were not awarded).

Disputes involved a wide range of economic sectors, although the transportation and storage sector was the most common with nine (24%) cases, closely followed by the information and communication sector with six (16%) cases, and manufacturing with five (13%) cases. Four (11%) cases involved the financial and insurance sector. Data on the relevant economic sector was not available in two (5%) cases. The case of *Borkowski and Rasia FZE v Armenia* involved two economic sectors, namely transportation and storage as well as construction and has been included within the transportation and storage figures in Table 5.6 .

Data is available for the breaches alleged by claimants from GCC member States in 12 (32%) out of the 38 arbitrations initiated. In one case, *ICRS v Jordan*, the breaches alleged were unclear, and data is not available for the remainder. In cases where data was available, expropriation, particularly indirect expropriation, was commonly alleged. The breaches were found in three (8%) cases, including arbitrary, unreasonable, and/or discriminatory measures (one (3%) case), and the FET protection/minimum standard of treatment (two (6%) cases). Jurisdiction was declined in four cases, and all claims were dismissed at the merits stage in seven (18%) cases. Seven (16%) arbitrations were settled or discontinued before a decision was made with respect to liability. The remainder of arbitrations initiated by claimants from GCC member States are pending, with the exception of *Agility v Pakistan*, for which data about breaches found is not available.

Figure 5.1 summarises the history of the GCC member States as home state of claimants' ISDS claims. As already mentioned, based on the limited available UNCTAD data and reliable secondary source data, claimants from the States have lodged 38 ISDS claims through established arbitration institutions, compared with 34 received by the States as respondents over a similar period of time. The first IIA-reliant case arose in 2005 (*Desert Line (Oman) v Yemen*), after which there appears to have been little inclination by investors from the States to publicly initiate claims for over a decade, except for three cases initiated by disparate Qatari investors in 2011. Then followed a period of almost complete inactivity for over a decade, until a mini-explosion of cases involving all States with multiple cases in some instances occurred from 2017 onwards. Part of the explanation for this surge could be due to the Qatari suite of cases which distorts the figures for the year 2020, but the trend appears to have continued. The slight downward trend from 2021 could well be attributable to the flow-on impact of the COVID-19 pandemic and its significant impact on global trade and economies. And, therefore, it is therefore quite likely that the downward trend in recent years could be corrected and actively reversed as economies begin to recover and foreign investment grows again, and as cases emerge from behind the cloak of confidentiality maintained by the majority of the leading arbitration tribunals.

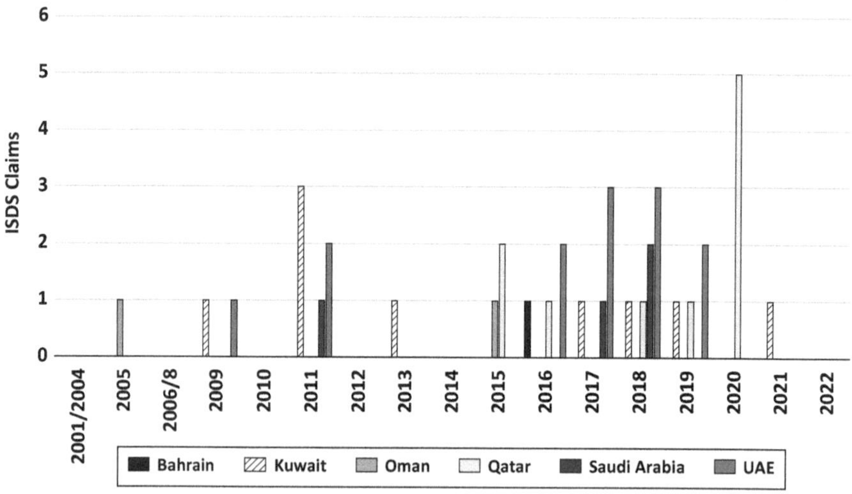

Figure 5.1 GCC member States as home state of claimants.

Source: Compiled by the authors as derived from UNCTAD data.

5.10 Concluding Remarks

In considering the above brief analysis of the performance of nationals of the GCC member States as investor/claimants in ISDS arbitrations, a few aspects stand out above the rest. Firstly, the success rate of claims is remarkably low – only three arbitrations are recorded as being successful, and one of those was annulled on appeal. The annulled arbitration originally proceeded under the OIC *Agreement*, while the remaining two currently (still) successful claims proceeded under BITs.

Secondly, the number of claims that have proceeded under the *OIC Agreement* and/or the *Arab Investment Agreement*, being in the majority overall, indicate a strong preference for those Islamic-based agreements, notwithstanding the issues with clarity of text and general agreement on substantive provisions, such as the definition and application of key terms, the operation of MFN provisions, and prior consent to arbitration. While it is noted that in some instances these two agreements were utilised in the absence of an applicable BIT or other IIA, they were also utilised where choice was available. What would also have to be of particular concern to any claimant is the record of the OIC Secretary-General in the non-appointment of arbitrators and the potential impact on the fate of a claim. If subsequent ICSID tribunals are persuaded by the majority's decision in *Itisaluna v Iraq*, claimants will potentially have to take a gamble anyway, on pursuing non-ICSID administered arbitration, or seek out relief in domestic litigation or state-to-state dispute settlement procedures.

Thirdly, evidence of the issue of "clean hands" can be seen in the awards rendered by tribunals.

As was stated in respect of the GCC member States as respondents in ISDS arbitrations, the States are likely to have increased the necessity of utilising investor–state arbitration in the future due to external environmental factors. Specifically, change may occur as a result of increased "economic competition" as a result of "high sovereign debt levels" caused by the domestic, regional, and international impact of the "COVID-19 pandemic and volatility in global oil markets."[102]

Accordingly, there would be merit in each GCC member State mitigating against the risk of adverse arbitral exposure by reviewing on behalf of their nationals participating in foreign investment their existing BITs and TIPs to review the scope of investment protections and limit the possibility of dispute settlement by arbitration. This is particularly important in the context of Shariah law and its influence upon the legal institutions and methods in the States.[103]

102 Sebastian Castelier, 'GCC States Race for Foreign Investment', *AL-Monitor* (22 February 2021) at <GCC states race for foreign investment - Al-Monitor: The Pulse of the Middle East>.

103 'International Construction Arbitration in the Middle East', *Aceris Law* (6 March 2021) at <International Construction Arbitration in the Middle East • Aceris Law LLC>.

Bibliography

AAN Digital Services Holding Company (KSC) v. Democratic Republic of the Congo (ICSID Case No. ARB/19/24, 11 September 2019).

Abd-El-Aziz Saleh Esmail Abdallah Al-Rashed, Awrad International Holding, International Holding Project Group and others v. Arab Republic of Egypt (ICSID Case No. ARB/18/31) (*'International Holding Group Project v Egypt'*).

'Agility Announces Arbitration Decision in Korek Case', *Agility, Press Release* (21 March 2023) at <Agility Announces Arbitration Decision in Korek Case | Agility>.

Agility Public Warehousing Company K.S.C. v. Republic of Iraq (ICSID Case No. ARB/17/7) (*'Agility v Iraq'*).

Agreement between the Government of the Republic of Armenia and the Government of the United Arab Emirates for the Promotion and Reciprocal Protection of Investments, signed 22 July 2016 (entered into force 21 November 2017).

Agreement between the Government of the Sultanate of Oman and the Government of the Republic of Bulgaria on the Promotion and Reciprocal Protection of Investments, signed 3 February 2007 (entered into force 22 October 2014).

Agreement between the Republic of Iraq and Japan for the Promotion and Protection of Investment, signed 7 June 2012 (entered into force 25 February 2014).

Agreement for the Reciprocal Promotion and Protection of Investments between the Government of the Sultanate of Oman and the Government of the Republic of Yemen, signed 20 September 1998 (entered into force 1 April 2000).

Alcor Holdings Ltd v The Czech Republic (Award, 2 March 2022) PCA Case No. 2018-45.

Ali Alyafei v. Hashemite Kingdom of Jordan (ICSID Case no. ARB/15/24, 11 June 2015), (*'Alyafei v. Jordan (I)'*).

Barucha, Nauzer, 'UAE Firms Sue India, desi co for Rs 5 lakh cr Over Mumbai Plots', *Times of India* (5 November 2015) in bilaterals.com at <https://www.bilaterals.org/?uae-firms-sue-india-desi-co-for-rs>.

Bohmer, Lisa, 'Egypt Round-Up: A Bifurcation Decision, A Provisional Measures Request, And New Legislation On Arbitration Awards and Agreements', *Investment Arbitration Reporter* (25 August 2021) at <Egypt Round-Up: A bifurcation decision, a provisional measures request, and new legislation on arbitration awards and agreements | Investment Arbitration Reporter (openathens.net)>.

Bohmer, Lisa, 'Tribunal Is In Place In Egyptian Real Estate Dispute, With Pierre Tercier Tapped to Chair', *Investment Arbitration Reporter* (6 August 2019) at <Tribunal is in place in Egyptian real estate dispute, with Pierre Tercier tapped to chair | Investment Arbitration Reporter (openathens.net)>.

Bohmer, Lisa, 'UNCITRAL Tribunal Dismisses Under-the-Radar Treaty Claim against Turkey', *Investment Arbitration Reporter* (19 October 2023) at <https://www-iareporter-com.eu1.proxy.openathens.net/articles/turkey-is-facing-under-the-radar-uncitral-arbitration/>.

Bohmer, Lisa, '[Updated with a Copy of the Award] UAE Based Agility Claims Victory in Commercial Telecoms Arbitration Involving Corruption Allegations – As Related ICSID Cases Continue to Unfold', *Investment Arbitration Reporter* (21 March 2023) at <[Updated with a copy of the Award] UAE-based Agility claims victory in commercial telecoms arbitration involving corruption allegations – as related ICSID cases continue to unfold | Investment Arbitration Reporter (openathens.net)>.

Castelier, Sebastian, 'GCC States Race for Foreign Investment', *AL-Monitor* (22 February 2021) at <GCC states race for foreign investment - Al-Monitor: The Pulse of the Middle East>.

Charlotin, Damien, 'An Update on the $1 billion Kharafi v. Libya Award', *Investment Arbitration Reporter* (4 October 2019) at <https://www-iareporter-com.eu1.proxy.openathens.net/articles/an-update-on-the-1-billion-kharafi-v-libya-award/>.

Charlotin, Damien, '[Corrected] French Court Annuls Finding of Lack of Jurisdiction Over Civil War Claims, But Upholds Remainder of Commercial Award in Favour of

Libya's National Oil Company, Libya and NOC Are Still Facing Trio of Arbitrations Arising From Same Dispute', *Investment Arbitration Reporter* (1 March 2021) at <[CORRECTED] French court annuls finding of lack of jurisdiction over civil war claims, but upholds remainder of commercial award in favour of Libya's National Oil Company; Libya and NOC are still facing trio of arbitrations arising from same dispute | Investment Arbitration Reporter (openathens.net)>.

Charlotin, Damien, 'Libya Round-Up: An update on Arbitration Cases Against the State'. *Investment Arbitration Reporter* (26 April 2022) at <https://www-iareporter-com.eu1.proxy.openathens.net/articles/libya-round-up-an-update-on-arbitration-cases-against-the-state/#topic-shortcode-S22176>.

Charlotin, Damien, 'Paris Appeal Court Confirms Lifting of Attachments against Sanctioned Libyan Entities in Battle for Enforcement of treaty Award', *Investment Arbitration Reporter* (9 February 2023) at <https://www-iareporter-com.eu1.proxy.openathens.net/articles/french-supreme-court-confirms-lifting-of-attachments-against-sanctioned-libyan-entities-in-battle-for-enforcement-of-treaty-award/>.

Charlotin, Damien, 'Uncovered: UNCITRAL Tribunal Finds That Sale of Investment Two Years Prior to Lodging the Arbitration Deprived Claimant of Investor States; Reservation of Right TO Bring Treaty Claim Is Deemed To Be Irrelevant', *Investment Arbitration Reporter* (22 March 2022) at <Uncovered: UNCITRAL tribunal finds that sale of investment two years prior to lodging the arbitration deprived claimant of investor status; reservation of right to bring treaty claim is deemed to be irrelevant | Investment Arbitration Reporter (openathens.net)>.

CTIP Oil & Gas International Limited v. Arab Republic of Egypt (ICSID Case No. ARB/19/27 (*'CTP Oil and Gas v Egypt'*).

Dahlquist, Joel, 'Qatari Businessman Contends that MFN Clause in Regional Treaty can Provide Foothold for an ICSID Claim Against Jordan', *Investment Arbitration Reporter* (15 June 2015) at <https://www-iareporter-com.eu1.proxy.openathens.net/articles/qatari-businessman-contends-that-mfn-clause-in-regional-treaty-can-provide-foothold-for-an-icsid-claim-against-jordan/>.

Dahlquist, Joel and Luke Eric Peterson, 'Investigation: Four Previously-Confidential Claims under the *OIC Agreement* Are Uncovered, as Controversy Continues Over Treaty's Use in Arbitration', *Investment Arbitration Reporter* (16 May 2019) at <https://www-iareporter-com.eu1.proxy.openathens.net/articles/investigation-4-previously-confidential-claims-under-oic-investment-agreement-are-uncovered-as-controversy-continues-over-treatys-use-in-arbitration/>.

Deepak, Girish, 'Kuwait Oil Company Reports win in LCIA Arbitration against Contractor', *Investment Arbitration Reporter* (21 June 2023) at <https://www-iareporter-com.eu1.proxy.openathens.net/articles/kuwait-oil-company-reports-win-in-lcia-arbitration-against-contractor/>.

Deepak, Girish, '[Updated With New Document] Iraq Round-Up: Iraq Joins Mauritius Convention And New York Convention, An Under-The-Radar 26 Billion USD Dispute And Updates On Other Pending Proceedings', *Investment Arbitration Reporter* (21 October 2021) at <[Updated with new document] Iraq Round-Up: Iraq joins Mauritius Convention and New York Convention, an under-the-radar 26 billion USD dispute, and updates on other pending proceedings | Investment Arbitration Reporter (openathens.net)>.

Desert Line Projects LLC v. Republic of Yemen (ICSID Case No. ARB/05/17 (*'Desert Line v Yemen'*).

Djanic, Vladislav, 'Banking Dispute Leads to South Sudan's Second Ever ICSID Arbitration', *Investment Arbitration Reporter* (9 October 2020) at <https://www-iareporter-com.eu1.proxy.openathens.net/articles/banking-dispute-leads-to-south-sudans-second-ever-icsid-arbitration/>.

DP World Limited v. Kingdom of Belgium (ICSID Case No. ARB/17/21) (*'DP World v Belgium'*).

'Egypt Defeats Hotel Investor', *Garrigues Newsletter* (27 December 2021) at <https://www.garrigues.com/en_GB/new/international-arbitration-newsletter-december-2021-regional-overview-middle-east-and-africa>.

'Egypt Reportedly Prevails in Treaty Arbitration', *Investment Arbitration Reporter* (15 November 2021) at <https://www-iareporter-com.eu1.proxy.openathens.net/articles/egypt-reportedly-prevails-in-treaty-arbitration/>.

Gaver, Craig, '"To the Centre": Itisaluna v. Iraq and ICSID's Entry into the OIC Debate', *Kluwer Arbitration Blog* (8 June 2020) at <"To the Centre": Itisaluna v. Iraq and ICSID's Entry into the OIC Debate - Kluwer Arbitration Blog>.

Ghaith Rashad Pharaon v. Republic of Tunisia (ICSID Case No. ARB/86/1 (*'Pharaon v Tunisia'*).

Government of the Hashemite Kingdom of Jordan and the Public Transport Regulatory Commission v. International Company for Railway Systems (ICRS) (ICC Case No. 16342/EC/ND, 6 February 2012) at <https://jusmundi.com/en/document/decision/en-the-government-of-the-hashemite-kingdom-of-jordan-and-the-public-transport-regulatory-commission-v-international-company-for-railway-systems-ii-award-monday-6th-february-2012>.

Hepburn, Jarrod, 'An Update on Investment Treaty Disputes Involving the Government of India', *Investment Arbitrator Reporter* (23 April 2018) at <https://www-iareporter-com.eu1.proxy.openathens.net/articles/an-update-on-investment-treaty-disputes-involving-the-government-of-india/>.

Hepburn, Jarrod, 'Investors Exchange Arguments with India over UNCITRAL/BIT Real Estate Dispute', *Investment Arbitration Reporter* (2 April 2017) at <https://www-iareporter-com.eu1.proxy.openathens.net/articles/investors-exchange-arguments-with-india-over-uncitralbit-real-estate-dispute/>.

Hepburn, Jarrod and Luke Eric Peterson, 'As Al Kharafi Group Try to Collect Billion Dollar Libya Award, Battles Flare in Egypt, France, and before Arab Investment Court', *Investment Arbitration Reporter* (23 November 2014) at <https://www-iareporter-com.eu1.proxy.openathens.net/articles/as-al-kharafi-group-try-to-collect-billion-dollar-libya-award-battles-flare-in-egypt-france-and-before-arab-investment-court/>.

Hepburn, Jarrod and Luke Eric Peterson, 'Investigation: As New Cases Emerge under Islamic Investment Treaty, Initial Viability of Claims Seems to Hinge on Willingness of Respondents to Appoint Arbitrators', *Investment Arbitration Reporter* (2 March 2017) at <https://www-iareporter-com.eu1.proxy.openathens.net/articles/investigation-as-new-cases-emerge-under-islamic-investment-treaty-initial-viability-of-claims-seems-to-hinge-on-willingness-of-respondents-to-appoint-arbitrators/>.

Hussain Sajwani, Damac Park Avenue for Real Estate Development S.A.E., and Damac Gamsha Bay for Development S.A.E. v. Arab Republic of Egypt (ICSID Case No. ARB/11/16) (*'Sajwani v Egypt'*).

International Company for Railway Systems (ICRS) v. Jordan (ICSID Case No. ARB/09/13) (*'ICRS v Jordan'*).

'International Construction Arbitration in the Middle East' *Aceris Law* (6 March 2021) at <International Construction Arbitration in the Middle East • Aceris Law LLC>.

'Investment Treaty Policy and Dispute Settlement', in *Middle East and North Africa Investment Policy Perspectives*(OECD Publishing, Paris, 2021) at <https://doi.org/10.1787/f78a2c1b-en>.

Itisaluna Iraq LLC, Munir Sukhitan International Investment LLC, VTEL Holdings Ltd., VTEL Middle East and Africa Limited v. Republic of Iraq (ICSID Case No. ARB/17/10, Award, 3 April 2020) (*'Itisaluna v Iraq'*).

Joseph K. Borkowski and Rasia FZE v. Republic of Armenia (ICSID Case No. ARB/18/28/0) (*'Borkowski v Armenia'*), Award, 20 January 2023.

Karbal, Mohamed, 'Libya: Oil and Gas Disputes: The Libyan Experience,' *Mondaq* (31 March 2021) at <Oil & Gas Disputes: The Libyan Experience - Oil, Gas & Electricity - Libya (mondaq.com)>.

'KOC Wins 77 Million Dollars in Arbitration Case Filed in London Court', *Kuwait Times* (21 June 2023) at <https://timeskuwait.com/news/koc-wins-77-million-dollars-in-arbitration-case-filed-in-london-court/>.

Konstantinidis, Ioannis, 'Deciphering the OIC Investment Agreement in Light of the Itisaluna v Republic of Iraq Award' (2022) 11(1) *International Review of Law*, 251–265.

'Kuwaitis Mount Multi-Billion Dollar Investment Arbitration Against Egypt', *Investment Arbitration Reporter* (20 September 2018) at <Kuwaitis mount multi-billion dollar investment arbitration against Egypt | Investment Arbitration Reporter (openathens.net)>.

Mohamed Abdulmohsen Al-Kharafi & Sons Co. v. The Republic of Libya and others (Final Award) ('Kharafi v Libya').

Omar Bin Sulaiman Abdul Aziz Al Rajhi v. The Sultanate of Oman (PCA Case No. 2017-32) (*'Bin Sulaiman v Oman'*).

Peterson, Luke Eric, 'After Obtaining a Jurisdictional Victory in 2013, Investor Later Concedes that Pakistani Investment Treaty is Not in Force and Drops its Arbitration', *Investment Arbitration Reporter* (11 August 2016) at <https://www-iareporter-com.eu1.proxy.openathens.net/articles/after-obtaining-a-jurisdictional-victory-in-2013-investor-later-concedes-that-pakistani-investment-treaty-is-not-in-force-and-drops-its-arbitration/>.

Peterson, Luke Eric, 'Damages Analysis: Investor Nets $900 Million Windfall for Libyan Resort That Was Never Built – and $30 Million in Moral Damages For Reputational Harm', *Investment Arbitration Reporter* (24 July 2013) at <Damages analysis: Investor nets $900 million windfall for Libyan resort that was never built - and $30 million in moral damages for reputational harm | Investment Arbitration Reporter (openathens.net)>.

Qatar National Bank (Q.P.S.C.) v. Republic of South Sudan and Bank of South Sudan (ICSID Case No. ARB/20/40), Proceedings, (*'Qatar National Bank v South Sudan'*).

Republic of Djibouti, Port de Djibouti SA and Djibouti Ports and Free Zone Authority v. Doraleh Container Terminal (DCT), DP World Djibouti FZCO and Dubai (International) Djibouti FZE (LCIA Case No. 142732) (*'Djibouti v DP World'*).

Salah, Fatma, 'Egypt Court Annuls Award against Libya on the Substantive Ground of Fundamental Error of Law', *Kluwer Arbitration Blog* (19 July 2020) at <https://arbitrationblog.kluwerarbitration.com/2020/07/19/egypt-court-annuls-award-against libya-on-the-substantive-ground-of-fundamental-error-of-law/>.

State General Reserve Fund of the Sultanate of Oman v Republic of Bulgaria (ICSID Case No. ARB/15/43, 22 October 2015) (*'SGRF v Bulgaria'*).

Treaty between the United States of America and the Republic of Armenia Concerning the Encouragement and Reciprocal Protection of Investment, signed 23 September 1992 (entered into force 29 March 1996).

Tsolova, Tsvetelia, 'Oman Fund Set to Seek Ruling against Bulgaria Over Bank Collapse-Source', *Reuters* (23 July 2015) at <https://www.reuters.com/article/bulgaria-oman-banking-idusl5n1013in20150722>.

UNCTAD, 'Investment Dispute Settlement Navigator' at <Investment Dispute Settlement Navigator | UNCTAD Investment Policy Hub>.

Unified Agreement for the Investment of Arab Capital in the Arab States, signed 26 November 1980 (entered into force 07 September 1981) (*'Arab Investment Agreement'*).

Wahab, Mohamed Abdel, 'Itisaluna and Others v Iraq: The OIC Agreement Conundrum: Consent to ICSID Arbitration and the MFN Clauses Saga' (2021) 36(1) *ICSID Review*, 1–13.

Yong, Lacy, 'India Faces $85billion Claim from UAE Investors', *Global Arbitration Review* (11 November 2015).

6 Intra-GCC Investor–State Arbitrations and Divergence in Approaches

6.1 Introduction

As demonstrated in the previous chapters, there is an increasing trend in both the number of arbitrations being brought against GCC member States and the incidence of claimants from a member State bringing about investor–state arbitrations against parties beyond or outside the GCC. However, very few arbitration claims have been generated within the GCC membership itself, that is, by claimants who are citizens of one State against another State as respondent. Where they have arisen, they all rely upon the *OIC Agreement*[1] as a basis of claim, and only occasionally on the *Arab Investment Agreement*[2] as well. It should be noted, however, that none of the States have individual BITs or other IIAs with each other. Kuwait and the UAE signed a BIT in 1966, but it appears to never have come into force.

The chapter examines these few intra-GCC arbitrations and in so doing endeavours to reveal whether there is a certain region-specific character that helps to explain why there may be so few compared to those in the wider extra-GCC arena in which individual GCC member States have participated – actively in some instances. The fact that one particular State participates in almost all the cases as the home state of the investor claimant distorts the overall picture significantly. At the same time the home state itself becomes intimately involved in those same cases, which adds a further unique element when compared with participation in extra-GCC arbitrations. The other fact that emerges from this examination is that none of the arbitrations have been withdrawn by virtue of an amicable settlement, as occurs frequently in the extra-GCC context, which might raise the question of whether there does exist or is emerging a pattern of particular characteristics in respect of the nature of ISDS-based arbitration disputes involving the States.

1 *Agreement on Promotion, Protection and Guarantee of Investments amongst the Member States of the Organization of the Islamic Conference*, signed 5 June 1981 (entered into force February 1988) (*'OIC Agreement'*).

2 *Unified Agreement for the Investment of Arab Capital in the Arab States*, signed 26 November 1980 (entered into force 7 September 1981) (*'Arab Investment Agreement'*).

DOI: 10.4324/9781003481072-6

Hence the chapter considers whether these factors reveal a region-specific character and/or a dichotomy with respect to attitudes and approaches by the States to investor–state dispute settlement, in part because of the unique socio-legal institutions and business practices within and between the States.

The chapter examines eight cases, only six of which are strictly intra-GCC. The chapter includes two cases which involve non-GCC participants, primarily because the circumstances surrounding those two cases are so intimately involved with a suite of intra-GCC cases, namely those involving the ongoing Qatar–Saudi Arabia, UAE, Bahrain, Egypt disputation across a number of fronts.

6.2 The Intra-GCC ISDS Disputes

Based on UNCTAD data, the GCC member States have been named as respondents in 33 ISDS arbitration disputes since 2001, and claimants from the States have initiated 38 investor–state arbitrations since 2005.[3] Yet, only six intra-GCC investor–state arbitrations have been initiated since 2017, five of which have been generated by Qatari entities and which relate to disputes arising from the recent Gulf diplomatic crisis and are still pending, namely *beIN Corporation v Saudi Arabia* in 2018, *Qatar Pharma and Al Sulaiti v Saudi Arabia* in 2019, and *Qatar Airways v Bahrain*, *Qatar Airways v Saudi Arabia*, and *Qatar Airways v United Arab Emirates* in 2020.

The first intra-GCC case, and the only instance not related to, or arising from, the recent Gulf diplomatic crisis and thus not generated by a Qatari investor, is the case of *Omar Bin Sulaiman Abdul Aziz Al Rajhi v The Sultanate of Oman (PCA Case No. 2017-32).*

3 UNCTAD, 'Investment Dispute Settlement Navigator' <Advanced Search | Investment Dispute Settlement Navigator | UNCTAD Investment Policy Hub>.

Table 6.1 Intra-GCC ISDS Cases

No.	*Year Initiated*	*Short Case Name*	*Summary*	*Outcome of Original Proceedings*
1	2020	Qatar Airways v Bahrain	Investment: licences and permits to conduct air transport activities. Claims arising from Government actions blocking Qatar Airways operations in the country, including closure of airspace and revocation of operating licences.	Pending
2	2020	Qatar Airways v Egypt	Investment: licences and permits to conduct air transport activities. Claims arising from Government actions blocking Qatar Airways operations in the country, including closure of airspace and revocation of operating licences.	Pending
3	2020	Qatar Airways v Saudi Arabia	Investment: licences and permits to conduct air transport activities. Claims arising from Government actions blocking Qatar Airways operations in the country, including closure of airspace and revocation of operating licences.	Pending
4	2020	Qatar Airways v United Arab Emirates	Investment: licences and permits to conduct air transport activities. Claims arising from Government actions blocking Qatar Airways operations in the country, including closure of airspace and revocation of operating licences.	Pending
5	2019	Qatar Pharma and Al Sulaiti v Saudi Arabia	Investment: investments in two locally incorporated pharmaceutical companies and three warehouses in Riyadh, Jeddah, and Dammam. Claims arising from the repudiation of long-term sales contracts with the Saudi Ministry of Health after Saudi Arabia suspended diplomatic relations with Qatar in 2017. The Ministry's measures included the failure to pay for supplied products contracts and the forced closure of warehouses.	Pending

(*Continued*)

Table 6.1 (Continued)

No.	*Year Initiated*	*Short Case Name*	*Summary*	*Outcome of Original Proceedings*
6	2018	beIN v. Saudi Arabia	Investment: broadcasting licence for pay TV in Saudi Arabia and ownership of local subsidiary, Al Oula Al Raeda Trading, for retail operations. Claims arising from Government measures to stop the claimant's broadcasting after Saudi Arabia suspended diplomatic relations with Qatar in 2017. Included non-renewal of claimant's pay TV broadcasting licence and the denial of licences required by the claimant's subsidiary.	Pending
7	2017	Bin Sulaiman v Oman PCA case no. 2017-32	Investment: in Oman construction sector. Details of claim not available.	Decided in favour of the State
8	2016	Al Jazeera v Egypt ICSID case no. ARB/16/1	Investment: investments in multimedia broadcasting operations. Claims arising from destruction of claimant's Egypt media business, by arrest and detention of employees, attacks on facilities, interference with transmissions and broadcasts, office closures, cancellation of broadcasting licence, and compulsory liquidation of local branch.	Pending

Source: compiled by the authors primarily from UNCTAD, *Investment Policy Hub* <Advanced Search | Investment Dispute Settlement Navigator | UNCTAD Investment Policy Hub>, and *Investment Arbitration Reporter*, <https://www-iareporter-com.eu1.proxy.openathens.net/>.

Very little information is available about the case of *Omar Bin Sulaiman Abdul Aziz Al Rajhi v The Sultanate of Oman (Bin Sulaiman v Oman)*. In 2017, Omar Bin Sulaiman Abdul Aziz Al Rajhi, head of a major Saudi business conglomerate and founder of the Al Rajhi Bank, lodged a multimillion-dollar investment claim against Oman with the Permanent Court of Arbitration (PCA) in London over an investment reportedly in Oman's construction sector and pursuant to the

OIC Agreement and proceeding under UNCITRAL Rules.[4] Both Oman and the OIC Secretary-General failed to appoint an arbitrator on behalf of Oman. At the claimant's request, the PCA named an appointing authority who then appointed an arbitrator. Oman originally raised a series of jurisdiction issues, which the tribunal rejected and allowed the case to proceed to the merits stage.[5] In December 2023, the Investment Arbitration Reporter confirmed that the arbitration concluded in May, rejecting all claims on the merits and awarding costs to Oman.[6]

6.3 The Gulf Diplomatic Crisis and the Qatari Disputations

On 5 June 2017, Saudi Arabia, the UAE, and Bahrain (in concert with Egypt) severed diplomatic and economic ties with Qatar, accusing it of destabilising the region with its alleged support for Islamist terrorist groups. The States issued an ultimatum that they would impose a land, sea, and air blockade on Qatar unless Qatar accepted a list of 13 demands within 10 days. Included among the demands were that Qatar scale down ties with Iran, sever all alleged ties with the Muslim Brotherhood, Hezbollah, al-Qaeda, and ISIL; shut down the Al Jazeera Media Network and cease funding of other media entities; align its political, economic, and military policies and strategies with those of its four neighbours; close a Turkish military base; and subject itself to monthly and then annual audits of its compliance with these demands.[7] Upon Qatar's refusal of the ultimatum, the States subsequently imposed the threatened blockade, bringing to a head a deteriorating relationship with Saudi Arabia in recent years over allegations of Qatar's support of terrorism, its patronship of Al Jazeera, and what was considered to be too "close [a] relationship with Saudi Arabia's regional rival, Iran".[8]

The blockade halted all direct trade relations and business activities between the four countries and Qatar and drastically impacted land, air, and sea traffic.

4 Luke Eric Peterson, 'OIC Round up: An Update on Pending Arbitration Cases Lodged under the OIC Investment Agreement', *Investment Arbitration Reporter* (11 August 2020) at <https://www-iareporter-com.eu1.proxy.openathens.net/articles/oic-round-up-an-update-on-pending-arbitration-cases-lodged-under-the-oic-investment-agreement/>.

5 Lisa Bohmer, 'Investor in Oman's Construction Sector Files for Annulment of Still-Confidential Award', *Investment Arbitration Reporter* (10 June 2012) at <https://www-iareporter-com.eu1.proxy.openathens.net/articles/investor-in-omans-construction-sector-files-for-annulment-of-still-confidential-award/>.

6 Lisa Bohmer, 'Uncovered: OIC tribunal dismisses arbitration claims against Oman', Investment Arbitration Reporter (5 December 2023) at <https://www-iareporter-com.eu1.proxy.openathens.net/articles/uncovered-oic-tribunal-dismisses-arbitration-claims-against-oman/>.

7 See 'Arab States Issue 13 Demands to End Qatar-Gulf Crisis', *Al Jazeera* (12 July 2017) at <https://www.aljazeera.com/news/2017/7/12/arab-states-issue-13-demands-to-end-qatar-gulf-crisis>. See also Patrick Wintour, 'Gulf Plunged into Diplomatic Crisis as Countries Cut Ties with Qatar', *The Guardian* (5 June 2017) at <https://www.theguardian.com/world/2017/jun/05/saudi-arabia-and-bahrain-break-diplomatic-ties-with-qatar-over-terrorism>.

8 'Qatar Airways Seeks $5 Billion Compensation from Arab Bloc over Airspace Ban', *Reuters* (22 July 2020) at <Qatar Airways seeks $5 billion compensation from Arab bloc over airspace ban | Reuters>.

Qatar Airways flights between the five countries and Qatar's airspace rights over Bahrain, the UAE, Saudi Arabia, and Egypt also ceased.[9]

The breakdown of this relationship contributed to the emergence of a range of disputes before international fora, including nearly all the intra-GCC disputes listed in Table 6.1.[10] ISDS arbitrations were initiated by Qatar Airways, Qatar Pharma, and beIN against Saudi Arabia, Qatar Airways against the UAE and Bahrain (and Egypt), and Al Jazeera against Egypt, all of which are still pending. In all these intra-GCC investor–state arbitrations, the applicable arbitration agreement was the *OIC Agreement*. In the case of the arbitrations brought by the Qatar Airways disputes with Saudi Arabia, the UAE, and Bahrain, the *Arab Investment Agreement* was also applied.

The Qatari Government has also pursued, and is continuing to pursue, relief in multiple dispute settlement fora at the state-to-state level, including the following:[11]

- initiation of a trade dispute against Saudi Arabia before the World Trade Organization (WTO) dispute settlement board in relation to the beIN dispute;
- claim against Bahrain, the UAE, Saudi Arabia, and Egypt to the International Civil Aviation Organization;
- arbitration proceedings against Bahrain, the UAE, Saudi Arabia, and Egypt, applying the Constitution of the Universal Postal Union in relation to the suspension of those services;
- claim against the UAE before the International Court of Justice alleging racial discrimination contrary to the *International Convention on the Elimination of All Forms of Racial Discrimination* ("CERD");
- proceedings against Saudi Arabia before the United Nations Committee on Elimination of Racial Discrimination.

However, the Qatari–Saudi, Emirati, and Bahraini relationships appear to have at least stabilised and even improved, following the GCC Summit at Al-Ula in January 2021 when Saudi Arabia, the UAE, and Bahrain agreed to restore diplomatic ties with Qatar following Saudi Arabia's reopening of its borders to Qatar. This improvement was likely promoted by Omani and Kuwaiti efforts and "reported concerns" that the Biden Administration may adopt a stronger approach to Saudi Arabia than the Trump Administration. But it should be noted that not all of the above state–state disputations have been fully resolved, with some still in a state of "suspension".

9 Lisa Bohmer, 'Easing of Qatar-Saudi Arabia Tensions Could Affect Treaty-Based Arbitrations', *Investment Arbitration Reporter* (14 January 2020) at <Easing of Qatar-Saudi Arabia tensions could affect treaty-based arbitrations | Investment Arbitration Reporter (openathens.net)>.

10 Ibid.

11 Ibid.

6.4 The Al Jazeera Arbitration

Strictly speaking, *Al Jazeera v Egypt* is not an intra-GCC dispute. But because of its inclusion as a core demand in the ultimatum presented to Qatar and its claim being intimately associated with the course of events that led eventually to the Qatari claims against the other GCC member States and Egypt for their actions as a joint enterprise, it is suggested that it warrants consideration in the same context as the other claims.

Qatari media organisation Al Jazeera is a broadcaster with global reach and with considerable influence in the Arab world, and arguably the most influential news source for the region. Al Jazeera has long been regarded by conservative Middle East rulers and governments as a somewhat radical and unrestrained generator of undesirable change and thus a destabilising influence. Saudi Arabia regards Al Jazeera as a propaganda tool of the Qatari government used to undermine the region's stability.

Following the Egyptian Revolution in 2013 and the overthrow of the Muslim Brotherhood government, the incoming government accused Al Jazeera of siding with the Brotherhood and advocating further revolution. The authorities moved to close down the organisation's Egyptian news operation, to arrest and imprison journalists and other staff, and eventually place them on trial, imprisoning three journalists and sentencing others in absentia.

On 28 April 2014, Al Jazeera served formal notice of dispute on Egypt, alleging that its actions in closing down its operations and its campaigns against its journalists were contrary to its obligations under international law generally and also in violation of the *Egypt–Qatar BIT* of 1999.[12] The notice described the actions in the following terms:

> Al Jazeera's offices in Egypt have been attacked by the military, police and gangs supporting the military government; while the network itself has been subjected to a sustained campaign of harassment and intimidation involving the jamming of transmissions and broadcasts, as well as the closure of offices and other facilities.
>
> Finally, Al Jazeera's licence to broadcast in Egypt has been cancelled and its local branch has become subject to a compulsory liquidation procedure.[13]

The notice asserted that the BIT required governments of both countries to afford investors fair and equitable treatment, full investment protection and security, and freedom from expropriation measures without payment of adequate compensation.

12 Luke Eric Peterson, 'Analysis: As Al Jazeera Media Network Notifies Egypt of Possible Arbitration Claim, What Legal Arguments Loom in Such a Case', *Investment Arbitration Reporter* (28 April 2014) at <https://www-iareporter-com.eu1.proxy.openathens.net/articles/analysis-as-al-jazeera-media-network-notifies-egypt-of-possible-arbitration-claim-what-legal-arguments-loom-in-such-a-case/>.

13 'Al Jazeera Serves Notification of Dispute on Egypt', *Carter Ruck*, Press Release (28 April 2014) at <https://www.carter-ruck.com/news/al-jazeera-notice-of-dispute-served-on-state-of-egypt/>

The BIT also obliges Egypt to treat Al Jazeera in a manner consistent with its obligations under international human rights treaties, including the right to freedom of expression, and the right not to be arbitrarily detained or to suffer inhuman or degrading punishment.[14]

After some delays a tribunal was eventually appointed on 17 February 2017. Al Jazeera soon thereafter sought provisional measures, including one relating to an imprisoned journalist. ICSID records that on 28 September 2021 the proceeding was suspended for one year at the request of the parties. No information has emerged since the due date for the suspension to lapse (and presumably for the arbitration to resume) to confirm the current status of the arbitral proceedings.

6.5 The Qatar Pharma Arbitration

In March 2019 Qatar Pharma and its founder and chairman, Ahmed Bin Mohammad Al Haie Al Sulaiti, brought claims arising out of the alleged repudiation of long-term sales contracts concluded between Saudi Arabia's Ministry of Health and the claimants, the closure of its Saudi manufacturing plants, and the seizure of its pharmaceutical product stock following Saudi Arabia's suspension of diplomatic relations with Qatar in 2017. According to the claimants, the Ministry's measures included a failure to pay for products supplied by the claimants under these contracts and allegedly forcing them to close their warehouses in the country.

The company, which is engaged in the manufacture and sale of intravenous infusions, dialysis solutions, and topical drugs, complained that its Saudi operations were brought to a standstill and formally closed down by the Saudi authorities as a result of the severance of diplomatic and trade relations. Qatar Pharma has alleged that the Saudi authorities seized USD24 million in pharmaceutical products delivered to the State without compensation.[15] It contends that the trade blockade led to the closure of its three manufacturing plants in Saudi Arabia, actions allegedly amounting to expropriation, a failure to provide full protection and security, and a failure to afford Qatar Pharma most-favoured-nation treatment.[16] Qatar Pharma alleges that it lost access to its Saudi facilities, resulting in expired medications, uncollected invoices, and loss of broader business. They profess to have suffered tens of millions of dollars in damages as a result. The claimants indicate that they served a notice of dispute on Saudi Arabia on 1 April of 2018, but that no response

14 Ibid.

15 Abby Cohen Smutny, David Hille, Preeti Bhagnani and Eric Lenier Ives, 'Strong Medicine: Using Investment Treaties to Mitigate Foreign Regulatory Risk in the Life Sciences', *White and Case* (3 October 2022) at <https://www.whitecase.com/insight-alert/strong-medicine-using-investment-treaties-mitigate-foreign-regulatory-risk-life>.

16 Luke Eric Peterson, 'Saudi Arabia Faces Another Investor Arbitration Claim under Organisation for Islamic Cooperation Investment Treaty – Brought by Qatari Pharma Firm Affected by Blockade', *Investment Arbitration Reporter* (29 March 2019) at <https://www-iareporter-com.eu1.proxy.openathens.net/articles/saudi-arabia-faces-another-investor-arbitration-claim-under-organisation-for-islamic-cooperation-investment-treaty/>.

was forthcoming from the Saudi side. As such, a request for arbitration was filed on 28 March 2019.

A tribunal was appointed by 20 October 2020. The arbitration may still be proceeding or it may also be in a suspended state following the declaration at the GCC Summit in January 2021 to resume diplomatic relations, and the intense and confidential negotiations between the respective parties to agree to a strategy to resume some degree of normal relations without any party losing too much face.

6.6 The beIN Arbitration: beIN or beouT

Qatari-based beIN Sports broadcaster has global live and subscription sports coverage and is one of the largest sport broadcasters in the Middle East and Asia. It holds exclusive licences with many European football leagues for the MENA and Oceania regions.

On 13 June 2017, Saudi Arabia banned beIN, shortly after the Gulf diplomatic crisis began. No clear explanation was given for Saudi Arabia's decision to ban the network. However, according to a *Reuters* news report at the time, the Saudi General Commission for Audiovisual Media had said it was acting out of "concern for the rights of its citizens and residents" without elaborating further, and that the ban only applied to the import of beIN Sports receivers and the sale and renewal of subscriptions to the sports channel.[17]

Soon thereafter, a pirated network broadcasting beIN Sports' programmes emerged from Saudi Arabia called "beoutQ", which in many instances simply constituted the superimposition of the Saudi logo over the Qatari logo in a sports broadcast. According to beIN, Saudi officials did nothing to combat beoutQ's piracy, but instead actively promoted the service, while local law firms have refused to represent beIN in domestic claims against beoutQ.[18]

The beIN Corporation submitted a Notice of Arbitration on 1 October 2018 in accordance with the UNCITRAL Rules and citing the *OIC Agreement*, and seeking damages in excess of USD1 billion, plus interest, costs, and arbitration costs. The claimant has sought to rely on Article 8 (the MFN clause) of the Agreement to submit the dispute pursuant to "Article 11 of the *Saudi Arabia-Austria BIT*".[19]

According to the Notice of Arbitration, the dispute arose from measures implemented by the respondent "following the suspension of diplomatic relations with Qatar in June 2017", specifically the revocation of beIN's

17 'Saudi Arabia Bans the Import, Sale, Renewal of BeIN Sports Receivers', *Reuters* (13 June 2017) at <https://www.reuters.com/article/us-gulf-qatar-sports/saudi-arabia-bans-the-import-sale-renewal-of-bein-sports-receivers-idUSKBN1940GD>.

18 Jarrod Hepburn, 'Saudi Arabia Faces $1 Billion Claim by Qatari Media Firm under OIC Investment Agreement, amidst Gulf Diplomatic Crisis', *Investment Arbitration Reporter* (1 October 2018) at <https://www-iareporter-com.eu1.proxy.openathens.net/articles/saudi-arabia-faces-1-billion-claim-by-qatari-media-firm-under-oic-investment-agreement-amidst-gulf-diplomatic-crisis/>.

19 *beIN Corporation v Kingdom of Saudi Arabia* (Notice of Arbitration (*'beIN v Saudi Arabia'*) UNCITRAL, 1 October 2018) [2].

> legal right to operate in the jurisdiction, prohibiting the broadcast of its channels (initially in tourist facilities and subsequently expanding to restaurants and cafes), prohibiting the importation and distribution of beIN set-top boxes, suspending all monetary transactions with beIN and blocking access to its websites and call center.[20]

Claimant beIN has also alleged that shortly after Saudi Arabia implemented those measures, ultimately preventing customers in the Kingdom from accessing its services, a broadcasting pirate, beoutQ ("a play on beIN's name meaning 'be out Qatar'"), commenced operations, "stealing beIN's proprietary media content and making it accessible via the internet and satellite broadcasting as if it were its own".[21] The Saudi government had "actively supported beoutQ, including by restricting or otherwise frustrating beIN's ability to pursue civil actions before the Saudi courts, by denouncing beIN's requests to investigate and prevent the pirate's illegal activities, and by organising public gatherings to view beoutQ's pirate broadcasts of the FIFA 2018 World Cup."[22] The claimant has further alleged that the Saudi Government had "pursued manifestly arbitrary and discriminatory competition law proceedings against beIN, subjected beIN employees to ongoing harassment, and disrupted beIN's coverage of major sporting events" and in consequence, that beIN had "been deprived of its rights under its licensing and contractual arrangements and of the value of its investments in Saudi Arabia."[23]

Reportedly, the beIN claim has occurred in the context of increasing "investment treaty claims relating to interference in foreign-owned media organisations due to their perceived political orientation", for example, *Cascade Investments v Turkey* (ICSID Case No. ARB/18/4) and *Al Jazeera v Egypt* (ICSID Case No. ARB/16/1).[24] It is likely that more of these types of disputes will be submitted to arbitration in the future in the context of increased economic digitalisation, the pervasive nature of digital media, and the shift towards developing new knowledge societies in the GCC member States.

Claimant beIN has relied on Article 8 of the *OIC Agreement* to argue that "in the event that Saudi Arabia offers more favourable rights and privileges to investors from a third country it must extend the same rights and privileges to investors covered by the OIC Agreement", entitling it to "any more favourable protections offered to investors under other investment treaties to which Saudi Arabia is a party, such as the right to more favourable dispute resolution provisions when submitting their disputes to arbitration".[25] In particular, beIN has sought a choice of dispute settlement mechanisms, specifically "ICSID arbitration, ad hoc arbitration under the UNCITRAL Rules, or any other agreed form of dispute settlement, being

20 Ibid [3] and [5].
21 Ibid.
22 Ibid [6].
23 Ibid [7].
24 Jarrod Hepburn (n 18).
25 *beIN v Saudi Arabia* (n 19), [78].

"more favourable to investors compared to the dispute resolution provisions of the OIC Agreement".[26]

There is speculation that beIN's reason for seeking to apply the *Saudi Arabia–Austria BIT* was because of concern over the view held by "certain OIC member states – and potentially the OIC Secretariat – that the OIC Investment Agreement does not contain any binding consent to investor-state arbitration" and that "the Secretary-General has apparently been reluctant to make default nominations in other cases, leaving several investor claims without fully-composed tribunals following the respondent state's own unwillingness to nominate arbitrators."[27] The reasons put forward in the Notice of Arbitration relating to this perceived deficiency of the *OIC Agreement* would seem to support this assertion, although claimants in other disputes (for example, *Bin Sulaiman v Oman*) were "successful in calling on the PCA, rather than the OIC Secretary-General, to act as appointing authority for claims under the *OIC Agreement*".[28])

Key among beIN's reasons to support this argument is concern that the OIC Secretary-General has somewhat of a history of failing to make the necessary appointments, and the absence of a designated "substitute appointing authority" effectively could prevent "the constitution of the arbitral tribunal" which was "less favourable than the treatment afforded to investors under the Saudi Arabia-Austria BIT".[29] Even if the OIC Secretary-General were to make the necessary appointments, he was a Saudi national who had held senior posts in the Government of Saudi Arabia, had expressed support for economic measures imposed upon Qatar, and would have been subject to the prospect of criminal action in Saudi Arabia for expressing pro-Qatari views.[30] Claimant beIN also argued that the UNCITRAL Rules allowed "for a more favourable procedural framework for international arbitration, and therefore more favourable treatment, for beIN under the Saudi Arabia-Austria BIT that it would obtain under the OIC Agreement".[31]

Claimant beIN submitted that the respondent has breached *OIC Agreement* guarantees in respect of adequate protection and security, treatment not less favourable than that accorded to investors of any third state, restrictions on expropriation, and free transfer of their investments and returns without discriminatory restrictions or any taxes or charges.[32] Because of the operation of the MFN clause, and the consequent protection of *the Saudi Arabia–Austria BIT*, the respondent has violated its guarantee of fair and equitable treatment, prohibition of impairment by arbitrary and discriminatory measures against the investments, full protection and security, restrictions of expropriation, and free transfer of payments.[33]

26 Ibid [79].
27 Jarrod Hepburn (n 18).
28 Ibid.
29 Ibid.
30 *beIN v Saudi Arabia* (n 19), [81].
31 Ibid [83]–[84].
32 Ibid [93].
33 Ibid [94].

By 11 August 2020, a tribunal was reported to have been constituted, 21 months after the lodgement of the arbitration claim. The arbitration is still apparently ongoing, and it remains to be seen as to what an arbitral tribunal may decide. Certainly, the claimant makes some strong arguments in relation to the respondent's alleged violation of the *OIC Agreement*. Nevertheless, it is still likely that the tribunal would follow the majority decision in *Itisaluna v Iraq* with respect to the extension of the MFN clause in Article 8 of the *OIC Agreement* to a choice of dispute settlement fora. If this view were adopted by the tribunal, it would likely be fatal to the claim, which is quite unfortunate given that based on the facts, the claimant would appear to have a *prima facie* legitimate claim.

The tribunal may consider attempted reliance on the *Saudi Arabia–Austria BIT* by virtue of the operation of the MFN clause to be valid. However, the more likely view is that it may be considered over-reach and/or cherry-picking. At the same time it is quite possible that the respondent in this case may well raise jurisdiction objections to an arbitration on the grounds that beIN is still a state-controlled entity by virtue of its Al Jazeera heritage – notwithstanding the declaration on beIN's website that the Al Jazeera Media Network disassociated itself from all sports activities in December 2013 and that the beIN Media Group was incorporated and became the new independent holding company of beIN Sports in January 2014.[34] The tribunal might also eventually record that the arbitration was concluded by agreement between the parties on grounds that remain confidential. This is an important consideration in the context of commercial culture (and generally in society) within the GCC.

6.7 The Qatar Airways Group Disputes

The Gulf diplomatic crisis has arguably been a central feature of intra-GCC disputes, with the Qatar Airways Group as claimant submitting multiple investment treaty disputes and submitting other claims to various dispute settlement fora. The Qatar Airways Group has submitted four treaty-based claims to arbitration during 2020, namely *Qatar Airways Group Q.C.S.C. v Kingdom of Bahrain*, *Qatar Airways Group Q.C.S.C. v Arab Republic of Egypt*, *Qatar Airways Group Q.C.S.C. v Kingdom of Saudi Arabia*, and *Qatar Airways Group Q.C.S.C. v United Arab Emirates*.

Qatar Airways is seeking no less than USD5 billion, after being prevented from using the airspace over Bahrain, Egypt, Saudi Arabia, and the UAE from 2017, claiming the ban infringed Qatar's sovereignty.[35] Specifically, Qatar Airways has alleged that from 5 June 2017, the respondents:

> took collective measures targeting Qatar Airways and its operations. These measures specifically targeted Qatar Airways, with the objective of shuttering

34 *beIN Media Group*, website, at <https://www.beinmediagroup.com/the-group/>.

35 *Reuters* (n 8).

> Qatar Airways' local operations, destroying the value of the airline's investments and causing widespread damage to Qatar Airways' global network of operations. In particular, these measures included but were not limited to, closing their airspace and airports to Qatar Airways' aircraft and revoking Qatar Airways' licenses and permits to operate the in the blockading states. These measures persist to date and continue to disrupt Qatar Airways' global operations.[36]

The Notices of Arbitration make clear that by imposing the measures against Qatar Airways, the blockading states have violated their obligations under the *OIC Agreement* and the *Arab Investment Agreement*, including by expropriating and failing to adequately protect and secure Qatar Airways' investments, discriminating against Qatar Airways, and failing to provide fair and equitable treatment to the airline and its investments.

Qatar has sought to apply both the *OIC Agreement* and the *Arab Investment Agreement*[37] (and the *Egypt–Qatar BIT* (1999) in the case of the claim against Egypt). The application of the *OIC Agreement* and the potential outcome of these claims are particularly significant because, although investors have attempted to rely on the dispute settlement provision, there is little information available about the outcome of these cases.[38] The *OIC Agreement* is significant in its capacity as a gap-filler in essence. It gives foreign investors an investment arbitration alternative in the absence of an applicable BIT, in disputes involving the Agreement partners and claimants from those states, for example in Saudi Arabia and Qatar.[39] In the four treaty-based claims initiated by the Qatar Airways Group, the arbitral rules are "UNCITRAL and/or ad hoc".[40]

This was very likely strategic. As Craig Gaver and Yusuf Kumtepe point out, the appointment of arbitrators under Article 17(2)(b) of the *OIC Agreement* requires the respondent to make an appointment, although the OIC Secretary-General can step in and "complete the composition" at the request of the claimant if the respondent

36 'Qatar Airways Launches Multibillion Dollar Investment Arbitrations against the UAE, Bahrain, Saudi Arabia and Egypt', *Qatar Airways Group* (22 July 2020) at <Qatar Airways launches multi-billion dollar investment arbitrations against the UAE, Bahrain, Saudi Arabia and Egypt | Qatar Airways>.

37 *Agreement between the Government of the Arab Republic of Egypt and the Government of the State of Qatar for the Reciprocal Promotion and Protection of Investments,* signed 2 December 1999 (entered into force 14 July 2006) ('*Egypt–Qatar BIT*' (1999)).

38 Ioannis Konstantinidis, 'Deciphering the OIC Investment Agreement in Light of the Itisaluna v Republic of Iraq Award', *Qatar University Press* (19 July 2021) at <https://journals.qu.edu.qa/index.php/IRL/issue/view/190> 251.

39 Craig D. Gaver and Yusuf Kumtepe, 'Checking in on the OIC Investment Agreement: New Arbitrations, but Slow Progress on Creating a Permanent Dispute Settlement Mechanism', *Kluwer Arbitration Blog* (17 March 2023) at <Checking in on the OIC Investment Agreement: New Arbitrations, But Slow Progress on Creating A Permanent Dispute Settlement Mechanism - Kluwer Arbitration Blog>.

40 'Qatar Airways v Egypt', *Investment Arbitration Reporter* (undated) <Qatar Airways v. Egypt | Investment Arbitration Reporter (openathens.net)>.

fails to do so.[41] However, the OIC Secretary-General has declined to do so in some instances, "reportedly under political pressure from some member states"; in order "[t]o overcome this problem, claimants have used the Agreement's MFN clause to import UNCITRAL Rules in other BITs where the Secretary-General of the Permanent Court of Arbitration ('PCA') is the appointing authority".[42] However, the preliminary award in the case of *D.S. Construction FZCO v Libya* was set aside by the Paris Court of Appeal in early 2021 on the basis "that the MFN clause in the Agreement cannot import dispute-settlement procedure from another treaty".[43] In any event, bypassing of ICSID resolves the potential exclusion of an ICSID review of the *OIC Agreement* disputes, following *Itisaluna v Iraq*.[44]

Assuming Qatar Airways does proceed with its treaty-based arbitrations, it may benefit from having instituted claims under both the *OIC Agreement* and *Arab Investment Agreement*, particularly given divergence in tribunal assessments regarding the application of the *OIC Agreement*, following the tribunal decisions in *Al-Warraq v Indonesia*[45] on the one hand and, more recently, *Itisaluna v Iraq* on the other.

However, the decision in *Itisaluna v Iraq* poses some significant challenges for Qatar Airways as the claimant to overcome if the relevant tribunals are of a similar mind to the *Itisalun*a tribunal, noting that they are not bound by the decision. Critically, that tribunal noted that the *OIC Agreement* "is not in every respect a model of clarity"[46] and further, determined that while Article 17(2) of the Agreement gave "consent to arbitration in general terms", that consent was conditional on the initiation and exhaustion of conciliation.[47] Respondents defending claims submitted to arbitration under the *OIC Agreement*, including the Qatar Airways Group disputes, may raise objections to jurisdiction including the initiation and exhaustion of conciliation efforts.[48] It is unclear whether or not this has happened in this case, and thus if conciliation efforts have not occurred, the tribunal may preclude the claim from proceeding. The present suite of cases, however, is seemingly different from *Itisaluna v Iraq* in that the arbitral rules to be applied are UNCITRAL and/or ad hoc, rather than the ICSID Convention, and thus, the claimant may have more success in overcoming potential barriers, specifically the double level of consent required to submit claims to arbitration under the ICSID Convention.[49]

41 Craig Gaver and Yusuf Kumtepe (n 39).

42 Ibid.

43 Ibid.

44 *Itisaluna Iraq and others v the Republic of Iraq* ('*Itisaluna v Iraq*') (ICSID Case No. ARB/17/10); see also Craig Gaver and Yusuf Kumtepe (n 39).

45 *Hesham Talaat M. Al-Warraq v the Republic of Indonesia ('Al-Warraq v Indonesia').*

46 *Itisaluna v Iraq* (ICSID Case No. ARB/17/10), (ICSID, Award, 3 April 2020) [158]; Ioannis Konstantinidis (n 38), 264.

47 *Itisaluna v Iraq* (n 44), [190]; Ioannis Konstantinidis (n 38), 264.

48 Ioannis Konstantinidis (n 38), 264.

49 Ibid, 264–5.

The current status of the Qatar Airways Group treaty-based investment claims is uncertain. The dispute may de-escalate or be discontinued, given the resumption of diplomatic relations and flights, for example, between Qatar and Saudi Arabia from 1 October 2021.[50] It may even just wither since there appears to be no indication that arbitrators have been appointed and tribunals formed. And if tribunals are formed, a jurisdictional challenge may soon arise with the respondents arguing that Qatar Airways is really a state-controlled entity and thus not eligible to pursue the matter as an ISDS or under either Agreement or under ICSID rules.

6.8 Qatar's State–State Strategy

The *Qatar Airways* disputes have been, and still are in some instances continuing to be subject to judicial and public scrutiny in a number of different dispute settlement fora, at both the investor–state level and the state–state level. In what must be viewed as a well-orchestrated and long-term campaign by Qatar, the dispute has been aired before general and specific international bodies from the United Nations downwards in order to eventually win the campaign, even if a few skirmishes might have remained "not won" along the way. Within these various fora, Qatar has generally requested that they be heard in public if that option is available. The initiation of the state–state submissions and hearings which have been initiated from early 2017 have generally preceded the lodgment of the Qatar Airways arbitration claims against Saudi Arabia, the UAE, and Bahrain (as well as Egypt) in 2020.

The potential for multiple legal actions to be taken in addition to ISDS would be of concern to the defendant states in these cases and serves to highlight the need for GCC member States to consider the overlap of IIAs with other treaty obligations and mitigate this risk by including, for example, fork-in-the-road provisions to avoid costly and time-intensive litigation arising out of one set of facts. There are indications that some state-to-state disputation is still in progress, albeit in a temporary state of suspension, as are the proceedings being adjudicated by the International Civil Aviation Organization.

The state-to-state campaign commenced with Qatar initiating separate proceedings before the WTO's Dispute Settlement Body (DSB) (comprising all members of the WTO) against Saudi Arabia, the UAE, and Bahrain. On 31 July 2017, Qatar notified the DSB that it had "requested consultations" (the WTO terminology for initiating dispute settlement procedures) with all three members in almost identical terms, concerning alleged violations of various provisions of the WTO's General Agreement on Trade and Tariffs 1994 (GATT 1994), General Agreement on Trade

50 'Qatar and Saudi Arabia Agree to Suspend Proceedings before the WTO's Appellate Body', *Investment Arbitration Reporter* (10 January 2022) at <Qatar and Saudi Arabia agree to suspend proceedings before the WTO's Appellate Body | Investment Arbitration Reporter (openathens.net)>; 'Qatar Airways to Resume Flights to Medina, Saudi Arabia with Four Weekly Flights Starting 1 October 2021', *Qatar Airways Group* (30 September 2021) at <Qatar Airways to Resume Flights to Medina, Saudi Arabia with Four Weekly Flights Starting 1 October 2021 | Qatar Airways Newsroom>.

in Services (GATS), and the Agreement on Trade-Related Aspects of Intellectual Property Rights (TRIPS Agreement). Although a dispute panel was requested in respect of the UAE "consultations", it appears that no proceedings were conducted, and the authority for the panel lapsed. Panels did not form in respect of the Saudi and Bahraini "consultations". The WTO still records the current status of all three as "in consultation on 31 July 2017".

However, on 1 October 2018, Qatar launched another "request for consultations" against Saudi Arabia, this time for alleged violations of the TRIPS Agreement in respect of its actions against beIN. On Qatar's request a panel was established with the stated measure before it of "Measures relating to the piracy by beoutQ, a broadcasting entity, of the proprietary content of beIN, a global sports and entertainment company headquartered in Qatar".[51] The panel circulated its report to DSB members on 16 June 2020. The panel determined that Saudi Arabia had acted inconsistently with (i) TRIPS Articles 41.1 (general obligations) and 42 (civil and administrative procedures and remedies) by measures that, directly or indirectly, resulted in preventing beIN from being able to enforce its IP rights through civil enforcement procedures before Saudi courts and tribunals; (ii) TRIPS Article 61 (criminal procedures) by not provid[ing] for criminal procedures and penalties to be applied to the operations of beoutQ; and (iii) TRIPS Article 73 (security exception): the panel concluded that the requirements for invoking TRIPS Article 73(b)(iii) were met in relation to inconsistencies with TRIPS Articles 41.1 and 42 of the "anti-sympathy measures". But the panel also made the damning formal note that:

> throughout the proceeding, Saudi Arabia took the position that, consistent with its severance of all relations with Qatar (including diplomatic and consular relations), and the essential security interests that motivated it to take that action, it would not interact, or have any direct or indirect engagement, with Qatar in any way in the dispute. Regarding the organizational meeting, the Panel decided to consult with the parties exclusively through a written procedure. The Panel also modified the standard Working Procedures to reflect the special circumstances.[52]

In late December 2021 both Saudi Arabia and Qatar agreed to the suspension of proposed appellate proceedings pursuant to the terms of the Al-Ula Declaration. Qatar also confirmed the suspension of any further proceedings to adopt the panel report, while the mutually agreed suspension remains in place.[53] On 20 January 2022, the UAE advised the WTO that it welcomes the statement by Qatar that it considers the proceedings and the dispute at an end. On its part, the UAE has

51 World Trade Organization, 'Saudi Arabia – Measures Concerning the Protection of Intellectual Property Rights', Report of the Panel, 16 June 2020, Doc. WT/DS567/R, 14.

52 Ibid, 14 and 15.

53 World Trade Organization, 'United Arab Emirates – Measures Relating to Trade in Goods and Services, and Trade-Related Aspects of Intellectual Property Rights', Communication from the Panel, 19 January 2022, Doc. WT/DS526/6.

decided not to seek the resumption of the proceedings, in order to give effect to the Al Ula Declaration, which requires the termination of all legal cases pending between the Parties.[54]

On 30 October 2017 Qatar commenced proceedings against Saudi Arabia, the UAE, and Bahrain before the Council of the International Civil Aviation Organization pursuant to Article 84 of the *Convention on International Civil Aviation* (1944) challenging the air travel blockades on the grounds that they violated the Convention.[55] The States as respondents raised preliminary objections to the Council's jurisdiction to hear the claims. On 29 June 2018, the Council rejected their claims. On 4 July 2018, Saudi Arabia, the UAE, and Bahrain responded by challenging the competency of the International Civil Aviation Organization to hear the dispute before the International Court of Justice (ICJ).[56] On 14 July 2021, the ICJ held that the International Civil Aviation Organization was competent to hear the matter.[57]

And on 8 March 2018, the UN Committee on the Elimination of Racial Discrimination received two submissions from Qatar respectively against Saudi Arabia and the UAE under Article 11 of the Convention on the Elimination of All Forms of Racial Discrimination.[58] Qatar again referred the matter to the Committee on 29 October 2018, following which the parties were invited to make submissions on issues of jurisdiction, admissibility, and the exhaustion of all available domestic remedies. In February 2020, the Chair of the Committee appointed members of separate ad hoc commissions for Saudi Arabia and the UAE.

Following the GCC's Al Ula Declaration at its Summit a week earlier, on 11 January 2021, Qatar requested the suspension of the proceedings. The Al Ula Declaration had apparently provided the parties with a deadline of one year to terminate the proceedings from the date of its adoption. Both respondents consented to the suspension.[59]

The Commission terminated the Saudi Arabia ad hoc commission on 19 January 2021 since neither state party had expressed a wish to resume the consideration

54 World Trade Organization, 'United Arab Emirates – Measures Relating to Trade in Goods and Services, and Trade-Related Aspects of Intellectual Property Rights', Communication from the United Arab Emirates, 20 January 2022, Doc. WT/DS526/8.

55 Vladislav Djanic, 'Qatar Airways Lodges Treaty-Based Arbitration Cases against Four Middle Eastern States', *Investment Arbitration Reporter* (22 July 2020) at <Qatar Airways lodges treaty-based arbitration cases against four Middle Eastern states | Investment Arbitration Reporter (openathens .net)>; see also UN News, 'UN Top Court Rules in Favour of Qatar in International Airspace Disputes' (14 July 2020) <UN top court rules in favour of Qatar in international airspace dispute | UN News>.

56 Vladislav Djanic (n 55).

57 UN News (n 55).

58 UN Committee on the Elimination of Racial Discrimination, 'Interstate Communications Qatar v. Kingdom of Saudi Arabia and Qatar v. United Arab Emirates', *UN Human Rights, Office of the High Commissioner* (undated) at <https://www.ohchr.org/en/treaty-bodies/cerd/inter-state-communications>.

59 Ibid.

of the dispute. A few days later, the UAE informed the Commission that, given the expiration of the one-year deadline following the conclusion of the Al Ula Declaration, "neither party has expressed within the indicated timeframe any wish to resume the proceedings",[60] and requested the proceedings to be terminated. On 23 December 2022, Qatar also requested the termination of the case. Finally, on 26 January 2023, the Commission, having noted that both state parties concerned requested the termination of the proceedings, decided to end its work, thus bringing to a close Qatar's UN commission campaign.[61]

On 11 June 2018, Qatar filed an application with the ICJ instituting proceedings against the UAE with regard to alleged violations of the International Convention on the Elimination of All Forms of Racial Discrimination (CERD) (1965). In public hearings, Qatar claimed and sought a declaration from the Court that the UAE committed violations of CERD by expelling, on a collective basis, all Qataris from the UAE; applying the travel bans; encouraging racial discrimination against Qataris and orchestrating a campaign of hatred against Qatar and Qataris; and failing to provide access to effective protection and remedies to Qataris to seek redress.[62]

Qatar requested the Court to direct the UAE to cease its ongoing violations and lift the travel bans, make full financial reparation for all material and moral damage caused by its internationally wrongful acts and omissions under the CERD, make a public apology, and offer assurances and guarantees of non-repetition.[63]

Both parties submitted requests for provisional measures, with the court approving those requested by Qatar and declining those requested by the UAE.[64] In its judgment delivered on 4 February 2021, the Court held by a majority of 11 to 6 that all 3 of Qatar's claims did not fall within the meaning of the Convention and that accordingly, the Court did not have jurisdiction *ratione materiae* in the present case under Article 22 of the Convention.[65]

On 20 September 2018, Qatar lodged notices with the PCA to initiate four separate arbitrations[66] against Bahrain, Egypt, Saudi Arabia, and the UAE, in each

60 Ibid.

61 Ibid. See also 'Qatar and Saudi Arabia Agree to Suspend Proceedings before the WTO's Appellate Body' (n 50).

62 International Court of Justice, 'Application of the International Convention on the Elimination of All Forms of Racial Discrimination (Qatar V. United Arab Emirates)', 4 February 2021, [22.2]

63 Ibid [22.2–4].

64 Ibid [8], [15].

65 Ibid [114]–[115].

66 *Arbitration Pursuant to Article 32 of the Constitution of the Universal Postal Union (The State of Qatar v. The Kingdom of Bahrain)* (PCA Case No. 2020-25), 20 September 2018, at <https://pca-cpa.org/en/cases/250/>; *Arbitration Pursuant to Article 32 of the Constitution of the Universal Postal Union (The State of Qatar v. The Arab Republic of Egypt)* (PCA Case No. 2020-26), 20 September 2020, at <https://pca-cpa.org/en/cases/251/>; *Arbitration Pursuant to Article 32 of the Constitution of the Universal Postal Union (The State of Qatar v. The Kingdom of Saudi Arabia)* (PCA Case No. 2020-27), 20 September 2020, at <https://pca-cpa.org/en/cases/252/>; *Arbitration Pursuant to Article 32 of the Constitution of the Universal Postal Union (The State of Qatar v. The United Arab Emirates)* (PCA Case No. 2020-28), 20 September 2018, at <https://pca-cpa.org/en/cases/253/>.

case invoking Article 32 of the Universal Postal Union (UPU) Constitution and asserting that the "four blockading states violated their international commitments when they suspended postal services with Qatar".[67] Tribunals for each arbitration were constituted on 29 May 2020. Pursuant to Article 153 of the UPU's General Regulations, the arbitration proceedings are confidential.

Counsel for Qatar in the PCA proceedings reported in February 2020 that Qatar secured an unprecedented resolution adopted by the UPU Council of Administration against the four States and in support of Qatar.[68] Although the UPU has called on the four states to re-establish direct postal relations with Qatar, none had heeded that call. Counsel's report also states that for more than a year, the four states have attempted to frustrate the PCA arbitration proceedings by refusing to cooperate in the appointment of their arbitrators for the arbitral tribunals. The UPU took note of their "continued lack of cooperation" in this regard.[69] Hence Qatar proposed the resolution before the Council to strongly urge the UPU's International Bureau to appoint the third arbitrator in the four arbitrations.

The PCA repository records that the proceedings against Egypt were terminated by the tribunal with the agreement of the parties on 6 October 2021, and those against Saudi Arabia were terminated on 15 February 2022. However, the proceedings against Bahrain and the UAE appear to be continuing.

In January 2021 the GCC member States held their Summit at the Saudi historic centre of Al-Ula. Some of the above state–state actions were resolved, but others were just suspended, and others still seem to be unresolved. Further resolution was achieved following the issuance of the Al-Ula Declaration from the Summit.

6.9 Concluding Remarks: A Region-Specific Character

In summary, the GCC has experienced just six entirely internal ISDS arbitrations, that is, where both the investor claimant and respondent have been nationals of a GCC member State. The first occurred as recently as 2017 – just six years ago – and all must still be seen as being in the "pending" category. Five of those cases involved a very similar set of factors or were joined by the one primary causation, namely the Gulf diplomatic crisis which led to the severance of diplomatic relations between Qatar on the one hand and Saudi Arabia, the UAE, and Bahrain on the other. Egypt has also been involved in two disputes involving the same causative factor, namely the Gulf diplomatic crisis, which has been the prime reason for including an analysis of their case involvements in this chapter.

Two issues in particular stand out from an analysis of the above arbitration cases. Firstly, the absence of principle and preparation on the part of the GCC member States, as both a union and as individual members of that union, to resolve

67 Lisa Bohmer, 'Easing of Qatar-Saudi Arabia Tensions Could Affect Treaty-Based Arbitrations' (n 9).

68 'Foley Hoag Helps Qatar Secure Unprecedented Resolution at the Universal Postal Union', *Foley Hoag* (27 February 2020) at <https://foleyhoag.com/news-and-insights/news/2020/february/foley-hoag-helps-qatar-secure-unprecedented-resolution-at-the-universal-postal-union/>.

69 Ibid.

(reasonably) amicably and promptly foreign investment disputes across their own borders. While the GCC reflects a solidarity to outsiders, reflecting perhaps the external regional threats that prompted its creation, the organisation's internal infrastructures and relationships have been exposed as rather wanting.

Secondly, the noble notion of brotherhood does not appear to be as strong and as widely held as the GCC would prefer and as it needs to be.

The Al-Ula Summit and the Declaration that emerged from it actually demonstrate those shortcomings. But also is an indication of the deteriorating situation confronting it that, if it continued to deteriorate, could threaten the whole fabric of the GCC itself. The Declaration reinforces that principle of solidarity and assert the following undertakings: for example, to:

- stand in solidarity to ensure that none shall in any way suffer its sovereignty to be encroached upon or security threatened;
- stand firm against any confrontation that could undermine their national or regional security;
- be united against any direct or indirect interference in any member's internal affairs;
- strengthen their media coordination in the context of the Gulf and Arab conventions concerning the media;
- strengthen their cooperation to combat terrorist entities, movements, and organisations, or any such actors that threaten the security or stability of any of their number.

In respect of the current disputes, the Declaration doesn't mince words and makes the following directive to its members:

> II. Further to the present Declaration, each of them is committed to bringing an end to any claims, complaints, measures, protests, objections or disputes of any sort against any other State party to the Declaration, including by dropping, withdrawing or rescinding them, and to stopping implementation of the measures announced on 10 Ramadan A.H. 1438 (5 June 2017), in accordance with the following parameters:
>
> 1. The measures announced on 10 Ramadan A.H. 1438 (5 June 2017), including those associated with or connected to land, air and sea transport, shall cease to be implemented within one week of the date of signature of the present Declaration.
> 2. All claims, complaints, measures, protests, objections and disputes shall be terminated at the end of the first year from the date of signature of the present Declaration. Such claims, complaints, measures, protests, objections and disputes shall be suspended or frozen with the entities in question (i.e. the courts, agencies, committees, authorities and other domestic, regional and international entities) within one week of the

signature of the present Declaration. Each State party to the present Declaration shall take implementing measures accordingly.

3. Owing to their commitment to sustaining the terms of the present Declaration, they shall refrain from taking or imposing any measures that could bring about a return to the situation before 5 June 2017.

It is noteworthy that the signatories to the Al-Ula Declaration include not only the six GCC member States but also Egypt, its signature "confirming the strengthening of diplomatic relations between Egypt and GCC states. This confirmation extends from the GCC Charter, which stipulates that coordination, cooperation and integration between the GCC states aims to reinforce and serve Arab interests".[70]

The impact of the above edict can be noticed with a number of state–state issues before international organisations suspended or withdrawn. However, the status of the actual investor–state arbitrations, including the one not related to the Gulf diplomatic crisis, remains uncertain.

In the view of the authors, the Al-Ula Declaration is a significant milestone and presents a possible opportunity for developing a regional or perhaps intra-GCC bilateral investment treaty framework. There is support for this assertion in the literature. For example, Nadder Kabbani argues that the Declaration was "an important first step towards reconciliation; yet much work needs to be done" namely, "greater coordination and integration of security, foreign policy and economic functions".[71] Given that investor–state arbitration and the IIA framework upon which it is based transcend both foreign and economic policy, and all GCC member States have demonstrated a desire to diversify their economies and shift towards knowledge-based societies, there is a strong argument to be made that coordination with respect to ISDS would be of benefit.

However, there is reason to suspect that the success of efforts in this regard will require a coordinated and conciliatory approach to what has historically been a fractious relationship. Qatar has been very strategic in its approach and legal response to the Gulf crisis, including the initiation of its investor–state arbitration and state-to-state disputes, and Saudi Arabia has certainly approached the qualified reconciliation marked by the Summit as a means to improve on "regionalized security arrangements", including "the perceived withdrawal of Washington from the Middle East" and neutralising the risk of Iran-related security issues as well as improving public relations.[72] There is reason to be cautious, however, of the façade of harmonious relations created by the Summit, as "intra-GCC differences

70 GCC Summit 41, *Gulf Cooperation Council*, Press Release (5 January 2021) at <https://gcc41.org/press-releases/the-al-ula-declaration>.

71 Nadder Kabbani, 'The Blockade on Qatar Helped Strengthen Its Economy, Paving the Way to Stronger Regional Integration', *Brookings* (19 January 2021) at <The blockade on Qatar helped strengthen its economy, paving the way to stronger regional integration | Brookings>.

72 Dania Thafer and Patrick Theros, 'What the Al-Ula GCC Summit Has (and Has Not) Accomplished' (indated) *Gulf International Forum* at <https://gulfif.org/what-the-al-ula-gcc-summit-has-and-has-not-accomplished/>.

and their underlying rivalries have not gone away, and could unexpectedly reappear in a future Gulf Crisis".[73] On this basis, and given the particular difficulties associated with reliance upon the defective *OIC Agreement*, it is suggested that if a union-based accord is difficult to achieve, the GCC member States work in country pairs to develop a strong BIT network with greater certainty in respect of the dispute settlement mechanism, which is capable of being utilised by aggrieved investor-claimants. Certainly, Qatar in particular has strong reasons to pursue this strategy to protect its nationals operating in other GCC territories.

The GCC has had a relatively complex approach to investor–state arbitration. While the member States subscribe to IIAs containing investment protections and dispute settlement mechanisms, there are significant gaps in the bilateral treaty network. Moreover, it is suggested that the two most significant treaties that can be relied upon in the absence of a more favourable BIT, namely the *OIC Agreement* and *Arab Investment Agreement*, are sub-optimal and underutilised. In addition, the dispute body contemplated by the *OIC Agreement* has yet to be established, while the Arab Investment Court appears to be underutilised. This is an interesting and somewhat contradictory position considering some obscurity in terms of reporting the relevant administering institution and a possible preference for the PCA, particularly for arbitrations conducted on an intra-GCC basis.

There are a number of examples discussed earlier and above where GCC member States named as respondents have tried to undermine or frustrate the dispute settlement process by, for example, not complying by failing to appoint an arbitrator or objecting to jurisdiction (as occurred in *Al Mehdar v. Egypt*). Perhaps unsurprisingly, there is evidence of an unwillingness of the OIC Secretary-General to step in and appoint arbitrators in circumstances where the respondent state has failed or declined to do so. However, the PCA has demonstrated a willingness to facilitate the constitution of tribunals by acting as an appointing authority. There are also examples of claimants attempting to apply the MFN provision in a multilateral investment agreement in order to obtain access to a more favourable BIT (as in *Alyafei v. Jordan (1)*). In some instances, claimants have experienced difficulty in enforcing awards, despite making seemingly *bona fide* attempts to settle prior (*Al-Kharafi v. Libya and others*). Together these actions demonstrate a consensus that both the substantive investment protections, dispute settlement protections, and broader IIA network need careful review and updating. More generally, there is a lack of transparency in the progress of claims submitted to arbitration, indicating a degree of disinclination in publicising disputes, which are not conducted or reported in as public a manner as in other treaty partnerships.

In addition, there is a fundamental disjunct between the number of claims submitted to arbitration on an extra-GCC basis and a marked reluctance to submit disputes to arbitration on an intra-GCC basis, outside of extenuating circumstances. This approach is vastly different from another significant regional treaty-based relationship, namely the USMCA (and formerly the NAFTA) partners, particularly

73 Ibid.

the United States, which has demonstrated an appetite for treaty change. Moreover, United States claimants are relatively much more likely to submit claims to arbitration, particularly to be administered by highly Western administering institutions, particularly ICSID. These factors suggest a region-specific culture that is characterised by a somewhat dichotomous attitude towards investor–state arbitration; a general wariness of the deficiencies of investment protection standards and the dispute settlement mechanism contained in the *OIC Agreement* and the *Arab Investment Agreement*; a reluctance to publicise disputes; and, from a foreign policy perspective, a certain complacency with antiquated agreements that arguably are not fit for purpose.

GCC member States are in the midst of a transformational period, undertaking programmes of economic diversification, together with investment in human capital and technology as they shift towards a digital economy. Part of this process involves investment in industry. CEO of the Qatar Development Bank Abdulaziz Al-Khalifa argues that industrial SMEs need access to money, training, and markets if the GCC is to leave its "single resource identity" behind.[74] Critically, the States are also seeking to attract foreign direct investment. Saudi Arabia, for example, is seeking to increase foreign direct investment from 0.7% to 5.7% of GDP as part of its Vision 2030.[75] One action taken to achieve this goal is the launch of Invest Saudi, an entity that brings together government entities, foreign investors, domestic investors, and private businesses and facilitates investment by, for example, issuing foreign investment licences.[76] Critically, however, the attraction and retention of foreign direct investment is only one aspect of the foreign policy puzzle.

The dispute settlement framework needs to be radically overhauled to meet possible increased demand in a manner that strikes a better balance between reflecting the unique socio-legal and economic objectives of the GCC member States and enhancing investor confidence in the region. Given the comparatively low rate of intra-GCC disputes, it is probably not necessary to have an intra-GCC investment treaty, although it may be of use in resolving disputes if there were, for example, a future Gulf crisis. It is suggested that the conclusion of intra-GCC BITs would be more beneficial and possibly more stable than a multilateral arrangement, although the broader *OIC Agreement* and *Arab Investment Agreement* have arguably enjoyed longevity. Certainly, there is an argument to be made for the States to develop a model investment treaty and update both the *OIC Agreement* and the *Arab Investment Agreement* in a significant way – although this is likely easier said than done given the multilateral nature of these agreements.

74 Alexandre Raffoul and Fatima Al Zahra Hewaidi, 'How Industrialisation Could Future-Proof MENA's Gulf Economies', *World Economic Forum* (28 June 2021) at <Industrialisation is key to GCC economic diversification | World Economic Forum (weforum.org)>.

75 'Invest in Saudi Arabia', *Kingdom of Saudi Arabia* (last updated 2022) at <https://www.investsaudi.sa/en/aboutSaudi>.

76 Ibid.

Certainly, there is a need for more precise language, particularly around consent to arbitrate, the appointment of arbitrators, and enforcement. In addition, the States would likely benefit from working further towards the establishment of an organ for the settlement of disputes under the *OIC Agreement* and consolidating and promoting the procedures of the *Arab Investment Court*. A review and consolidation of the other GCC investor–state dispute settlement adjudicatory centres would also be of benefit. It is suggested that a regional review and overhaul of the existing GCC-related BIT network would be beneficial so that duplication can be avoided and gaps can be addressed to avoid the application of treaties of last resort.

Bibliography

Agreement between the Government of the Arab Republic of Egypt and the Government of the State of Qatar for the Reciprocal Promotion and Protection of Investments, signed 2 December 1999 (entered into force 14 July 2006) (*'Egypt – Qatar BIT'*).

Agreement on Promotion, Protection and Guarantee of Investments amongst the Member States of the Organization of the Islamic Conference, signed 05 June 1981 (entered into force February 1988) (*'OIC Agreement'*).

'Al Jazeera Serves Notification of Dispute on Egypt', *Carter Ruck*, Press Release (28 April 2014) at <https://www.carter-ruck.com/news/al-jazeera-notice-of-dispute-served-on-state-of-egypt/>.

'Arab States Issue 13 Demands to End Qatar-Gulf Crisis', *Al Jazeera* (12 July 2017) at <https://www.aljazeera.com/news/2017/7/12/arab-states-issue-13-demands-to-end-qatar-gulf-crisis>.

Arbitration Pursuant to Article 32 of the Constitution of the Universal Postal Union (The State of Qatar v. The Kingdom of Bahrain) (PCA Case No. 2020-25) (20 September 2018) at <https://pca-cpa.org/en/cases/250/>.

Arbitration Pursuant to Article 32 of the Constitution of the Universal Postal Union (The State of Qatar v. The Arab Republic of Egypt) (PCA case No. 2020-26) (20 September 2020) at <https://pca-cpa.org/en/cases/251/>.

Arbitration Pursuant to Article 32 of the Constitution of the Universal Postal Union (The State of Qatar v. The Kingdom of Saudi Arabia (PCA Case No. 2020-27) (20 September 2020) at <https://pca-cpa.org/en/cases/252/>.

Arbitration Pursuant to Article 32 of the Constitution of the Universal Postal Union (The State of Qatar v. The United Arab Emirates) (PCA Case No. 2020-28) (20 September 2018) at <https://pca-cpa.org/en/cases/253/>.

beIN Corporation v Kingdom of Saudi Arabia (Notice of Arbitration, (*'beIN v Saudi Arabia'*) UNCITRAL, 1 October 2018).

'beIN Media Group' at <https://www.beinmediagroup.com/the-group/>.

Bohmer, Lisa, 'Easing of Qatar-Saudi Arabia Tensions Could Affect Treaty-Based Arbitrations', *Investment Arbitration Reporter* (14 January 2021) at <Easing of Qatar-Saudi Arabia tensions could affect treaty-based arbitrations | Investment Arbitration Reporter (openathens.net)>.

Bohmer, Lisa, 'Investor in Oman's Construction Sector Files for Annulment of Still-confidential Award', *Investment Arbitration Reporter* (10 June 2012) at <https://www-iareporter-com.eu1.proxy.openathens.net/articles/investor-in-omans-construction-sector-files-for-annulment-of-still-confidential-award/>.

Djanic, Vladislav, 'Qatar Airways Lodges Treaty-Based Arbitration Cases Against Four Middle Eastern States' *Investment Arbitration Reporter* (22 July 2020) at <Qatar Airways lodges treaty-based arbitration cases against four Middle Eastern states | Investment Arbitration Reporter (openathens.net)>.

'Foley Hoag Helps Qatar Secure Unprecedented Resolution at the Universal Postal Union', *Foley Hoag* (27 February 2020) at <https://foleyhoag.com/news-and-insights/news/2020/february/foley-hoag-helps-qatar-secure-unprecedented-resolution-at-the-universal-postal-union/>.

Gaver, Craig D. and Yusuf Kumtepe, 'Checking in on the OIC Investment Agreement: New Arbitrations, But Slow Progress on Creating A Permanent Dispute Settlement Mechanism', *Kluwer Arbitration Blog* (17 March 2023) at <Checking in on the OIC Investment Agreement: New Arbitrations, But Slow Progress on Creating A Permanent Dispute Settlement Mechanism - Kluwer Arbitration Blog>.

GCC Summit 41, 'Gulf Cooperation Council', *Press Release* (5 January 2021) at <https://gcc41.org/press-releases/the-al-ula-declaration>.

Hepburn, Jarrod, 'Saudi Arabia Faces $1 Billion Claim by Qatari Media Firm Under OIC Investment Agreement, Amidst Gulf Diplomatic Crisis', *Investment Arbitration Reporter* (1 October 2018) at <https://www-iareporter-com.eu1.proxy.openathens.net/articles/saudi-arabia-faces-1-billion-claim-by-qatari-media-firm-under-oic-investment-agreement-amidst-gulf-diplomatic-crisis/>.

Hesham Talaat M. Al-Warraq v The Republic of Indonesia, Award on Respondent's Preliminary Objections to Jurisdiction and Admissibility of the Claims (UNCITRAL, 21 June 2012) (*'Al-Warraq v Indonesia'*).

International Court of Justice, 'Application of the International Convention on the Elimination of All Forms of Racial Discrimination (Qatar V. United Arab Emirates)', 4 February 2021.

Invest Saudi, 'About Invest Saudi', *Kingdom of Saudi Arabia* (2023) at <https://www.investsaudi.sa/en/aboutSaudi>.

Itisaluna Iraq and others v the Republic of Iraq (ICSID Case No. ARB/17/10) ('*Itisaluna v Iraq*').

Jones, Tom, 'Saudi Arabia Faces Another Claim Over Qatar Blockade', *Global Arbitration Review* (29 March 2019) at <Saudi Arabia faces another claim over Qatar blockade - Lexology>.

Kabbani, Nadder, 'The Blockade on Qatar Helped Strengthen its Economy, Paving the Way to Stronger Regional Integration', *Brookings* (19 January 2021) at <he blockade on Qatar helped strengthen its economy, paving the way to stronger regional integration | Brookings>.

Konstantinidis, Ioannis, 'Deciphering the OIC Investment Agreement in Light of the Itisaluna v Republic of Iraq Award', *Qatar University Press* (19 July 2021) at <Deciphering_the_OIC_Investment_Agreement_in_Light_.pdf>.

Omar Bin Sulaiman Abdul Aziz Al Rajhi v. Oman (PCA Case No. 2017-32) ('*Bin Sulaiman v Oman*').

Peterson, Luke Eric, 'Analysis: As Al Jazeera Media Network Notifies Egypt of Possible Arbitration Claim, What Legal Arguments Loom in Such a Case', *Investment Arbitration Reporter* (28 April 2014) at <https://www-iareporter-com.eu1.proxy.openathens.net/articles/analysis-as-al-jazeera-media-network-notifies-egypt-of-possible-arbitration-claim-what-legal-arguments-loom-in-such-a-case/>.

Peterson, Luke Eric, 'OIC Round Up: An Update on Pending Arbitration Cases Lodged under the OIC Investment Agreement', *Investment Arbitration Reporter* (11 August 2020) at <https://www-iareporter-com.eu1.proxy.openathens.net/articles/oic-round-up-an-update-on-pending-arbitration-cases-lodged-under-the-oic-investment-agreement/?>.

Peterson, Luke Eric, 'Saudi Arabia Faces Another Investor Arbitration Claim under Organisation for Islamic Cooperation Investment Treaty – Brought by Qatari Pharma Firm Affected by Blockade', *Investment Arbitration Reporter* (29 March 2019) at <https://www-iareporter-com.eu1.proxy.openathens.net/articles/saudi-arabia-faces-anther-investor-arbitration-claim-under-organisation-for-islamic-cooperation-investment-treaty/>.

'Qatar Airways Launces Multibillion Dollar Investment Arbitrations against the UAE, Bahrain, Saudi Arabia and Egypt', *Qatar Airways Group* (22 July 2020) at <Qatar Airways launches multibillion dollar investment arbitrations against the UAE, Bahrain, Saudi Arabia and Egypt | Qatar Airways>.

'Qatar Airways to Resume Flights to Medina, Saudi Arabia with Four Weekly Flights Starting 1 October 2021', *Qatar Airways Group* (1 October 2021) at <Qatar Airways to Resume Flights to Medina, Saudi Arabia with Four Weekly Flights Starting 1 October 2021 | Qatar Airways Newsroom>.

'Qatar Airways Seeks $5 Billion Compensation from Arab Bloc Over Airspace Ban', *Reuters* (22 July 2020) at <Qatar Airways seeks $5 billion compensation from Arab bloc over airspace ban | Reuters>.

Raffoul, Alexandre and Fatima Al Zahra Hewaidi, 'How Industrialisation Could Future-Proof MENA's Gulf Economies', *World Economic Forum* (28 June 2021) at <Industrialisation is key to GCC economic diversification | World Economic Forum (weforum.org)>.

'Saudi Arabia Bans the Import, Sale, Renewal of BeIN Sports Receivers', *Reuters* (13 June 2017) at <https://www.reuters.com/article/us-gulf-qatar-sports/saudi-arabia-bans-the-import-sale-renewal-of-bein-sports-receivers-idUSKBN1940GD>.

Smutny, Abby Cohen, David Hille, Preeti Bhagnani and Eric Lenier Ives, 'Strong Medicine: Using Investment Treaties to Mitigate Foreign Regulatory Risk in the Life Sciences', *White and Case* (3 October 2022) at <https://www.whitecase.com/insight-alert/strong-medicine-using-investment-treaties-mitigate-foreign-regulatory-risk-life>.

Thafer, Diana and Patrick Theros, 'What the Al-Ula GCC Summit Has (and Has Not) Accomplished', *Gulf International Forum* at <What the Al-Ula GCC Summit Has (and Has Not) Accomplished - Gulf International Forum,at https://gulfif.org/what-the-al-ula-gcc-summit-has-and-has-not-accomplished/>.

UNCTAD, 'Investment Dispute Settlement Navigator' at <Advanced Search | Investment Dispute Settlement Navigator | UNCTAD Investment Policy Hub>.

Unified Agreement for the Investment of Arab Capital in the Arab States, signed 26 November 1980 (entered into force 7 September 1981) (*'Arab Investment Agreement'*).

UN Committee on the Elimination of Racial Discrimination, 'Interstate Communications Qatar v. Kingdom of Saudi Arabia and Qatar v. United Arab Emirates', *UN Human Rights, Office of the High Commissioner* (undated) at <https://www.ohchr.org/en/treaty-bodies/cerd/inter-state-communications>.

UN News, 'UN Top Court Rules in Favour of Qatar in International Airspace Disputes', *United Nations* (14 July 2020) at <UN top court rules in favour of Qatar in international airspace dispute | UN News>.

World Trade Organisation, 'Appellate Body' (10 January 2022) at <Qatar and Saudi Arabia agree to suspend proceedings before the WTO's Appellate Body | Investment Arbitration Reporter (openathens.net)>.

World Trade Organisation, 'Saudi Arabia – Measures Concerning the Protection of Intellectual Property Rights', *Report of the Panel* (16 June 2020), Doc. WT/DS567/R.

World Trade Organisation, 'United Arab Emirates – Measures Relating to Trade in Goods and Services, and Trade-Related Aspects of Intellectual Property Rights', *Communication from the Panel* (19 January 2022), Doc. WT/DS526/6.

World Trade Organisation, 'United Arab Emirates – Measures Relating to Trade in Goods and Services, and Trade-Related Aspects of Intellectual Property Rights', *Communication From The United Arab Emirates* (20 January 2022), Doc. WT/DS526/8.

7 Domestic Investment Protection and Promotion Legislative and Regulatory Frameworks in the GCC

7.1 Introduction

This chapter provides some local background and context to the ISDS disputation environments examined in the previous chapters, namely the GCC member States as respondents, and as the home states of claimants. It briefly reviews the various domestic legislative and regulatory regimes of the GCC member States as context for the promotion and protection of foreign direct investment and the international investment agreements (IIAs) that the States have ratified and that allow for investor–state dispute settlement. The chapter also considers whether the States' domestic regimes approach to the treatment of foreign investors differs from that of local or regional investors. The chapter then provides some brief background information on the status of FDI capital inflows and outflows in respect of the GCC member States.

Domestic investment protection and promotion legislation and regulations in the GCC are changing, starting to become more liberalised and modern in character. Some of the GCC member States have recently enacted, and even re-enacted, legislation addressing foreign direct investment, and others are in the process of reviewing related legislative regimes and at times longstanding legislation. The legislative and regulatory frameworks impacting upon foreign direct investment in each State broadly define key terms, set out the rules in relation to allowable foreign investment activities, and in some instances, address dispute settlement. Some legislation addresses important investment protections typically contained in IIAs, such as transfer of capital and profits and anti-expropriation versus expropriation in the public interest. This demonstrates a level of awareness of the potential for claims to arise which may challenge, for example, the legitimacy of a particular state policy or legal measure, as well as a desire to preserve state sovereignty in undertaking measures deemed necessary.

However, the drafting of these domestic protections is generally rather broad – potentially risking regulatory chill and arguably open to subjective and potentially inconsistent interpretation and application. Unfortunately, if disputes progress to international investment arbitration, there is a potential risk that legitimate regulatory activities undertaken by the GCC member States will be open to arbitral review. Gordon Blanke argues that despite the inclusion of investment protections and incentives, and "generally favourable, pro-investment language, the GCC

DOI: 10.4324/9781003481072-7

investment laws are not as advanced as the bilateral investment treaties (BITs) and multilateral investment treaties (MITs) that individual States have in place".[1] Blanke emphasises that the domestic legislation does not contain "provisions on equal and non-discriminatory treatment between local and foreign investors" and further, that not all the domestic foreign direct investment laws contain a dispute settlement provision allowing access to arbitration.[2] While some States are in the process of further amending their foreign direct investment legislative and regulatory regimes, there is arguably much more work to be done in terms of striking a better balance between investment protection, and certainly, more clarity is needed in terms of the dispute settlement process and the availability of domestic dispute resolution and international arbitration.

7.2 Domestic Legislative Frameworks and Environments

The GCC member States have taken different approaches to the domestic protection and promotion of foreign direct investment (FDI). The UAE and Saudi Arabia have embraced some elements of a Western approach to investment protection and promotion, while retaining some conflicting elements of national protection. The other States, particularly Kuwait and Qatar, have maintained a more conservative and traditional approach, while Bahrain and Oman are tending to become increasingly liberal. The majority of the States have sui generis foreign investment protection laws in place, which generally display similar core elements in common, albeit with variations in the content and degree of commitment of those elements, arguably indicating more of a degree of intra-State collaboration and intercourse at the ministerial and operative levels (which is common practice between the States) than GCC–State-level formal debate and agreement. Neither Bahrain nor the UAE currently have sui generis FDI laws in force. Bahrain has yet to create such a law, while the UAE repealed its 2018 FDI law in 2020 when it incorporated its provisions primarily into an upgraded commercial companies law, complemented by other standing commercial-related laws. Where such sui generis laws are in force, they are generally of fairly recent standing and have either generally arisen from contemporary commercial laws of long standing or replaced (as distinct from amended) earlier FDI laws of a vintage when the respective economies and associated FDI were of much smaller dimension and complexity. Hence, Kuwait's FDI law was first enacted in 2013, while the UAE's *Federal Law No. 2 of 2015 Concerning Commercial Companies*, as amended in 2017 and 2020, replaced the longstanding Federal Law No. 8 of 1984 and absorbed the FDI law created in 2018 and repealed in the 2020 amendments. These FDI laws and/or their commercial company counterparts are generally reinforced by related laws governing

1 Gordon Blanke, 'GCC Investment Laws: To Arbitrate or Not to Arbitrate, That Is the Question (Part 1)', *Practical Law Arbitration Blog* (7 February 2019) at <GCC investment laws: to arbitrate or not to arbitrate, that is the question (Part 1) | Arbitration Blog (practicallaw.com)>.

2 Ibid.

commercial activity, such as company registration, operation of agencies, property ownership, commercial banking and financial regulation, competition regulation, taxation, concealment of required information, and commercial arbitration, just to mention some. Most States also retain protectionist regimes to a greater or lesser extent in respect of local employment opportunity and preference by limiting or even excluding the recruitment of foreign staff into certain employment categories.

GCC member State regulators appear to intend to adopt a more culturally appropriate dispute settlement mechanism by, for example, incorporating a requirement for amicable settlement (Saudi Arabia) in domestic legislation and regulations governing FDI. While this is likely to accommodate the preferences of intra-GCC investors, it may not necessarily suit Western investors with a litigious mindset. However, there is recognition of the potential failure of a negotiated informal settlement and the initiation of domestic legal proceedings and arbitration, as well as a need to better delineate between the role and scope of arbitral tribunals and domestic legal institutions hearing such disputes (UAE). These provisions evidence a view held by the States that foreign investors from outside the GCC are much more likely to pursue relief in international arbitration, compared with investors from within the GCC. It lends credence to the argument that foreign investors from the other States have a disinclination to public, non-local, and formal dispute settlement proceedings and that international investment arbitration on an intra-GCC basis is undertaken more as a last resort, and for the most part, in times of regional discord. However, it must be emphasised that each of the States has adopted varying approaches in this respect.

The United States Department of State produces a regular series of annual reports on a broad spectrum of trade-related subject matter dealing with the relationships between, and performance of, its trading partners in respect of their US trading counterparts and investors. While the reports generally focus on the promotion of US interests and their access to foreign markets, they also provide revealing insights. Accordingly, brief extracts from the State Department's reports dealing with the respective GCC member States and their foreign direct investment regimes are included at the close of each State section.

7.3 The Kingdom of Bahrain

Investment policy oversight and review is led mainly by the Ministry of Industry and Commerce ("MOIC"), the Central Bank of Bahrain ("CBB"), and the Bahrain Economic Development Board ("EDB"), with the Board taking the role of promoting foreign investment in Bahrain and liaising with the different authorities to ensure that "a business-friendly environment is achieved with a focus of supporting both local and foreign investors".[3]

3 Fatima Al Ali and Saifuddin Mahmood, 'Foreign Direct Investment Regimes Bahrain 2023', *ICLG* (30 November 2022) at <Foreign Direct Investment Regimes Laws and Regulations Report 2023 Bahrain (iclg.com)>.

Bahrain is the only GCC member State yet to introduce a sui generis law for managing FDI.[4] The core statute of Bahrain's foreign investment legislative and regulatory framework is the *Commercial Companies Law No. 21 of 2001*, a lengthy statute of over 360 articles, which has been updated and amended in recent times, namely, in 2014, 2015, and 2018.[5] The Ministry of Industry and Commerce, being the responsible ministry, states that the Commercial Companies Law "regulates the affairs of public and closed joint stock companies, shareholding companies, limited liability companies, holding companies, the transformation and expiry of companies and the practice of foreign companies for their activities in the Kingdom".[6] Hence it generally includes all corporate entities in which foreign direct or indirect investment is likely to be involved.

A draft law is reportedly under consideration as part of the State's long-term strategic development plan, Vision 2030, which "aims to achieve the Kingdom's economic Vision 2030 by creating an attractive and safe environment for local and foreign investment and moving from an oil-based economy to a productive economy capable of competing globally"[7] and a "new investment policy that will aim to strengthen the national economy, create new jobs for Bahrainis, promote technological change and adhere to the State's general strategy for economic development".[8]

Pursuant to Articles 3, 4, and 5, the Commercial Companies Law applies to any commercial company irrespective of its form of incorporation and to any civil company with a commercial form regardless of its purpose. Accordingly, subsequent articles incorporate foreign investor references as appropriate. For example, Article (25), which deals with partnerships, includes the provision that "general partnership companies, of whatever types, may be established amongst Bahraini or non-Bahraini partners in accordance with the conditions and requirements prescribed by an order issued by the Competent Minister". Article (65) provides that Bahraini public shareholding companies may be established with the participation of foreign capital or expertise, subject to the Minister concerned with trade affairs, specifying the percentages of participation of foreign capital or expertise in certain sectors or activities.[9] Article (298) provides for the establishment of a holding

4 Gordon Blanke (n 1).

5 Bahrain, *Legislative Decree No. (21) of 2001, the Commercial Companies Law,* at <Ministry of Finance & National Economy (moic.gov.bh)> (see amended version at <Bahrain Business Laws | Commercial Companies Law>.

6 Bahrain, 'Regulations', *Ministry of Commerce and Industry* (undated) at <Regulations (moic.gov .bh)>.

7 'New Law Urged to Regulate Investment in Bahrain', *Zawya* (22 May 2022) at <New law urged to regulate investment in Bahrain (zawya.com)>.

8 Ibid.

9 Bahrain, *Law No. (50) of 2014 Amending Certain Provisions of the Commercial Companies' Law Promulgated by Legislative Decree No. (21) of 2001,* Article (65).

company for the purpose of owning shares in Bahraini or foreign shareholding companies or to participate in the establishment of such companies.[10]

However, specific provision addressing foreign companies is limited to Part XIII Foreign Capital Companies, comprising just two articles (Articles 345 and 345bis) and Part XIV Branches, Offices, and Agencies of Foreign Companies, comprising just five fairly brief articles (Articles 346–50).

Part XIII Article 345(a), as amended in 2015 and 2018, states in part that:

> a license may be issued approving the incorporation of companies provided for in this Law which are fully or partially owned by non-Bahraini partners to conduct business activities which are strictly conducted by Bahrainis or those which non-Bahrainis may not conduct without a Bahraini partner owning the majority of shares in the Company or to carry on any of those activities according to the Company's capital or the regions which the Company uses as headquarters to conduct its business activities.[11]

Article 345(b) empowers the Council of Ministers to issue the necessary authorisation or licence, while Article 345(c) empowers the Minister responsible for commercial affairs with the approval of the Cabinet of Ministers to approve the establishment of companies with foreign capital to carry out a specific activity which is not mentioned in section (a) where the Minister's approval is warranted by the strategic and economic importance or profitable benefits to the economy. Article 345(d) introduces further liberalisation, allowing a foreign capital company to be exempt from the minimum required share capital, for its capital to be in non-Bahraini currency, and for board of directors meetings and shareholder meetings to be held outside of Bahrain, provided the meetings still adhere to all regulations mentioned in the Law.

Part XIV Branches, Offices, and Agencies of Foreign Companies Article 347 was amended in 2014 to enable a company incorporated outside Bahrain to set up branches, agencies, or offices in Bahrain provided it first obtains a licence from the Ministry concerned with trade affairs and that the branch, agency, or office is registered with the Ministry's Commercial Registry.[12] UNCTAD explains that the 2014 Amendments had other impacts, namely, that the Article 347 amendments also meant that branches of foreign entities no longer require a Bahraini sponsor. With the exception of companies exclusively incorporated by the government, the new law also amended Article 75(d) so that the minimum number of founders required for a joint-stock company in Bahrain was reduced to two instead of seven.[13]

10 Bahrain, *Law No. (1) of 2018 Amending Certain Provisions of the Commercial Companies' Law Promulgated by Legislative Decree No. (21) of 2001,* Article (298).

11 Ibid, Article (345(a)).

12 *Law No. (50) of 2014* (n 9), Article (347).

13 'New Commercial Companies Law', *UNCTAD* (11 September 2014) at <Bahrain - New Commercial Companies Law | Investment Policy Monitor | UNCTAD Investment Policy Hub>.

An amendment to Part XII on 19 July 2016 allowed for "100% foreign ownership in residency, food, administrative services, arts, health and social work, information and communications, mining and quarrying, water supplying, real estate and technical activities, and manufacturing, among others."[14] According to the United States Department of State:

> Bahrain permits 100 percent foreign ownership of new industrial entities and the establishment of representative offices or branches of foreign companies without Bahraini sponsors or local partners. In 2017, the [Government] expanded the number of sectors in which foreigners are permitted to maintain 100 percent ownership in companies to include tourism services, sporting events production, mining and quarrying, real estate, water distribution, water transport operations, and crop cultivation and propagation. In May 2019, the [Government] loosened foreign ownership restrictions in the oil and gas sector, allowing 100 percent foreign ownership in oil and gas extraction projects under certain conditions.[15]

Noor Radhi et al. provide a useful summary of recent edicts impacting foreign investment in Bahrain, particularly activities in which foreign companies can participate and the percentage of allowable foreign ownership, notably:

- Prime Ministerial Edict No. 49 of 2016, detailing activities allowing 100% foreign ownership;
- Prime Ministerial Edict No. 50 of 2016, detailing activities allowing foreign ownership up to 49%;
- Prime Ministerial Edict No. 17 of 2018 as amended by Prime Ministerial Edict No. 16 of 2019, detailing activities allowing 100% foreign ownership, subject to certain conditions. Foreign ownership restriction can be waived in relation to certain activities that otherwise require 51% or more Bahraini ownership where the company concerned is present in at least three international markets, has capital of at least BHD20 million or equivalent in foreign currency, and the Bahraini company branch will have capital of at least BHD2 million.[16]

14 'Bahrain Passes a New Law Allowing 100% Foreign Ownership in Various Sectors', *UNCTAD* (19 July 2016) at <Bahrain - Bahrain passed a new law allowing 100% foreign ownership in various sectors. | Investment Policy Monitor | UNCTAD Investment Policy Hub>.

15 United States Department of State, '2023 Investment Climate Statements: Bahrain' (30 November 2022) at <Bahrain - United States Department of State>.

16 Noor Radhi, Fatima Al Ali, Saifuddin Mahmood and Hasan Alkoofi, Hassan Radhi & Associates *Thomson Reuters Practical Law* (1 July 2021) at <Doing Business in Bahrain: Overview | Practical Law (thomsonreuters.com)>. See also Bahrain, 'Guidebook of Commercial Activities Requirements', *Sijilat* (Version No. June 2023) at <Sijilat 2.61_en_Finial.pdf>.

On 3 April 2023, Bahrain announced the introduction of a "golden license" offering benefits to local and foreign companies bringing large-scale investment projects to Bahrain.[17] Companies with major investment and strategic projects creating more than 500 jobs in Bahrain, or with an investment value exceeding $50 million, will be eligible for the licence. Benefits include prioritised allocation of land, infrastructure, and services, easier access to government services, and support from government development funds. Other advantages include integrated cooperation with various government departments, a designated account manager from Bahrain's Economic Development Board, and potential review of existing laws or regulations where necessary and applicable.

Other laws which impact foreign direct investment in Bahrain include *Decree No. 40/1999 on the Appropriation of Land by Citizens of the Gulf Cooperation Council of Arab Gulf Countries* and *Decree No. 2/2001* with respect to *Ownership by non-Bahrainis of Constructed Property and Land.*[18] Fatima Al Ali and Saifuddin Mahmood note, for example, "GCC nationals are given Bahraini national treatment"; however "[f]oreign nationals and companies owned by foreign nationals are permitted to own real property in certain designated areas" and "may be required to undergo a security check".[19]

With regard to the relationship between domestic legislation relating to foreign direct investment and domestic resolution of investment disputes, the United States Department of State notes that there have been no expropriations in recent years:

> Arbitration procedures are largely a contractual matter in Bahrain. Disputes historically have been referred to an arbitration body as specified in the contract, or to the local courts. In dealings with both local and foreign firms, Bahraini companies have increasingly included arbitration procedures in their contracts. Most commercial disputes are resolved privately without recourse to the courts or formal arbitration. Resolution under Bahraini law is generally specified in all contracts for the settlement of disputes that reach the stage of formal resolution but is optional in those designating the BCDR. Bahrain's court system has adequately handled occasional lawsuits against individuals or companies for non-payment of debts.[20]

7.4 The State of Kuwait

Kuwait appears to have in place a fairly broad suite of legislative and regulatory instruments to regulate, control, or otherwise impact FDI across its full spectrum.

17 'Bahrain Foreign Direct Investment with World Partners and EU27', *EU–GCC Dialogue on Economic Diversification Gulf Cooperation Council (GCC) Countries,* April 2023, 21.

18 Fatima Al Ali and Saifuddin Mahmood, 'Foreign Direct Investment Regimes Bahrain', *ICLG* (30 November 2022) at <Foreign Direct Investment Regimes Laws and Regulations Report 2023 Bahrain (iclg.com)>.

19 Ibid.

20 United States Department of State (n 15).

According to Mohamed Salem Alhihi, the FDI regime in Kuwait has changed profoundly in recent years, having become more liberal and capable of adopting the concepts of a globalised economy. These are essentially opposite to the previous laws that had virtually excluded foreigners from having businesses in the country. Most of the national laws were aimed at sustaining the wealth of the country among the citizens and preserving the assets from departing over borders.[21]

The current primary legislative instrument in respect of FDI is *Decree Law No. 116 of 2013, the Kuwait Direct Investment Promotion Law*,[22] repealing the earlier law of 2001,[23] which was generally perceived as being largely ineffective in achieving its primary objective of encouraging foreign investment in the Kuwaiti market because of its fairly restrictive rather than facilitative provisions. The 2013 Law is meant to address at least some of those restrictions, particularly in respect of clarifying such elements as investor and permissible investment, capital and capital transfer, expropriation, and dispute resolution. Alhihi suggests that the key shortcoming of the earlier FDI law was the absence of "specific guidelines for the investors' rights and obligations and the procedures required to establish a business project in Kuwait".[24]

In very basic terms, the 2013 Law defines an "investor" as a "natural or legal person of any nationality", "direct investment" as "an investment where the Investor, individually or with the participation of another investor, employs his capital directly through an Investment Entity", and an "investment entity" as "an economic enterprise or activity that is licenced in accordance with this law by virtue of an investment".[25] "Capital" is defined as that which is employed or used directly for the purposes of direct investment through an investment entity subject to the Law and includes:

- funds, financial and commercial securities, be they local or foreign.
- machinery, tools, equipment, transportation means, and other technological devices;
- raw materials and intermediate goods required for the commencement of actual production or operations by the investment entity;
- intangible rights such as patents, trademarks, licences, registered trade names, and industrial and technological designs

21 Mohamed Salem Alhihi, 'Legal Assessment of the Kuwaiti Foreign Direct Investment Rules in Light of the WTO Rules' (2020) *Kuwait International Law School Journal* (8) Special Supplement 35, 41.

22 Kuwait, *Decree Law No. 116 of 2013 on Promoting Direct Investment in the State of Kuwait*, at <law1162013.pdf (kdipa.gov.kw)>.

23 Kuwait, *Decree Law No. 8 of 2001 on Regulating Direct Foreign Capital Investment In the State of Kuwait*, at <Microsoft Word - direct_investment.doc (kuwaitemb-australia.com)>.

24 Mohamed Salem Alhihi (n 21).

25 Kuwait, Law No. 116 of 2013 (n 22), Article 1.

- profits and proceeds of the invested capital if used for the increase of the capital or if they are employed or used for the purposes of direct investment through an investment entity licenced in accordance with the Law.[26]

The Law then devotes primary consideration to the establishment of a Direct Investment Promotion Authority and its role and responsibilities, and rules for the good corporate governance of the Authority whose purpose is to attract and promote both foreign and local direct investment in the country.[27] The aims of the Authority are again generally enunciated:

- develop and improve the national investment environment, facilitate procedures and remove hurdles encountered by investors, and provide assistance and support to encourage direct investment in the country;
- raise awareness regarding the importance of direct investment, especially foreign investment, and promotion of the Investment Law investment environment and available direct investment opportunities;
- encourage investors to transfer, settle, and use modern and sophisticated technologies, means of production and operations, management methods, and technical and marketing expertise and to encourage partnerships between Kuwaiti and foreign investors that foster the objectives of development.

The Law has some inbuilt flexibility for future policy developments in respect of allowable foreign investments, but it still preserves some business areas for Kuwaiti nationals. Article 11, for example, requires the Council of Ministers to produce a "Negative List" of investments that will be excluded from the scope of the Law and thus not attract its encouragements and benefits. The List is subject to updating in light of public policy with the Council of Ministers setting "the principles and rules regarding the investments of foreign corporate entities" in Kuwait,[28] but logic would dictate that areas not included on the List remain within the purview of the Authority. The List, not surprisingly, encompasses key areas of Kuwaiti industry and society, namely:

- oil and natural gas extraction; gas manufacture and mains distribution; manufacture of fertilisers and nitrogen compounds;
- real estate, excluding privately operated building development projects;
- security and investigation activities;
- public administration and defence; compulsory social security;
- activities of membership organisations;

26 Ibid.

27 Ibid, Articles 2–3. See also 'Kuwait Enacts the Direct Investment Promotion Law', *UNCTAD* (16 June 2013) at <Kuwait - Enacts the Direct Investment Promotion Law | Investment Policy Monitor | UNCTAD Investment Policy Hub>.

28 Kuwait, Law No. 116 of 2013 (n 22), Article 11.

- activities of hiring labour, including domestic labour.

Excluding the Negative List prohibitions, the Law nevertheless allows a certain degree of 100% foreign ownership of domestic companies under the following circumstances:

- a Kuwaiti company having one of the legal entity forms of companies per *Decree Law No. 25 of 2012, the Companies Law,* if incorporated for the purposes of direct investment. Foreign participation may amount to 100% of the capital of the company in accordance with the principles and rules of the Companies Law;
- a branch of a foreign company licensed to operate within Kuwait for the purpose of direct investment;
- representative offices having the sole purpose of preparing market studies and production possibilities, without engaging in a commercial activity or activity of commercial agents.[29]

Critically, Article 19 addresses expropriation, attempting to preserve acts undertaken in the public interest, stating that:

> No Investment Entity, licenced in accordance with the provisions of this Law, shall be confiscated pursuant to this Law nor be deprived of its property except in the public interest and only in accordance with the applicable laws and against compensation equivalent to the true economic value of the expropriated project at the time of expropriation, estimated in accordance with the economic situation prior to any threat of expropriation. The due compensation is to be paid as soon as the said decision is taken.

The Law's statement in respect of dispute settlement proceedings is very brief: Article 26 simply states that domestic courts are solely competent to consider any disputes arising between investment projects and third parties. However, the matter may be referred to arbitration by agreement between the parties. Relevantly, according to the United States Department of State, "Kuwait has had no recent cases of expropriation or nationalization involving foreign investments" and "[t]he last nationalization occurred in 1974".[30] However, the Department of State would have been referring only to those events impacting US citizens and companies. Kuwait has recently been subject to an indirect expropriation claim, among others, in international investment arbitration in *Bachar Kiwan v State of Kuwait* (ICSID Case No. ARB/20/53), for example, which is currently pending.

29 Ibid.

30 United States Department of State, '2022 Investment Climate Statements: Kuwait' (2022) <Kuwait - United States Department of State>.

However, other laws relating to business and public-private partnerships have some direct or indirect influence on FDI, as well as drawing a distinction between investment and domestic operation.[31] For example:

- the longstanding *Law No. 74 of 1979 Regulating the Ownership of Real Estate by Non-Kuwaitis* prevents foreign individuals and entities from obtaining ownership of real estate in Kuwait, although exception is made for diplomatic posts and associated official residences.[32] However, Article 3 allows other GCC nationals to own property if permanent residents;
- *Law No. 68 of 1980, the New Commercial Law*, generally prevents foreign individuals and entities from participating in a business enterprise in Kuwait except through a Kuwaiti agent or company in which at least 51% of the equity of such company is owned by GCC nationals.[33]

While the Commercial Law of 1980 does not govern foreign investment in a direct sense, Articles 23 and 24 can significantly negatively impact foreign investment. Article 23 does not allow foreigners to participate in any business-related venture in Kuwait unless partnered with one or more Kuwaiti individuals who shall own no less than 51%.[34] That article aims to grant the national (Kuwaiti) partners the majority of the capital and control over the management of any business projects. Article 24 also bans any foreign company from establishing a branch in the state of Kuwait and has restricted its practice of any business unless through a Kuwaiti agent.[35] However, Article 14 of the 2013 FDI Law specifically provides that foreign companies holding a licence issued under that Law are not subject to the restrictive ownership provisions of Articles 23 and 24 of the 1980 Commercial Law.

Aaron Dikos argues that the exceptions to the operation of restrictions impacting FDI within the Real Estate Ownership Law and Commercial Law of 1980 are very different in nature:

> Apart from exceptions pertaining to ownership of real estate by foreign governments for the purposes of their diplomatic missions, there are no practical exceptions to the restrictions imposed by the Real Estate Ownership Law. There is, however, a notable exception to the restrictions imposed by the Commercial Law, as well as a number of practical solutions that foreign

31 'Foreign Direct Investment (FDI) in Kuwait', *Lloyds Bank* (last updated April 2023) at <Foreign direct investment (FDI) in Kuwait - International Trade Portal (lloydsbanktrade.com)>.

32 Aaron Dikos, 'Foreign Investment in Kuwait', *Al Tamimi* (December 2018–January 2019) at <Foreign Investment in Kuwait - Al Tamimi & Company>.

33 Ibid.

34 Mohamed Salem Alhihi (n 21), 41.

35 Ibid.

investors can utilise in order to obtain more control of their investments in Kuwait which are currently in compliance with Kuwait law and practice.[36]

With respect to the relationship between foreign direct investment legislation and investor–state arbitration, the United States Department of State reported in early 2023:

> The recognition and enforcement of foreign arbitral awards occurs more expeditiously than the enforcement of foreign judgements. Enforcement of the former, however, must meet with the same reciprocity and procedural criteria of enforcing foreign judgements under Articles 199 and 200 of the Civil and Commercial Procedure Code No. 38 of 1980. Accordingly, an award passed by a foreign arbitral panel or tribunal may be enforced in Kuwait provided that: a) the country where the award has been rendered is a member of the New York Convention; b) the foreign award is rendered by a competent arbitrator in accordance with the laws of the country in which it was awarded; c) the parties have been promptly summoned to appear and duly represented before the arbitral tribunal which it was awarded; d) the award must become a res judicata according to the laws of the country in which it was awarded and e) the award must not be in conflict with an ordered judgement that has been rendered by a local court in Kuwait and additionally does not contradict mandatory provisions or constitute criminal conduct, or violations to morality or public policy, under Kuwait laws.[37]

7.5 The Sultanate of Oman

One of the more significant legislative instruments impacting FDI in Oman is *Royal Decree 50/2019, the Foreign Capital Investment Law*,[38] which replaced *Royal Decree 102/1994, the Foreign Capital Investment Law*.[39] The new Law is touted as:

- streamlining procedures and permits necessary to start foreign investment through the Ministry of Commerce and Industry's (MOCI) Investment Services Centre;
- expanding sectors open to foreign investors to include strategic projects contributing to development;
- offering advantages, guarantees, and incentives to attract foreign investment and granting the foreign investor the necessary guarantees for its investment project;

36 Aaron Dikos (n 32).

37 United States Department of State (n 30).

38 Oman, *Royal Decree 50/2019 Promulgating the Foreign Capital Investment Law*, at <https://mjla.gov.om/eng/legislation/decrees/details.aspx?Id=1091&type=L>.

39 Oman, *Royal Decree 102/1994 Promulgating the Foreign Capital Investment Law*, at <Oman - Foreign Investment Law | Investment Laws Navigator | UNCTAD Investment Policy Hub>.

- potential preferential treatment for foreign investors in accordance with the reciprocity principle;
- potential allocation of land and real estate required for an investment project by way of a long-term lease or usufruct.[40]

Amel Abdallah suggests that Royal Decree 102/1994 "had the aim of regulating the activities of all foreign investors and included different standards of protection".[41] Abdallah argues that, with respect to the 1994 Law, "[l]iberalization of admission was not the attitude of the Sultanate, as it preferred to retain a wide discretion regarding the admission of foreign investors, tempered only by considerations relating to the development of Omani society", noting however that the law was not "rigidly restrictive".[42]

The new 2019 FDI Law "significantly relaxed the rules and restrictions on foreign investment, streamlined the registration and licensing procedures for foreign investors and aligned foreign investor's rights and incentives to those given to local investors", the key change being allowing 100% foreign ownership in a number of sectors.[43] Article 1 defines "foreign investment" as "using direct foreign capital invested to create, expand, develop, finance, manage, or own an investment project", "investment project" as "any economic activity established in the Sultanate by a foreign investor individually, or in partnership with another foreigner or an Omani", and "foreign investor" as "every natural or legal non-Omani person who establishes an investment project in the Sultanate".[44] "Invested foreign capital" is defined very broadly as "all types of assets included in an investment project regardless of type, and which have a financial value, whether monetary, in kind, or intangible".[45]

Article 6 of the Law provides that foreign investors in the form of an "establishment or a company" can carry out foreign investment in permitted activities "by owning the invested foreign capital in whole or by contributing to it". Jeremy Poole and Salim Al Harthi argue that Article 6 contains a central pillar, namely: "[i]n order to carry on business in Oman, therefore a foreign investor is still required to establish a duly licensed presence in the Sultanate (or to operate through a duly licensed distributor)".[46] Article 8 requires some undertakings from foreign

40 'Oman: Adoption of New Foreign Capital Investment Law', *UNCTAD* (1 July 2019) at <https://investmentpolicy.unctad.org/investment-policy-monitor/measures/3417/oman-adoption-of-new-foreign-capital-investment-law>.

41 Amel Abdallah, 'A Critical Analysis of Omani Investment Law' (2015) (16) *Journal of World Investment & Trade* 506, 507.

42 Ibid, 511.

43 'Oman: New Foreign Capital Investment Law and Executive Regulations', *PWC Middle East (2020)* at <Oman: New Foreign Capital Investment Law and Executive Regulations - PwC Middle East>.

44 Oman, *Royal Decree 50/2019* (n 38), Article 1(h).

45 Ibid, Article 1(f)–(h).

46 Jeremy Pooley and Salim Al Harthi, 'A New Dawn for Foreign Direct Investment in Oman', *MENA Business Law Review – Special Edition: Foreign Investment Law* (January 2021) at <A New Dawn for Foreign Direct Investment in Oman | Law Firm Oman | SASLO>.

investors, stating that "the investment project shall undertake to protect the environment and matters relating to work ethics, and it shall undertake to preserve public health and safety, in accordance with the laws and regulations in force in the Sultanate". However, the use of discretionary and expansive language potentially invites subjective interpretation and application.

The Law directly addresses permittable foreign investment activities. Article 10 provides that an investment project can be established "for strategic projects contributing to achieving the development of the activities of public utilities and infrastructure, or new or renewable energy, roads, transportation, or ports", subject to "a decision of Oman's Council of Ministers on recommendation by the responsible minister". However, investment projects are prohibited from undertaking "any activities to achieve political or religious objectives, that involve discrimination between nationals or residents, or that prejudice public order or public morals".[47]

As is common with the other GCC member States, Oman also establishes a "Negative list" of areas of economic activity in which foreign investment and/or ownership is prohibited. Article 14 requires the responsible minister to regulate a "list of activities that are prohibited to be undertaken by foreign investment".[48] MOCI Ministerial Decision No. 72/2020, as the Law's executive regulations,[49] introduced further detail on the nature of the negative list as well as licencing requirements, conditions relevant to incentives, and other benefits and introduces the concept of a negative list of prohibited investments.[50] Ministerial Decision No. 209/2020 expanded upon that detail on the negative list which "aims to promote local products and entrepreneurship projects while providing priority to employer small and medium-sized enterprises".[51] As part of its longstanding "Omanisation" programme to generate business and employment opportunities for the Omani population, the list then detailed over 40 selected areas of economic activity, mostly small business-related, in which foreign investors are prohibited from investing. The areas include, for example, the transporting and sale of drinking water; service station operations and vehicle maintenance and repairs; retail sales across a broad spectrum dealing directly with the public; real estate, tourism, and hospitality; activities related to libraries and archives; aged care and childminding; and hairdressing.[52]

47 Oman, *Royal Decree 50/2019* (n 38), Article 11.

48 Ibid, Article 14.

49 Ministerial Resolution No. 72/2020 issuing the executive regulations of the Foreign Capital Investment Law, at <Ministry of Commerce and Industry: Ministerial Decree 72/2020 Promulgating the Executive Regulations of the Foreign Capital Investment Law – Qanoon.om (qanoon-om.translate .goog)>.

50 'New Executive Regulations of the Foreign Capital Investment Law', *UNCTAD* (14 June 2020) at <Oman - New Executive Regulations of the Foreign Capital Investment Law | Investment Policy Monitor | UNCTAD Investment Policy Hub>.

51 'Prohibiting Foreign Investment in Some Activities', *UNCTAD* (14 December 2020) at <Oman - Prohibiting foreign investment in some activities | Investment Policy Monitor | UNCTAD Investment Policy Hub>.

52 Ibid.

The dispute settlement provisions do not contain a "fork-in-the-road" clause and state that domestic courts "shall have the competence to examine any dispute arising between the investment project and others, and the cases of investment projects shall have urgency status when examined by these courts", although "[i]t is permitted to resolve differences and disputes by arbitration".[53] It is not clear what "urgency status" is or how it will be treated as a special category of disputes, and while the Law allows for disputes to be submitted to arbitration, it does not address the potential risk of multiple and parallel dispute settlement proceedings being initiated.

The Law outlines some foreign investment incentives. Article 18 permits the Council of Ministers to declare preferential treatment for a foreign investor and to also grant a collection of additional benefits to FDI projects that are established in the least developed areas in the Sultanate. This demonstrates an intention by the Sultanate to promote FDI, particularly in local areas deemed strategically important, such as Salalah in the south near the Yemen border. Article 19 allows for the designation of

> land and real estate required for the investment project through long term leases or by granting a usufruct right over them without adhering to the provisions of the Royal Decree Regulating the Usufruct of the Lands of the Sultanate and the Land Law.

The Law includes reference to the protection of FDI. Article 23 provides that "[i]t shall not be permitted to confiscate any investment project except with a judicial decision, nor impound its assets, freeze them, or hold them in custody or under guardianship except with a judicial decision", excepting taxes owed. Given that this provision still allows for confiscation if there is a judicial decision, it arguably invites potential arbitral tribunal review of the merits of judicial decisions in future investor–state arbitration proceedings, which would not be desirable from Oman's perspective. Hence, Article 24 sets out the rules in relation to expropriation, attempting to protect expropriations undertaken for the broadly expressed carve-out "public benefit":

> It is not permitted to expropriate an investment project except for public benefit in accordance with the Law on Expropriation for Public Interest, and in return for fair compensation to be quantified at the time of expropriation. The due compensation shall be paid without delay, and it shall not be permitted to terminate usufruct or lease contracts in cases of the privatisation of land and real estate, except in the cases prescribed by law, or by a judicial decision.

53 Oman, *Royal Decree 50/2019* (n 38), Article 17.

In respect of the transfer of capital returns from an investment project, the foreign investor has the freedom to carry out all transfers out of the Sultanate at any time.[54]

According to Abdallah, GCC investors have been encouraged to invest in Oman, for example, *Royal Decree 21/2004* allowed GCC-based investors to "own and rent buildings or land in Oman under some restrictions", although *Royal Decree 76/2010* partially removed those restrictions.[55] According to *Royal Decree 76/2010*,

> non-GCC investors, legal or natural persons, are not entitled to acquire the ownership of Omani land, but they might be granted usufructuary rights by ministerial decision under the following conditions: 1) their project should help in the development of the Sultanate; and 2) the right of usufruct should be for a limited period; and 3) the approval of the Cabinet is obtained where the contribution of Omanis or GCC nationals is less than 30 percent.[56]

Royal Decree 52/2019 Promulgating the Public Private Partnership Law provides that the "winning bidder [of a public-private tender] shall establish a project company whose sole purpose shall be the execution of the announced partnership project, and it is permitted for it to be owned wholly by non-Omani persons".

With respect to the relationship between domestic foreign direct investment dispute resolution and international arbitration, the United States Department of State records that Oman's interest in increased FDI and technology transfer makes expropriation or nationalisation unlikely, and that there are no recent examples of expropriation or nationalisation:

> Corporate entities in Oman are increasingly turning to arbitration to resolve their disputes, since arbitration is generally cheaper, quicker, and easier than: settling commercial disputes in the normal court system, where judges often lack expertise on technical commercial issues. An arbitral award is usually rendered in Oman within 12 months after the aggrieved party states in writing that a dispute has arisen. In contrast, court processes can often be much lengthier, particularly where technically complex issues are involved. Cases normally go through three tiers of justice (Primarily, Appeal, and Supreme), lengthening the process.[57]

54 Ibid, Article 26.

55 Amel Abdallah (n 41), 518.

56 Ibid, 521.

57 United States Department of State, '2023 Investment Climate Statements: Oman' (2023) <Oman - United States Department of State>.

7.6 The State of Qatar

The Qatari Government has recently enacted legislation in order to attract and promote FDI into the State.[58] One of the main instruments of domestic legislation concerned with FDI protection and promotion in Qatar is *Law No. (1) of 2019 on Regulating Non-Qatari Capital Investment in Economic Activity*.[59] Article (1) of the Act defines a "non-Qatari investor" as a "Non-Qatari person who invests in any of the projects in which a direct investment is permitted in accordance with the provisions of this Law", and further defines "non-Qatari capital" as:

> Cash, in kind money or pecuniary rights that Non-Qatari Investors invest in the State of Qatar including:
>
> 1 – Funds transferred through licensed banks and financial institutions.
> 2 – Physical assets imported for investment purposes;
> 3 – Profits, revenues and reserves generated from non-Qatari capital investment in a project whereby project capital has been increased or if invested in any of the permitted projects in accordance with the provisions of this Law.
> 4 – Moral rights such as licenses, patents and trademarks registered in Qatar.

The term "Company" is defined as "[a]ny company incorporated in accordance with the provisions of the above-mentioned Law of Commercial Companies".

Article (2) of the Act sets out the rules in relation to the percentage of foreign ownership:

> Without prejudice to legislations regulating Non-Qataris' practices of commercial businesses and professions, and the provisions of Article (4) hereof, a Non-Qatari investor may invest in all economic sectors even with a capital up to 100% in accordance with the Executive Regulations of this Law.

Non-Qatari investors seeking to obtain shares "above 49% in the company's capital" need to submit an application to the Ministry of Economy and Industry.[60] Although the Act details a time frame in which a decision on such application must be made, it also provides that lack of response is to be "deemed an implicit rejection".[61]

58 United States Department of State, '2022 Investment Climate Statements: Qatar' (2022) <Qatar - United States Department of State>.

59 Qatar, *Law No. (1) of 2019 on Regulating Non-Qatari Capital Investment*, at <Law no. 1 of 2019 on regulating non-Qatari Capital Investment_EN.pdf (unescwa.org)>, which repealed *Law No. (13) of 2000 on Regulating the Investment of Non-Qatari Capital in Economic Activity*.

60 Ibid, Article (3).

61 Ibid.

The Act creates a negative list excluding sectors from foreign investment, which is remarkably brief by comparison with the other GCC member States, but can also be remarkably wide in its discretionary interpretation, namely:

- Banks and insurance companies, unless otherwise excluded by a decision from the Council of Ministers.
- Commercial agencies.
- Any other fields for which a decision from the Council of Ministers is issued.[62]

Article (5) stipulates the requirements ("controls") for non-Qatari companies which are "executing business contracts in Qatar", requiring that:

"1 – The Company's branch in the State shall carry out the implementation.
2 – The contract shall be entered into with one of the ministries, government bodies, public authorities or institutions, or companies or institutions in which the State participates.
3 – Registration in the Commercial Register and obtaining a commercial licence for the company's branch through which the contract will be implemented, after awarding the business and before signing the contract.
4 – Fulfilling all requirements of the competent authorities in the State in accordance with the legislation's executive by such authorities throughout the term of the contract.
5 – Renewal of the commercial register and commercial licence issued for the company's branch throughout the term of the contract."

Article (7) sets out the rules in relation to the percentage of foreign ownership in listed Qatari companies. Non-Qatari investors may own not more than 49% of Qatari companies listed on the Stock of Exchange after the Ministry's approval of the proposed percentage. However, a non-Qatari investor may own more than the regulation 49% with the approval of the Council of Ministers based on a proposal from the Minister.

Chapter 3 of the Act sets out the rules relating to investment incentives, including, for example, the allocation of land, importation rights, exemption from income and customs taxes, and allowing for the granting of additional "incentives and privileges" for investment projects at the discretion of the Council of Ministers acting upon the Minister's advice.[63]

Articles (13)–(16) set out the rules in relation to FDI protection and transfers out of Qatar, transfers between foreign investors and local investors in respect of the investment, and dispute settlement. Article (13) contains a prohibition against expropriation, with attempted carve-outs for measures undertaken in the public interest, and combines this protection with an anti-discrimination measure:

62 Ibid, Article (4).
63 Ibid, Article (12).

> Neither directly nor indirectly, Non-Qatari investments shall be subject to expropriation nor any other similar procedures unless such measures are taken for public interest, implemented in a non-discriminating manner, and in return for a prompt and reasonable compensation in accordance with the same legal procedures applied in case of Qatari citizens.

The provisions relating to free transfer of capital, monies, and profits from Qatar are rather broadly drafted, stating that:

1 – Non-Qatari Investors may transfer all amounts relevant to their investment from and to any external destination without any delay. Transfers shall include:
   a. Investment revenues.
   b. Amounts generated from partial or entire sale or liquidation of investment.
   c. Amounts resulting from the settlement of investment disputes.
   d. Compensation stated in Article (13) hereof.

2 Money transfers can be executed in any exchangeable currency at the exchange rate prevailing on the date of transfer.[64]

Provisions in respect of dispute settlement are, again, very brief and broadly drafted. Article (16) allows for disputes, other than labour disputes, to be determined by arbitration or by any other means of settling disputes in accordance with the law.

Article (17) requires non-Qatari investors to meet obligations in respect of public health, environmental management, and security and requires those investors to "not engage in any acts affecting public order or decency in the State".

Another law relevant to foreign direct investment in *Qatar is Law No. (16) of 2018 on the Regulation of Non-Qataris' Ownership and Usage of Real Estate.*[65] Article (2) states that:

> Non-Qataris may own the Real Estates and make use thereof in the zones, in accordance with the terms, controls, advantages and procedures, specified by a Decision issued by the Council of Ministers, upon the Committee's proposal.
>
> In all cases, the right of use granted to Non-Qatari shall not lapse by his death, and it shall be transferred to his heirs, unless otherwise agreed on by the two parties.

Frank Lucente explains that the foreign ownership of real estate law allows non-Qataris, including natural and legal persons, to hold "freehold ownership as well as usufruct rights (leasehold rights for 99 years) in real estate in certain designated

64 Ibid, Article (14).

65 Al-Sulaiti Law Firm, 'Qatar Real Estate Laws' at <alsulaitilawfirm.com>.

areas in Qatar".[66] The *Qatar Financial Centre Real Estate Ownership Regulations*, issued on 6 September 2021, also contemplate real estate ownership by non-Qataris, and the Cabinet has issued a resolution (no. (28) of 2020), for example, which specifies areas in which foreigners can invest in property.[67]

With respect to the relationship between foreign direct investment legislation and investor–state arbitration, the United States Department of State notes:

> Under current legislation (Law 1/2019 and Law 16/2018), the government protects foreign investment and property from direct or indirect expropriation, unless for public benefit, in a non-discriminatory manner, and after providing adequate compensation. Law 8/2022 covers the rules of expropriation for public benefit. The same procedures are applied to the expropriated property of Qatari citizens. Expropriation is unlikely to occur in the investment zones where foreigners may purchase or obtain rights to property. However, the law does not restrict the expropriation power in these areas. The Cabinet approved three expropriation decisions between 2021–2022.
>
> The Qatar Financial Centre (QFC) features an Alternative Dispute Resolution Centre. Although primarily concerned with hearing commercial matters arising within the QFC itself, the QFC has expanded the centre's jurisdiction to accept other disputes at its discretion …
>
> Qatar's arbitration law (Law 2/2017), based on the United Nations Commission on International Trade Law, gives the QICDRC the jurisdiction to oversee arbitration cases in Qatar in line with recent local and international developments. There is no set duration for dispute resolution and the time to obtain a resolution depends on the case.[68]

7.7 The Kingdom of Saudi Arabia

Saudi Arabia's primary foreign investment statute is the *Foreign Investment Law, 2000* issued by *Royal Decree No. M/1, of 5.1.1421H the Foreign Investment Law*. This Decree replaced a much earlier *Royal Decree No. M/4, the Foreign Capital*

66 Frank Lucente, 'Ownership of Real Estate in Qatar by Foreigners', *Al Tamimi & Co* (May 2019) at <Non-Qatari Individuals: Investment in Real Estate and Succession Planning - Al Tamimi & Company>.

67 *Qatar Financial Centre Real Estate Ownership Regulations* (Version No. 1 – August 2021), at <QFCRA_13173_VER1.pdf (thomsonreuters.com)>; Addleshaw Goddard, 'The Qatar Financial Centre Issues New Real Estate Ownership Regulations' (13 September 2021) at <The Qatar Financial Centre Issues New Real Estate Ownership Regulations | Addleshaw Goddard LLP>.

68 United States Department of State, '2023 Investment Climate Statements: Qatar' (2023) at <Qatar - United States Department of State>.

Investment Law, of 1 January 1979.[69] The 2000 Law defines a foreign investor as "[t]he natural person of non-Saudi nationality or otherwise the body corporate, where all partners are non-Saudi nationals", and "foreign investment" as "[i]nvestment of Foreign Capital in a licenced activity under this Act".[70] "Foreign capital" is a non-exhaustive definition which includes:

1. Money, securities, and commercial instruments.
2. Foreign investment profits if they are invested to increase the capital, expansion of existing projects or establishment of new projects.
3. Machinery, equipment, supplies, spare parts, means of transportation, and production requirements relevant to the investment.
4. Legal rights i.e., licences, intellectual properties, technical know-how, administrative skills and production techniques.[71]

The Law creates a General Investment Authority, responsible for issuing licences for foreign capital investments (undefined).[72] The Authority is an "investment promotion agency" responsible for

> making improvements to increase the Kingdom's competitiveness as an investment destination; building upon the quality of service and value proposition offered to investors; and offering new investment opportunities to attract businesses and investors alike to help advance Saudi Arabia's economic diversification agenda.[73]

The Authority is now the Ministry of Investment of Saudi Arabia; originally created for the purpose of regulation, it now focusses particularly on promoting and facilitating investment.[74] Its stated mission is to "promote Saudi Arabia as a world-class investment destination, attract and retain investors, and expand their investments; for the benefit of a sustainable national economic growth"; with a vision "[t]o place Saudi Arabia among the top performing markets for investments".[75] A significant element of its role is to facilitate economic

69 Saudi Arabia, *Royal Decree No. M/1 of 5.1.1421.H, the Foreign Investment Law* (corresponding to 10 April 2000), Article 18, at <Saudi Arabia - Foreign Investment Law | Investment Laws Navigator | UNCTAD Investment Policy Hub>.

70 Ibid, Article 1.

71 Ibid.

72 Royal Decree No. M/1 of 2000 (n 69), Article 2.

73 'Saudi Arabian General Investment Authority (SAGIA)', *World Economic Forum* (2023) at <Saudi Arabian General Investment Authority (SAGIA) | World Economic Forum (weforum.org)>.

74 United States Department of State, '2021 Investment Climate Statements: Saudi Arabia' (2021) at <Saudi Arabia - United States Department of State>.

75 'MISA at a Glance', *Saudi Arabian Ministry of Investment* (2023) at <MISA at a Glance | Ministry of Investment>.

diversification, among other objectives, in line with Saudi Arabia's Vision 2030 objectives.[76]

According to Article 4 of the Act's implementing regulations ("Executive Rules"), foreign investment projects licenced under the Act can be either "firms owned by a national and foreign investor" or "firms wholly owned by a foreign investor".[77]

The Act creates a foreign investment "Negative List", with Article 3 stating that "[t]he Council shall have the authority to issue a list of activities excluded from foreign investment". Annex B of the Act's implementing regulations details a comprehensive list of economic and societal sectors and activities that are excluded from foreign investment, including:

Manufacturing Sector

- Most of the oil exploration, drilling, and production sector.
- Manufacturing of military equipment, devices, and uniforms, and civilian explosives.

Services Sector

- Catering to military sectors.
- Security and detective services.
- Real estate investment in Makkah and Madina.
- Tourist orientation and guidance services related to Hajj and Umrah.
- Recruitment and employment services, including local recruitment offices.
- Real estate brokerage.
- Printing and publishing activities, except for areas with international classifications
- Audiovisual and media services.
- Telecommunications services, except for those with international classifications
- Land and air transportation.
- Satellite transmission services.
- Services rendered by midwives, nurses, physiotherapists, and paramedics
- Fisheries.
- Blood banks, poison centres, and quarantines.[78]

However, according to the United States Department of State, in their assessment, "foreign minority ownership in joint ventures with Saudi partners may be allowed in some of these [excluded] sectors".[79]

76 Ibid.

77 *Executive Rules to the Saudi Arabian Foreign Investment Law,* Article 4, at <https://www.saudiembassy.net/foreign-investment-act-and-executive-rules>.

78 Ibid, Annex (B).

79 United States Department of State, '2023 Investment Climate Statements: Saudi Arabia' (2023) <Saudi Arabia - United States Department of State>.

Articles 7 and 11 of the Act address transfer issues and expropriation respectively, and these provisions are materially mirrored in the Act's implementing regulations, although only as examples in the provision relating to equal treatment of national projects and foreign investment projects.[80] Foreign investors are afforded

> the right to reallocate his share as derived from the selling of his equity, or from the liquidation surplus or profits generated by the facility, out of the Kingdom or to use by any other legal means, and he shall also be entitled to transfer the required amounts to settle any contractual obligations pertaining to the project.[81]

The Act determines that disputes between the foreign investor and the Saudi Government or the investor's Saudi partners are meant to be "settled amicably" before a governmental disputes settlement committee.[82] In the event that a dispute cannot be resolved amicably, the dispute "shall be settled through arbitration according to the *Arbitration Act* and its executive rules issued by Royal Decree No. (46) dated 12.7.1403 H".[83] This provision seemingly does not require complainant foreign investors to submit disputes to the Dispute Settlement Committee in the first instance but seemingly offers a potential way to have disputes heard locally.

In April 2022 the Saudi Ministry of Investment announced that it was in the process of "drafting a new Investment Law that will provide for the equal treatment of local and foreign investors in respect of direct investments in the Kingdom", supporting "the principle of competitive neutrality and fairness, and to ensure equal opportunities in the treatment of direct investments made by public and private investors".[84] The draft law is apparently undergoing a process of public consultation, but local reports indicate that its key objectives include facilitating and protecting the entry procedures for foreign investors, supporting the principle of competitive neutrality and fairness, and ensuring equal opportunities in the treatment of foreign direct investments made by public and private investors.[85] In this regard, the most distinctive objective of the draft is said to be the standardisation of the rights of foreign investors with those of Saudi investors and promoting equal treatment.[86]

80 *Executive Rules to the Saudi Arabian Foreign Investment Law* (n 77).

81 Royal Decree No. M/1 of 2000 (n 69), Article 7.

82 Ibid, Article 13.

83 *Executive Rules to the Saudi Arabian Foreign Investment Law* (n 77), Article 26.

84 'New Investment Law to Treat Saudi and Foreign Investors Equally', *Sovereign Group Blog Saudi Arabia* (29 April 2022) at <New Investment Law to treat Saudi and foreign investors equally - The Sovereign Group>.

85 Suhaib Hammad and Ebaa Tounesi, 'A General Introduction to Foreign Investment Regulation in Saudi Arabia', *Lexology* (3 October 2023), at <https://www.lexology.com/library/detail.aspx?g=f56ae9f1-600e-4ce3-8d08-13e66a5259ca>.

86 Ibid.

Another important law impacting foreign direct investment in Saudi Arabia is the *Royal Decree No. M/15, on Real Estate Ownership and Investment by Non-Saudis*, of 19 July 2000.[87] The Law contemplates the ability of non-Saudi natural and corporate persons to obtain property. Article 5(2) of the Law defines the term "non-Saudi" rather broadly, to mean:

a) A natural person not holding Saudi nationality.
b) A non-Saudi company.
c) A Saudi company founded, co-founded, or partially owned by a natural or corporate person not holding Saudi nationality, with the exception of the following:
    i. Banks and real estate financing companies licensed by the Saudi Arabian Monetary Authority …
    ii. Listed companies not engaged in real estate activities …
    iii. Entities [so] specified by the Council of Ministers …
d) Persons or categories so listed … by the Council of Ministers.

In 2011, Saudi Arabia eased the Law to allow foreign residents to purchase and own property in the Kingdom.[88] This was perceived as a means by which to "revive the country's moribund real estate market".[89] Saudi Arabia reportedly intends to further liberalise foreign property ownership laws in an effort to attract foreign investment in real estate and as part of the broader economic diversification programme it has embarked upon, with the new law "in its final stages and will be made public in a short period".[90] The new law will reportedly be broader and more comprehensive than the current law, and foreign investors will have the option of purchasing any type of property, pursuant to the regulations, and previous exclusions impacting the foreign purchase of property located in cities of religious significance may be removed.[91]

Saudi Arabia has also introduced an "anti-concealment law", promulgated by *Royal Decree No. M/4, the Anti-Concealment Law* of 20 August 2020, which replaced an earlier Anti-Concealment Law of June 2004.[92] The purpose of the Anti-

87 Saudi Arabia, *Royal Decree No. M/15 dated 17.04.1421H* (corresponding to 19 July 2000), *the Law of Real Estate Ownership and Investment by Non-Saudis*, at <https://www.moj.gov.sa/Documents/Regulations/pdf/En/37.pdf>.

88 'Amendments to Law on Real Estate Ownership and Investment by Non-Saudis', *UNCTAD* (30 May 2011) at <Saudi Arabia - Amendments to Law on Real Estate Ownership and Investment by Non-Saudis | Investment Policy Monitor | UNCTAD Investment Policy Hub>.

89 Staff reporter, 'Saudis Allow Foreigners to Own Property; but Market Remains Tight', *International Business Times* (3 March 2011) at <Saudis allow foreigners to own property; but market remains tight (ibtimes.com)>.

90 'New Law Allowing Foreigners to Buy All Kinds of Properties in KSA Soon: Top Official', *Arab News* (27 March 2023) at <https://www.arabnews.com/node/2276401/business-economy/1000>.

91 Ibid, citing Real Estate General Authority Chief Abdullah Alhammad.

92 'Saudi Arabia's New Anti-Concealment Law', *Baker McKenzie* (February 2021) at <New Anti-Concealment Law (bakermckenzie.com)>.

Concealment Law is to prevent evasion of the Saudi Arabian foreign investment legislation, continuing "a legal prohibition that dates back to 1989" relating to "schemes or practices designed to evade" such laws.[93] According to Article 2, "concealment" means "an agreement or arrangement whereby a person enables a non-Saudi to practice an economic activity in the Kingdom that he is not licenced to practice by using the licence or approval issued in his favor". An "economic activity" is defined broadly as "[a]ny for-profit activity that requires approvals or licences from the competent authorities, be it an investment or service provision activity, or commercial, professional, industrial, agricultural or otherwise".[94]

Other laws impacting upon foreign investment in Saudi Arabia include the "Companies Law, the Labour Law, the Social Insurance Law, the Income Tax Law, the Bankruptcy Law, the Competition Law and other Gulf Cooperation Council laws specific to certain sectors".[95]

With respect to the relationship between domestic disputes and investor–state arbitration, there is reason to believe that potential complainants have a preference for international arbitration, although there are significant hurdles to overcome in this regard and this may change over time. According to the United States Department of State:

> The Embassy is not aware of any cases in Saudi Arabia of expropriation from foreign investors without adequate compensation. Some small- to medium-sized foreign investors, however, have complained that their investment licenses have been cancelled without justification, causing them to forfeit their investments…
>
> Traditionally, dispute settlement and enforcement of foreign arbitral awards in Saudi Arabia have proved time-consuming and uncertain, carrying the risk that sharia principles can potentially supersede any foreign judgements or local precedents. Even after a decision is reached in a dispute, effective enforcement of the judgement can be lengthy. In several cases, disputes have caused serious problems for foreign investors. In cases of alleged fraud or debt, foreign partners may also be jailed to prevent their departure from the country while awaiting police investigation or court adjudication. Courts can in theory impose precautionary restraint on personal property pending the adjudication of a commercial dispute, though this remedy has been applied sparingly.[96]

93 Ibid.

94 Saudi Arabia, *Royal Decree No. M/4 of 1.1.1442H* (corresponding to 20 August 2020), *the Anti-Concealment Law*, Article 1.

95 Suhaib Hammad and Ebaa Tounesi, 'The Foreign Investment Regulation Review: Saudi Arabia', *The Law Reviews* (21 October 2022) at <The Foreign Investment Regulation Review - The Law Reviews>.

96 United States Department of State, '2023 Investment Climate Statements: Saudi Arabia' (2023) (n 79).

7.8 The United Arab Emirates

The UAE is pursuing a programme of economic diversification and has recently enacted or updated laws designed to both liberalise previously restrictive foreign ownership laws in certain sectors and promote foreign direct investment, but to still maintain what it perceives as the appropriate degree of management and control consistent with its own federal priorities. The United States Department of State, for example, asserts that, while the "UAE has signalled throughout 2021 its intention to develop a more commercially friendly legislative environment to strengthen foreign investment ... its onshore regulatory and legal framework "continues to generally favor local Emirati investors over foreign investors".[97]

The UAE currently has a set of major legislative instruments in force that drive and impact foreign direct investment, namely:

- *Federal Law No. 2 of 2015 Concerning Commercial Companies* ("2015 Commercial Companies Law"), as amended (most recently in 2020);[98]
- *Federal Law No. 18 of 1981 on the Regulation of Commercial Agencies* ("2018 Agencies Law"), as amended (most recently in 2020);[99]
- *Federal Decree-Law No. 25 of 2022 on the Regulation and Development of Industry* ("2018 Industry Development Law");
- *Federal Law No. 6 of 2018 on Arbitration* ("2018 Arbitration Law").

For a short period of time the UAE also possessed a sui generis foreign investment law with *Federal Decree-Law No. 19 of 2018 Concerning Foreign Direct Investment* ("2018 FDI Law"). The 2018 FDI Law was reportedly promulgated "in response to the issue of amendments to Article 10 of the 2015 Commercial Companies Law in 2018, relating to the maximum stake that foreign investors could hold in UAE Limited Liability Companies".[100] Article 10 stipulated that at least 51% of the shares in any corporate entity established "onshore" in the UAE (that is, outside a free trade zone (FTZ)) must be owned by an Emirati.[101] Consequently, foreign investors seeking to establish a corporate entity in the UAE were either restricted to doing so "offshore" in an FTZ allowing 100% foreign ownership, or establishing an onshore company with an Emirati entity and with a holding limited to 49% at most.

97 United States Department of State, '2023 Investment Climate Statements: United Arab Emirates' (2023) <United Arab Emirates - United States Department of State>.

98 *Federal Law No. 2 of 2015 Concerning Commercial Companies* ('2015 Commercial Companies Law'), as amended by *Federal Decree-Law No. 18 of 2017* and *Federal Decree-Law No. 26 of 2020.*

99 *Federal Law No. 18 of 1981 on the Regulation of Commercial Agencies*, as amended by *Federal Law No. 14 of 1988*, *Federal Law No. 13 of 2006*, *Federal Law No. 2 of 2010,* and *Federal Law No. 11 of 2020.*

100 Tareq Na'el Al-Tawil, Venugopal Prabhakar Gantasala and Walaaeldeen Ibraheem, 'The Potential Impact of the 2020 UAE FDI Decree and Side Agreements' (2021) *ICSID Review – Foreign Investment Law Journal* 36(3), 518, 519.

101 Christopher Williams, 'UAE Foreign Direct Investment Law', *Bracewell* (25 July 2019) at <https://bracewell.com/insights/uae-foreign-direct-investment-law-0>.

The objectives of the 2018 FDI Law, as specified in Article 2, were to enhance the investment environment and attract higher levels of foreign direct investment, particularly that which targeted priority sectors. Foreign capital, defined in Article 4, was rather broad, including funds transferred to the State through banks and financial companies licenced in the State, which are used in a foreign direct investment project; the profits and returns of a foreign direct investment in the state used in the establishment of new investment projects or increasing the capital of an existing FDI project; and local or foreign securities and commercial paper. Article (5)(1) established a specialist unit to be concerned with proposing foreign direct investment policies record keeping in relation to FDI projects, improving the investment environment, assessing the performance of such investments in the UAE, and reporting on investment, among other activities.

Foreign investors were permitted to invest in economic sectors and activities as determined from time to time by the UAE Council of Ministers, thereby creating its "positive list" of permitted areas of investment.[102] That list was subject to amendment by addition or removal of areas as determined by the Council. Areas of economic activity excluded by the Council encompassed the exploration and production of petroleum materials; investigations, security, military sectors, arms, explosives, and military equipment manufacture, devices, and clothing; banking and financing activities, payment systems and dealing with cash; insurance services; Hajj (pilgrimage) and Umrah services, employment and recruitment services for staff and servants; water and electricity services; services related to fisheries; postal, telecommunications services, and audio and video services; land and air transport services; printing and publishing services; commercial agents' services; medical retail such as private pharmacies; and blood banks, venom, and quarantine centres (thereby at the same time creating a Negative List).[103] The Council had discretion to approve a foreign direct investment project not included in the Positive List, and in so doing determine the project's legal form, permitted foreign ownership percentage, minimum share capital, local employment requirements, and any other incentives or exemptions from the Companies Law and other federal laws.[104]

The 2018 FDI Law was repealed in 2020 as part of a significant number of amendments introduced into the 2015 Commercial Companies Law in September of that year.[105] However, it needs acknowledgement because of its significance as sui generis legislation and what it represented in terms of a shift in the UAE's approach to FDI. It had served its purpose, having been warmly welcomed by both local and foreign media and the business environment when it was introduced.[106]

102 *Federal Decree-Law No.19 of 2018 on Foreign Direct Investment,* Article 7(3).

103 Ibid, Article 7(1) and (2).

104 Ibid, Article 7(4).

105 *Federal Decree-Law No. 26 of 2020 Amending Certain Provisions of Federal Law No. (2) of 2015 on Commercial Companies,* Article 6(2).

106 See 'Update on Foreign Direct Ownership and Investment in the UAE', *K & L Gates* (27 November 2020) at <https://www.jdsupra.com/legalnews/update-on-foreign-direct-ownership-and-36235/>.

The stated purpose of the 2015 Commercial Companies Law, as most recently amended in 2020, is to contribute to the development of the business environment, the UAE's capabilities, and economic status by regulating companies in light of international standards, particularly with respect to governance, the protection of shareholders' and partners' rights, corporate social responsibility, and relevantly, "supporting the flow of foreign investment".[107] The provisions apply to both domestic companies and "to the foreign companies which exercise any activity or have any branches or representation offices in the State".[108] However, companies operating in FTZs within the Emirates are not subject to the Law to the same extent, according to Article 5(1), unless they also engage in activities beyond the FTZ.

The 2020 enacted changes were widespread, replacing a broad range of articles. Significantly, they repealed Article 10 which limited foreign ownership to 49%, and Article 329 which had required a foreign company to have an Emirati national as agent, or all partners as Emirati if a company. The 2020 amendments were reportedly introduced in part to ameliorate a key issue, namely the "operationalization of the FDI Law depended primarily on local decisions at each of the Emirates". They also removed restrictions to facilitate further mergers and acquisition activity. Tahan Thraya and Jad Taha summarise the key changes as follows:

- remove the minimum local ownership requirement applicable to limited liability companies (LLCs) and joint stock companies (JSCs);
- allow for the operation of local branches without the appointment of a UAE national local service agent;
- enable previously restricted corporate board seats to be occupied by foreign nationals;
- ease previously imposed restrictions on general assembly meetings, giving shareholders of both LLCs and JSCs greater flexibility to call and hold general assembly meetings (including a lower ownership threshold requirement for calling such meetings and the ability to hold such meetings electronically).[109]

On 17 March 2020 the UAE Cabinet of Ministers issued *Resolution No. 16 of 2020 Concerning the Determination of the Positive List of Economic Sectors and Activities Eligible for Foreign Direct Investment and Percentage of Their Ownership.*[110] The *Positive List* defined foreign investors as "a natural or moral

107 *Federal Law No. 2 of 2015* (n 98), Article (2)

108 Ibid, Article (3).

109 Tahan (Tom) A. Thraya and Jad A. Taha, 'The UAE Recalibrates Its Foreign Direct Investment Framework with 100% Foreign Ownership and Other Landmark Changes to Its Commercial Companies Law', *Mayer Brown* (1 December 2020) at <The UAE Recalibrates its Foreign Direct Investment Framework with 100% Foreign Ownership and Other Landmark Changes to its Commercial Companies Law | Perspectives & Events | Mayer Brown>.

110 'The "Positive List" Has Been Officially Published', *UNCTAD* (last updated 20 April 2023) at <United Arab Emirates - The "Positive List" has been officially published | Investment Policy Monitor | UNCTAD Investment Policy Hub>.

person who has not the UAE nationality and invests in the State in accordance with the Federal Law No. (19) of 2018 on Foreign Direct Investment".[111] It sets out the permitted investment sectors and mandates the legal forms which FDI projects can take, namely limited liability companies, including those with a single owner, and private joint stock companies, including those with a single owner.[112] Importantly, Article 4 states that "[t]he foreign investor shall own 100% of Foreign Direct Investment Project in the economic activities referred to in Article (2) hereof, except as provided for in the [2015 Commercial Companies Law]".[113]

The issuance of the Federal Laws and the "Positive List" thus has resulted in a relaxation of foreign ownership laws in the specified sectors. Natasha Teja suggests that the introduction of the List, particularly the 100% foreign ownership allowance in respect of certain business activities, was a "significant departure from the tightly government-controlled business sector that preceded it".[114] Mohammed Al-Shukairy notes that "[t]he UAE is being bold in terms of the approach to foreign investment, especially against the backdrop of historical requirement of having significant parts of its business held by family backed conglomerates and other local investors" and continues to say that "[t]his has very much been part of the local landscape".[115]

FDI is subject to restrictions and conditions as set out in the "Positive List", in addition to any further restrictions and conditions determined by the licencing authority and by legislation in force. Some of the restrictions and conditions particularised in the List are rather vague and ambiguous, requiring more precision in definition and scope. For example, in the agricultural sector, those named include "use modern technology, bring high added-value, contribute in research & development, meet the requirements of licensing entities in the State". Article (7) sets out the rules relating to the minimum percentage of nationals, stating that the minimum percentage employed in the FDI project is subject to the relevant *regulation* made by the Ministry of Human Resources and Emiratization.[116]

Federal Law No. 6 of 2018 on Arbitration (Arbitration Law) "annuls articles 213–218 of the UAE Civil Procedures Law No. 11 of 1992 which tackled some provisions of arbitration in the UAE".[117] Reportedly, the purpose of the Arbitration Law was to better align UAE law with the UNCITRAL Model Law on International Commercial Arbitration, with the objective of securing the UAE's status "as an

111 UAE Cabinet of Ministers Resolution No. 16 of 2020 *Concerning the Determination of the Positive List of Economic Sectors and Activities Eligible for Foreign Direct Investment and Percentage of their Ownership,* Article 1.

112 Ibid, Articles 2 and 3.

113 Ibid, Article 4.

114 Natasha Teja, 'Foreign Ownership in UAE Remains Low Despite FDI Reforms' (2022) *International Financial Law Review.* (14 April 2022), at <https://www.iflr.com/article/2a647zxame68p5g8dagow/foreign-ownership-in-uae-remains-low-despite-fdi-reforms>.

115 Ibid, citing Mohammed Al-Shukairy.

116 UAE Cabinet of Ministers Resolution No. 16 of 2020 (n 111), Article 7.

117 UAE, *Federal Law No. 6 of 2018, on Arbitration* (12 May 2023) at <UAE federal law on arbitration - The Official Portal of the UAE Government>.

international hub for arbitration disputes".[118] Importantly, Article 2(1) applies to "any arbitration which is carried out in the State, unless the parties agree on the application of the provisions of another Arbitration Law, provided that it is not contrary to the public order and public morality of the State". According to Articles 2(2)–(3), the Arbitration Law applies to any international commercial arbitration conducted outside of the UAE or to "any arbitration arising from a dispute on a contractual or non-contractual legal relationship organised by the Law in force in the State; unless whatever is excluded by a special provision". The Law also provides that "the parties waive their rights to arbitration should they not raise an objection before addressing any claim or defence on the merits of the dispute if the matter is referred to the courts"; it increased tribunal power and limited "court intervention specifically in matters relating to awarding interim measures".[119]

In terms of the application of the FDI legislation, there seems to be limited exposure to expropriation claims and residual issues with the settlement of investment disputes. According to the United States Department of State in 2023:[120]

> Mission UAE is not aware of foreign investors subjected to any expropriation in the UAE in the recent past. There are no federal rules governing compensation if expropriations were to occur. Individual emirates would likely treat expropriations differently. In practice, authorities would be unlikely to expropriate, unless there was a compelling development or public interest need to do so…
>
> Foreign investors continued to raise concerns regarding the resolution of investment disputes and the difficulty of enforcing arbitration awards. Onshore dispute resolution can be difficult and uncertain, particularly when involving politically connected local parties, and payment following settlements is often slow. Disputes are generally resolved by direct negotiation and settlement between the parties themselves, arbitration, or recourse within the legal system.

7.9 The GCC Member States and FDI Capital Flows

This section endeavours to provide a brief background to the foregoing review of the States' domestic legislative and regulatory frameworks for the protection of FDI inflows while being mindful of the history of ISDS disputation explored in the previous chapters. It is suggested that it adds substance to the argument conveyed in this study that the frequency of ISDS cases will increase in the future, and that State reviews of both their IIAs and their domestic frameworks would be timely.

118 'Arbitration Law Update', *Davidson & Co* (January 2019) at <Arbitration Law Update - Federal Law No. 6 of 2018 - Davidson & Co (davidsoncolaw.com)>.

119 Ibid.

120 United States Department of State, '2023 Investment Climate Statements: United Arab Emirates' (2023) (n 97).

Appreciation of the imperative for diversification of their national economies away from heavy, if not almost entire reliance in some instances on oil-based incomes towards more knowledge-based societies has been on the GCC States' agendas over the last two decades or so. Martin Hvidt, writing in 2013, suggested at the time that

> the policy response to pre-empt the Arab Spring uprising indicates that these regimes easily give up their well-argued and planned policies when under pressure and fall back on established ways of doing business, namely through patronage and the predominant role of the public sector.[121]

However, he adds that the States "[currently] seem not only to give political priority to economic diversification, but also to pursue such a strategy in real terms".[122] The impact of the global financial crisis, the COVID-19 pandemic, major regional conflicts, and suggestions of other looming global financial crises have added to the economic diversification imperative.

Commitment to economic diversification has driven the States to devise and implement strategies to attract foreign capital into the States. At the same time the multigenerational global demand for oil and the accompanying boom in oil prices have enabled the States to build up significant national reserves. As a consequence, the States are currently experiencing significant – by any standard – inflows of capital and generating equally significant outflows for investment projects.

UNCTAD, in its 2023 World Investment Report, calculates the individual FDI inflows and outflows for the respective States as shown in Table 7.1.

Table 7.1 GCC Economies: FDI Inflows and Outflows 2021 and 2022

GCC Economy	*FDI Inflows 2021 (Millions of Dollars)*	*FDI Inflows 2022 (Millions of Dollars)*	*FDI Outflows 2021 (Millions of Dollars)*	*FDI Outflows 2022 (Millions of Dollars)*
Bahrain	17,797	1,951	64	1,948
Kuwait	567	758	−1,366	99
Oman	4,021	3,716 (estimate)	−398	−520 (estimate)
Qatar	1,093	76	160	2,384
Saudi Arabia	19,286	7,886	23,860	18,826
UAE	20,667	22,737	22,546	24,833

Source: derived from UNCTAD, 'World Investment Report 2023' (5 July 2023) <World Investment Report 2023: Investment and sustainable energy (unctad.org)>.

121 Martin Hvidt, 'Economic Diversification in GCC Countries: Past Record and Future Trends', *London School of Economics and Political Science*, Kuwait Programme on Development, Governance and Globalisation in the Gulf States (January 2013) at <http://eprints.lse.ac.uk/id/eprint/55252>.

122 Ibid.

According to the World Bank, FDI flows to Saudi Arabia fell by 59% to USD7.9 billion and FDI "[f]lows to the UAE increased by 10 per cent to $23 billion – the highest ever recorded" from 2021 to 2022.[123] Critically, however, while the UAE enjoyed significant FDI inflows in 2022, it was exceeded by its outflows. Of the smaller economies, Oman was the strongest performer in terms of FDI inflows in 2022.

In terms of outflow potential, Vinnie Lauria argues that the States share a commonality, namely "their lineup of sovereign wealth funds with assets running from many billions to hundreds of billions of US dollars" and further, that these funds "are the main drivers of outbound investment".[124] Lauria estimates the size of the States' sovereign wealth funds (SWFs) as Bahrain USD30 billion (Mumtalakat); Kuwait USD708 billion (Kuwait Investment Authority); Oman USD40billion (Oman Investment authority); Qatar USD461 billion (Qatar Investment Authority); Saudi Arabia USD607 billion (Public Investment Fund); and UAE USD2,024 billion (4 × SWFs).[125]

These capital resources, even on the simplest plane, reveal a significant investment environment which will involve both public and private entities as both recipients and initiators of development projects which may carry an inherent risk of evolving into ISDS arbitration claimants or respondents.

7.10 Concluding Remarks

This chapter briefly discussed the salient aspects of the legislative and regulatory frameworks of each GCC member States in respect of FDI. The States have enacted stand-alone foreign direct investment legislation in the recent past, with the exception of Bahrain, and in some instances, are reportedly in the process of drafting new legislation governing this activity and reflecting foreign investment policy (Saudi Arabia and Bahrain). The purpose of enacting and/or modernising their respective FDI legal and regulatory regimes is to protect and promote FDI in the region. However, on the whole, these regimes are lacking the precision and clarity needed to foster consistency and coherence in terms of outcomes for investor claimants. They also unnecessarily expose the States to having to defend executive/judicial decisions, potentially in more than one dispute settlement proceeding.

Contained within these frameworks are investment protections similar to those typically contained within IIAs, chiefly anti-expropriation obligations, with attempted carve-outs for matters in the public interest. The domestic FDI frameworks also contain dispute settlement mechanisms, although there are significant issues that both investor claimants and respondent states must grapple with in terms of these dispute settlement proceedings.

123 UNCTAD, 'World Investment Report 2023' (5 July 2023) 13, at <World Investment Report 2023: Investment and sustainable energy (unctad.org)>.

124 Vinnie Lauria, 'How the Gulf Is Changing Global Capital Flows', *Entrepreneur Asia Pacific* (27 March 2023) at <How The Gulf Is Changing Global Capital Flows | Entrepreneur>.

125 Ibid.

Generally, greater clarity with respect to access to domestic remedies and investment treaty arbitration is required. There is a need for legislators to precisely address the requirements for access or as a pre-condition to investment treaty arbitration, including the institution and/or exhaustion of local remedies and review of arbitral tribunal decisions by domestic courts. There is also a need for legislators to address the finality, priority, and/or primacy of decisions made by domestic legal institutions and those of arbitral tribunals and perhaps assess whether their respective foreign investment legislative regimes may benefit from including so-called fork-in-the-road clauses. There is also a need to clarify the respective domestic litigation processes and timeframes.

As it stands, there is reason to anticipate that increased levels of FDI may result in the duplication of settlement procedures on a domestic basis and through international arbitration because the domestic frameworks do not contain a fork-in-the-road clause (for example in Oman) or prior exhaustion of domestic remedies before submitting claims to international arbitration. Instead, claims may be submitted to arbitration by agreement (for example, in Kuwait). This requires remediation because the States may be in the less than desirable position of having to defend multiple claims in different fora, arising out of the one cause of action and potentially allowing for arbitral tribunal or even superior courts of record in other countries review of domestic judicial decisions. However, this is a delicate balance to strike, as investor claimants may perceive the ability to pursue remedies in multiple fora, or in a choice of fora, as particularly desirable when operating in GCC-host states.

Alternatively, claimants investing in GCC member States may seek to bypass domestic dispute settlement entirely in cases where alternative forms, including investor–state arbitration, are available, more favourable, and potentially more lucrative. Unfortunately, this potentially invites international arbitral tribunal review of domestic machinations and regulatory chill. It does however, go some way to mitigating against imbalance in domestic dispute settlement procedures due, for example, to a foreign claimant's unfamiliarity with business practices in the region as well as legal institutions and methods in the Gulf. However, the legislation does not go far enough in terms of delineating between access to domestic and international arbitration remedies. The States stand to gain from amending their current legislative frameworks to address these issues.

In terms of the apparent dichotomy between disputes settled on an intra-GCC basis, compared to those resolved on an extra-GCC basis, it could be argued that the domestic foreign direct investment legislative and regulatory regimes generally reflect an intention to allow extra-GCC investor-claimants access to domestic remedies, in addition (and potentially in parallel) to international arbitration.

The dimension of the flow of investment capital into, from, and within the respective GCC member States from public (sovereign wealth funds) and semi-public (government-related entities) and private investors (at times also closely related to government entities) inevitably leads to significant development and growth in the nature, range, and complexity of investment projects. This in turn may well lead to further ISDS cases emerging from or into the region, particularly in the areas involving new and emerging technologies or greenfield investments.

This possible or likely scenario, it is suggested, would strengthen the merit of the States reviewing both the ISDS arbitration provisions in their various IIAs and BITs as well as their FDI, arbitration, and related legislative frameworks.

Bibliography

Abdallah, Amel, 'A Critical analyses of Omani Investment Law' (2015) 16 *Journal of World Investment & Trade*, 506–531.

Al Ali, Fatima and Saifuddin Mahmood, 'Foreign Direct Investment Regimes Bahrain 2023', *ICLG* (30 November 2022) at <Foreign Direct Investment Regimes Laws and Regulations Report 2023 Bahrain (iclg.com)>.

Alhihi, Mohamed Salem, 'Legal Assessment of the Kuwaiti Foreign Direct Investment Rules in Light of the WTO Rules' (2020) 8 *Kuwait International Law School Journal*, 35–68, Special Supplement 35.

Al-Tawil, Tareq Na'el, Venugopal Prabhakar Gantasala and Walaaeldeen Ibraheem, 'The Potential Impact of the 2020 UAE FDI Decree and Side Agreements' (2021) 36(3) *ICSID Review – Foreign Investment Law Journal*, 518–535.

'Amendments to Law on Real Estate Ownership and Investment by Non-Saudis', *UNCTAD* (30 May 2011) at <Saudi Arabia - Amendments to Law on Real Estate Ownership and Investment by Non-Saudis | Investment Policy Monitor | UNCTAD Investment Policy Hub>.

'Arbitration Law Update', *Davidson & Co* (January 2019) at <Arbitration Law Update - Federal Law No. 6 of 2018 - Davidson & Co (davidsoncolaw.com)>.

'Bahrain, Commercial Companies Law', *Economic Development Board* at <Bahrain Business Laws | Commercial Companies Law>.

'Bahrain Foreign Direct Investment with World Partners and EU27', *EU– GCC Dialogue on Economic Diversification Gulf Cooperation Council (GCC) Countries* (21 April 2023).

'Bahrain: Guidebook of Commercial Activities Requirements', *Sijilat* (Version No. June 2023) at <Sijilat 2.61_en_Finial.pdf>.

'Bahrain, Law No. (50) of 2014 Amending Certain Provisions of the Commercial Companies', *Law Promulgated by Legislative Decree No. (21) of 2001.*

'Bahrain, Legislative Decree No. (21) of 2001, the Commercial Companies Law' at <Ministry of Finance & National Economy (moic.gov.bh)>.

'Bahrain Passes a New Law Allowing 100% Foreign Ownership in Various Sectors', *UNCTAD* (19 July 2016) at <Bahrain - Bahrain passed a new law allowing 100% foreign ownership in various sectors. | Investment Policy Monitor | UNCTAD Investment Policy Hub>.

'Bahrain, Regulations Ministry of Commerce and Industry' (undated) at <Regulations (moic .gov.bh)>.

Blanke, Gordon, 'GCC Investment Laws: To Arbitrate or Not to Arbitrate, That is the Question (Part 1)', *Practical Law Arbitration Blog* (7 February 2019) at <GCC investment laws: to arbitrate or not to arbitrate, that is the question (Part 1) | Arbitration Blog (practicallaw.com)>.

Dikos, Aaron, 'Foreign Investment in Kuwait', *Al Tamimi* (December 2018–January 2019) at <Foreign Investment in Kuwait - Al Tamimi & Company>.

'Foreign Direct Investment (FDI) in Kuwait' *Lloyds Bank* (April 2023) at <Foreign direct investment (FDI) in Kuwait - International Trade Portal (lloydsbanktrade.com)>.

Hammad, Suhaib and Ebaa Tounesi, 'A General Introduction to Foreign Investment Regulation in Saudi Arabia', *Lexology* (3 October 2023) at <https://www.lexology.com/library/detail.aspx?g=f56ae9f1-600e-4ce3-8d08-13e66a5259ca>.

Hammad, Suhaib and Ebaa Tounesi, 'The Foreign Investment Regulation Review: Saudi Arabia', *The Law Reviews* (21 October 2022) at <The Foreign Investment Regulation Review - The Law Reviews>.

'Kuwait, Decree Law No. 116 of 2013 on Promoting Direct Investment in the State of Kuwait' at <law1162013.pdf (kdipa.gov.kw)>.

'Kuwait, Decree Law No. 8 of 2001 on Regulating Direct Foreign Capital Investment In the State of Kuwait' at <Microsoft Word - direct_investment.doc (kuwaitemb-australia .com)>.

'Kuwait Enacts the Direct Investment Promotion Law', *UNCTAD* (16 June 2013) at <Kuwait - Enacts the Direct Investment Promotion Law | Investment Policy Monitor | UNCTAD Investment Policy Hub>.

Lucente, Frank, 'Ownership of Real Estate in Qatar by Foreigners', *Al Tamimi & Co* (May 2019) at https://www.tamimi.com/law-update-articles/non-qatari-individuals -investment-in-real-estate-and-succession-planning/>.

'MISA at a Glance', *Saudi Arabian Ministry of Investment* (2023) at <MISA at a Glance | Ministry of Investment>.

Natasha, Teja, 'Foreign Ownership in UAE Remains Low Despite FDI Reforms' (2022) *International Financial Law Review*. (14 April 2022), at <https://www.iflr.com/article/2a647zxame68p5g8dagow/foreign-ownership-in-uae-remains-low-despite-fdi-reforms>.

'New Commercial Companies Law', *UNCTAD* (11 September 2014) at <Bahrain - New Commercial Companies Law | Investment Policy Monitor | UNCTAD Investment Policy Hub>.

'New Executive Regulations of the Foreign Capital Investment Law', *UNCTAD* (14 June 2020) at <https://investmentpolicy.unctad.org/investment-policy-monitor/measures /3548/oman-new-executive-regulations-of-the-foreign-capital-investment-law>.

'New Investment Law to Treat Saudi and Foreign Investors Equally', *Sovereign Group Blog Saudi Arabia* (29 April 2022) at <New Investment Law to treat Saudi and foreign investors equally - The Sovereign Group>.

'New Law Allowing Foreigners to Buy All Kind of Properties in KSA Soon: Top Official', *Arab News* (27 March 2023) at <New law allowing foreigners to buy all kind of properties in KSA soon: Top official (arabnews.com)>.

'New Law Urged to Regulate Investment in Bahrain', *Zawya* (22 May 2022) at <New law urged to regulate investment in Bahrain (zawya.com)>.

Noor Radhi, Fatima Al Ali, Saifuddin Mahmood and Hasan Alkoofi, Hassan Radhi, 'Associates Thomson', *Reuters Practical Law* (1 July 2021) at <Doing Business in Bahrain: Overview | Practical Law (thomsonreuters.com)>.

'Oman: Adoption of new Foreign Capital Investment Law', *UNCTAD* (1 July 2019) at <https://investmentpolicy.unctad.org/investment-policy-monitor/measures/3417/oman -adoption-of-new-foreign-capital-investment-law>.

'Oman: New Foreign Capital Investment Law and Executive Regulations', *PWC Middle East* (2020) at <Oman: New Foreign Capital Investment Law and Executive Regulations-PwC Middle East>.

'Oman, Royal Decree 50/2019 Promulgating the Foreign Capital Investment Law' at <https://mjla.gov.om/eng/legislation/decrees/details.aspx?Id=1091&type=L> .

'Oman, Royal Decree 102/1994 Promulgating The Foreign Capital Investment Law' at <Oman - Foreign Investment Law | Investment Laws Navigator | UNCTAD Investment Policy Hub>.

Pooley, Jeremy and Salim Al Harthi, 'A New Dawn for Foreign Direct Investment in Oman', *MENA Business Law Review – Special Edition: Foreign Investment Law* (January 2021) at <A New Dawn for Foreign Direct Investment in Oman | Law Firm Oman | SASLO>.

'Prohibiting Foreign Investment in Some Activities', *UNCTAD* (14 December 2020) at <https://investmentpolicy.unctad.org/investment-policy-monitor/measures/3627/prohibiting-foreign-investment-in-some-activities>.

'Qatar, Law No. (1) of 2019 On Regulating Non-Qatari Capital Investment' at <Law no. 1 of 2019 on regulating non-Qatari Capital Investment_EN.pdf (unescwa.org)>.

'Qatar, Law No. (16) of 2018 on the Regulation of Non-Qataris' Ownership and Usage of Real Estate' at <Law No. (16) of 2018 on the Regulation of Non-Qataris' Ownership and Usage of Real Estate.pdf (almeezan.qa)>.

Saudi Arabia, 'Executive Rules to the Saudi Arabian Foreign Investment Law' at <https://www.saudiembassy.net/foreign-investment-act-and-executive-rules>.

Saudi Arabia, 'Royal Decree No. M/1 of 5.1.1421.H, the Foreign Investment Law (corresponding to 10 April 2000)' at <Saudi Arabia - Foreign Investment Law | Investment Laws Navigator | UNCTAD Investment Policy Hub>.

Saudi Arabia, 'Royal Decree No. M/4 of 1.1.1442H (corresponding to 20 August 2020), the Anti-Concealment Law'.

Saudi Arabia, 'Royal Decree No. M/15 dated 17.04.1421H (corresponding to 19 July 2000), the Law of Real Estate Ownership and Investment by Non-Saudis' at <https://www.moj.gov.sa/Documents/Regulations/pdf/En/37.pdf.>

'Saudi Arabia's New Anti-Concealment Law', *Baker McKenzie* (February 2021) at <New Anti-Concealment Law (bakermckenzie.com)>.

'Saudis Allow Foreigners to Own Property; But Market Remains Tight', *International Business Times* (3 March 2011) at <Saudis allow foreigners to own property; but market remains tight (ibtimes.com)>.

Tahan, Tom, A. Thraya and Jad A. Taha, 'The UAE Recalibrates its Foreign Direct Investment Framework with 100% Foreign Ownership and Other Landmark Changes to its Commercial Companies Law', *Mayer Brown* (1 December 2020) at <The UAE Recalibrates its Foreign Direct Investment Framework with 100% Foreign Ownership and Other Landmark Changes to its Commercial Companies Law | Perspectives & Events | Mayer Brown>.

'The "Positive List" Has Been Official Published', *UNCTAD* (20 April 2023) at <United Arab Emirates - The "Positive List" has been officially published | Investment Policy Monitor | UNCTAD Investment Policy Hub>.

'The Qatar Financial Centre Issues New Real Estate Ownership Regulations', *Addleshaw Goddard* (13 September 2021) at <https://www.addleshawgoddard.com/en/insights/insights-briefings/2021/real-estate/qatar-financial-centre-issues-new-real-estate-ownership-regulations/>.

UAE Cabinet of Ministers Resolution No. 16 of 2020, *Concerning the Determination of the Positive List of Economic Sectors and Activities Eligible for Foreign Direct Investment and Percentage of their Ownership.*

UAE, *Federal Law No. 2 of 2015 Concerning Commercial Companies.*

UAE, *Federal Decree-Law No.19 of 2018 on Foreign Direct Investment.*

UAE, *Federal Decree-Law No. 26 of 2020 Amending Certain Provisions of Federal Law No. (2) of 2015 on Commercial Companies.*

UAE, *Federal Law No. 6 of 2018, on Arbitration.*

UNCTAD, 'World Investment Report 2023' (5 July 2023) at <World Investment Report 2023: Investment and sustainable energy (unctad.org)>.

United States Department of State, '2023 Investment Climate Statements: Bahrain' (30 November 2022) at <Bahrain - United States Department of State>.

United States Department of State, '2022 Investment Climate Statements: Kuwait' (2022) at <Kuwait - United States Department of State>.

United States Department of State, '2023 Investment Climate Statements: Oman' (2023) at <Oman - United States Department of State>.

United States Department of State, '2022 Investment Climate Statements: Qatar' (2022) at <Qatar - United States Department of State>.

United States Department of State, '2023 Investment Climate Statements: Saudi Arabia' (2023) at <Saudi Arabia - United States Department of State>.

United States Department of State, '2023 Investment Climate Statements: United Arab Emirates' (2023) at <United Arab Emirates - United States Department of State>.

Williams, Christopher, 'UAE Foreign Direct Investment Law', *Bracewell* (25 July 2019) at <https://bracewell.com/insights/uae-foreign-direct-investment-law-0>.

8 ISDS, Islamic Law-Based Investment Agreements and Islamic Finance Principles

8.1 Introduction

This chapter considers the ISDS regime and its application to dispute outcomes that may be particularly relevant to ISDS in the Gulf Cooperation Council (GCC) region and other Islamic countries. It explores the question of whether ISDS can be Shariah compliant, particularly in view of the extensive development and acceptance of Islamic finance and banking principles within both the Islamic and Western economies and investment regimes.

The discussion investigates the extent to which Islamic finance principles can be incorporated by tribunals into the application of ISDS arbitration, initially with the two leading Islamic-based international arbitration agreements, notably the *Arab Investment Agreement* and the *OIC Agreement*, and considers whether these Agreements might be appropriate vehicles for the application of Islamic finance in international investment and relations. The chapter is explorative in seeking solutions to ISDS and Arab-based investment agreements through Islamic finance principles.

8.2 International Perspective and Background

The GCC union is a cooperation agreement that was established in 1981 between the six GCC member States. The purpose of the GCC Charter was to set out the key objectives of the States and to hold court in the international arena as a regional entity. The Preamble to the Charter is embedded with a statement outlining a respect for the shared religious views of its member States, stating that each State is "fully aware of the ties of special relations, common characteristics and similar systems founded on the creed of Islam which bind them".[1] The impact of religious beliefs on the States is important as the Charter deals with all aspects of business and commerce. For example, Article 4 of the Charter lists the key field of its collective cooperation as economic and financial affairs, commerce, customs and communications, and education and culture.[2] The Charter is a comprehensive document set out over 22 articles and deals primarily with establishing a Council and the main objectives

1 GCC Charter, Preamble, <https://www.gcc-sg.org/en-us/AboutGCC/Pages/Primarylaw.aspx>.
2 Ibid, Article 4.

DOI: 10.4324/9781003481072-8

of the union. The GCC has its own Supreme Council, Ministerial Council, and Secretariat General,[3] with Article 7 declaring the Supreme Council as the highest authority in the GCC[4] and Article 8 listing the main functions of the Supreme Council. The Ministerial Council is formed of the Foreign Ministers of the States or other delegated ministers and is primarily concerned with proposing policies and recommendations.[5] The Secretariat General is led by a Secretary-General who is appointed by the Supreme Council and is assisted by a number of staff.[6] Thus, despite the variances in the governance structures of the States, there has been a conscious effort to develop a GCC Charter that is democratic and representative of all member States. The aim of the articles of the Charter is to set out how the states can collectively govern a single common market.

The GCC Charter embodies the GCC's strong desire to develop national laws and regulations to bring it and its member states on par with legislative and regulatory developments in the international arena. The Economic Agreement between the GCC member States, adopted by the GCC Supreme Council in December 2001, states in its Preamble a desire to "enhance the economy of the GCC member States in the light of recent global economic developments which require further integration among the Member States to strengthen their negotiating position competitive capacity in international markets".[7] The Agreement covers trade, international economic relations, the GCC common market, scientific and technical research, development, and infrastructure. In relation to international economic relations, the Agreement focusses on securing better terms and more favourable conditions in their international economic relationships by conducting economic relations in a collective manner when dealing with other countries, blocs, and regional groupings, as well as other regional and international organisations. Article 2 of the Agreement states the GCC members shall come to an understanding to:

3 Ibid, Article 6. The Article states: "*Organization of the Cooperation Council – The Cooperation Council shall have the following main organizations. 1. The Supreme Council to which shall be attached the Commission for Settlement of Disputes. 2. The Ministerial Council. 3. The Secretariat General*". Each of these organisations establishes sub-agencies as may be necessary".

4 Ibid, Article 7. The Articles states: "*Supreme Council – The Cooperation Council shall be formed of the six states that participated in the Foreign Ministers' meeting held in Riyadh on 4 February 1981. The Supreme Council is the highest authority of the Cooperation Council and shall be formed of heads of member states. Its presidency shall be rotatory based on the alphabetical order of the names of the member states. The Supreme Council shall hold one regular session every year. Extraordinary sessions may be convened at the request of any member seconded by another member. The Supreme Council shall hold its sessions in the territories of member* states. *A Supreme Council's meeting shall be considered valid if attend by two-thirds of the member states*".

5 Ibid, Articles 11–13.

6 Ibid, Articles 14–16.

7 *Economic Agreement between the GCC States*, adopted by the GCC Supreme Council (22nd Session; 31 December 2001) at <https://www.worldtradelaw.net/document.php?id=fta/agreements/GCC_FTA.pdf>.

> negotiate collectively in a manner that serves the negotiating position of the Member States, collectively conclude economic agreements with trading partners, unify import and export rules and procedures and unify commercial exchange policies with the outside world.[8]

The GCC has made considerable efforts to develop international relations, most notably with the EU and US, along with others.[9] The GCC is currently the EU's fifth largest export market, and the EU is the GCC's second largest trading partner[10] and follows the main international provisions of the WTO's General Agreement on Trade and Tariffs (GATT), and Agreement on the Trade-Related Aspects of Intellectual Property Rights (TRIPs Agreement). In the case of the GCC, these have been supplemented by further negotiations regarding international provisions concerning intellectual property.

The GCC has outstanding free trade agreements with the EU and the US. The EU is a uniquely large economic and political partnership between a significant number of European countries that are collectively represented in the global arena.[11] The US has the largest economy in the world and, similar to many of the EU countries, exports and imports goods around the globe. The GCC and US have set up a joint committee, the US–GCC Strategic Cooperation Forum, as part of their Framework Agreement for Trade, Economic, Investment and Technical Cooperation of 2012 to examine opportunities for enhancing economic, commercial, investment, and technical cooperation leading to a comprehensive free trade agreement, as set out in their Framework Agreement.[12] The main impetus for a free trade agreement is largely due to an increased effort to raise the volume of trade and investment between the GCC and the US.[13]

The negotiations for a free trade agreement between the GCC and the EU began in 1988.[14] The purpose behind the trade agreement is similar to that of the framework trade agreement between the GCC and the US, which is to harmonise investment rules in the GCC to allow corporations to participate more directly in oil, banking, investment, and other industries. However, political issues have slowed

8 Ibid, Article 2, International Economic Relations.

9 Other initiatives and agreements include the Australia–GCC Free Trade Agreement (FTA) negotiations, New Zealand–GCC FTA, Singapore–GCC FTA, India–GCC FTA, and ASEAN–GCC FTA. Other countries include Turkey, South Korea, Iran, China, and Pakistan.

10 For further details on the working of the EU, see 'Your Gateway to the EU' *European Union*, at <http://europa.eu/about-eu/index_en.htm>.

11 For further details on the working of the EU, see 'Your Gateway to the EU', *European Union*, at <http://europa.eu/about-eu/index_en.htm>.

12 *Framework Agreement for Trade, Economic, Investment and Technical Cooperation between the Cooperation Council for the Arab States of the Gulf and the Government of the United States of America*, signed 25 September 2012 (not yet in force), ('US-GCC Framework Agreement') at <https://ustr.gov/sites/default/files/uploads/agreements/Trade%20Investment/U.S.-GCC%20TIFA%20Final%20Text%20--%20English%209-25-12.pdf>.

13 United States Trade Representative, at <http://www.ustr.gov/about-us/press-office/press-releases/2012/september/ustr-kirk-announces-agreement-gcc>.

14 'EU Trade Relations with the Gulf Region', *European Commission*, at <https://policy.trade.ec.europa.eu/eu-trade-relationships-country-and-region/countries-and-regions/gulf-region_en>.

down the progress of the GCC–EU trade agreement.[15] Nonetheless, trade still continues, and ISDS clauses are invoked when there is a state–state level dispute. The debatable issue would be on the status of a Shariah ruling and if it would be binding on the tribunals. This largely depends on the Shariah governance frameworks and the level of superiority given to Shariah-led decisions. The situation is jurisdictional-based and in the GCC, the status of Shariah law pronouncements is ambiguous. Therefore, there needs to be a practical solution to resolve the issue of ISDS by examining the legal environment and structure. Proactive efforts to bolster the position of Shariah law through Islamic finance principles could be the best way forward to enforce Shariah rulings in arbitration tribunals.

The GCC is currently negotiating several trade agreements, as are the EU and the US. Trade agreements aim to remove trade barriers across different economic sectors to increase trade between countries and regional blocs such as the GCC, the EU, and the US. Trade agreements between the GCC, the EU, and the US will have spill-over effects for the GCC as they raise key questions for both the EU–GCC Free Trade Agreement and US–GCC Framework Agreement.[16] For example, will the US and EU be on an equal footing or will one triumph over the other, will third-party countries like the GCC member States be expected to adopt new standards as a result, and will it lead to more competition? Both the EU and the US have included investor–state dispute settlement (ISDS) in their agreements. ISDS enables foreign investors to circumvent domestic legal processes and hold governments in foreign states to account in arbitration tribunals, since they are unable to go through the WTO dispute settlement process, nevertheless in effect creating a form of corporate sovereignty. Sovereignty is itself a contentious issue, with all three entities, the US, EU, and GCC, having very different political structures and as a result raising distinct individual and regional sovereignty issues. ISDS poses a series of sovereignty threats as it puts foreign investors on par with nations, giving them authority to seek compensation directly from states with some draconian measures such as powers to seize state assets.[17]

ISDS has an added layer of issues with the GCC member States since a question arises as to whether ISDS is, or can be, compatible with Shariah law. Further

15 Rym Ayadi, 'EU-GCC Trade and Investment Relations: What Prospect of an FTA between the Two Regions?', *CEPS* (24 October 2013) at <http://www.ceps.eu/book/eu-gcc-trade-and-investment-relations-what-prospect-fta-between-two-regions>. Valentina Kostadinova, 'What Is the Status of the EU-GCC Relationship?', *Gulf Research Center Papers* (July 2013) at <http://eu-gcc.kcorp.net/common/publicationfile/29.pdf>.

16 *US-GCC Framework Agreement (n 12).*

17 United Nations Conference on Trade and Development (UNCTAD), World Investment Report, 2013, Global Value Chains: Investment and Trade for Development, 110, at <http://unctad.org/en/publicationslibrary/wir2013_en.pdf>.

analysis will be conducted in this chapter on the implications of ISDS on the States, as all have accepted ISDS as an acceptable dispute settlement mechanism.[18] Investment carries with it risk; foreign investment would in turn carry higher risks as investors would be acting in markets with different political and legal structures. If the risk is too speculative, then it potentially falls under the Islamic principle of *gharar*.[19] In terms of Shariah references to international business and ISDS, the Quran has clear statements regarding honouring agreements and the need for certainty while forbidding *riba* and *gharar*. The clearest reference can be found in the chapter Surah Al Baqarah, at verse 275:

> Those who consume interest cannot stand [on the Day of Resurrection] except as one stands who is being beaten by Satan into insanity. That is because they say, "Trade is [just] like interest." But Allah has permitted trade and has forbidden interest. So, whoever has received an admonition from his Lord and desists may have what is past, and his affair rests with Allah. But whoever returns to [dealing in interest or usury] – those are the companions of the Fire; they will abide eternally therein.

Through trade, different models of contractual arrangements have emerged which, although are Shariah compliant, allow a trader or investor to earn some return on the capital that has been invested without breaching the prohibition on interest. It is the distinction between return on investment and interest that has been the cornerstone of the Islamic finance industry, which warrants examination in relation to ISDS and whether Islamic finance can be the solution to how tribunals apply ISDS clauses and award damages accordingly.

Therefore, the key to a successful application of ISDS in the Gulf States is striking a balance between permissible trade and circumventing *riba* and *gharar*, similar to the manner in which Shariah-compliant models have evolved in Islamic finance. In an international context, ISDS is at the heart of most trade agreements and the greater the protection, the more trade can take place through foreign direct investment. When a developing country can demonstrate compliance with ISDS procedures and consistency in application, there are obvious advantages as foreign companies and multinationals are more willing to invest where they have confidence that there is a robust legal route. Currently it is the UNICTRAL rules that prevail, although this chapter focusses on the varying approaches to ISDS tribunals and the potential impact of Islamic finance principles on the development of a more Shariah-compliant approach.

18 'Assessing Investment Policies of Member Countries of the Gulf Cooperation Council Stocktaking Analysis', *MENA-OECD Investment Programme* (5 April 2011), 57, at <http://www.oecd.org/mena/investment/Preliminary%20assessment%20GCC%20invt%20policies.pdf>.

19 Abdulrahim Al Saati, 'The Permissible *Gharar* (Risk) in Classical Islamic Jurisprudence' (2003) 16(2) *Islamic Economics*, 3–19, 3.

Arbitration has been approved as a primary source in the Quran as an acceptable dispute resolution mechanism. As there is no express or even implied rule against settling commercial disputes by arbitration, Islamic law accepts arbitration as a dispute settlement mechanism that can be applied to international investment disputes.[20] The pertinent question is how to resolve ISDS disputes in compliance with Islamic law.

8.3 The Influence of Shariah Law in the GCC

To fully examine the impact of ISDS in the GCC and the consequential challenges it creates from a Shariah law perspective, it is imperative to lay the foundational steps on which a potential Shariah law-complaint ISDS system can be built while also accounting for the competing interests of the international heavyweights. Islamic finance has crossover application to ISDS proceedings, and given the unique religious commonality of the GCC region in constitutional law, there is an opportunity for the GCC to lead on a Shariah-compliant ISDS approach.

In terms of composition, the GCC is a union of 6 states in the Middle East that have undergone many changes over the last 30 years. The union was founded on 26 May 1981, and the continued aim of the union is to promote coordination between member States in all fields in order to achieve unity. The main impetus behind the union was in response to three main issues, namely, the perceivable security threats to the different Gulf Arab regimes from the Iran–Iraq conflict around the time of formation, the Soviet communist threat from Afghanistan, and to be better protected against security threats.[21] A failed coup attempt in Bahrain in 1981,[22] a series of bombings in Kuwait in 1983,[23] and the Iran–Iraq War caused regional instability and spearheaded the strong commitment by its members to the newly established GCC.[24]

Therefore, the creation of the GCC addressed a number of security concerns for its member States, and enhancing security protection has been and continues to be a primary concern. Along with the geographical commonalities which they share, the States are the world's biggest oil producers and, collectively, are dependent,

20 Amel Abdallah, *Islamic Sharia and Arbitration in GCC States: The Way Ahead* (Qatar University Press, 2020).

21 Abdulrhman Hussain, *So History Doesn't Forget: Alliances Behaviour in Foreign Policy of the Kingdom of Saudi Arabia, 1979–1990* (AuthorHouse UK, 2012); Neil Patrick, 'The GCC: Gulf State Integration or Leadership Cooperation?' (2011) *London School of Economics and Political Science*, Kuwait Programme on Development, Governance and Globalisation in the Gulf States, at <http://www.lse.ac.uk/IDEAS/.

22 Toby Matthiesen, *The Other Saudis, Shiism, Descent and Sectarianism* (Cambridge University Press, 2014) 118; Gabriel Gorodetsky, *Soviet Foreign Policy, 1917–1991: A Retrospective* (Routledge Cavendish, 2014) 206; Miriam Joyce, *Bahrain from the Twentieth Century to the Arab Spring* (Palgrave McMillan, 2012), 105–6.

23 Haim Shaked and Daniel Dishon (eds), *Middle East Contemporary Survey*, vol. 8 (1983–84) (The Moshe Dayan Center, 1986).

24 David Partington, *The Middle East Annual: Issues and Events*, vol. 2 (G. K. Hall & Co., 1982) 178.

to varying degrees, on oil production.[25] Before analysing ISDS regimes in the GCC, understanding the structure of the GCC Charter is relevant to forming a complete picture of how deeply rooted the States are in Islamic values. The number of national and international memberships for each State can be linked to the weight Shariah law holds in legislative matters. The six States can be distinguished in respect to the level of Shariah compliance observed. The strictest following of Shariah law is by Saudi Arabia which cites Shariah as the constitution of the state. Below Saudi Arabia is Oman which has Shariah as the basis of legislation. Qatar follows behind Oman with Shariah considered to be the main source of law and lastly Bahrain and Kuwait have Shariah as a main source of law.

8.4 The Elephant in the Room – ISDS and the GCC

The ISDS has at its core a rigid dichotomy between the critical view that ISDS clauses give corporations and foreign investors corporate sovereignty against the business standpoint that the clauses are vital to protecting foreign investment in countries where judicial systems are unpredictable.[26] The main fear of ISDS clauses is that they could lead to governments being held to ransom by wealthy corporations, as ISDS would allow firms to sue authorities for compensation over policies that adversely affect them. This has serious ramifications for domestic sovereignty and the rule of law. In an international context, both for the contracting states and non-contracting states, the impact of ISDS on the ability of states to make laws challenges fundamental principles of constitutional law and democracy. The root of all the fears about the investment agreements is that the number of ISDS cases will rise further if more and more deals are concluded with ISDS clauses, and consequently, the threat created by corporate sovereignty will increase. This raises a key question on infrastructure limitations in the GCC. The success or failure, for that matter, of an ISDS process is contingent upon the expertise and experience of the judicial system that is making the decision. If there is a lack of expertise and/or precedent, where is the solid foundation of knowledge from which to answer principle questions?

8.4.1 Is ISDS Shariah Compliant?

ISDS has an added layer of issues with the GCC member States as a question arises as to whether ISDS is compatible with Shariah law. The States have accepted ISDS as an acceptable dispute settlement mechanism in existing agreements.[27] Investment

25 Martin Hvidt, 'Economic Diversification in GCC Countries: Past Record and Future Trends' (2013) *London School of Economics and Political Science*, Kuwait Programme on Development, Governance and Globalisation in the Gulf States, at <http://www.lse.ac.uk/IDEAS/>.

26 See 'Reforming Investment Dispute Settlement: A Stocktaking', *UNCTAD Series on Issues in International Investment Agreements* (March 2019, Issue 1) at <https://investmentpolicy.unctad.org/publications/1194/reforming-investment-dispute-settlement-a-stocktaking>.

27 MENA-OECD Investment Programme (n 18), 57.

carries with it risk; foreign investment would in turn carry higher risks as investors would be acting in markets with different political and legal structures. If the risk is too speculative, then it potentially falls under the Islamic principle of *gharar*.[28] The outcome of the Al Jazeera and Egypt ISDS case, for example, could set new ground for international disputes in the region as both states have Shariah as part of their constitution. Therefore, how the arbitration process deals with principles of *gharar* and *riba* will be relevant to other countries in the Middle East region and beyond.

8.4.2 The Trojan Horse – Corporate Sovereignty Impact on the GCC

The GCC is a collection of rentier states, as discussed earlier. They have similar autocratic monarchies and political and cultural identities, which are historically rooted in Islamic beliefs.[29] Unlike other international bodies, the GCC is unique in that all its member States are Islamic states. Each individual State has varying degrees of Shariah law incorporated in its constitution. ISDS will have spill-over effects for the GCC as it has yet to finalise the EU–GCC FTA and several other international agreements. The power dynamics between the US and EU will be a deciding factor for determining what powers will be available to investors to bring ISDS claims against foreign countries.

ISDS clauses in international agreements will bind the GCC member States and have a significant impact on a number of sectors including financial services, intellectual property, and the energy sector. The tribunals would require a new regulatory environment of governance, accountability, and transparency. This leaves the GCC in quite the conundrum. Neither of its FTAs with the US or EU have reached a conclusion, so the negotiating power the GCC will have is something that requires the States to be proactive and mitigate ahead of the deal.

The main issues with ISDS and subsequently the threat to corporate sovereignty are three-fold. The first issue is the lack of clarity on arbitrator powers which in essence arises because of the vague formulation of major treaty provisions. The lack of clarity on arbitrator powers has created a Pandora's box for arbitrators to allow and deal with a wide range of interpretations. Following on from this is the arbitration process, much of which is in secret; therefore the risk of inconsistencies in similar cases is heightened. There is an absence of effective review mechanisms for appeal processes; there is an annulment committee procedure available for arbitrations conducted by the International Centre for the Settlement of Investment

28 *Riba* is the doctrine on the prohibition of interest payments, undue profits, or excessive gain from a transaction, and *gharar* deals with risk, speculative transactions, ambiguity, or excessive uncertainty in contracts. See Rodney Wilson, 'The Development of Islamic Finance in the GCC', *London School of Economics and Political Science* (2009) Working Paper, Kuwait Programme on Development, Governance and Globalisation in the Gulf States, 27, at <http://eprints.lse.ac.uk/id/eprint/55281>.

29 See Abdulhadi Khalaf and Giacomo Luciani (eds), 'Constitutional Reform and Political Participation' (2006) *Gulf Research Center*, at <https://cadmus.eui.eu/handle/1814/13235>.

Disputes.[30] However, this is limited to challenging the validity of an award and whether the challenge can lead to the annulment of the award.[31] Thirdly, as a result of how ISDS is incorporated into trade agreements and is dealt with by the arbitration process, there are serious implications for national sovereignty within each State, their democratic governance, and the rule of law within national legal systems.[32] In theory, a foreign arbitral award can be enforced given the ratification of the 1994 New York Convention by a State; however there is no conclusive answer on enforceability. Consequently, the remaining sections will assess the potential solution that Islamic finance can offer to ISDS arbitration proceedings.

8.5 Islamic Finance and Its Products

8.5.1 Islamic Finance Overview

Islamic finance is very much enshrined in ethical guidelines that are deeply rooted in a religion by which it must abide.[33] In Islamic teachings, money is a measure of value as opposed to a commodity.[34] Therefore, in line with Islamic teachings, the money should be put to practical use, invested to create wealth, and not be a commodity of itself.[35] It is the earning of a passive return on capital which is identified as the backbone of the definition of the prohibition of *riba*.[36] In its simplest terms, Shariah expressly prohibits the making of money from money, but rather requires the creation of real value for the participants of a transaction.[37] The same prohibition of interest applies to debt whereby the risk and responsibility are the debt are shared between all contractually obligated parties.[38]

30 'Updated Background Paper on Annulment for the Administrative Council of ICSID', *International Centre for the Settlement of Investment Disputes (ICSID)* (2016) at <https://icsid.worldbank.org/resources/publications/background-papers-annulment>.

31 Ibid, 9–10.

32 Robert French, 'ISDS: A Cut above the Courts?', *Civil Liberties Australia* (2 September 2014) at <http://www.cla.asn.au/News/isds-a-cut-above-the-courts/>.

33 Usman Hayat, 'Islamic Finance: Ethics, Concepts, Practice', *CFA Institute Research Foundation* (1 November 2014) at <http://www.cfainstitute.org/learning/foundation/research/Documents/islamic_finance_ethics_concepts_practice.pdf>.

34 Abu Ahmad, 'The Time Value of Money Concept in Islamic Finance', *American Journal of Islamic Social Sciences* (2012) 23(1) 66–89, at <http://uaelaws.files.wordpress.com/2012/05/the-time-value-of-money-concept-in-islamic-finance.pdf.

35 Abdullah Saeed, *Islamic Banking and Interest: A Study of the Prohibition of Riba and Its Contemporary Interpretation* (Brill Academic, 2012).

36 Hussein Elasrag, 'Principals of the Islamic Finance: A Focus on Project Finance', *Munich Personal RePEc Archive* (18 April 2011) at <http://mpra.ub.uni-muenchen.de/30197/1/MPRA_paper_30197.pdf>.

37 Ibid.

38 Abbas Mirakhor and Iqbal Zaidi, 'Profit-and-Loss Sharing Contracts in Islamic Finance', *Handbook of Islamic Banking* (April 2007) at <http://202.154.59.182/mfile/files/Economics/Handbook%20of%20Islamic%20Banking/Chapter%204%20Profit-and-loss%20sharing%20contracts%20in%20Islamic%20finance.pdf>.

Islamic finance is defined as Shariah-compliant financial transactions which can be used as an alternative to conventional western banking methods.[39] Islamic finance emerged in the early 1960s with the objective of providing alternative financial contracts in conformity with Shariah principles as necessitated by primary and secondary sources of Islam. The Mit Ghamr Local Savings Bank in Egypt in 1963 is widely accepted as the first modern attempt at Islamic banking.[40] Dubai established the first Islamic Bank in 1975, known as the Dubai Islamic Bank.[41] Therefore, similar to the developments of intellectual property in the GCC, Islamic finance is also relatively new in the context of financial banking in the Gulf region.[42] The developments of Islamic finance in the GCC run parallel with the oil boom[43] over the last three decades; the GCC states have heavily invested in developing Shariah-compliant banking.[44]

Islamic finance has developed through a series of fatwas that are passed by Islamic scholars and jurists. A fatwa is a result of human interpretation of the Shariah. A fatwa can be passed based on the interpretation of texts and recordings from primary and secondary Shariah sources. They are not viewed as the ordained

39 Mahyuddin Khalid, 'Development of the Malaysian Islamic Financial System', *Universiti Teknologi Mara (2013)* at <https://www.scribd.com/presentation/116822528/Development-of-the-Malaysian-Islamic-Financial-System>; T. Beck, 'Islamic vs. Conventional Banking: Business Model, Efficiency and Stability', *Journal of Banking Finance* (2013) (372), 433–447, at <http://ac.els-cdn.com/S0378426612002920/1-s2.0-S0378426612002920-main.pdf?_tid=b6195f62-96c4-11e4-a4db-00000aacb361acdnat=1420673414_a5be4510b722d8a1b52b95eed93067d7>.

40 Shariq Nisar, 'The Practices of Islamic Banking and Finance: A Historical Perspective' (2003) at <http://www.shariqnisar.com/images/My_writings/Islamic%20Finance%20History.pdf>; Mohamed Ariff, 'Islamic Banking', *Asian-Pacific Economic Literature (1988) 2(2) 46*–62, at <http://www.nzibo.com/IB2/Islamic%20Banking%20-%20Mohammed%20Ariff.pdf>; Mehmet Asutay, 'Reflecting on the Trajectory of Islamic Finance: From Mit Ghamr to the Globalisation of Islamic Finance', *Afro Eurasian Studies* (2013) 2(2) 5–14, at <http://www.afroeurasianstudies.net/dosyalar/site_resim/veri/0344147.pdf>.

41 Rodney Wilson (n 28); John R. Presley (ed), *Directory of Islamic Financial Institutions* (Routledge: Banking and Finance, 2012). See also Dubai Islamic Bank at <https://www.dib.ae/business>.

42 'Shariah-Compliant Funds: A Whole New World of Investment', *PricewaterhouseCoopers Global Financial Services Islamic Finance Programme* (2009) at <https://www.pwc.com/en_US/gx/financial-services/islamic-finance-programme/pdf/shariah-compliant-funds.pdf>.

43 'Oil Boom in GCC Region Shifts Economic Landscape', *World Finance* (2014) at <http://www.worldfinance.com/banking/oil-boom-in-gcc-region-shifts-economic-landscape>; Ibrahim Warde, *Islamic Finance in the Global Economy* (Edinburgh University Press, 2000) electronic version at <http://www.iefpedia.com/english/wp-content/uploads/2011/03/2000-Ibrahim-Warde-Islamic-finance-in-the-global-economy-Edinburh-University-Press1.pdf>; Clement Henry and Rodney Wilson, *The Politics of Islamic Finance* (Edinburgh University Press, 2004); Wafik Grais and Matteo Pellegrini, 'Corporate Governance and Shariah Compliance in Institutions Offering Islamic Financial Services', *World Bank,* Policy Research Working Paper 4054 (21 June 2013) at <http://elibrary.worldbank.org/doi/pdf/10.1596/18; 13-9450-4054>.

44 Iqbal Khan, 'Islamic Banking', *Global Islamic Finance* (2009) at <http://theislamicfinanceandbanking.wordpress.com/islamic-finance-iqbal-khan/>. See also Cyril Garbois, Cyril Gourp, Alexander von Pourk and Mukund Bhatnagar, 'The Future of Islamic Banking', *AT Kearney* (2012) at <http://www.atkearney.com/documents/10192/654853/Future+of+Islamic+Banking.pdf/27167edf-a96d-4465-b88a-83beb25ed4bd>; Rodney Wilson (n 28).

word of Allah (SBTH) but rather a permissible method of analysing and/or combining different Shariah principles to come to a decision. Fatwas are issued by Shariah boards to rule on whether a new Islamic finance product is Shariah compliant or to amend an existing fatwa. Interestingly, there is no prescribed religious hierarchy in the Quran or Sunnah for the field of Islamic scholars who interpret the different sources of Shariah law. Therefore, the decisions require enforcement by banks, legislation, and financial institutions to make them binding.

The central findings from the Islamic finance sector on how the products are structured, the compliance mechanisms in place, the role of supervisory boards, and public confidence will be utilised to make recommendations for the investment arbitration sector.

8.5.2 Founding Principles of Islamic Finance

> There is nothing prohibited except that which God prohibits … to declare something permitted prohibited is like declaring something prohibited permitted.[45]

Islamic finance, at its core, is an ethical and equitable mode of finance, the origins of which can be traced back to Shariah principles found in the Quran and Sunnah.[46] The Quran, the highest source of Islamic law, unconditionally prohibits sinful (*haram*) activity[47] and *riba*[48] in financial transactions. However, although the Quran and Sunnah are unequivocally clear on what defines *haram* activity, there is no unanimity about the limitations or scope of the prohibition of *riba*.[49] This is largely due to the interpretation of the leading Quranic verse on *riba* found in Surah Baqarah at verse 275 and also at eight other verses.[50] *Riba* and *gharar* are at the heart of the connection between Islamic finance and intellectual property, for example, as both sectors prohibit transactions that involve *riba* and *gharar*.

Islamic finance is not a sector that is seamless in its governance, nor is it exempt from conflict. The differences in interpretation of Shariah raise issues for the harmonisation of Islamic finance products. Some divergence is unavoidable, given

45 Salahuddin Ali Abdul Majwood, *The Biography of Imam Iba Al Qayim* (translated by Abdul Rafi-Adewala) (Darussalam Publishers & Distributors, 2007). Also quoted in Abdulkader Thomas, *Interest in Islamic Economics: Understanding Riba* (Routledge, 2006) 63.

46 Mufti Muhammad Taqi Usmani, *An Introduction to Islamic Finance* (Arham Shamsi, 2004).

47 This includes direct or indirect investment with certain types of business areas that involve profit making from alcohol, pork products, betting, and gambling. See the Quran (Sahih International Translation) at verses 2:173, 2:219, 5:3, 5:90, 6:145, and 16:115, at <www.quran.com>.

48 Ibid, at verse 2:275.

49 Ahmad Shafaat, 'Islamic Perspectives, Chapter One', *Riba in the Quran* (2005) at <http://www.islamicperspectives.com/Riba1.htm>; Abdulkader Thomas (n 56); Shoiab Ghias, 'Juristic Disagreement: The Collective Fatwa against Islamic Banking in Pakistan', in Karen Hunt-Ahmed (ed), *Contemporary Islamic Finance: Innovations, Applications and Best Practices*, Chapter 6 (John Wiley & Sons, 2009); Ibrahim Warde (n 43).

50 See the Quran (n 47), at verses 2:275–80, 3:130, 4:161, and 30:39.

that the cultural, political, economic, and social beliefs in individual countries will differ from others.[51]

There are a number of Shariah scholars who specialise in Islamic finance and derive the necessary Islamic jurisprudence known as fiqh.[52] Islamic jurisprudence is recognised in the Quran as a method of understanding the way of the Prophet Muhammed.[53] Based in Jeddah, Saudi Arabia, the Islamic Fiqh Academy comprises leading scholars who make decisions on permissible Islamic finance products.[54] The International Fiqh Academy has played a pivotal role in the development of Islamic finance. The Dow Jones Islamic Index[55] and Islamic bonds, known as sukuks, are two key changes that have been synonymous with the expansion of Islamic financial markets. The Dow Jones Islamic Index Sharia Supervisory Board includes the five most eminent Shariah scholars in modern-day Islamic finance, namely, Sheikh Nizam Yaquby, Dr Mohammed Daud Bakar, Sheikh Dr Mohamed A. Elgari, Shaykh Abdul Sattar Abu Ghuddah, and Sheikh Yusuf Talal DeLorenzo. Dr Bakar is currently a member of the Shari'ah Advisory Council of many financial institutions in Malaysia and around the world, including the Central Bank of Malaysia, the Securities Commission of Malaysia, the International Islamic Financial Market in Bahrain, the Accounting and Auditing Organization for Islamic Financial Institutions (AAOIFI) in Bahrain, and HSBC (Malaysia). The scholars are all from different countries as a purposeful attempt to give the Dow Jones Islamic Index as wide a remit for investment as possible. It also needs to be noted that the scholars are from countries that are leaders in the Islamic finance market, such as Malaysia, Saudi Arabia, and Bahrain.[56]

8.5.3 Islamic Finance Products

There are a number of Shariah-compliant frameworks that are in existence across the Islamic finance market. In relation to its impact on ISDS, there are a number of relevant Shariah-compliant practices that have overcome the inevitable dichotomy that arises when Islamic law principles are married to Western concepts. In order to make recommendations on how Islamic finance can engender better compliance with ISDS processes, the main Islamic finance products are considered in terms of the rationale behind each product and the role of Shariah boards in promulgating the Shariah-compliant frameworks.[57] Further, as the purpose of analysing Islamic

51 Ishrat Husain, 'Islamic Finance Industry: Positioned for Growth', 2nd Pakistan Islamic Banking Conference, Karachi, 8 November 2006.

52 Fiqh is the consensus opinion of a group of scholars and exists in all aspects of Shariah. For Islamic finance fiqh is concerned with consensus opinions pertinent to Shariah-compliant financial products.

53 See the Quran (n 47), at verses 2:129, 2:159, 2:231, and 62:2.

54 Natalie Schoon, *Islamic Banking and Finance* (Spiramus Press, 2010) 144.

55 See Dow Jones Islamic Market Indices at <http://www.djindexes.com/islamicmarket/>.

56 Ibid.

57 There are a number of other Shariah-compliant frameworks such as Bai' al-Inah, known as a sale with a buyback agreement; however, this is outside the scope of the research. The various other types of Islamic finance products will provide the framework for further research and will include safeguarding property for another (*wadia*), a surety (*kafala*), and loan agreements (*qard hasssan*).

finance products is to identify the role Islamic finance can play in further developing ISDS protection in the GCC, Islamic finance is analysed to propose potential application to ISDS.

8.5.4 Equipping ISDS through Islamic Finance

International trade agreements have brought into play investor-to-state dispute settlement mechanisms (ISDS) and corporate sovereignty. The GCC member States need to develop the requisite knowledge and expertise in ISDS and corporate sovereignty by developing clear parameters for both in respect to *riba* and *gharar*. ISDS has serious ramifications for domestic sovereignty and the rule of law as it impacts on the ability of states to make laws, challenging fundamental principles of constitutional law and democracy.

Nonetheless, the States will struggle to justify the compensatory remedies of ISDS proceedings as compliant with Shariah law as there are no frameworks or internal infrastructures in place to control the level of damages that can be sought. Al Jazeera of Qatar, for example, relied on the ISDS included in the 1999 bilateral investment treaty between Egypt and Qatar.[58] Al Jazeera has argued that Egypt has breached the treaty, and the outcome of the proceedings will be relevant to the remaining GCC States and the international application of ISDS. But the geopolitical motives on both sides relating to the circumstances driving the disputation and consequent arbitration make it difficult to reconcile it with Shariah law principles. What the case also spotlights is that there are issues with judicial expertise, arbitration court structures, and transparency in ISDS proceedings in the GCC and neighbouring states such as Egypt where new areas of law are being developed.

ISDS mechanisms can be better equipped in the GCC and neighbouring states by integrating Islamic finance principles into the international agreements. Islamic finance can be utilised to create frameworks and benchmarks for ISDS processes that align with Shariah law. Most importantly, the frameworks would avoid *riba* and *gharar*, which are at the heart of Islamic finance methodology.

Nations involved in international agreements, both bilateral and multilateral, have sought to include ISDS provisions in the agreements as an arbitration action. ISDS enables foreign investors to circumvent domestic legal processes and hold governments in foreign states to account in international arbitration tribunals, in effect creating a corporate sovereignty.[59] Sovereignty is itself a contentious issue, as different states and regions have very different political structures, resulting in individual sovereignty issues. ISDS poses a series of threats to national sovereignty as it puts investors on par with nations, giving them authority to seek compensation

58 *Agreement between the Government of the Arab Republic of Egypt and the Government of the State of Qatar for the Reciprocal Promotion and Protection of Investments*, signed 2 December 1999 (entered into force 14 July 2006) ('Egypt – Qatar BIT'). See also Shawn Donnan, 'Al Jazeera sues Egypt for $150m after crackdown on journalists', Financial Times (26 June 2014) at <http://www.ft.com/cms/s/0/7ff2210c-cec0-11e3-ac8d-00144feabdc0.html#axzz3CNLGmNPk>

59 'The TTIP of the Anti-Democracy Iceberg', *Friends of the Earth Europe* (October 2013) at <http://www.foeeurope.org/sites/default/files/foee_factsheet_isds_oct13.pdf>.

directly from states with powers such as seizing state assets.[60] Therefore, within the ambit of Islamic finance law, future GCC developments must consider the potential positive impact that Islamic finance modelling can play in ISDS mechanisms.

Islamic finance can deal with access to arbitration, filtering frivolous and obviously unmeritorious claims, and laying down certain mandatory steps before resorting to ISDS. The recommendations include carefully drafting definitions such as who can be defined as an investor, what constitutes fair and equitable treatment, the remit of national treatment, direct and indirect expropriation, umbrella clauses, and public policy exceptions.

8.6 Shariah and the Relevance of Contract Law

Contract law is relevant to drafting definitions and utilising Islamic contract law rules when examining the role Islamic finance principles can play in arbitration decisions for ISDS mechanisms. How the award is calculated and how the contract clauses are examined and interpreted will all bear relevance to creating a Shariah-compliant framework for ISDS. There are a number of Quranic references in relation to contract law. Quranic references relevant to contract law include Surah Al-Mā'idah, verse 1, "*O you who have believed, fulfill [all] contracts*".[61] Further references focus on honouring contractual promises and documenting the contract.[62] In considering contract law it is useful to have a comparator. In English contract law there are seven key elements which make up contract formation: agreement, consideration, intention to create legal relations, form, capacity, consent, and legality. Even where all the required elements of a contract are met, a contract will not have legal effect under Shariah law if it contains an attribute

60 UNCTAD (n 17).

61 See the Quran (n 47), at verse 5:1.

62 Ibid, at verse 2:282: *"O you who have believed, when you contract a debt for a specified term, write it down. And let a scribe write [it] between you in justice. Let no scribe refuse to write as Allah has taught him. So let him write and let the one who has the obligation dictate. And let him fear Allah, his Lord, and not leave anything out of it. But if the one who has the obligation is of limited understanding or weak or unable to dictate himself, then let his guardian dictate in justice. And bring to witness two witnesses from among your men. And if there are not two men [available], then a man and two women from those whom you accept as witnesses – so that if one of the women errs, then the other can remind her. And let not the witnesses refuse when they are called upon. And do not be [too] weary to write it, whether it is small or large, for its [specified] term. That is more just in the sight of Allah and stronger as evidence and more likely to prevent doubt between you, except when it is an immediate transaction which you conduct among yourselves. For [then] there is no blame upon you if you do not write it. And take witnesses when you conclude a contract. Let no scribe be harmed or any witness. For if you do so, indeed, it is [grave] disobedience in you".* See also the Quran at verses 2:177, 4:12, 4:33, 5:89, 9:1, 9:111, 17:34, and 23:8.

of gambling,[63] alcohol,[64] or forbidden meat.[65] Reaching agreement, first of all, in Shariah law is not as straightforward as one party making an offer which the other accepts given the influence of the doctrines of *riba*[66] and *gharar*.[67] *Riba* is the doctrine on the prohibition of interest payments, undue profits, or excessive gain from a transaction, and *gharar* deals with risk, speculative transactions, ambiguity, or excessive uncertainty in contracts.[68]

Key elements of the general theory of contract are evident in the Quran, chapter Surah An-Nisā', verse 4, which emphasises mutual consent and gainful exchange.[69] The Sunnah further expands on the obligations of contracting parties to fully disclose the value of their bargain and any defects that exist:

> both the buyer and the seller give the option of either confirming or cancelling the bargain three times, and if they speak the truth and mention the defects, then their bargain will be blessed, and if they tell lies and conceal the defects, they might gain some financial gain but they will deprive their sale of (Allah's) blessings.[70]

As GCC member States have embarked on international contracts and treaties, *riba* and *gharar* have played a significant role in financial transactions, and this is what can distinguish an Islamic law-based ISDS approach from current practice.

8.7 The Arab Investment Agreements

Arab investment agreements would be the best fit for an Islamic law-based ISDS approach. UNCTAD reports that 19 ISDS cases have been initiated relying on the *OIC Agreement*.[71] But this number is conservative and would include only publicly reported cases, and would thus exclude unreported cases or cases conducted under private or commercial arbitration bodies and so-called "under the counter cases".

63 Ibid, at 2:219, 5:3, 5:90, 5:91, and 5:92. The link between intellectual property and gambling comes from the potential for royalties to be deemed so uncertain as to be like gambling, and therefore further research on the relationship between intellectual property and gambling within an Islamic context will shed light on how a potential reward for risk can exist. See also Steven Jamar, 'The Protection of Intellectual Property under Islamic Law,' *Capital University Law Review* (1992) 21, 1079–104.

64 See the Quran (n 47), at verses 2:219, 5:3, 5:90, 5:91, 5:92, and 16:67.

65 Ibid, at verses 2:259, 5:3, 6:121, 6:145, 16:14, and 22:37.

66 See Quran 4:161 *"And [for] their taking of usury while they had been forbidden from it, and their consuming of the people's wealth unjustly. And we have prepared for the disbelievers among them a painful punishment"*.

67 Abdulrahim Al Saati (n 19), 3.

68 Rodney Wilson (n 28), 27.

69 See the Quran (n 47), at verse 4:29.

70 *Sahih al-Bukhari*, Chapter Number 34, Hadith number 327, at <https://sunnah.com/bukhari>.

71 United Nations Conference on Trade and Development (UNCTAD), 'Investment Dispute Settlement Navigator: Treaty' (2022) at <Investment Dispute Settlement Navigator | UNCTAD Investment Policy Hub>.

The *Investment Arbitration Reporter* has recently listed 22 cases relying on that Agreement.[72] The new ISDS cases in 2020 relying on the *OIC Agreement* and the *Arab Investment Agreement* with four cases each were primarily from the Qatar group of claims arising out of the Gulf diplomatic crisis.[73] The main challenge is the lack of public information on the arbitration hearings and the level of transparency, given they are held in private.

The fundamental principles at the core of the *OIC Agreement* are investment, promotion, and protection by conferring a broad range of rights on investors. The Agreement contains provisions for investment protection and includes guarantees for adequate protection and security, incentives, freedom of movement of personnel, most-favoured-nation protection rights, protection against expropriation, free transfer and disposition of capital, compensation for the violation of rights, and national treatment.[74] *Al Warraq v Indonesia*[75] is the first case initiated under the *OIC Agreement* in August 2011 whereby Saudi investor Hesham Talaat M. Al-Warraq brought a case against Indonesia for claims arising out of the Indonesian Government's bailout of a bank in which the claimant had allegedly invested. Since then, more than 20 other arbitrations have been initiated under the Agreement.[76]

Similarly, the Arab Investment Court (AIC), established under the *Arab Investment Agreement*, has jurisdiction to settle investment disputes. *Tanmiah v Tunisia*[77] was the first AIC case, and since then, there have been 6 cases at least in which the Court or a tribunal appointed under the Agreement has rendered a decision.[78] The prevailing applicable arbitration rules in *Tanmiah v Tunisia* followed the United Nations Commission on International Trade Law (UNCITRAL).

72 Case Profiles, *Investment Arbitration Reporter* (undated) at <https://www.iareporter.com/arbitration-cases/?fwp_treaty=oic-investment-agreement&fwp_arbitration_cases_sort=year_desc&fwp_per_page=100>.

73 UNCTAD, 'Investment Policy Hub' (2022) at <Advanced Search | Investment Dispute Settlement Navigator | UNCTAD Investment Policy Hub>.

74 *Organisation of Islamic Cooperation Agreement on Promotion, Protection and Guarantee of Investments among Member States of the Islamic Conference,* signed 5 June 1981 (entered into force February 1988) ('*OIC Agreement*').

75 *Hesham T.M. Al Warraq v Republic of Indonesia* ('*Al-Warraq v Indonesia*') at <https://www.italaw.com/cases/1527>.

76 Walid Ben Hamida, 'A Fabulous Discovery: The Arbitration Offer under the Organization of Islamic Cooperation Agreement Related to Investment' (2013) 30(6) *Journal of International Arbitration* 637–63.

77 *Tanmiah for Consultancy Management & Marketing v. Republic of Tunisia and the Organising Committee for the Mediterranean Games* (Arab Investment Court Case No. 1/1) at <https://www.italaw.com/cases/1072>.

78 Gordon Blanke, 'Investment Arbitration in the Middle East: Basic Trends and Developments (Part 2)', *Thomson Reuters Practical Law Arbitration blog* (17 September 2018) at <http://arbitrationblog.practicallaw.com/investment-arbitration-in-the-middle-east-basic-trends-and-developments-part-2/>.

8.7.1 The ISDS Clause in the OIC Investment Agreement

In *Al Warraq v Indonesia*, there was some contention on the applicability of ISDS in the *OIC Agreement* articles. There was some uncertainty as to whether the Agreement provided a viable ISDS mechanism. The two main articles to consider are Articles 16 and 17. Article 16 states investors have the right to:

> resort to its national judicial system to complain against a measure adopted by its authorities against him, or to contest the extent of its conformity with the provisions of the regulations and laws in force in its territory, or to complain against the non-adoption by the host state of a certain measure which is in the interest of the investor, and which the state should have adopted, irrespective of whether the complaint is related, or otherwise, to the implementation of the provisions of the Agreement to the relationship between the investor and the host state.

Article 17, which provides the arbitration procedure, refers to the "parties to the dispute", which led the respondents in Al-Warraq to contest the application of Article 17 to State–State dispute resolution only, and not extend it to ISDS as this was outside the scope and would be ultra vires. However, on reviewing rules of treaty interpretation under Articles 31 to 33 of the Vienna Convention on the Law of Treaties (VCLT), the tribunal found that despite the ambiguity in the drafting of Article 17, it was in compliance with the overall objectives and intention of the *OIC Agreement* to extend to ISDS arbitration as well as state to state[79]. The Agreement doesn't discuss what this means for corporate sovereignty and the repercussions for the rule of law where the relevant states have a constitutional commitment to Islamic law. An analysis of some recent cases will be made followed by recommendations for Islamic finance-compliant processes.

8.7.2 The OIC Agreement's Most-Favoured-Nation (MFN) Clause

The MFN clause in the *OIC Agreement* guarantees investors the entitlement to be treated at least as favourably as other investors of the contracting state under other agreements. MFN clauses are used in investment treaty arbitrations by claimants seeking to gain from more generous protections than the ones granted in the international investment agreements under which the claims have been brought.[80] In *Omar Bin Sulaiman Abdul Aziz Al Rajhi v The Sultanate of Oman*,[81] UNICTRAL rules are relied on and as such the MFN clause applies; however, given that both

79 Ioannis Konstantinidis, 'Deciphering the OIC Investment Agreement in Light of the Itisaluna v. Republic of Iraq Award' (2022) 11(1) *International Review of Law.*

80 Ibid.

81 *Bin Sulaiman v. Oman, Omar Bin Sulaiman Abdul Aziz Al Rajhi v The Sultanate of Oman* (PCA Case No. 2017-32).

states are GCC members and that the case is still pending, the question arises as to why Islamic arbitration rules are not the preferred mode of application.

In *Itisaluna Iraq LLC and others v Republic of Iraq*, the tribunal was faced with the question of attempting to define the scope of the MFN clause in article 8 of the *OIC Agreement* in relation to whether article 8 extends to an International Centre for Settlement of Investment Disputes (ICSID) arbitration because of Article 17(4) of the Iraq–Japan bilateral investment treaty (BIT) ISDS clause[82]. In Al Warraq v. Indonesia,[83] the tribunal took a liberal interpretation of Article 8 of the Agreement, consequently highlighting consistency issues with the scope of the Agreement's MFN clause. Given that ISDS arbitration is not bound by principles of binding precedent as can be found in litigation, the impact of diverging interpretations of the MFN clause lends weight to the argument for an alternative approach to arbitration tribunals, especially where both parties have Islamic law as a source of law. The current agreements draw attention to inherent flaws in the most common modes of arbitration rule application and the influence of bilateral and free trade agreements.

8.7.3 A Hybrid Islamic Finance Legal Framework

Islamic finance operates, by its nature, as a hybrid legal framework. Although compliance with Shariah law is compulsory, legitimate concerns arise when considering jurisdiction and choice of law in ISDS tribunals. Almost all international agreements have template clauses for mandatory arbitration and jurisdiction of choice. An example in which Shariah law has been relied on as the jurisdiction of choice, can be seen in *Beximo Pharmaceuticals Ltd v Shamil Bank of Bahrain* [2004]. The case was heard in the Court of Appeal in England on the status of a dual Shariah and English governing clause. For the role of Islamic finance in ISDS tribunals and awards, the Beximo case throws quite the spanner in the works as, on applying the *Rome Convention on the Law Applicable to Contractual Obligations (1980)*, the choice of law provision only exists for a national system of law. Shariah law was defined as a non-national law and as a result, it was English law that was binding on the parties. Despite changes to the Rome Convention to include non-national laws, English law prevails as the governing law.[84]

Considering Islamic finance-compliant frameworks in ISDS mechanisms, Shariah law as the choice of law, despite the amendments, remains problematic. However, Islamic finance law as a national law in the GCC for ISDS could be more effective. All laws that do not contravene Islamic law principles are deemed permissible, and given the popularity of English law, there is an opportunity here

82 Gordon Blanke, 'The OIC Agreement and Its MFN clause: A Question of Scope', *Thomson Reuters Practical Law Arbitration Blog* (24 July 2020) at <The OIC Agreement and its MFN clause: a question of scope | Arbitration Blog (practicallaw.com)>.

83 *Al Warraq v Indonesia* (n 85).

84 Mohammed, F. (2015), 'The Adjudication of Islamic Finance Cases: The UK Experience', in Islamic Commercial Law Report 2016.

for the GCC States to develop a uniform Islamic finance law of choice as a code of conduct to reflect equitable maxims and the prohibition of *riba* and *gharar*.[85]

8.8 Concluding Remarks – Can Islamic Finance Offer a Solution?

The GCC shares certain commonalities which make developments in the region relevant to many other countries that share similarities in religious influence, societal and cultural norms, economic progression, and development. The developing GCC member States are struggling to meet international standards, and a successful Shariah-compliant ISDS framework will impact how the States move forward with ISDS protection within their constitutional religious obligations. Further, there is potential for it to impact other Islamic states and as a result lead to more informed negotiation in trade agreements with developed states. It will also meet the overall objective of developing a framework within which Islamic states can improve the level of ISDS protection offered without alienating their own distinct Shariah-based constitutional obligations.

There are systematic flaws in the GCC member States adopting ISDS approaches which have been nothing short of a complete overhaul of domestic laws, modified to reflect foreign laws from colonial occupation or taken from donor countries. As can be seen from the research, each State has differing levels of national Shariah compliance and international agreement commitments to ISDS. There is a strong dichotomy that exists between the religious characteristics of each State and the ISDS clauses that exist under Western legal principles, and therefore the foreign laws, as they stand, are unsuitable for the States and require modification. There is a significant paucity of research in developing a Shariah-compliant ISDS framework in the GCC, and therefore one of the fundamental aims of this research is to act as a catalyst for further research in this area.

International trade agreements have brought into play ISDS and corporate sovereignty. The GCC member States need to develop the requisite knowledge and expertise in ISDS and corporate sovereignty by developing clear parameters for both in respect to *riba* and *gharar*. ISDS has serious ramifications for domestic sovereignty and the rule of law as it impacts the ability of states to make laws, challenging fundamental principles of constitutional law and democracy. Nonetheless, the States will struggle to justify the compensatory remedies of ISDS proceedings as compliant with Shariah law as there are no frameworks or internal infrastructures in place to control the level of damages that can be sought. What the Al Jazeera case law spotlights, for example, is that there are issues with judicial expertise, arbitration court structures, and transparency in ISDS proceedings in the GCC and neighbouring states such as Egypt where new areas of law are being developed.

85 J. Colón, 'Choice of Law and Islamic Finance' (2011) 46(2) *Texas International Law Journal* 411–35.

Islamic finance has managed to grow as an industry despite not all Islamic countries adhering to Shariah at the same constitutional level. Applying this to the GCC member States, each State has its own Islamic finance institutions with Islamic scholars that sit on Shariah boards with the main role of acting as an independent body of specialised jurists to direct, review, and supervise Islamic finance products.[86] The States are paving the way forward in recognising the relationship between Islamic finance and ISDS.

There are four main Islamic finance structures that can be translated into an integrated ISDS approach. These are to develop Shariah board-based infrastructures, improve consumer and investor protection, promote regulatory cooperation, and build human capital. By developing Shariah-compliant ISDS infrastructures, the GCC will start to take control over the sector and promote fit-for-purpose control mechanisms through setting up internal auditing committees, introducing governance ethics, initiating periodic reviews, and giving assurances for ISDS.

The premise of adopting Islamic finance structures to promote better ISDS approaches is two-fold, namely, it is based on learning the role of Shariah law in promoting a more compliant ISDS sector and, secondly, addressing the shortcomings in Islamic finance in order to overcome these in the approach to ISDS. There are aspects of Islamic finance products that can form the basis of ISDS proceedings.

Islamic finance is not without its faults. However, rather than reject Islamic finance because of its shortcomings, such as lack of transparency, the level of independence observed by Shariah boards, and accountability measures, the GCC and its member States have an opportunity to learn from both the strengths and weaknesses of the Islamic finance sector to pioneer a Shariah-compliant ISDS approach for Muslim countries.

There is a pressing need to have an authoritative and common platform to resolve ISDS disputes that relate to the GCC member States and other countries that have Shariah law as a constitutional law influence, with Islamic finance being the relevant tool to extract Islamic finance methodologies and apply them in a modern commercial context. Arbitration systems are split into domestic and international systems, with the main relevance to ISDS being international arbitration. To cater to dispute settlement mechanisms, commercial disputes can be dealt with by Islamic finance by providing Shariah-modelled arbitration clauses that can set out procedural rules, conduct, and appropriate rules for the form, effect, and interpretation of the tribunal decision as a national law in the GCC member States.

86 Bashar Malkawi, 'A Bright Future: Towards an Enhanced Shariah Supervision in Islamic Finance', *European Financial Review* (28 February 2014) at <https://www.europeanfinancialreview.com/bright-future-enhanced-shariah-supervision-islamic-finance/>.

Bibliography

Abdallah, Amel, *Islamic Sharia and Arbitration in GCC States: The Way Ahead* (Qatar University Press, 2020).

Agreement between the Government of the Arab Republic of Egypt and the Government of the State of Qatar for the Reciprocal Promotion and Protection of Investments, signed 2 December 1999 (entered into force 14 July 2006) *('Egypt – Qatar BIT').*

Ahmad, Abu, 'The Time Value of Money Concept in Islamic Finance', *American Journal of Islamic Social Sciences* (2012) 23(1) at <http://uaelaws.files.wordpress.com/2012/05/the-time-value-of-money-concept-in-islamic-finance.pdf.

Al Saati, Abdulrahim, 'The Permissible *Gharar* (Risk) in Classical Islamic Jurisprudence' (2003) 16(2) *Islamic Economics*, 3–19.

Ariff, Mohamed, 'Islamic Banking', *Asian-Pacific Economic Literature* (1988) 2(2) at <http://www.nzibo.com/IB2/Islamic%20Banking%20-%20Mohammed%20Ariff.pdf>

'Assessing Investment Policies Of Member Countries Of The Gulf Cooperation Council Stocktaking Analysis', *MENA-OECD Investment Programme* (5 April 2011) at <http://www.oecd.org/mena/investment/Preliminary%20assessment%20GCC%20invt%20policies.pdf>.

Asutay, Mehmet, 'Reflecting on the Trajectory of Islamic Finance: From Mit Ghamr to the Globalisation of Islamic Finance', *Afro Eurasian Studies* (2013) 2(2) at <http://www.afroeurasianstudies.net/dosyalar/site_resim/veri/0344147.pdf>.

Ayadi, Rym, 'EU-GCC Trade and Investment Relations: What Prospect of an FTA between the Two Regions?', *CEPS* (24 October 2013) at <http://www.ceps.eu/book/eu-gcc-trade-and-investment-relations-what-prospect-fta-between-two-regions>.

Beck, T., 'Islamic vs. conventional Banking: Business Model, Efficiency and Stability', *Journal of Banking & Finance* (2013) 37(2) at <http://ac.els-cdn.com/S0378426612002920/1-s2.0-S0378426612002920-main.pdf?_tid=b6195f62-96c4-11e4-a4db-00000aacb361&acdnat=1420673414_a5be4510b722d8a1b52b95eed93067d7>.

Bin Sulaiman v. Oman, Omar Bin Sulaiman Abdul Aziz Al Rajhi v The Sultanate of Oman (PCA Case No. 2017-32).

Blanke, Gordon, 'Investment Arbitration in the Middle East: Basic Trends and Developments (Part 2)', *Thomson Reuters Practical Law Arbitration blog* (17 September 2018) at <http://arbitrationblog.practicallaw.com/investment-arbitration-in-the-middle-east-basic-trends-and-developments-part-2 />.

Blanke, Gordon, 'The OIC Agreement and its MFN Clause: A Question of Scope', *Thomson Reuters Practical Law Arbitration Blog* (24 July 2020) at <The OIC Agreement and its MFN clause: a question of scope | Arbitration Blog (practicallaw.com)>.

Case Profiles, *Investment Arbitration Reporter* (undated) at <https://www.iareporter.com/arbitration-cases/?fwp_treaty=oic-investment-agreement&fwp_arbitration_cases_sort=year_desc&fwp_per_page=100.

Colón, J., 'Choice of Law and Islamic Finance' (2011) 46(2) *Texas International Law Journal*, 411–435.

Donnan, Shawn, 'Al Jazeera Sues Egypt for $150m after Crackdown on Journalists', *Financial Times* (26 June 2014) at <http://www.ft.com/cms/s/0/7ff2210c-cec0-11e3-ac8d-00144feabdc0.html#axzz3CNLGmNPk>.

Dow Jones Islamic Market Indices at <http://www.djindexes.com/islamicmarket/>.

Economic Agreement between the GCC States, adopted by the GCC Supreme Council (22 Session; 31 December 2001) at <https://www.worldtradelaw.net/document.php?id=fta/agreements/GCC_FTA.pdf>.

Elasrag, Hussein, 'Principals of the Islamic Finance: A Focus on Project Finance', *Munich Personal RePEc Archive* (18 April 2011) at <http://mpra.ub.uni-muenchen.de/30197/1/MPRA_paper_30197.pdf>.

'EU Trade Relations with the Gulf Region', *European Commission* at <https://policy.trade.ec.europa.eu/eu-trade-relationships-country-and-region/countries-and-regions/gulf-region_en>.

Framework Agreement for Trade, Economic, Investment and Technical Cooperation between the Cooperation Council for the Arab States of the Gulf and the Government of the United States of America, signed 25 September 2012 (not yet in force), (*'US-GCC Framework Agreement'*) at <https://ustr.gov/sites/default/files/uploads/agreements/Trade%20Investment/U.S.-GCC%20TIFA%20Final%20Text%20--%20English%209-25-12.pdf>.

French, Robert, 'ISDS: A Cut above the Courts?' *Civil Liberties Australia* (2 September 2014) at <http://www.cla.asn.au/News/isds-a-cut-above-the-courts/>.

Garbois, Cyril, Cyril Gourp, Alexander von Pourk and Mukund Bhatnagar, 'The Future of Islamic Banking', *AT Kearney* (2012) at <http://www.atkearney.com/documents/10192/654853/Future+of+Islamic+Banking.pdf/27167edf-a96d-4465-b88a-83beb25ed4bd>.

GCC Charter at <https://www.gcc-sg.org/en-us/AboutGCC/Pages/Primarylaw.aspx>.

Ghias, Shoiab, 'Juristic Disagreement: The Collective Fatwa Against Islamic Banking in Pakistan', in Karen Hunt-Ahmed (ed), *Contemporary Islamic Finance: Innovations, Applications and Best Practices*, Chapter 6 (John Wiley & Sons, 2009).

Gorodetsky, Gabriel, *Soviet Foreign Policy, 1917–1991: A Retrospective* (Routledge Cavendish, 2014).

Grais, Wafik, and Matteo Pellegrini, 'Corporate Governance and Shariah GCC Compliance in Institutions Offering Islamic Financial Services', *World Bank*, Policy Research Working Paper 4054 (21 June 2013) at <http://elibrary.worldbank.org/doi/pdf/10.1596/18; 13-9450-4054>.

Hayat, Usman, 'Islamic Finance: Ethics, Concepts, Practice', *CFA Institute Research Foundation* (1 November 2014) at <http://www.cfainstitute.org/learning/foundation/research/Documents/islamic_finance_ethics_concepts_practice.pdf>.

Henry, Clement and Rodney Wilson, *The Politics of Islamic Finance* (Edinburgh University Press, 2004).

Hesham T.M. Al Warraq v Republic of Indonesia (*'Al-Warraq v Indonesia'*) at <https://www.italaw.com/cases/1527>.

Husain, Ishrat, 'Islamic Finance Industry: Positioned for Growth', 2nd Pakistan Islamic Banking Conference, Karachi, 8 November 2006.

Hussain, Abdulrhman, *So History Doesn't Forget: Alliances Behaviour in Foreign Policy of the Kingdom of Saudi Arabia, 1979–1990* (AuthorHouse UK, 2012).

Hvidt, Martin, 'Economic Diversification in GCC Countries: Past Record and Future Trends' (2013) *London School of Economics and Political Science*, Kuwait Programme on Development, Governance and Globalisation in the Gulf States at <http://www.lse.ac.uk/IDEAS/>.

Joyce, Miriam, *Bahrain from the Twentieth Century to the Arab Spring* (Palgrave McMillan, 2012).

Khalaf, Abdujllah and Giacomo Luciani (eds), 'Constitutional Reform and Political Participation' (2006) *Gulf Research Center* at <https://cadmus.eui.eu/handle/1814/13235>.

Khalid, Mahyuddin, 'Development of the Malaysian Islamic Financial System', *Universiti Teknologi Mara* (2013) at <https://www.scribd.com/presentation/116822528/Development-of-the-Malaysian-Islamic-Financial-System>.

Khan, Iqbal, *Islamic Banking* (Global Islamic Finance, 2009) at <http://theislamicfinanceandbanking.wordpress.com/islamic-finance-iqbal-khan/>.

Kostadinova, Valentina, 'What is the Status of the EU-GCC Relationship?', *Gulf Research Center Papers* (July 2013) at <http://eu-gcc.kcorp.net/common/publicationfile/29.pdf>.

Konstantinidis, Ioannis, 'Deciphering the OIC Investment Agreement in Light of the Itisaluna v. Republic of Iraq Award' (2022) 11(1) *International Review of Law*, 251–270.

Majwood, Salahuddin, *The Biography of Imam Iba Al Qayim* (translated by Abdul Rafi-Adewala) (Darussalam Publishers & Distributors, 2007).

Malkawi, Bashar, 'A Bright Future: Towards an Enhanced Shariah Supervision in Islamic Finance', *European Financial Review* (28 February 2014) at https://www.europeanfinancialreview.com/bright-future-enhanced-shariah-supervision-islamic-finance/

Matthiesen, Toby, *The Other Saudis, Shiism, Descent and Sectarianism* (Cambridge University Press, 2014).

Mirakhor, Abbas and Iqbal Zaidi, 'Profit-and-Loss Sharing Contracts in Islamic Finance', *Handbook of Islamic Banking* (April 2007) at <http://202.154.59.182/mfile/files/Economics/Handbook%20of%20Islamic%20Banking/Chapter%204%20Profit-and-loss%20sharing%20contracts%20in%20Islamic%20finance.pdf>.

Mohammed, F., *The Adjudication of Islamic Finance Cases: The UK Experience* (Islamic Commercial Law Report, 2016).

Nisar, Shariq, 'The Practices of Islamic Banking and Finance: A Historical Perspective' (2003) at <http://www.shariqnisar.com/images/My_writings/Islamic%20Finance%20History.pdf>.

'Oil Boom in GCC Region Shifts Economic Landscape' (2014) *World Finance* at <http://www.worldfinance.com/banking/oil-boom-in-gcc-region-shifts-economic-landscape>.

Organisation of Islamic Cooperation Agreement on Promotion, Protection and Guarantee of Investments among member States of the Islamic Conference, signed 5 June 1981 (entered into force February 1988) (*'OIC Agreement'*).

Partington, David, *The Middle East Annual: Issues and Events*, vol 2, 178 (G. K. Hall & Co., 1982).

Patrick, Neil, 'The GCC: Gulf State Integration or Leadership Cooperation?' (2011) *London School of Economics and Political Science*, Kuwait Programme on Development, Governance and Globalisation in the Gulf States at <http://www.lse.ac.uk/IDEAS/.

Presley John R., (ed), *Directory of Islamic Financial Institutions* (Routledge: Banking and Finance, 2012). Dubai Islamic Bank at https://www.dib.ae/business.

'Reforming Investment Dispute Settlement: A Stocktaking', *UNCTAD Series on Issues in International Investment Agreements* (March 2019, Issue 1) at <https://investmentpolicy.unctad.org/publications/1194/reforming-investment-dispute-settlement-a-stocktaking>.

Saeed, Abdullah, *Islamic Banking and Interest: A Study of the Prohibition of Riba and Its Contemporary Interpretation* (Brill Academic, 2012).

Sahih al-Bukhari, 'Chapter Number 34, Hadith number 327' at https://sunnah.com/bukhari>.

Schoon, Natalie, *Islamic Banking and Finance* (Spiramus Press, 2010).

Shafaat, Ahmad, 'Islamic Perspectives, Chapter One' (2005) *Riba in the Quran* at <http://www.islamicperspectives.com/Riba1.htm>.

Shaked, Haim and Daniel Dishon (eds), *Middle East Contemporary Survey, 1983–84*, vol. 8 (The Moshe Dayan Center, 1986).

'Shariah-Compliant Funds: A Whole New World of Investment' (2009) *PricewaterhouseCoopers Global Financial Services Islamic Finance Programme* at <https://www.pwc.com/en_US/gx/financial-services/islamic-finance-programme/pdf/shariah-compliant-funds.pdf>.

Tanmiah for Consultancy Management & Marketing v. Republic of Tunisia and the Organising Committee for the Mediterranean Games (Arab Investment Court Case No. 1/1) at <https://www.italaw.com/cases/1072>.

'The Quran (Sahih International Translation)' at <www.quran.com>.

'The TTIP of the Anti-Democracy Iceberg', *Friends of the Earth Europe* (October 2013) at <http://www.foeeurope.org/sites/default/files/foee_factsheet_isds_oct13.pdf>.

UNCTAD, 'Investment Policy Hub', *UNCTAD* (2022) at <Advanced Search | Investment Dispute Settlement Navigator | UNCTAD Investment Policy Hub>.

UNCTAD, 'World Investment Report, Global Value Chains: Investment and Trade for Development' (2013) at <http://unctad.org/en/publicationslibrary/wir2013_en.pdf>.

United Nations Conference on Trade and Development (UNCTAD), 'Investment Dispute Settlement Navigator', *UNCTAD* (2022) at <Investment Dispute Settlement Navigator | UNCTAD Investment Policy Hub>.

United States Trade Representative at <http://www.ustr.gov/about-us/press-office/press-releases/2012/september/ustr-kirk-announces-agreement-gcc>.

'Updated Background Paper on Annulment for the Administrative Council of ICSID' (2016) *International Centre for the Settlement of Investment Disputes, (ICSID)* at <https://icsid.worldbank.org/resources/publications/background-papers-annulment>.

Usmani, Mufti Muhammad Taqi, *An Introduction to Islamic Finance* (Arham Shamsi, 2004).

Warde, Ibrahim, *Islamic Finance in the Global Economy* (Edinburgh University Press, 2000). electronic version at <http://www.iefpedia.com/english/wp-content/uploads/2011/03/2000-Ibrahim-Warde-Islamic-finance-in-the-global-economy-Edinburh-University-Press1.pdf>.

Wilson, Rodney, *The Development of Islamic Finance in the GCC* (London School of Economics and Political Science, 2009), Working Paper, Kuwait Programme on Development, Governance and Globalisation in the Gulf States at <http://www.lse.ac.uk/IDEAS/programmes/kuwait/home>.

'Your Gateway to the EU European Union' at <http://europa.eu/about-eu/index_en.htm>.

9 Reflections and Recommendations

9.1 Introduction

This chapter draws together the key research outcomes as reported in the previous chapters. It also reflects on possible changes in the regional ISDS regime that might emerge in the short-term future. In this regard, it takes account of commentary and specific suggestions from the Gulf Cooperation Council (GCC) member States, namely Bahrain and Kuwait, in the context of UNCTAD's and UNCITRAL's Working Group III ongoing campaign for review and reform of the current investor–state dispute settlement (ISDS) regime.

The GCC member States are increasingly entering into international investment agreements (IIAs) containing substantive investment protections and dispute settlement mechanisms. They are also increasingly subject to investor–state arbitrations, and these trends are expected to continue in the future, particularly in light of the adoption of economic diversification policies. There are indications that claimants from the States are becoming more likely to initiate investor–state arbitrations. Intra-GCC investor–state arbitrations are less common but have increased in recent years due in part to the Qatar Airways and related disputes arising out of the Gulf crisis. Intra-GCC investor–state disputes may continue to increase as a mechanism by which complainants can seek relief outside of domestic courts and with little risk of a favourable award being subject to appeal, being annulled, being set aside, or being the subject of counterclaims.

The GCC is becoming increasingly open to foreign investment. Therefore, it would benefit from improving and consolidating its legal remedies and institutions to match the continuing increased demand and to protect itself and its member States from exposure to disingenuous, vexatious, and frivolous claims. In particular, it would be prudent for the States to attempt to limit the scope of operation of the substantive investment provisions in applicable IIAs and reduce the availability of recourse to arbitration. This can be achieved by a careful review of current arbitration treaties, particularly the *OIC Agreement*,[1] which seems to be used as an option of last resort, and in some instances as a gateway to more favourable

1 *Organisation of Islamic Cooperation Agreement on Promotion, Protection and Guarantee of Investments among Member States of the Islamic Conference*, signed 5 June 1981 (entered into force February 1988) ('*OIC Agreement*').

DOI: 10.4324/9781003481072-9

bilateral investment treaties (BITs). The States may also benefit from the adoption of a cautious approach to the drafting of new treaties containing investment provisions and dispute settlement mechanisms.

9.2 Themes in GCC Investor–State Arbitrations

There are some common themes in dispute settlement involving GCC member States, including but not limited to the absence of an intra-GCC BIT framework as well as substantive investment protection issues, namely imprecision and defective or vague procedural mechanisms. More specifically, these include nationality issues, clean hands, non-appointment of arbitrators (and contention about the legitimacy of the Permanent Court of Arbitration (PCA) intervention) and frustration of process, multiplicity of proceedings/priority issues between arbitral awards and domestic courts of superior review, and reliance on most-favoured-nation (MFN) clauses to import substantive investment protections and consent to submit to arbitration (including ICSID arbitration). A number of these issues go to jurisdictional considerations/objections, including *ratione personae*, *ratione materiae*, *ratione voluntatis*, and *ratione temporis*. Critically however, these considerations may also be relevant in the merits phase of an arbitration. These issues are not strictly limited to the States, but they are certainly strong themes running through their significant cases.

"Unclean hands" is a theme that emerged in at least two case studies examined in Chapter 4, namely *Bank Melli v Bahrain*[2] and *Kiwan v Kuwait*.[3] There are direct and indirect methods of creating accountability for potential claimants, which are explored by Martin Jarrett, Sergio Puig and Steven Ratner.[4] They argue that policy-makers can pursue this objective by addressing particular aspects of ISDS. Though arguably imperfect, the GCC and its member States can protect themselves against adverse exposure to investor–state arbitration by expressly excluding investments that are made unconscionably or illegally or are tainted by fraud. Such a provision should make a distinction between unconscionable, illegal, or fraudulent actions undertaken contemporaneously with the investment or at a later point and address when the temporal nexus is relevant to the preliminary objections, merits, and award phase. This undertaking would avoid doubt about the application of equitable considerations and limit the ability of a tribunal to take an inconsistent approach. However, while the States may attempt to use such a device to prevent claimants' access to arbitration, on a jurisdictional basis, for example, claimants

2 *Bank Melli and Bank Saderat v The Kingdom of Bahrain* (PCA Case No. 2017-25) ('*Bank Melli v Bahrain*').

3 *Bachar Kiwan v State of Kuwait* (ICSID Case No. ARB/20/53) ('*Kiwan v Kuwait*').

4 Martin Jarrett, Sergio Puig and Steven Ratner, 'Towards Greater Investor Accountability: Indirect Actions, Direct Actions by States and Direct Actions by Individuals' (2023) *Journal of International Dispute Settlement*, Vol. 14(2), 259–80. < https://academic.oup.com/jids/article/14/2/259/6449423>.

could still institute costly and time-intensive arbitrations before a tribunal could decline to hear the dispute on jurisdictional grounds.[5]

From a procedural perspective, the GCC could establish a union-level arbitration centre that properly reflects the paramountcy of the Shariah within the member States and promotes a credible Middle Eastern dispute settlement institution within a traditionally European and North American centric system. To be a credible alternative to the ICSID-dominated dispute settlement process and instil confidence in foreign investors, the centre would need a permanent pool of independent arbitrators remunerated by the centre and who would be precluded from working on other matters from which panels would be constituted. Critically, the centre should have an appellate or review capacity, and the States would be required to enforce awards.

The GCC and its member States can also improve their outcomes in the context of ISDS by requiring claimants to first initiate and exhaust regional remedies, including non-adversarial dispute settlement, in a GCC-level arbitration centre, as a precondition to instituting investor–state arbitration. Alternatively, they could also include the incorporation of "fork-in-the-road" provisions which require investors to make a binding election on whether to pursue claims in domestic courts or seek relief through investment arbitration.[6] The States could explore the options available for taking action against claimants directly or by giving domestic nationals impacted by the actions of investors the capability of holding investors to account through the creation of standing for third parties, for example.[7] These policy tools, however, may be somewhat limited in requiring proper conduct by investors given the sectors and, in some cases, such as *Bank Melli v Bahrain* and *Kiwan v Kuwait*, by the causes of action from which disputes arise in the Arabian Gulf.

The OIC Secretary-General has also demonstrated some reluctance in appointing a default arbitrator when a respondent state has failed to do so. In some instances, this situation occurred because of appointment time limitations, and "political pressure" from some OIC members relating to an objection to consent to arbitrate, prompting the PCA to intervene and designate an appointing authority upon request by frustrated claimants.[8] The PCA has certainly demonstrated a willingness to intervene in both intra-GCC and extra-GCC cases to facilitate the constitution of tribunals when respondent states and the OIC Secretary-General

5 Ibid.

6 Ibid.

7 Ibid.

8 Yusuf Kumtepe, and Riccardo Loschi, 'Investment Dispute Settlement Body of the Organisation of Islamic Cooperation: A Dead End for Claims under the OIC Investment Agreement?', *Kluwer Arbitration Blog* (29 December 2019) at <Kluwer Arbitration Blog>; referring to Jarrod Hepburn and Luke Eric Peterson, 'Investigation: As New Cases Emerge under Islamic Investment Treaty, Initial Viability of Claims Seems to Hinge on Willingness of Respondents to Appoint Arbitrators', *Investment Arbitration Reporter* (2 March 2017).

have failed to act. In the intra-GCC case of *Bin Sulaiman v Oman*,[9] the claimant ultimately requested assistance from the PCA with respect to constituting a tribunal (arbitration seated in London).[10] The PCA designated an appointing authority to make an appointment.[11] Similarly, in *beIN v. Saudi Arabia*,[12] the PCA nominated an appointing authority, who proceeded to make an appointment.

The issue of non-appointment of arbitrators demonstrates some reservations held by respondent states in so far as playing their role in facilitating the dispute settlement process and is at odds with their conclusion of IIAs, including BITs and other treaties with investment provisions (TIPs). From the authors' perspective, it does seem somewhat as though they are attempting to frustrate the process at the expense of denying claimants with legitimate claims from treaty-based arbitration. The OIC Secretary-General's failure to intervene in certain circumstances is evidence of a failed stop-gap measure within the treaty itself. It demonstrates an appetite for treaty negotiation and conclusion, but an aversion to honouring, at the least, the dispute settlement mechanism, evidencing evasive behaviours. This is not always the case, however, and examples of this behaviour suggest a need to remedy this deficiency.

The disinclination of host states to always comply with procedural requirements is an important consideration in the context of the dichotomy between approaches to initiating investor–state arbitration on an extra-GCC or intra-GCC basis. Investor–state arbitrations in which the *OIC Agreement* is employed are significant because the Agreement has been applied in all known intra-GCC disputes and in 15 of the 38 arbitrations initiated by claimants from GCC home states, either in its own right or in addition to another IIA.[13] One possible reason for significant reliance upon the ISDS mechanism contained within the *OIC Agreement* is the lack of additional or alternative IIAs, including BITs, due perhaps to the nationality of claimants.

The application and interpretation of the *OIC Agreement* are the subject of contention, since its language is somewhat ambiguous and anachronistic. Moreover, while the Agreement contemplates such disputes to be determined by a bespoke permanent body, no such body exists, although steps have reportedly been taken to establish such a body, including an appellate mechanism in response to the

9 *Omar Bin Sulaiman Abdul Aziz Al Rajhi v The Sultanate of Oman* (PCA Case No. 2017-32) ('*Bin Sulaiman v Oman*').

10 Damien Charlotin, 'Breaking: Paris Court Finds That PCA Secretary General Lacked Power to Step into Libya Arbitration When OIC Secretary General Failed to Appoint Arbitrator', *Investment Arbitration Reporter* (26 March 2021) at <Breaking: Paris Court finds that PCA Secretary General lacked power to step into Libya arbitration when OIC Secretary General failed to appoint arbitrator | Investment Arbitration Reporter (openathens.net)>.

11 Jarrod Hepburn and Luke Eric Peterson (n 8).

12 *beIN Corporation v Kingdom of Saudi Arabia (Notice of Arbitration, ('beIN v Saudi Arabia') UNCITRAL, 1 October 2018)*).

13 United Nations Conference on Trade and Development (UNCTAD), 'Investment Dispute Settlement Navigator' (2022) at <Investment Dispute Settlement Navigator | UNCTAD Investment Policy Hub>.

institution of increasing claims applying the Agreement.[14] Parties to the Agreement include the GCC member States named as respondents and claimants from GCC home states who are parties to an *OIC Agreement* dispute.

Although the *OIC Agreement* has some redeeming features, it is arguably sub-optimal. The Agreement notably includes a fork-in-the-road provision requiring claimants to make an exclusive election about where to pursue relief. While it contemplates the creation of an organ to hear investor–state arbitration applying the Agreement, no such organ exists, although reportedly, steps have been taken to agree to establish a "permanent investment dispute settlement mechanism" and to revise the substantive provisions of the Agreement.[15] As such, dispute settlement under the Agreement is conducted on an ad hoc basis. Article 8 of the Agreement sets out the most-favoured-nation (MFN) rules,[16] while Article 16 addresses the pursuit of relief in domestic litigation or arbitration, requiring claimants to essentially elect one or the other, and Article 17 deals with dispute settlement rules and procedures, including the appointment of arbitrators.

The *OIC Agreement* in particular is vague and imprecise. The dispute settlement organ and dispute settlement mechanisms in particular need to be reworked. Reform efforts are underway but given that it has been prolifically used in intra-GCC disputes, perhaps GCC member States would benefit from establishing their own intra-GCC IIA complete with a dispute settlement organ and appellate or review mechanism. These may be easier to achieve and more effective, from the GCC's perspective, than reform efforts concentrated on improving a large multilateral agreement that is somewhat antiquated and that no longer suits the GCC's purpose.

The domestic legislative and regulatory regimes governing foreign direct investment in the GCC member States are evolving and attempting to address some elements of investor–state dispute settlement, namely anti-expropriation protections, with carve outs for acts undertaken in the public interest. However, they are weak, vague, and imprecise particularly with respect to dispute settlement mechanisms. There is a strong need for the States to delineate between domestic relief avenues and investor–state arbitration and to address, among other matters, whether initiation and exhaustion of the former are a prerequisite of access to investor–state arbitration, priority, and finality of proceedings including avenues for appeal. It is evident, from an examination of their respective domestic legislation regimes, that this in particular is lacking and requiring attention.

The GCC member States have evinced intentions to diversify and attract foreign direct investment, although to varying degrees and with varying levels of urgency. Overall, the GCC is increasingly subject to investor–state arbitration and nationals from the States are increasingly instituting claims. While limited, intra-GCC

14 Joel Dahlquist and Luke Eric Peterson, 'Governments Working to Rein in Use of OIC Investment Treaty's Investor-State Arbitration Offer', *Investment Arbitration Reporter* (3 April 2019), at <Governments working to rein in use of OIC investment treaty's investor-state arbitration offer | Investment Arbitration Reporter (openathens.net)>.

15 Ibid.

16 See discussion of national treatment and most-favoured-nation (MFN) in Chapter 3.

investor–state disputes are also increasing, particularly in light of the emerging Qatar Airways series of disputes following the recent Gulf diplomatic crisis. The so-called Gulf diplomatic crisis is significant because, as reflected in the Qatar Airways suite of investor–state disputes (among others), it also involved Egypt, an extra-GCC state. The damages being claimed, where data is available, are significant, and therefore there is much to be gained through reform. However, since all disputes arising from the Gulf diplomatic crisis are supposedly terminated by virtue of the Al-Ula Summit Declaration, perhaps the real test of the GCC's approach to ISDS is yet to come.

The GCC is a party to historical IIAs that could benefit from a careful review and the inclusion of substantive investment provisions which operate on a narrower basis and limit access to arbitration in the first instance. There are a number of tools available to GCC member States at the regulatory, bilateral treaty-making, and regional levels. There is a strong argument for the GCC to develop a model BIT, which would go some way towards improving consistency and promoting regional interests. However, it is acknowledged that this may be difficult to achieve in practice for a number of reasons, particularly the at times fractious relationships and underlying tensions within the GCC itself. There is also the possibility that such a model may have limitations in practice depending on the bargaining equality (or rather, inequality) between the GCC and its BIT partners in the treaty-making process; and whilst there are some indications of the adoption of consistency in treaty-making practices, the adoption of a "common approach" towards ISDS may be beneficial.[17] Further examination of the content of existing treaties with BIT partners would be useful in determining the likely success of a model BIT in this regard.

The GCC and its member States would also arguably benefit from the creation of a GCC-level arbitration body, but one with features necessary to promote the rule of law and inspire confidence in investors and respondent States. These features would include an appellate/review capacity and improved procedural features regarding, for example, the appointment of independent arbitrators, their independent remuneration, and security of tenure. This would need to be supported by measures designed to enhance the recognition and enforcement of awards within the States to give it full effect in terms of meeting the objectives. It is likely that the creation of such a body would promote consistency in the settlement of disputes involving the States and their nationals, particularly in the circumstances where there has been a plethora of local and competing dispute settlement bodies established by the States. It would also go some way to promoting the paramountcy of Shariah and offering an Arab alternative to what has traditionally been a Western dispute settlement system. Again, the creation of such a body may be difficult to achieve in practice due to the complexity of the GCC and the nature of the dynamic

17 Wolfgang Alschner, Dimitry Skougarevskiy and Mengyi Wang, 'Champions of protection? A text-as-data analysis of the bilateral investment treaties of GCC countries'(2016) 5(3) *International Review of Law* 1–19.

relationships between its members. It would, however, be particularly effective in terms of the settlement of intra-GCC disputes which are seemingly increasing.

There are also a number of instrument-level design options open to the GCC member States in terms of addressing and reducing the risk of exposure to adverse investor–state arbitration. A particular theme that emerged from the above-mentioned *Bank Melli v Bahrain* and *Kiwan v Kuwait* case studies was that of "unclean hands". The GCC could address this risk in future IIAs by expressly denying jurisdiction in cases where the claimant has made a tainted investment or otherwise acted illegally or fraudulently. It could also include or strengthen the existing requirement for investors to act in accordance with local laws, by including an obligation to make *bona fide* investments. Provisions would need to specify the impact of nefarious activities in relation to the jurisdiction, merits, and damages phases and would not be able to exclude, for example, an aggrieved investor from instituting proceedings notwithstanding their likely failure. Therefore, it would be necessary for such measures to be made as part of a series of improvements, including, for example, the inclusion of a "fork-in-the-road" provision or, in the alternative, a requirement for exhaustion of local remedies in the first instance. These steps, while difficult to achieve on a practical level, may go some way to protecting the GCC and its member States from costly arbitration.

The non-appointment of arbitrators, the apparent refusal of the OIC Secretary-General to act, and the subsequent intervention in certain extra-GCC cases are significant procedural issues plaguing cases in the region. A further issue is the imprecision of the language adopted in the *OIC Agreement*. The interpretation and application of the Agreement in extra-GCC investor–state arbitrations demonstrate the different approaches adopted by arbitral tribunals over time, given this uncertainty. This has created an undesirable situation where investor-claimants seeking to apply the Agreement are forced to overcome several hurdles to firstly constitute a tribunal and then ultimately, to overcome objections to jurisdiction raised by GCC respondent states in order to reach the merits phase. While there is a strong argument that the GCC member States can use these deficiencies to remedy the asymmetry created by the treaty, it does little to promote and protect foreign direct investment and fails totally with respect to delivering timely and consistent investor–state dispute settlement.

In the case of *Al-Warraq v Indonesia*, Indonesia objected to the jurisdiction of the tribunal, arguing that Article 17 of the *OIC Agreement* did not contain the consent of a State party to arbitrate disputes with a private individual.[18] The tribunal acknowledged that the opening phrase of the Article had been "ambiguously drafted", finding that "it is implicit in the language of Articles 16 and 17, and consistent with the object and purpose of the Agreement, to conclude that Article

18 *Hesham Talaat M. Al-Warraq v The Republic of Indonesia* ('*Al-Warraq v Indonesia*') (Award on Respondent's Preliminary Objections to Jurisdiction and Admissibility of the Claims 21 June 2012), [49] and [52].

17 provides for investor-state arbitration".[19] Indonesia also argued that Article 17 only allowed for the possibility of conciliation (by consent) and arbitration (if conciliation fails) until the prescribed organ for settling such disputes is established, arguing that the organ in question was the International Islamic Court of Justice. Accordingly, arbitration could not take place and, further, the claimant could not avail itself of the protection offered under the Agreement because of "illegal conduct" in contravention of Article 9.[20] Indonesia further argued that the appropriate forum was the domestic courts and that the MFN provision could not be used to introduce an investor–state arbitration provision, or to provide consent to arbitration when none in fact existed.[21] The tribunal found that conciliation was not a precondition to arbitration and the two forms of dispute settlement could be used "sequentially or alternatively".[22] The tribunal also found that Article 17 was "an open offer by the state parties to investors, that can be accepted and the arbitration initiated", without the need for additional express consent.[23] The tribunal rejected the assertion that the International Islamic Court of Justice was the organ contemplated within Article 17 of the Agreement.[24]

The case of *D.S. Construction v Libya* demonstrates the serious, and even potentially fatal, impact of the non-appointment of an arbitrator upon what might otherwise be a legitimate arbitration claim. In this case, the PCA determined it had competence to intervene and consequently designated an appointing authority leading to the appointment of an arbitrator after the respondent and the OIC Secretary-General failed to do so. Libya as the respondent party reportedly objected to both the constitution of the tribunal and its action in proceeding to decide the arbitration on the merits. Libya sought judicial intervention from a domestic court in the seat of arbitration (Paris), seeking determination that the PCA's designation was improper and the tribunal determination invalid. The Paris Court of Appeal annulled the preliminary award, relevantly finding that the *OIC Agreement* did not allow for the PCA Secretary-General to intervene if the OIC Secretary-General declined to make an appointment and further that the Agreement's MFN clause did not operate to import the respondent's consent to arbitration from another IIA.

A Saudi investor and business entity and his family appear to have experienced the above-mentioned potentially fatal consequence of respondent and OIC Secretary-General refusal to appoint. Hashem Al-Mehdar reportedly initiated three arbitrations against Egypt, in respect of which both Egypt and the OIC Secretary-General declined to nominate the required arbitrators.[25] Although local media

19 Ibid [75].
20 Ibid [53]–[54].
21 Ibid [58].
22 Ibid [79].
23 Ibid [81].
24 Ibid [88].
25 See Joel Dahlquist and Luke Eric Peterson, 'Investigation: Four Previously-Confidential Claims under the *OIC Agreement* Are Uncovered, as Controversy Continues over Treaty's Use in Arbitration', *Investment Arbitration* Reporter (16 May 2019) at <https://www-iareporter-com.eu1.proxy

reported Al Mehdar had informally settled those claims to enable projects to continue, with *Hashem Al Mehdar v Arab Republic of Egypt (4)*,[26] lodged in 2018, he is apparently still pursuing those original or related claims and applying the *OIC Agreement*.

The potential fragility of a tribunal's status and stability under the *OIC Agreement* has also been demonstrated by the cases of *Itisaluna v Iraq*[27] and *Navodaya v Gabon*,[28] in both of which the respondent parties endeavoured to interpret the wordings of Article 8 and Article 17 of the *OIC Agreement* to challenge the jurisdiction of the respective tribunals. In both cases, the respondents argued that consent in writing to submit a dispute to ICSID arbitration cannot be derived or inferred from another instrument by operation of Article 8 as the Agreement's MFN clause.

In the case of *Itisaluna v Iraq*, the tribunal found that Article 8 does not incorporate the requisite consent from the *Iraq–Japan BIT* into the Agreement, upholding Iraq's *ratione voluntatis* objection. The tribunal noted that it could not, in its "interpretative process", fracture the "multilateral character of a multilateral treaty". It also found that Articles 16 and 17 of the Agreement had to be read together, rather than in isolation, and that it was plainly evident that the Agreement contemplated recourse to ISDS.

The respondent in *Itisaluna v Iraq* argued that Article 17(2) of the OIC Agreement amounted to "consent to arbitration in general terms" but not "consent to ICSID arbitration, as required by Article 25(1) of the ICSID Convention". Critically, the tribunal found that "Article 8(1) of the OIC Agreement is subject to exception and limitation, both express and by necessary implication, that exclude its application to incorporate an ICSID consent to arbitration clause from another treaty". The tribunal also cautioned against over-reach and found public policy considerations to be important in its consideration, stating

> a distinction has to be made between the legitimate extension of rights and benefits by means of the operation of the clause, on the one hand, and disruptive treaty-shopping that would play havoc with the policy objectives of underlying specific treaty provisions, on the other hand.[29]

The *Itisaluna v Iraq* tribunal also found that "resort to conciliation" and the "failure of the process" were preconditions for accessing arbitration. The respondent in *Novadoya v Gabon*, however, advanced a similar argument, namely, that

.openathens.net/articles/investigation-4-previously-confidential-claims-under-oic-investment-agreement-are-uncovered-as-controversy-continues-over-treatys-use-in-arbitration/>.

26 Ibid.

27 *Itisaluna Iraq LLC and others v Republic of Iraq* (ICSID Case No. ARB/17/10) ('*Itisaluna v Iraq*').

28 *Navodaya Trading DMCC v. Gabonese Republic* (PCA Case No. 2018-23) ('*Navodaya v Gabon*').

29 *Itisaluna v Iraq*, (n 27), (Award, 3 April 2020), 211–220, citing *Emilio Augustín Maffezini v. The Kingdom of Spain*, ICSID Case No. ARB/97/7, Decision of the Tribunal on Objections to Jurisdiction, 25 January 2000, 62–63.

conciliation was a precondition to the submission of claims to arbitration, but the tribunal rejected this in contrast to the decision in *Itisaluna v Iraq*.

In *Navodaya v Gabon*, Gabon argued that Article 17 only dealt with state-to-state disputes but that this condition could only apply until an organ to settle such disputes was established, specifically the International Islamic Court of Justice which could only settle inter-state disputes. The argument was rejected by the tribunal, which found that the Islamic Court of Justice statutes had not been ratified, similar to the findings in *Al-Warraq v Indonesia.*

9.3 A *Sui Generis* Culture and Region-Specific Character

The GCC is a complex and at times fractious union, and each of the member States, while sharing some commonalities including the influence of Shariah, has varying economies, foreign policies, legal regimes, and commercial practices, which is reflected in their treaty-making processes. The States are at times in conflict, have unequal bargaining power, and have different levels of appetite and exposure to ISDS. They also act in coordination, in some instances, with extra-GCC states, notably Egypt in the context of the flights blockade at the heart of the Qatar Airways suite of disputes. The GCC's approach to ISDS must therefore be understood in this context. The GCC itself has entered into relatively few TIPs, perhaps because of difficulties achieving consensus among the members.

There are significant differences between the individual GCC member States in respect of the number of BITs into which they have entered and TIPs, demonstrating a far greater appetite for concluding BITs, although some States are more balanced in their approach (notably Saudi Arabia). It is unclear as to why this is the case. The States have demonstrated divergence in their treaty-making practices on an individual basis. For example, Saudi Arabia, Oman, and Bahrain have entered into relatively few IIAs, particularly BITs, whereas Qatar, Kuwait, and especially the UAE have entered into more. The divergence between union-level and individual State treaty-making practices may go some way to explaining why there is seemingly no model treaty in existence. While a model treaty BIT may improve consistency, it is probably unlikely to be achievable in practice because of differences in approaches to ISDS and cultural issues such as tribal rivalries, for example.

One could expect to see that States with more BITs and TIPs would likely be subject to higher levels of disputes. However, according to UNCTAD, and the limits already stated on that data, Saudi Arabia, which has entered into the fewest IIAs, has been named as respondent in the most claims initiated. It is however, one of the most advanced economies in the union and the aberration may be explained in those terms. In terms of claims by investor-claimants from the States, there appears to be divergence between the approach of claimants from Saudi Arabia, Bahrain, and Oman, whose nationals seem somewhat disinclined to pursue relief in investor–state arbitration compared to the other States. However, that is probably not surprising given their treaty-making practices and suggests a culture of reservation. Investors from Kuwait, the UAE, and Qatar have had more of an appetite to institute arbitration and this is consistent with their treaty-making practices. Critically, the data does suggest that, within the GCC, there are two groups adopting different approaches to both treaty-making practices and the institution of arbitration.

Except for Qatar, claimants from GCC home states seem to have exhibited a marked disinclination to pursue claims through investor–state dispute settlement mechanisms against GCC host states. This might indicate a culture of conducting business and resolving disputes outside of the ISDS framework on an intra-GCC basis. This is consistent with the sophisticated and non-Western socio-legal constitution within the States, in which the conclusion of a contract need not be deemed as the settlement of conditions but rather as establishing a foundation for further negotiation.

It is expected that intra-GCC arbitrations will increase in the future, due in part to the diversification policies being adopted by GCC member States, particularly Saudi Arabia. As such, it is arguably both a natural and desirable consequence to create a regional-level dispute settlement body that can adjudicate disputes in a central forum, while preserving the paramountcy of the Shariah and being versed in the nuances of contractual engagement and socio-legal constructs within the GCC. Such a body needs a panel of independent arbitrators with security of tenure from across the GCC to avoid potential conflict of issue and conflict of interest problems arising. In the absence of an intra-GCC IIA and dispute settlement body, or alternatively, a strong intra-GCC BIT framework, the States would do well to endeavour to work with their *OIC Agreement* partners to resolve this difficulty by clarifying the intended scope of operation of the MFN clause, specifically addressing dispute settlement provisions, the organ contemplated by Article 17 of the Agreement, and the domestic review of arbitral appointments and/or decisions.[30]

Figure 9.1 provides a basic comparison of the GCC member States as respondents in ISDS arbitrations against home state of claimants in ISDS claims. As mentioned above, based largely on the UNCTAD parameters (with occasional secondary source refinement), claimants as citizens from the States have lodged 38 ISDS claims through established arbitration institutions, compared with 34 received by the States as respondents over a similar period of time. And at first glance, Figure 9.1 might be considered to show a profile not all that different from that of the States as respondents. However, restraint should be followed in trying to establish a nexus or causal relationship between the two situations. Bahrain and Oman, as two of the smaller economies within the GCC, reveal a similar distribution between respondent and claimant with small numbers in both States. Qatar would show a similar pattern if the suite of Qatar Airways cases is discounted to a single instance. Kuwait, albeit with much larger numbers, also shows an approximate equivalence between the respondent and home state status. But what

30 Mohamed S Abdel Wahab and Kabir Duggal, *The Resurgence of the Unified Arab Investment Agreement and the Organisation for Islamic Cooperation Investment Agreement: A Dawn of a New Chapter on Investment Protection?* (BRILL, 2022) 13.

is striking is the different situation between the two largest economies in the GCC. Saudi Arabia has experienced more than twice as many arbitrations as a respondent (eleven) than it has as an investor home state (four). The UAE, on the other hand, is just the reverse, with twice as many arbitrations as an investor (13) compared with as a respondent (6).

Also worthy of note is that the practice within the GCC member States of initiating IIA-based arbitrations has only gained some momentum since 2015, with only the occasional instance over the decade beforehand. The corresponding figures for the number of claims against the States as respondents reveal a similar pattern, albeit with occasional instances arising over a 20-year period beforehand.

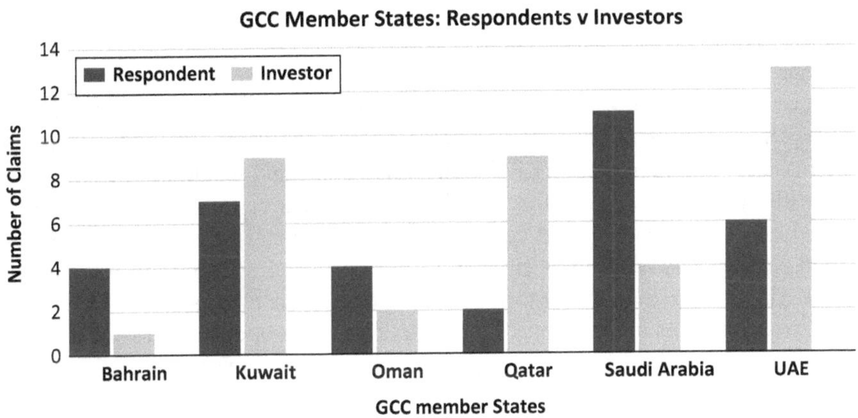

Figure 9.1 GCC member States as respondents and claimant home states.

Source: compiled by the authors derived from UNCTAD data.

There are very few instances of intra-GCC disputes submitted to arbitration, and this is possibly a cultural and societal issue. Qatari claimants seemingly have fewer reservations with respect to initiating investor–state dispute arbitrations on an intra-GCC basis, perhaps reflective of fallout from the Gulf crisis, but care must be taken in drawing conclusions about broader practices. Certainly, there is reason to watch developments in this regard carefully. While a regional IIA capable of filling the gaps within an *OIC Agreement* with defects would be beneficial for investor-claimants, it is perhaps unlikely to be achieved in practice because the Al-Ula Summit and Declaration have not resolved underlying tensions between the union, particularly involving Qatar. There is a strong reason for GCC member States to therefore pursue bilateral IIA relationships with fellow members, particularly in the case of Qatar which may need to protect its own investors operating in other States in the future.

The United Nations classifies the GCC member States as "developing economies" and "net fuel exporters" in Western Asia.[31] It is likely that these classifications may change in the future, as the GCC economies shift away from hydrocarbon exports and embrace knowledge-based economies, warranting future research. Nevertheless, currently, the States face significant challenges with respect to ISDS. Of significant concern to developing countries, including the States, is that, according to UNCTAD, a significant number of ISDS claims initiated in 2021 were instituted by developed economies and principally Western investors, predominantly hailing from the United States, Western Europe, and Canada.[32] In these circumstances, the States may consider the inclusion of ISDS provisions in future regional and bilateral trade agreements as undesirable. Certainly, the track record of successful claims by investor/claimants from the States would warrant questioning the current merit of the ISDS regime and be thus a catalyst for at least a review of their prevailing approach to the incorporation of ISDS provisions in their current form or negotiating a more favourable approach when negotiating future agreements. Such a response may not be achievable in the short term but may be in the fullness of time in respect of bilateral agreements and would not be inconsistent with the approaches of other developing countries or even highly developed countries. But it is hardly practicable in respect of regional agreements. The States could alternatively revise their limited approach to entering into IIAs at the union level. This may go some way towards mitigating against the potential hegemony of developed states in treaty-making practices, and if properly addressing a GCC-centric dispute settlement organ, may balance the scale, so to speak, of the possible "Westernisation" of disputes.

There is growing awareness within developing economies of the need to recalibrate their approaches to ISDS. In recent years a number of developing states, including those from broader Asia, have become critical of ISDS and rejected the process, as well as the tribunals that deliver it, in favour of alternative dispute resolution models.[33] In 2010 South Africa declared its intention to withdraw from its 20 BITs with ISDS provisions, and immediately gave effect to that declaration. Indonesia made a similar declaration in respect of its 67 BITs, and cancelled its BIT with the Netherlands in March 2014, as the first symbolic step.[34] Ecuador, Venezuela and Nicaragua have opted to terminate BITS with ISDS provisions, Romania attempted to withdraw from the BIT with Sweden, and the Philippines have excluded ISDS provisions in the *Japan–Philippines Economic Partnership*

31 United Nations, 'World Economic Situation and Prospects 2023' (25 January 2023) at <World Economic Situation and Prospects 2023 | Department of Economic and Social Affairs (un.org)>.

32 UNCTAD, 'Facts on Investor-State Arbitrations in 2021: With a Special Focus on Tax-Related ISDS Cases (July 2022) at <IIA Issues Note, No. 1, 2022 - Facts on Investor-State arbitrations in 2021: With a special focus on tax-related ISDS cases (unctad.org)>.

33 Leon Trakman and Kunal Sharma, 'Locating Australia on the Pacific Rim: Trade, Investment and the Asian Century' (2015) 12(1) *Transnational Dispute Management, (TDM)*.

34 See David Price, 'Indonesia's Bold Strategy on Bilateral Investment Treaties: Seeking an Equitable Climate for Investment?' (January 2017) *Asian Journal of International Law*.

Agreement.[35] Conversely, China "traditionally restricted investor-state provisions in BITs until its more recent emergence as a leading capital exporter".[36]

This recalibration is not limited, however, to just developing economies. For example, Australia has recently had a skittish approach to investment and trade agreements, including an ISDS provision, adopting a sceptical and conservative non-adoption approach under the former Labour Government, backed by a Productivity Commission Report advocating the avoidance of ISDS provisions.[37] The current Australian Government has adopted a case-by-case approach to the adoption of ISDS provisions.

More generally, the GCC member States have demonstrated a desire to contribute to ISDS reform at the multilateral level. Bahrain and Kuwait have made recent submissions in 2019 to UNCITRAL's Working Group III with respect to possible reform of ISDS. Bahrain's submission focused on reform of "procedural aspects of ISDS", noting that the mandate of Working Group III was limited to such issues and arguing that as such it "misses the opportunity to consider substantive reform of international investment agreements".[38] While Bahrain acknowledged that there are many benefits of ISDS, it identified several issues of concern including "conflicts of interest", the "diversity crisis" in respect of arbitrators, "costs and duration of ISDS disputes", and questionable "consistency and coherency of ISDS jurisprudence". These are not necessarily uncommon criticisms, however, as Bahrain as an Arab developing country (and the other States) has likely experienced marginalisation in practice. Bahrain also demonstrated reservations about the possible establishment of a permanent "multilateral investment court system" advocated by the European Commission.[39] Bahrain notably submitted that the Working Group should "consider whether ICSID's proposed amendments to its rules and regulations address the criticisms made against ISDS", advocating for reform instead of the establishment of a "permanent investment court". Bahrain suggested the following options for reform of procedural issues: the creation of "binding codes of conduct" led by the arbitration institutions, increased diversity in tribunals (specifically promoting women and arbitrators from developing economies), the creation of joint interpretative committees instead of an appellate capacity, the creation of a class of ICSID arbitrators for the purpose of hearing annulment matters, and the broadening of grounds for annulment through the creation of a model provision.[40]

In its submission, Kuwait adopted a somewhat different approach, reflecting the breadth of ISDS experiences within the GCC. Of particular interest, Kuwait

35 Trakman (n 33).

36 Ibid.

37 Ibid.

38 United Nations Commission on International Trade Law Working Group III (Investor-State Dispute Settlement Reform) Thirty-eighth session Vienna, 14–18 October 2019: Submission from the Kingdom of Bahrain on the Possible Reform of Investor-State Dispute Settlement (ISDS). UNGA doc. A/CN.9/WG.III/WP.180.

39 Ibid.

40 Ibid.

addressed the consideration of "the development of a code of conduct" for arbitrators and in its submission, drew particular attention to the issue of "[n]epotism and patronage on the basis of family, religious, sectarian or partisan political considerations".[41] Kuwait made a statement highly relevant to cultural considerations, which reflects on the culture pervading GCC member States, stating:[42]

> Kuwait is a developing State where family and clan reign supreme and ties of kinship (blood and marriage) are paramount. In that respect, it resembles most States in the Middle East region. Such a situation can be a major obstacle to progress and development. Conflict of interest resulting from nepotism, patronage or cronyism is a feature of tribal society.

9.4 Concluding Remarks: Strategies for Treaty-Based Investor–State Arbitration Optimisation

Treaty-making practices could be improved by the creation of a model BIT by the GCC for utilisation on either a regional or member State basis. This would likely promote consistency and improved construction of treaty provisions. However, this is also likely to be difficult to achieve in practice given the GCC's unique constitution and, at times, conflict and divergence between its member States, as highlighted by the geopolitical conflict situation that resulted in the Qatar Airways disputes. There is also a risk that the GCC's treaty partners would seek to promote their own national interest and policy agendas in the treaty-making process, potentially at the expense of the GCC and its member States. The creation of a model treaty would go some way towards mitigating against this risk and there is reason to investigate whether or not a *de facto* model BIT exists, in future studies. Unfortunately, this analysis fell outside the scope of the present study. Analysis of the language of existing BITs with the model BITs of the GCC and the States' treaty partners may be beneficial for assessing this risk and the degree to which it can be addressed by the adoption of consistent treaty-making practices.

There are also a number of specific provisions that the GCC and its member States can incorporate within IIAs to achieve these objectives. The investment protections can be limited to exclude more disingenuous claims by incentivising foreign companies to establish a local company and requiring those companies to invest capital in the host state with which they are engaged through a careful construction of the definitions of "investor" and "investment". There is a real risk that foreign companies may object to the introduction of strengthened

41 Submission from the Government of Kuwait on the Possible Reform of Investor-State Dispute Settlement (ISDS), United Nations Commission on International Trade Law Working Group III (Investor-State Dispute Settlement Reform), Thirty-ninth session, New York, 30 March–3 April 2020, UNGA doc.A/CN.9/WG.III/WP.186, at <Kuwait submission to UNCITRAL Working Group III 30 December 2019.pdf>.

42 Ibid.

requirements around local ownership or other relationships. However, there is precedence for this undertaking in other jurisdictions, for example, Article 1(b) of the 2019 Netherlands Model Investment Agreement, in which the definition of "investor" means among other things "any legal person constituted under the law of that Contracting Party and having substantial business activities in the territory of that Contracting Party". Subsection 1(c) of Article 1 goes on to provide a non-exhaustive list of indications of what constitutes substantive business activities:

Indications of having "substantive business activities" in a Contracting Party may include:

(i) the undertaking's registered office and/or administration is established in that Contracting Party;
(ii) the undertaking's headquarters and/or management is established in that Contracting Party;
(iii) the number of employees and their qualifications based in that Contracting Party;
(iv) the turnover generated in that Contracting Party; and
(v) an office, production facility and/or research laboratory is established in that Contracting Party.

These indications should be assessed in each specific case, taking into account the total number of employees and turnover of the undertaking concerned, and taking account of the nature and maturity of the activities carried out by the undertaking in the Contracting Party in which it is established. While the definition of substantive activities could be strengthened to require companies to be headquartered, invest capital, and employ local staff in the relevant host country, it is an example of how the States could take active steps to limit companies from instituting arbitrations through manipulation of corporation laws.

The Gulf crisis was reportedly resolved, or at least considerably eased, at the GCC Summit in January 2021, when Bahrain, the UAE, Saudi Arabia, and Egypt, interestingly, partially restored their relationship with Qatar. However, it remains to be seen what impact this restoration will have on the investor–state claims brought by Qatar Airways, Qatar Pharma, and beIN, noting that these disputes are still pending. The respondent States may have avoided the time and expense involved in defending multiple actions if there was a local remedies requirement contained in the *OIC Agreement*, for example. Although, at least in this particular case, the claims made by Qatar and the Qatari companies are arguably best addressed in external dispute settlement fora. The establishment of a regional-level dispute settlement centre with jurisdiction and competence to hear investor–state disputes, including mandatory reference of intra-GCC disputes thereto, may be a prudent middle road in terms of allowing claimants to seek relief while preserving the integrity of domestic judicial institutions and decisions and avoiding unnecessary multiplicity of proceedings.

With an expected growth in intra-GCC arbitrations in the future, due in part to the diversification policies of the GCC member States, it is arguably both a natural and desirable consequence to create a regional-level dispute settlement body that can adjudicate disputes in a central forum, while preserving the paramountcy of the Shariah and being versed in the nuances of contractual engagement and socio-legal constructs within the GCC. Such a body would require a panel of independent arbitrators with security of tenure from across the GCC to avoid potential conflict of issue and conflict of interest problems arising.

The GCC member States may benefit from collaborating with the OIC treaty partners to establish a formalised dispute settlement organ and provide more clarity about the intention of treaty partners with respect to the dispute settlement mechanism, the purpose and scope of the MFN clause, and the availability and preconditions for accessing arbitration. Certainly, there is evidence that this is happening, although in the view of the authors, this is unlikely to impact the Qatar Airways Group treaty-based disputes. The OIC has taken steps towards reform of the somewhat problematic agreement, issuing Resolution No. 2/46-E, and via a meeting of the Intergovernmental Experts Group on the Establishment of a Permanent Organ & Mechanism for Settlement of Investment Disputes (October 2022, Casablanca); "[t]he group aims to finalize the Draft Protocol to present to the States by March 2023".[43]

Notwithstanding these developments, changes to the *OIC Agreement* are likely to take time and, in some respects, the Agreement needs a significant overhaul. The GCC member States would benefit from a careful review of their existing BIT network and an examination of the possible (though rare) exposure to intra-GCC disputes submitted to arbitration in the absence of an applicable BIT, especially those seeking to apply the Agreement. The States may also benefit from concluding a modern IIA between themselves, including investment protection provisions and a dispute settlement mechanism, together with a permanent dispute settlement body (or reliance on an existing one) capable of hearing such disputes, complete with an appellate/review body and clearly defined appellate procedures. This would be an elegant treaty-based solution for disputes initiated on an intra-GCC basis in the absence of an applicable BIT. However, it is for the time being probably unlikely because of the limited number of disputes conducted on this basis. Changes to access to arbitration under the Agreement are probably more likely at this stage. The appointment of arbitrators, the objections to jurisdiction, and the outcome of the Qatar Airways Group treaty-based disputes will therefore be most instructive in this reform process.

43 Gaver, Craig and Yusuf Kumtepe, 'Checking in on the OIC Investment Agreement: New Arbitrations, but Slow Progress on Creating a Permanent Dispute Settlement Mechanism', *Kluwer Arbitration Blog* (17 March 2023) at <https://arbitrationblog.kluwerarbitration.com/2023/03/17/checking-in-on-the-oic-investment-agreement-new-arbitrations-but-slow-progress-on-creating-a-permanent-dispute-settlement-mechanism/>.

Bibliography

Bachar Kiwan v State of Kuwait (ICSID Case No. ARB/20/53) (*'Kiwan v Kuwait'*).

Bank Melli and Bank Saderat v The Kingdom of Bahrain (PCA Case No. 2017-25) (*'Bank Melli v Bahrain'*).

beIN Corporation v Kingdom of Saudi Arabia (Notice of Arbitration, ('beIN v Saudi Arabia')) UNCITRAL, 1 October 2018.

Charlotin, Damien, ' Breaking: Paris Court Finds That PCA Secretary General Lacked Power to Step Into Libya Arbitration When OIC Secretary General Failed to Appoint Arbitrator', *Investment Arbitration Reporter* (26 March 2021) at <Breaking: Paris Court finds that PCA Secretary General lacked power to step into Libya arbitration when OIC Secretary General failed to appoint arbitrator | Investment Arbitration Reporter (openathens.net)>.

Dahlquist, Joel and Luke Eric Peterson, 'Governments Working To Rein In Use of OIC Investment Treaty's Investor-State Arbitration Offer', *Investment Arbitration Reporter* (3 April 2019) at <Governments working to rein in use of OIC investment treaty's investor-state arbitration offer | Investment Arbitration Reporter (openathens.net)>.

Dahlquist, Joel and Luke Eric Peterson, 'Investigation: Four Previously-Confidential Claims under the *OIC Agreement* are Uncovered, as Controversy Continues Over Treaty's Use in Arbitration', *Investment Arbitration Reporter* (16 May 2019) at <https://www-iareporter-com.eu1.proxy.openathens.net/articles/investigation-4-previously-confidential-claims-under-oic-investment-agreement-are-uncovered-as-controversy-continues-over-treatys-use-in-arbitration/>.

Gaver, Craig and Yusuf Kumtepe, 'Checking in on the OIC Investment Agreement: New Arbitrations, But Slow Progress on Creating A Permanent Dispute Settlement Mechanism', *Kluwer Arbitration Blog* (17 March 2023) at <https://arbitrationblog.kluwerarbitration.com/2023/03/17/checking-in-on-the-oic-investment-agreement-new-arbitrations-but-slow-progress-on-creating-a-permanent-dispute-settlement-mechanism/>

Itisaluna Iraq LLC and others v Republic of Iraq (ICSID Case No. ARB/17/10) (*'Itisaluna v Iraq'*).

Jarrett, Martin, Sergio Puig and Steven Ratner, 'Towards Greater Investor Accountability: Indirect Actions, Direct Actions by States and Direct Actions by Individuals' (2023) *Journal of International Dispute Settlement*, Vol. 14(2), 259–80.

Kumtepe, Yusuf and Riccardo Loschi, 'Investment Dispute Settlement Body of the Organisation of Islamic Cooperation: A Dead End for Claims under the OIC Investment Agreement?' *Kluwer Arbitration Blog* (29 December 2019) at <Kluwer Arbitration Blog>; referring to Jarrod Hepburn and Luke Eric Peterson, 'Investigation: As New Cases Emerge Under Islamic Investment Treaty, Initial Viability of Claims Seems To Jing On Willingness Of Respondents To Appoint Arbitrators' *Investment Arbitration Reporter* (2 March 2017) at <Investigation: As new cases emerge under Islamic investment treaty, initial viability of claims seems to hinge on willingness of respondents to appoint arbitrators | Investment Arbitration Reporter (openathens.net)>.

Navodaya Trading DMCC v. Gabonese Republic (PCA Case No. 2018-23) (*'Navodaya v Gabon'*).

Omar Bin Sulaiman Abdul Aziz Al Rajhi v The Sultanate of Oman (PCA Case No.2017-32) (*'Bin Sulaiman v Oman'*).

Organisation of Islamic Cooperation Agreement on Promotion, Protection and Guarantee of Investments among member States of the Islamic Conference, signed 5 June 1981 (entered into force February 1988) (*'OIC Agreement'*).

Price, David, 'Indonesia's Bold Strategy on Bilateral Investment Treaties: Seeking an Equitable Climate for Investment?' (January 2017) *Asian Journal of International Law*, Vol. 17(1), 124–151.

Trakman, Leon and Kunal Sharma, 'Locating Australia on the Pacific Rim: Trade, Investment and the Asian Century' (2015) 12(1) *Transnational Dispute Management, (TDM)*, 1–20.

UNCTAD, 'Facts on Investor-State Arbitrations in 2021: With a Special Focus On Tax-Related ISDS Cases' (July 2022) at <IIA Issues Note, No. 1, 2022 - Facts on Investor-State arbitrations in 2021: With a special focus on tax-related ISDS cases (unctad.org)>.

United Nations, 'World Economic Situation and Prospects 2023' (25 January 2023) at <World Economic Situation and Prospects 2023 | Department of Economic and Social Affairs (un.org)>.

'United Nations Commission on International Trade Law Working Group III (Investor-State Dispute Settlement Reform), Thirty-ninths session, New York' (30 March – 3 April 2020), Submission from the Government of Kuwait on the Possible Reform of investor-State dispute settlement (ISDS), UNGA doc.A/CN.9/WG III/WP.186 at <Kuwait submission to UNCITRAL Working Group III 30 December 2019.pdf>.

'United Nations Commission on International Trade Law Working Group III (Investor-State Dispute Settlement Reform) Thirty-eighth session Vienna' (14–18 October 2019), Submission from the Kingdom of Bahrain on the Possible Reform of Investor-State Dispute Settlement (ISDS). UNGA doc. A/CN.9/WG.III/WP.180.

United Nations Conference on Trade and Development (UNCTAD), 'Investment Dispute Settlement Navigator', *UNCTAD* (2022) at <https://investmentpolicy.unctad.org/investment-dispute-settlement>..

Wahab, Mohamed S. Abdel and Kabir Duggal, *The Resurgence of the Unified Arab Investment Agreement and the Organisation for Islamic Cooperation Investment Agreement: A Dawn of a New Chapter on Investment Protection?*, vol. 13 (BRILL, 2022).

Index

Page numbers in **bold reference tables.
**Page numbers in *italics* reference figures.

Index of Arbitrations

Agility v Iraq (2017) **128**, 131
Agility v Pakistan (2011) **129**, 131, 159–160
Al Awamleh and others v Qatar (2018) **102**
Alcor v Czech Republic (2018) **146**, 151
Alcoser and Lucidos de Yeso v Kuwait (2019) **90**
Alghanim v Jordan (2013) **129**
Aljarallah v Turkey and TMSF (2019) **123**, 130
Al Jazeera v Egypt (2016) **141**, **165**–167
Almasryia v Kuwait (2018) 62, **91**, 93, 116
Al Mehdar v Egypt (2018) **143**, 144
Al Tamimi v Oman (2011) 51–52, **99**, 115
Al-Kharafi v Libya (2011) **129**, 133, 135, 158
Al-Tuwairqi v Pakistan (2018) **143**
Al-Warraq v Indonesia (2011) 12, 26–28, 37, 46–47, 58, 71, 143–**144**, 159, 243–244, 258–259
Alyafei v Jordan (2015) 71, 138, **141**
Attila Dogan v Oman (2016) **99**, 100

Bachar Kiwan v Kuwait (2020) 48, **90**, 103, 114
Bank Melli Iran and Bank Saderat Iran v Bahrain (2017) 85–89
Bank Melli v Bahrain (2017) **84**, 89, 114–115, 253
Bawabet v Egypt (2011) **129**
beIN v Saudi Arabia (2018) 30, **87**, 110, **139–140**, **168**–172, 255
Benabderrahmane v Qatar (2022) **102**, 116
Beximo Pharmaceuticals Ltd v Shamil Bank of Bahrain (2004) 245
Bin Sulaiman v Oman (2017) **98**, **144**, **169**, 244, 255
BM Muhendislik v United Arab Emirates (2017) **111**–113
Borkowski and Rasia FZE v Armenia (2018) 147, 153

Central Bank of Iran v Bahrain (2021) **84**–85
Conseil Economique v Kuwait (2018) **92**–93
CTIP Oil & Gas v Egypt (2019) **146**, 150

Dalal v United Arab Emirates (2019) 111
Desert Line v Yemen 125, 135–137, 159
DP World v Belgium (2017) **147**, 158
DSG v Saudi Arabia (2019) **103**, 108
D.S. Constructions v Libya (2017) 30, **148**, 179, 259

Ed Züblin v Saudi Arabia (2003) **103**, 108

Ghaith Pharaon v Tunisia (1986) 13–14, 143

Hashem Al Mehdar v Arab Republic of Egypt (2018) 144, 259
HOCHTIEF Infrastructure v Saudi Arabia (2018) **106**
Holman v Johnson (1775) 97

ICRS v Jordan (2009) **125**, 126, 154
Impregilo v United Arab Emirates (2001) 8–9, 83, 110 **112**
International Holding Project Group and others v Egypt (2018) **128**
Itisaluna Iraq and others v Iraq (2017) 7, 12, 66, 145, **147**, 154, 245, 256

KGL v Egypt (2021) 126, **128**
Khadamat v Saudi Arabia (2018) 63–64, **107**, 109
Kiwan v Kuwait (2020) 48–49, **90**, 103, 114, 116, 253

MAKAE Europe v Saudi Arabia (2017) 49–50, **107**, 109
Maria Lazareva v The State of Kuwait (2018) **93**
MTN v Yemen (2009) **143**, 145
Muhendislik v Saudi Arabia (2023) **103**

Naftiran Intertrade v Bahrain (2022) **84**
National Gas v Egypt (2011) **149**
Navodaya v Gabon (2018) 61, 67, **147**, 260–261
Nile Douma v Egypt (2016) 126

OHL and others v Kuwait (2017) **92**, 115
Omar Bin Sulaiman Abdul Aziz Al Rajhi v the Sultanate of Oman (2017) **144**, **167**, 169, 244, 255

PCCW Cascade (Middle East) v Saudi Arabia (2022) **99**, 116
Perenco Ecuador Ltd v Republic of Ecuador (2014) 50
Pezold and others v Republic of Zimbabwe (2015) 50
Pharaon v Tunisia (1986) 13–14, 143

Qatar Airways v Bahrain (2020) **84**, **168**, **171**
Qatar Airways v Egypt (2020) **168**, **171**
Qatar Airways v Saudi Arabia (2020) **104**, **168**, **171**
Qatar Airways v United Arab Emirates (2020) **89**, **168**, **171**
Qatar National Bank v South Sudan and the South Sudan Bank (2020) 138–139
Qatar Pharma and Al Sulaiti v Saudi Arabia (2019) **140**, **168**

Ras Al Khaimah Investment Authority v India (2106) **148**

Sajwani v Egypt (2011) **149**
Samsung v Oman (2015) **99**, 105
Samsung v Saudi Arabia (2017) **107**, 109
SGRF v Bulgaria (2015) **136**, 138
Soufraki v United Arab Emirates (2002) 47–48, 110, **112**
State General Reserve Fund (SGRF) of Oman v Bulgaria (2015) **136**, 138
Strategic Infrasol and Thakur Family Trust v India (2016) **148**, 152
Sumrain v Kuwait (2019) **90**, 92

Taheri v United Arab Emirates (2021) **111**–112
Tanmiah v Tunisia (2003) 9, 243
Trasta v Libya (2019) **146**

Waleed Aljarallah v Turkey (2020) 130

Index of Arbitration Agreements

Bahrain–Iran BIT (2002) 83
Bahrain–United States FTA (2006) 22

Cambodia–UAE CEPA (2023) 44
Czech Republic–UAE BIT (1994) 151

Egypt-Kuwait BIT (2001) 62, 115
Egypt-Qatar BIT (1999) 30, 159, 172
EU–GCC proposed FTA 235

France–Kuwait BIT (1989) 48–49, **54–55**, **65**, 68, 95–97

Germany–Saudi Arabia BIT (1996) 115

Iraq–Japan BIT (2012) 28, 66, 245, 260
Iraq–Kuwait BIT (2013) 7, 131
Italy–Jordan BIT (1996) 71, 142
Italy–United Arab Emirates BIT (1995) 110, 115, 150–151

Kuwait–Iraq BIT (1964) 44
Kuwait–Pakistan BIT (1983) **129**, 131
Kuwait–Syria BIT (2001) 95

Netherlands–Chile BIT (1998) 52

Oman–Bulgaria BIT (2007) 137
Oman–Yemen BIT (1998) 59, 136

Panama–Qatar BIT (2010) 102

Saudi Arabia–Austria BIT (2001) 174, 176–177
Saudi Arabia–France BIT (2002) 49 **54**, **56**, **60**, **65**, 68, **73**

Turkey–Kuwait BIT (2010) 131

United Arab Emirates–Italy BIT (1995) 9, 47, 82

United Arab Emirates–Kuwait BIT (1966) 21
United States–Armenia BIT (1992) 153
United States–Oman FTA (2009) 43, 51, 54, **56**, 59, **60**, **65**

General Index

AAN Digital Services Holding 127
admissibility 88
Agreement on the Trade-Related Aspects of Intellectual Property Rights (TRIPs Agreement) 230
Ahli United Bank 85
Al Jazeera 240
Al-Mehdar, Hashem 259–260
Al-Ula Declaration 177, 181–182, 257
Al-Ula Summit 171
Al-Waseet Group 94
anti-discrimination 65, 68; most-favoured-nation (MFN) provisions **70**; national treatment standard **70**
Arab Investment Agreement see Unified Agreement for the Investment of Arab Capital in the Arab States
Arab Investment Court 34
Arab regional unity 23
arbitral review 45
arbitral tribunals 3
arbitration 5, 8–9, 36, 92–93; in the Quran 233
arbitration provisions for dispute resolution **72–73**
Australia 265

Bahrain 30, 261; bilateral investment treaties (BITs) 20–21; *Commercial Companies Law No 21 of 2001* 195–198; domestic legislation 194–198; golden license 198; as home state of claimants 126; as home state of investor **126**; marginalisation 265; Ministry of Industry and Commerce (MOIC) 194–195; money laundering 96–97; Prime Ministerial Edict No. 17 of 2018, 197; Prime Ministerial Edict No. 49 of 2019, 197; Prime Ministerial Edict No. 50 of 2016, 197; reform of ISDS 261; as respondent **84**, 93–94; *Vision 2030*, 195
beoutQ 174
bilateral investment treaties (BITs) 1, 6, 19–25, 36, 257, 264; Arab Investment Court 34; French-related BITs 43

Cairo Regional Centre for International Commercial Arbitration (CRCICA) 132
capital, defined 199
capital flows, foreign direct investment (FDI) 214–215
Central Bank of Iran 89
CET *see* common external tariff
China 265
claimants *see* home states of claimants
"clean hands" issues 42, 96–97, 145
common external tariff (CET) 22
Communications & Media Commission (CMC), Iraq 131
contract law, Shariah law 241–242
control 50, 109
Convention on the Settlement of Investment Disputes between States and Nationals of Other States 47–48
Corpbank 137–138
corporate sovereignty 235–236
Court of Cassation 133–134
CRCICA *see* Cairo Regional Centre for International Commercial Arbitration
critics of international investment agreements (IIAs) 9–10

decided in favour of investor, outcomes of cases 80
decided in favour of neither party, outcomes of cases 80
decided in favour of state, outcomes of cases 80
default arbitrators 254
Democratic Republic of Congo (DRC) 127
developing economies 264–265; non-systemic risk 5
diplomatic protection 3
direct investment, defined 199
discontinuance 92
discontinued, outcomes of cases 80
dispute resolution 70–73; by arbitration provisions **72–73**
Dispute Settlement Body (DSB) 180
Dispute Settlement Navigator 12–14, 79–80
diversification 217
diversity, international investment agreements (IIAs) 45

doctrine of legitimate expectations 57
domestic legislative frameworks and environments 193–194, 224–225; Bahrain 194–198; Kuwait 198–203; Oman 203–207; Qatar 208–211; Saudi Arabia 211–216; United Arab Emirates 217–218
Down Jones Islamic Index Sharia supervisory Board 239
DSB *see* Dispute Settlement Body
Dubai Islamic Bank 237
(Dutch) Model BIT 52

EC–GCC Cooperation Agreement 25
Economic Agreement 229
Economic Development Board (EDB), Bahrain 194
economic diversification 217
Ecuador 264
EDB *see* Economic Development Board
EFTA *see* European Free Trade Association
Egypt 259
European Commission 265
European Free Trade Association (EFTA) 8
European Union 230
expropriation 61–65; non-expropriation **64**; Oman 206

fair and equitable treatment (FET) 42–43, 57–59, 95
Fast International Trading Group 106
fatwas 237–238
FDI *see* foreign direct investment
FET *see* fair and equitable treatment
Financial and Economic Committee 24
fiqh 239
First Gulf Asia Holdings Ltd 47
foreign capital, United Arab Emirates 213
foreign direct investment (FDI) 193–194, 256; Bahrain 195; capital flows 216–218; Kuwait 199–203; Oman 203–207; Saudi Arabia 211–216; United Arab Emirates 217–218
foreign investment 204, 252
foreign investors: defined 204; United Arab Emirates 213, 216
foreign ownership, Qatar 209–211
fork-in-the road provisions 254, 258; *OIC Agreement* 256
Framework Agreement for Trade 230
France: anti-discrimination **68–69**; arbitration provisions **73**; definition of investments **55**; definition of investors **54**; fair and equitable treatment (FET) **60**; non-expropriation provisions **64**
free trade agreements (FTAs) 1, 10, 22
French-related BITs 43
FTAs *see* free trade agreements
Future Bank 85–89

GATT *see* General Agreement on Trade and Tariffs
GCC Commercial Arbitration Centre 23–24
GCC Deputy Ministers of Finance 24
GCC Economic Agreement of 2001 23
GCC Financial and Economic Committee 24
GCC-level arbitration body 257
GCC *see* Gulf Cooperation Council
General Agreement on Trade and Tariffs (GATT) 230
gharar 232, 235, 238, 240, 246
Gulf Cooperation Council (GCC) 1, 5; introduction to ISDS 8–9; member states 6–8
Gulf Cooperation Council (GCC) Charter 228–230
Gulf diplomatic crisis 257; Qatari disputations 170

home states of claimants 124–126, 152–155, 258; Bahrain **126**; Gulf Cooperation Council (GCC) member states 152–155; Kuwait 126–127; Oman 135–138; Qatar 138–142, **168–169**; Saudi Arabia 142–143; United Arab Emirates 145–154
hybrid Islamic finance legal framework 245–246

ICSID Convention (1965) 21
IIAs *see* international investment agreements
illegality, Future Bank 85–89
Indonesia: bilateral investment treaties (BITs) 6
industrial SMEs 37
Intercontinental Bank of Lebanon 132
international arbitration 10
International Centre for Settlement of Investment Disputes (ICSID) Rules and Regulations 6–7
International Fiqh Academy 239

international investment agreements (IIAs) 1–3, 6, 43–46, 252, 257; background and context 6–8; definition of investments 46–54; definition of investors 46–54
intra-GCC ISDS disputes 160–161, 180, 184, 186, 252, 256–257, 260–261, 264
invested foreign capital, defined 204
investment arbitration, in Gulf region 9–12
investment entity, defined 199
investment project, defined 204
investment protection laws 192; *see also* domestic legislative frameworks and environments
investments, defined 46–54, **56–57**
investment treaties 2, 44
investors: defined 46–52, **56**, 199, 266–267; non-Qatari investors 208–211
investor-state arbitrations 252; themes in 253, 258
Iran, Future Bank 88
Iraq, Communications & Media Commission (CMC) 131
Iraq Telecom 132
ISDS clauses 234–236; *OIC Agreement* 244
ISDS provisions 2–6
Islamic-based investment treaties 25–26; *Arab Investment Agreement see Arab Investment Agreement*; *OIC Agreement see OIC Agreement*
Islamic finance 236–240, 246–247; equipping IDS through 240–241; hybrid Islamic finance legal framework 245–246
Islamic principles: fatwas 237–238; fiqh 239; *gharar* 232, 238, 240, 246; *riba* 232, 235–236, 238, 240, 246; Shariah law 233–234

Japan–Philippines Economic Partnership 6, 264
Jordan: *Judicial Arbitration in Civil and Commercial Matter Law (1995)* 98

Keppel Seghers Engineering of Singapore 83
KOC *see* Kuwait Oil Company
Korek Telecom 131
Kuwait 98–100, 257–258; bilateral investment treaties (BITs) 20–21; *Code of Civil and Commercial Procedure (1980)* 98; *Decree Law No. 25 of 2012, the Companies Law* 201; *Decree Law No. 116 of 2013, the Kuwait Direct Investment Promotion Law* 199–203; Direct Investment Promotion Authority 200; *Direct Investment Promotion Law* 199–203; domestic legislation 198–203; foreign direct investment (FDI) 193, 202–203; as home state of claimants 126–127; ICRS v Jordan 126, **130**, 159; Kuwait Oil Company (KOC) 127; *Law No. 68 of 1980, the New Commercial Law* 202; *Law No. 74 of 1979 Regulating the Ownership of Real Estate by Non-Kuwaitis* 202; Negative List 200–201; Real Estate Ownership Law 202–203; reform of ISDS 252–255; as respondent **90–91**

LAS *see* League of Arab States
LCIA *see* London Court of International Arbitration
League of Arab States (LAS) 31
Lebanese Arbitration Centre 132
legal personality 27
legitimate expectations 57
LERCO *see* Libyan Emirates Oil Refining Company
Libya: Trasta Energy Ltd 144
Libyan Emirates Oil Refining Company (LERCO) 150–151
local remedies rule 3
London Court of International Arbitration (LCIA) 127
Low, Jho 94–95

MENA region *see* Middle East-North Africa (MENA) region
MFN clause *see* most-favoured-nation (MFN) provisions
Middle East-North Africa (MENA) region 7
Ministerial Council 229
Mit Ghamr Local Savings Bank 237
MNF clause 27–28
MOCI *see* Ministry of Commerce and Industry
model BIT 49
Model Investment Agreement, 2019 262
MOIC *see* Ministry of Industry and Commerce
most-favoured-nation (MFN) provisions 58, 65, 67, 154–155, 256; anti-discrimination **68**; *OIC Agreement* 244–245
multilateral treaties 260

nationality 27, 42, 46, 51–52, **55**
national treatment standard 65; anti-discrimination **68**
Negative List: Kuwait 200–201; Oman 205; Saudi Arabia 213
net fuel exporters 264
Netherlands 264
New York Convention (1958) 21
Nicaragua 264
no details available, outcomes of cases 80
non-appointment of arbitrators 255, 258
non-expropriation provisions **64–65**
non-Qatari investors 208–211
non-Saudi 215
non-systemic risk 5

OIC Agreement. see Organisation of Islamic Cooperation Agreement on Promotion, Protection and Guarantee of Investments among Member States of the Organisation of the Islamic Conference (OIC Agreement)
Oman 255; bilateral investment treaties (BITs) 20–21; domestic legislation 203–207; expropriation 206; as home state of claimants **136**, 138–140; Ministerial Decision No. 72/2020 205; Ministerial Decision No. 214/2020 205; Ministry of Commerce and Industry (MOCI) 203; Negative List 205; Omanisation programme 205; Oman Refineries and Petroleum Industries Company (ORPIC) 100; as respondent **84**; *Royal Decree 21/2004* 207; *Royal Decree 50/2019, the Foreign Capital Investment Law* 203–207; *Royal Decree 52/2019 Promulgating the Public Private Partnership Law* 207; *Royal Decree 102/1994, the Foreign Capital Investment Law*, Oman 203–207; urgency status 206
Orange Telecom (France) 131–132
Organisation of Islamic Cooperation Agreement on Promotion, Protection and Guarantee of Investments among Member States of the Organisation of the Islamic Conference (OIC Agreement) 7, 10, 12, 25–31, 38, 43, 46, 47, 72, 242–243, 252, 255–256, 258, 259, 263, 267; anti-discrimination 65–**68**, 70; arbitration provisions **72–73**; fair and equitable treatment (FET) 59; investments **56**; ISDS clauses 244; most-favoured-nation (MFN) provisions 58, 244–245; non-expropriation provisions **55**; OIC Secretary-General 254–255; Qatar Airways Group 177–180; Resolution No. 2/46-E 268
ORPIC *see* Oman Refineries and Petroleum Industries Company

Paris Court of Appeal 259
Paris Tribunal de Grande Instance 134
PCA *see* Permanent Court of Arbitration
pending, outcomes of cases 80
Permanent Court of Arbitration (PCA) 29–30, 36, 98, 254–255
Pharaon, Ghaith 8, 125
Philippines 6
preferential treatment provisions, Arab Investment Agreement 32
protectionist regimes 194

Qatar 257; arbitration law 211; bilateral investment treaties (BITs) 20; domestic legislation 208–211; foreign ownership209–211; Gulf diplomatic crisis 167, 170; as home state of claimants 125, 140–141, **168**; *Law No. (1) of 2019 on Regulating Non-Qatari Capital Investment in Economic Activity* 208–210; *Law No. (16) of 2018 on the Regulation of Non-Qataris' Ownership and Usage of Real Estate*210–211; non-Qatari investors 208–211; *Qatar Financial Centre Real Estate Ownership Regulations* 211; as respondent **102**, 106; state-state strategy 180
Qatar Airways Group 30, 257, 268; intra-GCC ISDS disputes 177–180
Qatar Financial Centre (QFC) 211
Quran: arbitration 233; contract law 241–242

Rasia FZE 153
ratione materiae 42
ratione personae 42, 49, 51, 155
ratione temporis 53
ratione voluntatis 66
Real Estate Ownership and Investment by Non-Saudis, Saudi Arabia 215
reform of ISDS 265
regimes, defined 44
region-specific character 261–266
Resolution No. 2/46-E, *OIC Agreement* 267

respondents: Bahrain **84**; Gulf Cooperation Council (GCC) member states 92–93, *113*; Kuwait **90–91**; Oman **98**; Qatar **102**, 106; Saudi Arabia **103–104**; United Arab Emirates **111–112**
riba 232, 235–236, 238, 240, 246
risk, non-systemic risk 5
Rome Convention on the Law Applicable to Contractual Obligations (1980) 245
Rule 43 Settlement and Discontinuance 81
Rule 44 Discontinuance 81

Saudi Arabia 30, 142–145, 261–262; bilateral investment treaties (BITs) 20–21; disputes with Qatar 175–176; domestic legislation 211–216; as home state of claimants 142–145; Ministry of Investment 212; Negative List 213; non-Saudi 215; as respondent **104–105**; *Royal Decree No. M/1, of 5.1.1421H the Foreign Investment Law* 211–214; *Royal Decree No. M/4, the Anti-Concealment Law* 215–216; *Royal Decree No. M/15, on Real Estate Ownership and Investment by Non-Saudis* 215
Saudi Arabia: anti-discrimination 68–**70**; *Arbitration Act*, 214; arbitration provisions **74**; definition of investors **55**; fair and equitable treatment (FET) **60**
Secretariat General 23–24, 229
Sematel 133
Shariah law 37, 231–234, 246; contract law 241–242; *gharar* 232, 235, 238, 240, 246; ISDS clauses 234–235; *riba* 232, 235–236, 238, 240, 246
South Sudan 138
state-state strategy, Qatar 175–179
state-to-state dispute settlement mechanisms 3–4
sui generis culture 257–262
sui generis laws 193, 195; United Arab Emirates (UAE) 217
Supreme Council 229

Tanmiah for Consultancy Management & Marketing (Tanmiah) 34–35
themes, in investor-state arbitrations 253–257
TIPs *see* treaties, with investment provisions
trade agreements 231
Trasta Energy Ltd 144–145
treaties, with investment provisions (TIPs) 115, 255, 257
treaty-based investor-state arbitration optimisation, strategies for 262–264
TRIPs Agreement *see* Agreement on the Trade-Related Aspects of Intellectual Property Rights
Tunisia 8–9
Turkiye **86**, 112, 133

UNCITRAL *see* United Nations Commission on International Trade Law
unclean hands 253, 258
UNCTAD *see* United Nations Conference on Trade and Development
Unified Agreement for the Investment of Arab Capital in the Arab States (Arab Investment Agreement) 7, 10–11, 25–26, 30–35, 38, 43, 111, 136, 242–243; anti-discrimination **69–70**; arbitration provisions **72**; definition of investors **54**; fair and equitable treatment (FET) **55**; investments **56**; non-expropriation provisions **64**
union-level arbitration centres 254
United Arab Emirates (UAE) 108–110, 261, 263; bilateral investment treaties (BITs) 202015 Commercial Companies Law (2015), 216–217; disputes with Qatar 178; domestic legislation 217–218; *Federal Decree-Law No. 19 of 2018 Concerning Foreign Direct Investments* (2018 FDI Law) 217–218; *Federal Law No. 6 of 2018 on Arbitration* 217, 220; foreign direct investment (FDI) 193; as home state of claimants 145, **146–149**; Positive List 219; *Resolution No. 16 of 2020 Concerning the Determination of the Positive List of Economic Sectors and Activities Eligible for Foreign Direct Investment and Percentage of Their Ownership* 219–220; as respondent **111–112**; United Nations 264
United Nations Commission on International Trade Law (UNCITRAL) 6, 243, 265
United Nations Committee on the Elimination of Racial Discrimination 171
United Nations Conference on Trade and Development (UNCTAD) 19,

43; Investment Dispute Settlement Navigator 12–14, 79–80
United States 230; Bahrain 197–198; Department of State 194; free trade agreements (FTAs) 22; Oman 207; Qatar 211; Saudi Arabia 216; United Arab Emirates 217; United States–GCC Framework Agreement 231; United States–GCC Strategic Cooperation Forum 230; United States–Mexico–Canada Agreement 10

VCLT *see* Vienna Convention on the Law of Treaties
Venezuela 264
Vienna Convention on the Law of Treaties 50, 244

weapons of mass destruction (WMD) 86
World Bank, International Centre for Settlement of Investment Disputes (ICSID) Rules and Regulations 6–7
World Trade Organisation (WTO): Agreement on the Trade-Related Aspects of Intellectual Property Rights (TRIPs Agreement) 230; Dispute Settlement Body (DSB) 180; General Agreement on Trade and Tariffs (GATT) 230

Yemen: United Arab Emirates (UAE) 145
Yemeni Arbitral Award 59
Yemeni Commercial Court 58, 136

FSC
www.fsc.org
MIX
Papier | Fördert gute Waldnutzung
FSC® C083411

Kolibri 360 GmbH
Ferdinand-Jühlke-Straße 7
99095 Erfurt, Deutschland
produktsicherheit@kolibri360.de